HIT THE SIGN AND WIN A FREE SUIT OF CLOTHES FROM HARRY FINKLESTEIN

BERT RANDOLPH SUGAR

FOREWORD BY BILL VEECK

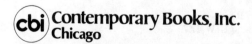 **Contemporary Books, Inc.**
Chicago

Library of Congress Cataloging in Publication Data

Sugar, Bert Randolph.
   Hit the sign.

   Includes index.
   1. Sports—United States—History.   I. Title.
GV583.S93   1978   796'.0973   78-57447
ISBN 0-8092-7787-5

Copyright © 1978 by Bert Randolph Sugar
All rights reserved
Published by Contemporary Books, Inc.
180 North Michigan Avenue, Chicago, Illinois 60601
Manufactured in the United States of America
Library of Congress Catalog Card Number: 78-57447
International Standard Book Number: 0-8092-7787-5

Published simultaneously in Canada by
Beaverbooks
953 Dillingham Road
Pickering, Ontario L1W 1Z7
Canada

This book is dedicated to those many men known as "promoters," whose ideas were hills from which to look as opposed to caves in which to hide. These men left more in the world they touched than they ever took out.

Contents

Foreword

I'm usually confused, sometimes embarrassed, by introductions to books. Probably because I invariably get the impression (based on my own reading habits, I suppose) that they aren't really meant for reading unless: (1) the piece that follows is so dull or obscure as to require explanation in advance, or (2) the introduction is necessary to explain why the book happened to be written in the first place.

This time, fortunately, I don't feel trapped. Not exactly, that is. At most I feel slightly superfluous. For, whatever I may end up trying to "con" you with, Bert Sugar has done better in more fascinating detail.

Under the guise of studying and analyzing "promotions" and "promoters," the author has produced a delightful and instructive study—maybe *history* is better—of major team sports (plus the fight game) in our, at least my, times; with emphasis (in his wacky and somewhat cynical style) on the historical oddities that have usually accompanied the evolution of our commercial games.

Come to think of it, he's probably right; the changes that have transpired more often than not have come about through the efforts of a comparatively few guys who figured that the wondrous world of fun and games beats working. A few guys whose motives ranged from desperation (eating being fun) to feeding giant-size egos—with a gamut of stops in between.

The author selected an unusual device to highlight his study. Both "promoters" and "promotion" have always occupied an interesting, often ambiguous, niche in society. According to Cicero (or was it another of the ancient gossip columnists?), the great Nero—promotion-wise only, you understand—had some problems in producing his spectacles when one of the subcontractors hired by the emperor to provide a palliative for his restless populace took it on the duffy (cash box in hand, of course), when his supply of Christians ran short, and substituted a few ringers to make up his quota of lion's food (several of whom were recognized by friends and relatives sitting in the cheaper seats).

And of more recent vintage, the *Oxford English Dictionary* (high-class, huh?) defines "promote" in the most complimentary terms: "promote; pro + movere to move forward, advance and in its preferred definition: to advance (a person) to a position of honour, dignity, or emolument; 2nd: to further the growth, development, progress, or establishment of (anything); to help forward (a process or result)"—etc., etc., etc.

And as for "Promoter": "1450–1530 . . . A comforter to them that are desolate, a promoter to the righteful, an helper to the synful."

Of course one explanation for the present somewhat less than glowing reputation of the word may be found in a few of the definitions that follow, including "one who helps secure the passage of a local or private act of Parliament; who takes the requisite steps for the formation of a joint stock company; and later: one whose job was to prosecute or denounce offenders against the law (a professional accuser, an informer)."

It's easy to see why some of those raps wouldn't exactly endear the hustlers of the world to their fellow man. But, as it is reported later on, in 1876, "A promoter, quoad promoter, is not necessarily a bad man." So there.

Now, having given the matter considerable thought over the years (undoubtedly a defense mechanism), I haven't reached the conclusion that the opprobrium often wreaked on the self-avowed "promoter" is someone else's defense mechanism. Strangely enough, the same tactics that are looked on askance when attributed to a "scuffler" are applauded as highly imaginative salesmanship when there is a physical product involved.

A *promoter* by definition too often seems to hustle intangibles—hopes, dreams, the emphemeral idea of fun—while the *salesman* has a tangible product (good, bad, or indifferent) to peddle. The promoter uses ingenuity, modern communications, ideas, and, above all, the unusual, instead of an organization complete with all the "tried and true" sales techniques. Obviously there's a risk, but then sometimes the rewards for winning make the game worthwhile, etc., etc., etc. And besides, if larceny doesn't work . . . well, there's always another day.

Maybe "promoters" and "promotions" would be better off separated from the more stodgy salesmen. After all, your large companies, computers and all, are now in the process of developing their own departments of promotion, which somehow seem to escape the taint still attached to every card-carrying promoter.

Before anyone says "He protesteth too much," allow me to let you in on a secret: Of course I do. I can't deny that I have used these pages for self-service. After all, I've never denied being a hustler. Strangely enough, I'm proud of the title. I find it both honorable and admirable. I find nothing wrong with adapting (some say stealing) old ideas for new situations or trying new techniques to improve old situations.

Change just for the sake of change is anathema—worse, it's stupid; but to protect and defend tradition when it becomes a stinking dead albatross hanging around the neck of progress is even more self-defeating. That's when new ideas must replace tired custom—if disaster is to be avoided, or at least minimized.

In the pages that follow, you will find that almost from their inception, sports have provided a continuously changing panorama: New ideas adopted, old discarded as changing techniques were needed to meet the changing times. Throughout, however, there has continued to be a noticeable skein of real or quickly manufactured tradition. Tradition's a saleable product. All these changes have been wrought by a comparatively few entrepreneurs—most of whom I have at one time or another, in one or another place, been privileged to watch at close quarters.

For thirty years I saw Abe Saperstein work his magic. George Halas, C. C. Pyle, George Marshall, Johnny Blood, Red Grange, Paul Brown, Curly Lambeau—the names and faces come into focus only to be replaced by our latter-day Saints as football has skyrocketed from its most modest beginnings. One-time holder of an official fight promoter's license in the old Milwaukee days, I can also boast a lifetime in baseball that has provided an overflowing cornucopia of laughs while watching—occasionally participating in—the vagaries of what has been known as "The Grand Old Game."

I wouldn't have missed a minute of it: heartaches, bankruptcy, even an occasional success, and all. Maybe that's the reason *Hit the Sign and Win a Free Suit of Clothes from Harry Finklestein* is very true, very poignant, and very memorable to this alleged foreworder.

By the way, if you've gotten this far. Well . . . thanks.

Bill Veeck

Introduction

The title of this book is representative of the many signs that once dotted the stadium landscape during the nineteenth century and the first four decades of the twentieth century. They came in all sizes and shapes, advertising every conceivable product and service. And some not so conceivable. Those best remembered not only advertised their wares but also tied them into the game itself, offering awards of free merchandise or cash to the player hitting the sacred sign. Some of those that dealt in this form of participatory advertising were the Abe Stark sign in Ebbets Field ("Hit Sign/Win Suit"), the Stoney's sign in Toronto's Maple Leaf Park ("Hit the Hole and Win $2,000 Cash") and the plumbing-supply outfit in Sacramento's Edward Field ("Hit the Toilet Seat and Win $20.").

But signs have contributed more than clothes and cash to the lore and legend of sports. They have also contributed to its rich fabric. In fact, they have even become part of the sports idiom by providing the inspiration for the oft-used term "bullpen." The ubiquitous Bull Durham sign, featuring a rampaging bull in stop-action, appeared on almost all outfield fences before the turn of the century. Utility players would take chairs and sit in the shadow of the sign, passing the time of day "until further notice"; which, in the early days of baseball, rarely came. The sign and the covey of players beneath it became so common a sight that the players became known as the "bullpen." And the bullpen it has stayed, thanks to Bull Durham and its advertising signs.

Those signs are almost all gone now. For with the erection of all-purpose scoreboards—all in the wonderful name of "progress"—has come something not as devoutly wished. The character patterned after Clarence Darrow in the *drame a clef Inherit the Wind* mused, "When they invented the telephone, they took away our privacy." Just so, when they constructed those giant electronic scoreboards-*cum*-advertising billboards, they took away the delicious anticipation of waiting for the next number to be dropped into place; they took away the sign stealers secreted somewhere way up there in the scoreboard; and they took away the old signs that made the scoreboards of yesteryear what they were—the "H's" and "E's" camouflaged as part of the Chesterfield sign and the Abe Stark and Stoney's signs. They took them all away in the name of "progress."

But the signs, and their residual remembrances, continue to serve as a symbolic reminder that some sort of a relationship existed between sports and business. One that was thought to be just as far removed from the field of action as the fence signs were. And although they have come down, to be replaced by multimillion-dollar omnibus scoreboards that do everything but make coffee, the very fantasy they inspired—that the commercial camel had kept its wet nose out of the sports tent—has also come tumbling down.

For sports are no longer just the physical game played on the field. There is also a financial game played off the field with wins and losses replaced by dollars and cents; and won-lost columns secondary to the debit and credit columns. Today sports has become a willing handmaiden to business, as obvious as the electronic scoreboards overlooking stadia everywhere.

Historically, it was ever thus. Since the first Roman gladiator laced on his first *cestus*, men have operated behind the scenes with hyperthyroidal bustling and brilliant hoopla to make sports a business—their business, as they turned their feverish *chutzpah* into cold cash.

And in so doing, these dreamers of dreams have taken on the promotion of sports with all the evangelical verve of a tent-show preacher moving bottles of snake-oil elixir; and they sculpted the face of sports. While some promoters, after a few creative droppings, have ricocheted to earth like Icarus, several have flown in the face of gaseous edicts—such as "It has never been done before"—and not allowed their wings to be clipped. Their promotions have soared and taken wing as these men have climbed mountains (many of which were made from their own molehills) and turned that ephemeral phenomenon known as a "promotion" into a reality.

The very first Prometheus of the Pleasure Principle and Patron Saint of all those who hold dear the precepts of promotion was none other than Phineas (a Biblical name meaning "brazen mouth") Taylor Barnum. Barnum ushered in that great era of American showmanship one hot August day in 1835 when he placed on public exhibition Joice Heth, "a 161-year-old colored woman" he displayed in Niblo's Garden as "unquestionably the most astonishing and interesting curiosity in the World!

Nurse to General George Washington (the Father of Our Country) . . . and was the first person who put clothes on the unconscious infant . . . and 'raised him.'" Never mind that it was later disclosed that Joice Heth was a hoax; Barnum had discovered the underlying principle of promotion: that people will pay for that intangible known as pleasure and entertainment.

His inspiration was the spark that was to set promoters everywhere afire. But none more so than in the world of sports. There the many pros and "cons" who claimed his mantle as lineal descendants, rightfully or illigitimately, turned their restless intellects and turbulent energies to the inexact science of promotion, carving niches in the face of sports to rival any Borglum etched on Mt. Rushmore. These men, who read like a "Who's Who in Ballyhoo," include such names as: "Cash and Carry" Pyle, Tex Rickard, Gary Davidson, Sonny Werblin, Abe Saperstein, Jerry Perenchio, George Marshall, Bill MacPhail, Don King, George Halas, and, of course, Bill Veeck. These men turned the stadia and the arenas of the twentieth century into midways; and in so doing changed sports from a game into a business.

These are the men who left a legacy—a schizoid legacy of flair, fame, fortunes, and sometimes even failure. It was a lasting legacy; one we hope we've captured in *Hit the Sign and Win a Free Suit of Clothes from Harry Finklestein*.

No book purporting to possess the magnitude of this one could have been attempted—let alone accomplished—without help. Those who have been kind enough to lend their support, their time, and their anecdotes include the cast of characters below, many of whom are included within the pages of *Hit the Sign*:

Hank Aaron, Vernon Alden, Muhammad Ali, Peter Bavasi, Howard Berk, Dick Boke, Teddy Brenner, Michael Burke, John F.X. Condon, Fred Corcoran, Dick Costello, Guido Cribari, Dan Daniel, Fred Danzig, Gary Davidson, Dave Dixon, Bobby Douglas, Lew Eskin, James T. Farrell, Larry Fleisher, Art Flynn, David Foster, Hy Goldberg, Eddie Gottlieb, Harold "Red" Grange, Ruth Gray, George Halas, Barry Halper, Tom Heinsohn, Bill Himmelman, Robert Holmen, Tony Isidore, Jim Jordan, Cliff Kachline, Don King, Barney Kremenko, Ike Kuhns, Jack Landry, George Lois, Bernie London, Nat Loubet, Carl Lundquist, Alec Mackenzie, Bill Madden, Art Mazansky, Jack McCafferty, Jim Morgan, Dave Neft, LeRoy Neiman, Floyd Patterson, Jerry Perenchio, Maurice Podoloff, Harvey Pollack, Shirley Povich, Harold Rosenthal, Stan Rosensweig, Irving

Rudd, Mrs. Clare Ruth, Rudie Schaffer, Gene Schoor, Burt Schultz, Hank Schwartz, Frank Scott, Milt Shermet, Joel Siegel, Ira Smith, Walter "Red" Smith, Cy Spengler, Peter Spengler, Jim Squiers, Francis Stann, Howie Starkman, John Steadman, Mike Storen, Sam Taub, Don Wall, Charles Tate, Phil Tocantins, Mike Veeck, Jimmy Walsh, Larry Williams, Lee Williams, Pat Williams, David Wolf, Dick Young, Dave Zinkoff, and the public relations departments of The Curtis Division of Standard Brands, The David Crystal Company and The Staley Starch Company, and to Bill Veeck, for services above and beyond the call of duty.

Bert Randolph Sugar
June 7, 1978

The care and feeding
of a new franchise

When sportswriter-turned-baseball executive Ford Frick originally came up with the brainstorm of establishing a Hall of
Fame in the designated birthplace of baseball, Cooperstown,
New York, he should have added an asterisk. For if the real
truth were known, the home of Abner Doubleday bears the same
relationship to baseball as Santa Claus does to Christmas and
the Easter Bunny to Easter. They are all delightful, childlike
symbols; but hoaxes nevertheless.

"Baseball" was, according to Mark Twain, "the very symbol,
the outward and visible expression of the drive and push and
rush and struggle of the raging, tearing, booming nineteenth
century." And just as it provided a metaphor for a burgeoning
nation destined to become the greatest in the world, it also
provided Americans with heroes. Cap Anson, Charley Comiskey,
King Kelly, Hoss Radbourne, Kid Nichols, and a whole raft of
others were celebrated in song and product. The Missouri
Pacific Railroad even named nine whistle-stops along its route
after the St. Louis Browns starting team.

For all its popularity, however, baseball still suffered from an
inferiority complex. The game Albert G. Spalding and others
called America's National Game was, in reality, an extension of
an English schoolboy game called "rounders," which could be
traced as far back as the age of the first Elizabeth. The America
of the 1900s was confident and cocksure, casting about for its
own identity though already sure of its place in history. The

1

country that gave the world the telephone, the phonograph, flickering films, the electric light, and even chewing gum was not about to acknowledge that *their* National Game was an import.

Caught in an upsurge of patriotism, the lords of baseball established a national commission of seven men in 1905 for the avowed purpose of determining the true origins of the game. Actually these seekers of truth viewed it as their solemn duty to promote—by whatever means necessary—evidence that would prove beyond a doubt that baseball was an American institution and disavow the British origins of our National Game.

For the next three years—while the commission scrounged for a hook to hang an invention on—the dispute raged. One brand of cigarette even issued buttons proclaiming: "I'm The Guy That Discovered Baseball." Finally, one of the members of the commission, A. G. Mills, former president of the National League of Professional Baseball Clubs, provided them with a rationale, no matter how tenuous.

That hook was a man whom Mills sponsored as the man who "designed or christened" the game of baseball—Major General Abner Doubleday. The general was well known for his contributions at Fort Sumter and Gettysburg, but not his contributions to baseball. But Doubleday had another qualification: he had also been a member of the same Grand Army of the Republic post as Mills, the famous Lafayette Post of New York. Mills had been personally responsible for escorting Doubleday's body back to New York's city hall after his death in Mendham, New Jersey, in 1893. Now Mills sought to make his friend immortal.

The "celebrated baseball commission of 1907" unanimously declared: "First—That baseball had its origin in the United States. Second—That the first scheme for playing it, according to the best evidence obtainable to date, was devised by Abner Doubleday, at Cooperstown, New York, in 1839."

The unwitting inventor of The National Game was supposed to have "standardized the game in 1839 by drawing up a set of rules and designing a playing field." Dead for fifteen years and in no position to contest the posthumous honor, Doubleday had never given anyone any indication that he had been in a position to "design" or "christen" the game. Enrolled at West Point the year he was supposed to have invented baseball, he never alluded to his brush with sports history in any of his correspondence or the sixty-seven diaries he compiled during his remaining fifty-four years.

The fact that the game of baseball had first been referred to in

2

A Little Pretty Pocket-Book published in London in 1744 and republished in New York in 1762; that Robin Carver's *Book of Sports*, printed in 1834, showed sketches of the game on Boston Common and possessed a set of printed rules; and that the identical rules credited to Doubleday are found in a rule book for the English game of rounders, published in London in 1827, were merely technicalities. An American was needed, and Doubleday filled the bill in the greatest promotion baseball has ever perpetrated.

Today the National Baseball Hall of Fame and Museum stands on the spot where Abner Doubleday supposedly "christened" the National Game. An old baseball, resembling an ossified mummy's head, attests less to his singular accomplishment than to baseball's ability to promote its all-American ancestry.

But the promotion doesn't end there.

In 1935, when National League President Frick conceived the idea of constructing the Baseball Hall of Fame, he petitioned the Clark Foundation—funded by the Singer Sewing Machine family—to generate a grant for the construction of the building. The foundation granted the money—less as a promotion for baseball than as a promotion for the town of Cooperstown and Otsego County—and organized baseball didn't have to pay the freight. That's the anatomy of a real promotion.

If baseball were true to its heritage and followed its roots as faithfully as Alex Haley did his, then the Hall of Fame would be some six hundred miles due west of Cooperstown, New York. It would be in the city of Milwaukee, Wisconsin, pretentiously called by its chamber of commerce "The Beer Capital of the United States."

Baseball started out as a natural extension of the brewery business. The original foundations of the hundred-year-old game are as firm as the foundations of the local brewery, most of baseball's early investors being saloon owners and liquor interests. The very first "major" league—the National Association of Professional Baseball Players—was founded in a saloon.

Beer was so much a part of the very fabric of baseball that a device known as a German Disturber was part of most games during the 1880s. The German Disturber was a keg of beer with a dipper attached, located at third base. Any player reaching third was entitled to quench his thirst with a dipperful of beer.

Through the late 1870s, 1880s, and early 1890s, teams in St. Louis, Baltimore, Brooklyn, Cincinnati, New York, and Louisville were owned by brewers, saloonkeepers, or distillers. To reflect the proper priorities of the times, a Cincinnati team actually resigned from the league because of the rule prohibiting the sale of liquor in its park.

Al Spink—a St. Louis sportswriter who later founded *The Sporting News*—one day revisited the baseball fields of his youth, the area at Grand Avenue in north St. Louis christened Sportsman's Park. There he found a small ball park and "gazed with awe and admiration on a grandstand that would seat 800 persons and bleachers that would seat 800 more." The ball park was vacant on this day in 1881. Once it had proudly housed the St. Louis Browns of the National League, a team which had finished second and fourth the first two years of the league's existence. Then, in the winter of 1877, while the owners awaited the arrival of four new players acquired in secret negotiations from the Louisville Grays, a betting scandal erupted that more seriously threatened the existence of organized baseball than any before or since. The four were expelled from baseball for "hippodroming"—or throwing games. St. Louis, bereft of the star players it had secretly acquired, dropped out of the league.

Now Spink approached the owner of the ball field and offered to buy him out. Disgusted with the bleak outlook for baseball in St. Louis, the owner quickly accepted the offer. Spink and a friend pooled their life savings of $500 and set out for Grand Avenue to complete the deal.

En route, the two stopped off at Chris Von der Ahe's for a glass of beer. Von der Ahe's was a combination saloon and grocery store, an outgrowth of a small boardinghouse he had run for German laborers. Von der Ahe struck up a conversation with the two strangers on the nature of their mission in that part of town. Without any hesitation, they discussed their plans for buying the ball park and bringing a major league team to St. Louis. "Suppose you give him your last $500," Von der Ahe asked, "and get the park. What will you do then?" The two men looked at each other. They hadn't thought it through that completely. But Von der Ahe, known as "Vondy," had. He knew that all those people would need something to slake their thirst on hot summer days. He suggested that they "organize a regular corporation. I'll join you in that and get others to join." And so the park, soon to be named Spink's Sportsman's Park, and the St. Louis Browns baseball club of the American Association were to become part of a corporation formed that very afternoon, with Vondy as its president and Al Spink as its secretary.

Von der Ahe constructed an amusement park adjacent to the ball park, complete with chute-the-chutes, horse races, bands, girl trumpeters, colored dancing waters, and a statue of himself. He also installed a Tivoli-type beer garden and sold tickets for everything in combination. The endeavor was an immediate success—with Von der Ahe giving more thought to who was perspiring at the refreshment stands than to what was transpiring on the field. But it soon prospered on the field as well and, by 1885, the St. Louis Browns had become an institution, winning four consecutive American Association pennants, including the winner-take-all World Series from the champion Chicago White Stockings team of the National League. After every game, Von der Ahe could be seen backing up his grocery wagon to the ball park and loading it up with bags containing the gate receipts for the trip to the bank.

Today that ancestral umbilicus between baseball and breweries still exists. All twenty-six teams are sponsored in one way or another by breweries. One team, the St. Louis Cardinals, is owned by a beer company, lock, stock and barrel, and another team has resigned itself to the obvious by calling itself the Milwaukee Brewers.

Marketing is salesmanship with a scalpel. In some hands it is an operative tool that allows for the delicate slicing up of the population into potential target audiences for goods and services; in other hands it becomes a bludgeon, capable of destruction and even self-mutilation. Marketing is one of the current "buzz words" used with the same frequency a lady of the evening applies rouge to her cheeks. It is used by many but becomes few. When properly used, this tightly integrated effort takes many forms, including production, distribution, customer satisfaction, and advertising. But most importantly, it translates into one proposition and one proposition alone: "Up Your Sales!"

Those who were weaned on movies take it as an article of faith that most meetings where marketing decisions are determined are either (a) chaired by someone who looks like Sidney Greenstreet and punctuates his bombastic statements by spitting on his desk, or (b) attended by junior execs in grey flannel suits who accompany every new thought-drop with hosannas of "Let's Run that One Up the Flagpole and See Who Salutes!"

Nothing could be further from the truth. Most marketing decisions are made by no more than two or three people sitting around a desk involved in masturbatory gymnastics. So it was on a cold day in January, 1974, when two executives of the John Labatt Company in London, Ontario, sat down to mental exercises that would take on the form of a three-dimensional chess game. It was six in the evening when Don McDougall, the young president of Labatt's, and Ed Bradley, the marketing director, took two beers from the handy refrigerator adjacent to the conference table and sat down to discuss the perplexing problem facing them. Labatt's, Canada's largest brewery and its 32nd largest industry, with sales totaling more than $727,000,000 was seeing its supremacy challenged in Toronto by its archcompetitor, Molson's. For any national beer, Ontario, the most populous province, and Toronto, the largest city, are linchpins to its overall success. Long the number two beer in both Toronto and Ontario, Molson's had recently overtaken Labatt's by a 42 to 32 percent share of the Toronto market.

Breweries have traditionally sought tie-ins with sports, a "macho" vehicle which appeals to their target audience: males 21–49. Much of Molson's success is traceable to its alliance with sport. In 1960, it had picked up the sponsorship of the weekly Hockey Night in Canada, a Saturday night program with nationalistic overtones. Molson's had found that if you scratch a hockey fan he bleeds deeply and, with the expansion of the hockey season to almost eight months of the year and the addition of the popular Canada-USSR series in the early 1970s, Molson's was tapping the benefits of hockey's loyal followers where it counted most, at the beer stores and pubs. Labatt's had countered with sponsorship of Canadian football and consequently suffered from two inherent liabilities: the football season overlaps the hockey season and the Canadian brand of football is inferior to that played by the National Football League, which is available to most Canadians on American TV.

Labatt's needed something more. McDougall and Bradley mulled over the available marketing opportunities. "Obviously a bridge tournament wasn't the answer," thought McDougall outloud.

McDougall knew that there had to be something. But what? No concrete decision came out of the two hours of brainstorming except to invite other members of the management team to come back with new promotional ideas. But something eventually came in over the transom. On July 2, 1974, a vice-president of a Toronto investment firm phoned to ask Labatt's if they had any interest in joining a venture to buy the financially troubled Cleveland Indians with an eye towards moving them to Toronto.

Beer and baseball. Of course! It was a natural: a long and rich

6

tradition that had been overlooked. Not only were most beer sales made in the warm weather months—months which belonged exclusively to baseball—but baseball was a natural vacuum in Canada, a ripe area for commercial exploitation.

"Hey, this could be the answer," thought McDougall. But after some preliminary discussions he found there "was no substance" to the proposal to bring the Indians to Toronto. All Labatt's was interested in, according to McDougall, was securing "the advertising rights," a deal which fell through because "we came to the conclusion it wouldn't have been beneficial to our company." Even if it didn't come to fruition, however, the Cleveland foray did implant an idea in McDougall's mind and a glint in Labatt's eye. McDougall was energized by the proposal enough to initiate a feasibility study. This concluded that the combination of beer and baseball would be good for Labatt's and Toronto, in that order. And bad for Molson's.

Once he zeroed in on his target of getting a major league franchise for Toronto, McDougall went public and avowed his purpose of purchasing a team for Canada's largest city. "Baseball in Toronto has a storied past that we should resurrect because a generation of Torontonians do not fully appreciate it."

That "storied past" had seen Toronto teams win fourteen championships over seventy-eight years before dropping out of the International League in 1967. During that time such baseball greats as Nick Altrock, Ike Boone, Dan Brouthers, Bill Carrigan, Bill Dineen, High Duffy, Bob Elliott, Buck Freeman, Charley Gehringer, George Gibson, Burleigh Grimes, Elston Howard, Carl Hubbell, Wee Willie Keeler, Ralph Kiner, Napoleon Lajoie, Tony Lazzeri, Heinie Manush, Frank McCormick, Steve O'Neill, Dick Rudolph, Rip Sewell, Urban Shocker, and Dixie Walker had all suited up in Toronto Maple Leaf uniforms. Managers such as Sparky Anderson, Ed Barrow, Chuck Dressen, Lee Fohl, Dan Howley, Joe Kelley, Luke Sewell, George Stallings, and Dick Williams had directed the Maple Leafs. And—as another footnote to McDougall's "storied past"—Babe Ruth hit his only minor league home run in Toronto. Baseball and Toronto were as much a "natural" as baseball and beer.

Twice before Toronto had flirted with going "big league." A. G. Spalding, former player turned equipment manufacturer, had paid a visit to Toronto in 1886 and suggested that it apply for a franchise in the National League—probably more to expand his company's business prospects in Canada than because of any great desire to expand the National League. But Toronto finessed the offer and applied instead for membership in the International League. Many years later, Maple Leaf owner Jack Kent Cooke—known as Canada's Bill Veeck—tried to bring one of the floating franchises to Toronto. After successively failing to detour either the Boston Braves, St. Louis Browns, or Philadelphia Athletics from their appointed rounds, he joined in the formation of the stillborn Continental League in 1959. This idea died aborning when the major leagues took notice and voted to expand the very next year, grabbing the choicest of the previously staked-out Continental League territories: New York City and Houston, consigning Toronto to the minors. For the moment.

The very first step towards acquiring the big-league label and franchise in Toronto was the construction of a ball park. Frank Lane, who at the time was general manager of the Chicago White Sox, told a gathering of baseball fans in 1954, "A major league franchise is a civic project. The important thing is to get a stadium, a municipal stadium, and then submit your bid."

The construction of stadia has often meant much to cities. As former American League President Joe Cronin once told the New York *Times'* Joe Durso: when he first broke in with the Washington Senators, Yankee Stadium was one of New York's primary tourist attractions, as much a part of America as "Amber fields of grain." "Friends of mine from San Francisco came to New York," recalled Cronin, "and went to see the Statue of Liberty and Yankee Stadium."

Toronto was without a ball park of Yankee Stadium's majestic proportions. In fact, Toronto was without a stadium of any proportions, including the major leagues minimum requirements. Something had to be done, and construction of a stadium was the first olive out of the jar towards bringing major league baseball to Toronto.

Ontario Place is a 96-acre playland strung out along the shores of Lake Ontario like a string of pearls. Built at a cost of $23,000,000 in 1974, it combines restaurants, theaters, playgrounds, a marina, and even one ultra-movie theater that looks like a gigantic golf ball floating in the lake. Adjacent to the amusement park complex is the Canadian National Exhibition Stadium, named for the huge fair that takes over Toronto for four weeks during August and September. Called more familiarly CNE Stadium or Exhibition Stadium, it would be the carrot for bringing major league baseball to Toronto.

Determined to bring CNE Stadium up to major league standards, the Metro Council voted $15,000,000 to expand it in 1974. The expansion to the stadium skeleton was to consist of an L-shaped portion that would form the baseball stands and a double-deck on the north stands for the football stands. The stadium was to house the Toronto Argonauts of the Canadian Football League and, hopefully, a major league baseball team. It would seat 40,000 for baseball and 54,000 for football.

McDougall had his stadium, his study, and his support. What he needed now was a team. The story of how he would get one unfolded slowly, like a thousand-petal lotus.

Since that summer day in 1974, when the potential sponsorship of the Cleveland Indians was brought to him, McDougall had cast around for a franchise. But now the specie he sought was different. It was not sponsorship he wanted for Labatt's; it was ownership.

McDougall was not alone in trying to land a franchise for Toronto. Others had determined that baseball, with or without beer, was a fundamentally sound idea and were now fishing in the same waters for a franchise. Metro Chairman Paul Godfrey, responsible for appropriating the $15,000,000 for the renovation of CNE Stadium, approached the major league owners at the 1975 All-Star game in Milwaukee to plead Toronto's case. R. Howard Webster, chairman and president of the *Toronto Globe and Mail* and a member of the Montreal Expos' board of directors, made his intentions known through Gerry Snyder, who had helped secure a National League franchise for Montreal. The management of Maple Leaf Gardens, Ltd., also was searching for a team. It was every group for itself.

If anyone was more interested than Labatt's in acquiring a franchise, no one was more active. First McDougall called the general manager of the Baltimore Orioles "to find out whether rumors of the possible sale of the Orioles were true." They were. From November 1974, through January of the following year, Labatt's negotiated with Oriole owner Jerry Hoffberger for the sale of the team. It soon became evident however, that Hoffberger—a beer baron himself—didn't want to sell the ball club without the brewery, the National Brewing Company. Labatt's was only interested in acquiring a baseball franchise. Not another brewery. (Ironically, after Labatt's broke off negotiations, one of its rivals, Carling-O'Keefe, bought out National, but not the Orioles.)

There were other rumors. One of baseball's premier—if not majestic—franchises, the San Francisco Giants, had fallen upon hard times and could be had.

The Giants traced their proud ancestry back to 1880, when Jim "Smiling Jeems" Mutrie, a former player, and John B. Day, a businessman whose interests included a wholesale tobacco and liquor business, sat next to each other at a game between the Brooklyn Atlantics and the New York Mutuals. Finding that their interests in sponsoring a club were as mutual as the team on the field, they formed the Metropolitan Exhibition Company on the spot. Their first venture was the New York Mets, an independent team. In 1882 they joined the American Association and, hedging their bets, the following year took over the dead Troy (New York) Haymaker franchise and entered a team in the National League, forming the first baseball "syndicate." The National League team, which played its games at the old Polo Grounds at 110th Street and Fifth Avenue, became known as the Giants in 1888 when the stovepipe-hatted Mutrie, then the manager of the team, remarked that his tall, broad-shouldered, troops were "Giants in action as well as stature."

Giants they became, a proud nickname for a proud team. Throughout the remainder of the nineteenth century and into the twentieth, the Giants were to become what *Baseball Magazine* called "the best known team in the world." These were the Giants of Buck Ewing, Tim Keefe, Jim McGraw, "Iron Man" Joe McGinnity, Christy Mathewson, Frankie Frisch, Bill Terry, Mel Ott, Carl Hubbell, and Willie Mays. The Giants have more players in the Hall of Fame, more victories, and more winning seasons than any other team in the history of baseball. These were indeed Giants.

It was a proud and mighty franchise that, regardless of its place in the standings, waxed fat in its Polo Grounds' headquarters and hindquarters through many a change in ownership: from Day and Mutrie to Andrew Freedman to John T. Brush and his son-in-law Harry Hemstead to Charles A. Stoneham and his son Horace. But their performance in the World Series left something to be desired. Fourteen times they had won the National League pennant, but had only four World Series wins to go with them as the climax to a successful season. And then, finally, in 1954, they won the Series against the Indians and improbable odds.

It was to be their last hurrah. In 1955 they were third, by 1956 sixth, and by 1958 the New York Giants were gone.

10

Following Horace Greeley's advice and Walter O'Malley's Brooklyn Dodgers, the Giants migrated to San Francisco after the 1957 season, thus ending seventy-five years of wedded bliss between New York and the National League. There were now the San Francisco Giants. In a take-off of Bill Terry's famous question, Brooklyn was no longer "still in the league"—and neither was New York.

The city of San Francisco greeted the Giants with open arms and plans for a new stadium: Candlestick Park. Built on fill which had once been San Francisco's trash dump on its good days, the new stadium would pose as a wind tunnel for nearby Lockheed Corporation. The winds were capricious, the players—including Willie Mays and Orlando Cepeda—exciting, the fans delirious. The Giants had struck California's richest vein since John Marshall discovered gold on his land near Sutter's Mill more than one hundred years before.

Playing to more than one and three-quarter million fans that first year—and only slightly fewer in succeeding years—the Giants began to mirror their success in the stands with their success on the field, first climbing back to respectability and then to the top of the mountain in 1962, when they won the National League pennant and came within one hit of winning the Series—Willie McCovey's drive that just failed to clear Bobby Richardson's outstretched glove.

But what did San Francisco blasé fans care? They had beaten the Dodgers in the play-offs and owned the National League. And Horace Stoneham was delighted. He had a lock on the Bay Area sports gold mine. Or at least he did until 1968, when another prospector, Charlie O (for "Owner") Finley brought the tatterdemalion Kansas City Athletics west to Oakland to pan the same waters.

Territorial rights had always been somewhat ambiguous. Dating from the establishment of the Brooklyn franchise in 1890, it was always thought that a body of water delineated a club's territorial claim. Thus, Brooklyn was able to enter the same league as New York because they were separated by the East River; anything on one side theoretically belonged to the Giants and on the other to Brooklyn's new team, the Superbas. Although Stoneham might have claimed territorial rights to the entire Bay Area in 1968, he somehow felt the distance between San Francisco and Oakland was made greater by the body of water that separated them. And he extracted no tribute.

After 1962, El Dorado's luster began to tarnish. The Giants never again won, finishing second five straight times as perennial bridesmaids, while the Dodgers were winning pennants with some regularity. Then there was Candlestick Park. The seagulls, the summertime fogs, and icy winds that wafted in from the bay were bad enough. Added to these was an unexpected hazard, the safety of the patrons. From the beginning, muggings had been a regular occurrence in the ill-lighted further reaches of the desolate parking lots. Over the years, this petty crime wave burgeoned but remained endemic until one day it burst forth inside the previously sacrosanct environs of the park itself. Six wives of bank executives were robbed at knife point in their reserved seats. This well-publicized incident merely typified the combat-like atmosphere at Candlestick. The lunatics were now in charge of the asylum. And if these problems weren't bad enough, Finley's A's were coming up like thunder across the bay. Soon, Bay Area fans were dividing their affections and the Giants' attendance had been cut in half.

By 1971, the original roles were reversed. A 21-year-old sensation named Vida Blue won nine of his first ten games and became an immediate drawing card. The A's won the first of five straight Western Division championships. The rout was on. In these five years the Giants suffered losses of $6,700,000, including $3,500,000 during 1974 and 1975, when their attendance slipped to 519,991 and 522,919—the worst in either league.

Coupled with all their other troubles, the Giants seemed to make their own. San Francisco native Joe DiMaggio felt that "their public relations and promotion have been very bad. I know of many instances where their ticket-office people acted like they were doing fans a favor when they sold them tickets to a game. They were saying to people 'We've got the only game in town and you've got to come and see us.'" Even Willie Mays, who went west with the Giants in 1958, saw much the same promotional vacuum and believed it contributed to their ultimate ruin. He traced that downfall back long before the Oakland A's arrived on the other side of the Bay. "It started before that when the Giants were really riding high and drawing a million and a half fans or more. The club should have had a strong promotional program under way. If you don't promote and stay after people when things are going good," Willie philosophized, "You'll find they've gone and forgotten you when things are not so good." And things were, in Willie's words, "not so good."

Even the city of San Francisco tried to ameliorate the Giants' plight. Instead of a lifesaver, however, the city fathers tossed the

12

drowning team an anchor. Faced with the threatened defection of the football 49ers, who were crying about the inadequacies of Kezar Stadium, the city enlarged the seating capacity of Candlestick from 44,000 to 58,000 and installed artificial turf. The Giants, who preferred natural turf and weren't filling the 44,000 seats with anything more than seagulls and their droppings, went to court to forestall the "improvements," but lost. The city then instituted a surcharge of 50¢ on every ticket over $2, giving the Giants one more bill they couldn't pay.

At first the Giants tried to stem the losses by peddling expensive ball players like Willie Mays and Willie McCovey. Then they borrowed to keep operating—a million dollars from the Bank of America and half a million from the National League. Even this wasn't enough. The team was in arrears on its loans, its rent, and its taxes. There remained only one answer: sell the franchise and the other properties in Arizona and Minnesota. And sell them immediately.

And so, in May 1975, the National Exhibition Company—the quaintly named corporation formed some seventy-two years before—was put on the block. Before McDougall and Labatt's entered the picture, the attorneys for the Giants and the National League had talked to some 35 prospective purchasers—including the Seibu Railway Co. of Tokyo, which had bid $18,000,000 for the team and then withdrawn it. McDougall would be the thirty-sixth, but still he was hesitant to turn this particular stone because of what he called "legal ramifications."

In an effort to pursue every available lead, McDougall met with the legal advisors for the team and for Horace Stoneham as well in September 1975. The meeting was "disastrous." Although both parties "left the door open," McDougall felt that "chances for an agreement didn't look too good."

Two months later the unlikeliest of matchmakers since Dolly Levi Gallagher stepped forward and indicated that McDougall should try again. The matchmaker was none other than Walter O'Malley, the man who had brought his Dodgers west and who had seduced Stoneham into the same bargain some twenty years before. McDougall had "assumed O'Malley was against the move of the Giants," but he had underestimated the man.

Walter O'Malley is not only the uncrowned king of the National League: he *is*, to all intents and purposes, the moving force in the major leagues. And he understood one thing: money. Where money was involved, "natural" rivalries took a back seat. The National League was in no position to loan the Giants any more. In fact, the league's borrowing power was somewhat taxed. With no takers in San Francisco—or anywhere else for that matter—O'Malley was looking to help the league, and himself, out of an impossible situation. McDougall remembers the meeting: "O'Malley was most encouraging. He suggested we make an offer to the National League because he figured the league would eventually have to take over the Giants."

McDougall promptly went back to Toronto and framed a proposal. The initial offer was $12,500,000; $10,000,000 for the team and $2,500,000 for legal costs incidental to paying off the remaining lease on Candlestick Park. The Giants had signed an agreement in 1960 pledging to keep the team in San Francisco and leasing Candlestick for thirty-five years at the rate of $125,000 a year. At the end of 1975 there were nineteen more years to run on the lease, of $2,375,000. Finally, after a negotiation that resembled Dr. Doolittle's "Push-me-Pull-you," the offer was firmed up at $13,500,000; $8,000,000 for the team and $5,500,000 to be put in escrow for legal costs attendant to moving the club to Toronto. Stoneham and the National Exhibition Company accepted the offer "in principle" on January 9, 1976.

Meanwhile, McDougall was shoring up his financial fences preparatory to purchasing the Giants and moving them to Toronto. He engineered a tripartite arrangement with financier R. Howard Webster and the Canadian Imperial Bank of Commerce. Labatt's and Webster's Vulcan Fund would both own 45 percent of the team and The Commerce 10 percent. "It's a viable business proposition with tremendous earnings potential," said McDougall, saying nothing about the public relations value to a beer company seeking to increase its own franchise.

Almost before the cheering in Toronto had died away, some of the "legal ramifications" that McDougall had originally feared loomed as stumbling blocks to the transfer of the team. The new mayor of San Francisco, George Moscone, went into Superior Court and obtained a temporary injunction blocking the proposed franchise move. For the next two months, as the case played to larger audiences than the normal Candlestick Park crowd, the Giants' financial linen was aired in public as Moscone sought desperately to find a purchaser who would pledge to keep the team in San Francisco.

Behind all the last-minute legal maneuvering was the fine hand of "Chub" S. (for Stoneham) Feeney, president of the National League. Baseball has always been a sport where blood is much thicker than water, and no clan was thicker than the Stonehams. Horace owned the Giants, and his sister's son Chub, former vice president of both the New York and San Francisco Giants, was now the league president. Feeney was involved in what Glenn Dickey of the *San Francisco Chronicle* saw as a rather interesting "conflict of interests." According to Dickey, if the San Francisco Giants were to move to Toronto—or any other place, for that matter—Feeney would "have been forced to move the National League head office to some other city." So the National League continued to pay mere lip service to the Toronto bid while keeping the door open for any and all bidders who would keep the team—and Feeney—in San Francisco.

Finally, on February 2, 1976, the very last day of the life of the restraining order, Moscone came up with what seemed to be a Band-Aid remedy. He had mated San Francisco businessman Robert Lurie with Robert Short, former owner of the Minneapolis Lakers of the National Basketball Association and the Washington Senators, late of the American League, twice removed. Together they had come up with $8,000,000, matching Labatt's basic offer to the Giants. The judge ordered the Giants to keep their hearts as well as their behinds in San Francisco.

The National League—viewing Short as a scalawag who had poisoned the waters before—imposed three conditions on the purchase and the Lurie-Short partnership. First, Lurie was to cast "any tie-breaking vote in the operation of the club and in league matters." Second, the city was to rescind the 50¢ surcharge. Third, the city was to supply security services in and around Candlestick Park. The latter items were quickly accepted by Moscone, but the first one stuck in Short's craw and he pulled out of the picture on March 2nd. The deal was falling through again, until Lurie managed to persuade an Arizona meat packer named Bud Herseth to pledge the money necessary to take over Short's position. The cavalry had arrived in the nick of time. The National League quickly approved the sale. The Giants stayed in San Francisco but not, ironically, Feeney, who was forced by a palace revolution to move the league offices to New York. The Mighty Casey at Labatt's had struck out. At least temporarily.

Like the girl who is all dressed up with no place to go, Don McDougall and his syndicate had no place to go on March 2, 1976. But another party was being planned and within one month they were to become part of this one.

If the National League had a problem with its San Francisco franchise, the American League was doubly blessed. Across the Bay, the A's were in trouble now. Concomitant with the steady

decline of Giants' attendance, in a classic case of product canni-
balism, the Oakland club had seen their number fall to the point
where the two teams together drew less than the Giants once
had alone. Then there was the Seattle problem. Seattle and
Kansas City had entered the American League in 1969 as part of
a major expansion to twelve teams. After only one year, however, the franchise shuffled off to Milwaukee. This solved one of
baseball's long-standing problems—how to replace the erstwhile
Milwaukee Braves—by creating a new set of problems. Some
trade-off! The state of Washington, the city of Seattle, and King
County responded in the only way baseball truly understands,
with an antitrust suit against organized baseball of gigantic
proportions: $32,500,000 in treble damages.

Nevertheless, the Seattle problem seemed solvable, especially
in 1976. The Chicago White Sox were destitute and in definite
need of either a sale, a shift, or both. The reasoning around the
league office was that if the White Sox moved to Seattle, in three
years the Oakland franchise would be moved to Finley's hometown of Chicago. All would be solved without any need for
expansion.

This scenario overlooked one pivotal character, however: Bill
Veeck. Among other clubs, Veeck had once owned the White Sox
and now had an option to buy them again. But Veeck was loved
by no one, except the fans and sometimes the press. Certainly
not the owners. They looked upon this tieless maverick as an
intruder into the most exclusive club in the world—their own.
Here was a man they had once frozen out of baseball—and they
had no desire to allow him back in. Especially not now. Not
when he represented a monkey wrench in their carefully laid
plans to move into a new territory and eliminate the lawsuit.

When Veeck presented his request for a transference of
ownership at baseball's winter meetings in 1975 he was received
with something less than open arms. In fact, he was almost
"armed." After voting down his request, the owners threw him a
bone. If he could come up with another $1,200,000 and change
the entire capitalization of his investing group—all within a
week's time—they might consider his application. It was obvious
that they had decided on putting as many financial hurdles as
possible in front of the one-legged genius and then—after grant-
ing the franchise to Seattle—explain that he couldn't clear them.
But they had either underestimated Veeck or didn't remember
his ability to make the impossible happen.

One week later Veeck was back. He had proved the impossible
was possible, even without adequate time. He had managed to

dance to the tune of their financial fandango. Characteristically, the owners voted his request down again. They had Danny Kaye waiting in the wings with a $10,000,000 certified check, able and more than willing to buy the team and transfer it to Seattle. But at this point John Fetzer, owner of the Detroit Tigers, had had enough. He made a plea for a second vote. "Gentlemen," said Fetzer, "I have been in this league for twenty years and I have seen one slipshod deal after another. We cannot allow this to happen any longer. We rush in here to vote and then we want to run out for drinks. There has been much soul-searching over this deal and it has set a precedent. We have left these people over a barrel. We told them to go do it—and they did it. Now, let's not cry over the spilled milk or moan about it." Shamed into voting a second time, the owners finally approved the transfer of the White Sox to Veeck, 10–2.

They had now met one moral issue head-on, and miraculously both their morals and their heads had triumphed. But what of Seattle? There still was the $32,500,000 suit to contend with. Lee MacPhail, president of the American League, insisted, "We don't want to go to court, but we aren't afraid of a lawsuit."

But if MacPhail wasn't "afraid of a lawsuit," there were plenty of owners who were. So, following the course of least resistance, they quickly voted to admit Seattle, setting the price at $6,300,000 for an expansion franchise, which was to enter the American League in 1977 as the thirteenth club.

But just as there are men who rent themselves out as the "fourteenth man" for dinners in France so that no table comes complete with the same unlucky number who sat around the table at the Last Supper, the American League now had thirteen clubs and desperately needed a "fourteenth" to fill out its own table and balance its schedule. The solution to the dilemma was right there in front of them. Sensing an opening for Toronto at the major league table, McDougall and Metro Chairman Godfrey had been campaigning at the winter meetings.

They were not without support. While, unbelievably, no one in command in the National League had ever been to Toronto, several in the American were familiar with the city. Muriel Kauffman, co-owner of the Kansas City Royals and wife of president Ewing Kauffman, a member of the league's franchise committee, was a native Torontonian whose father had been a member of the Ontario legislature. Dick O'Connell, general manager of the Boston Red Sox, who had known Toronto back in the days when it had the Bosox Triple-A farm team, expressed the belief that "Toronto is a major league city." Charlie Finley expressed himself in his own fashion when Toronto made its presentation: "Don't let those guys get out of the room. Award them something! Anything!"

They did. On March 29, the American League voted 11-1 to expand to Toronto, scant minutes before the National League decided that they too would lay claim to the city north of the border, for no other reason than the natural rivalry it would breed between Montreal and Toronto. But the National League was hindered by two considerations: any expansion required a unanimous vote, and Commissioner Bowie Kuhn had attempted to tie the tail of Washington's reentry into the majors on Toronto's kite, bringing both down. Kuhn, who had once served as a summertime employee behind the scoreboard in Washington's Griffith Stadium, had personally pledged to several congressmen that he would bring baseball back to Washington. But it was not to be so, at least not in the National League, which voted the dual entry of Washington and Toronto down. Toronto belonged to the American League, and within two days, the Toronto franchise belonged to Labatt's—in tandem with Webster's Vulcan Assets Dominion, Ltd. and the Canadian Imperial Bank of Commerce—for $7,000,000, $6.5 million less than the Giants would have cost them.

Because baseball, like nature, abhors a vacuum, expansion is a natural procedure, physically acting as a crowbar—to pry up baseball's physical boundaries. Expansion has been part of baseball's digestive process since the first expansion teams—Washington and Los Angeles—were added to the American League in 1961. Now Toronto and Seattle would become the ninth and tenth new teams to be added in the last seventeen years, taking major league baseball to every large metropolitan area on the North American continent and making it, in marketing terms, an international product.

Labatt's long search for a marketing "hook" they could exploit was over. Major league baseball and the label "big league" finally belonged to Toronto. Never mind that the team wasn't the transplanted San Francisco Giants with their established stars, their glamorous history, and their built-in rivalry with their fellow National League entry, Montreal. Never mind that the National League appeared to be a stronger league with more top stars and larger-drawing teams. It was major league baseball—even if it was expansion baseball.

The most successful expansion franchise from a marketing point of view was the New York Mets. National League fans in

New York were orphaned when the Dodgers and Giants left town. They had lost their sense of identity, and worse, their heritage. But even in their grief they wouldn't be caught dead in Yankee Stadium. Watching those guys in pinstripes who won all the time was "like rooting for U.S. Steel." Or so the reasoning went.

Dodger and Giant fans never flocked to a winner. They stayed with their teams year after year, come hell or high jinx. And so, when the Dodgers and Giants went west after drawing 1,682,000 fans between them in 1957, you would have thought some of those baseball-starved fans would have given in to an old urge and surreptitiously crept into Yankee Stadium, even if it was just for a "fix" to keep their old habit going. But the Yankees, as one official of the team now remembers, "offended a lot of people in the old days." Even though they were on their way to their ninth pennant in ten years, they actually drew 68,700 *fewer* fans in 1958 than they had the previous year when the Dodgers and Giants provided competition.

The Yankees also were insensitive enough to successfully alienate entire groups of their own fans. They were a "lily-white" team—even with Elston Howard playing catcher and token black. National League fans who had come to appreciate the contributions of players like Jackie Robinson, Roy Campanella, Don Newcombe, Junior Gilliam, Sandy Amoros, Monte Irvin, Reuben Gomez, and Willie Mays not only accepted and applauded blacks and Latin Americans, they expected them. Minority groups—especially those who happened to be living near Yankee Stadium—demanded them. It was obvious to all, except the Yankees, that it would be an important plus in marketing the team.

In fact, to review the Yankees' past mistakes would only serve as the basis for a case history in "The Mismanagement of a Franchise" for study at the Harvard Business School. After fifteen of the most glorious years in baseball history, the Yankees threw Babe Ruth out the door. The only team to give him a job after he finished his playing career was, ironically, the Brooklyn Dodgers. The Yankees forbade banners in their stately pleasure palace and, when one was espied, the culprits were descended upon with all the efficiency of S.S. troops, confiscating the offending bedspread or sheet that had been lovingly hand-lettered and throwing the culprits out of the park bodily. They put Casey Stengel, the man made out of gingerbread who looked like he stepped right out of the pages of a Hans Christian

Andersen fairy tale, out to pasture. And then, even after the Mets had come to town and the message should have been heard loud and clear, they then proceeded to fire Yogi Berra, who, in the eyes of many New Yorkers, had the charm of all seven of Snow White's dwarfs rolled into one.

When the Mets were formed out of whole cloth in 1961, their first moves were to (A) acquire the Polo Grounds, the Giants former field, to play in until their new stadium was finished; (B) obtain St. Petersburg, the Yankees' former training site, as theirs; (C) hire Casey Stengel as their manager; (D) draft one of the most popular of all Dodgers, Gil Hodges, from Los Angeles; or (E) all of the above? Answer (E) is correct.

From Day One, the Mets—dubbed "Amazin'" by Stengel— were the darlings of the press and the public. Even though there were some hesitant expectations for respectability, they were far outweighed by the nostalgic umbilicus the Mets formed to New York baseball fans; particularly the vestigial remainder of Dodger and Giant fans.

The entire success of the Mets lay in packaging. They had been astute enough not to predicate their marketing on the team. That would have been foolhardy. Instead, they based their success on their appeal to the fans. It was the Mets' fans themselves who were truly "Amazin'." Some were caught up in the role reversal of rooting for the underdog. In those days, when Avis was trying the same approach on its competitor Hertz, this group of fans saw in the Mets an identifiable champion for all its lost causes. When they won—which was infrequent—the fan vicariously saw himself beating up on his landlord or boss or someone else in authority, something he never could do with the Yankees. The younger fan, searching for his own identity, didn't want to cheer for the team of his parents, but wanted a team of his own. That "team" was to be the Mets. Finally, there was the old National League and Hate-the-Yankees fan, who had waited four long years for something to fill his rooting void. Together they came out to the Polo Grounds to cheer even the weakest of ground balls, carry their illegible banners around the stands, and follow their heroes, typified by the incomparable and incompetent Marvin Eugene Throneberry, whose very initials formed an anagram of the team's name. These fans were what *New York Daily News* columnist Dick Young called The New Breed. And they were the making of the franchise.

Now McDougall needed some semblance of structure and muscularity to the team. He needed a front office. Many applied for the job of general manager. But one who did not was Peter Bavasi, vice president and general manager of the San Diego Padres. Baseball has traditionally eaten its young. The Carpenters, Griffiths, Veecks, O'Malleys, and Bavasis are prime examples of second generation baseball families. But Peter was different. He had not fallen heir to a business, but he was pedigreed nevertheless, working his way into the game through the kind offices of his father.

Peter Bavasi had traveled with Emil "Buzzie" Bavasi as he climbed up the Dodger chain from Valdosta, Georgia; to Vero Beach, Florida; to Durham, North Carolina; to Nashua, New Hampshire; and finally to Montreal, Brooklyn and Los Angeles. All the while, as he moved from town to town, much like a "service brat," he was "hanging around," keeping his ears open and his mouth shut and getting an informal education in baseball. From this early childlike Walter Mittyesque existence, for which any boy could gladly trade his entire baseball card collection, Peter Bavasi learned baseball by osmosis.

Some of his earliest memories are of his father negotiating with players; of Andy High, the great Dodger scout, coming up to suburban Scarsdale to meet with his father; and even—when the family lived in Nashua, New Hampshire—of Roy Campanella and Don Newcombe visiting their home on a Sunday after Campanella had hit a couple of home runs. A local chicken farmer had offered twenty baby chicks for every homer hit on Sunday. "Campie had so many of those baby chicks, I think he finally ended up giving them all to his mother," the now-older little boy remembers. "And she had one of the largest chicken farms in New Jersey."

Peter augmented this informal education with a formal one, attending St. Mary's University in California, from which he graduated with a BA in philosophy in 1964. He joined the Dodger organization in the winter of 1964 to "work for Buzzie," first as business manager of the Dodgers' Albuquerque farm club in the Class AA Texas League, then as general manager of their Santa Barbara farm club in the Class A California League, and finally returning to Albuquerque to serve as general manager of the club in 1968.

It was while he was in his final year at Albuquerque that Peter Bavasi merged the old with the new: his past remembrances with his present capacity. Weaned on baseball, Brooklyn-style, he fondly remembered the Ebbets Field of his early years: Gladys Gooding at the organ playing "Follow the Dodgers," the Sym-Phony Band marching through the stands playing music which bore no resemblance to any recognizable tune, and Hilda Chester ringing her cowbells. Now he wanted some of the same atmosphere at Albuquerque. Because the team was nicknamed the Dodgers, he got in touch with artist Willard Mullin, who had created the famed Brooklyn Bum, and had him work up a similar character with a sombrero and a serape to serve as the new Albuquerque logo. They would be the Albuquerque Bums. Peter O'Malley, the president of the parent club, told Bavasi that he "shouldn't use the Bum, 'cause it's not our image now." But image-schmimage, Bavasi didn't say anything; he just did it, and the second-place Albuquerque Bums drew 20 percent more fans than they had the previous year when they had won the pennant.

By the next year Peter Bavasi had moved to the major leagues. Only it wasn't to Los Angeles, but to San Diego, where he joined his own padre, Buzzie, as director of minor league operations for the Padres. Then, three years later, he ascended to the job of general manager. At the age of 30, he was the youngest general manager in major league history.

Don McDougall had spent two months looking for a general manager, one who, the board of directors had instructed him, must be a man young enough to relate to the youth image of the team and yet, on the other hand, be steeped in baseball knowledge and tradition. It sounded like the job requirements for an account executive in a Madison Avenue advertising agency: the applicant must be 25 with thirty-five years of experience. If there was such a hybrid, Peter Bavasi was it. One day in May 1976, McDougall called Bavasi *Père* to sound him out on his son's availability. Buzzie asked Peter "What do you think?" Peter, who was going to call the Toronto club anyway to recommend Eddie Robinson, gave a half-hearted demurrer: "Oh, the hell with that. I've been through this three or four times. And anyway, I love you and San Diego . . . I'll stay with this!" Over the previous three years, by his own admission, he had been taking over more and more of the operations; not taking it away from Buzzie, but having it given to him by Buzzie. Besides, the two of them owned a piece of the team, a gift from Ray Kroc, owner of the Padres.

But the more Peter thought about it, the more he was fascinated. First of all, he had always been, no matter what, his father's man. He didn't know if he could establish his "baseball legs" on his own, and he wanted a chance to test his own ability. Secondly, and from a point of very personal pride, if he were to become the general manager and general factotum of the Toronto expansion team, it would mark the first time in baseball history that a father and son had run two baseball franchises at the same time. And so, Peter Bavasi pursued the inquiry from McDougall for reasons of family pride as well as personal accomplishment.

After a month of negotiating, McDougall, in the name of the board of directors, offered Peter a five-year, $65,000-a-year contract with a noninterference clause to go out and "do his own thing." And on June 18, 1976, Peter Bavasi was introduced at a hastily called press conference as the chief executive officer of the Toronto Whatchamacallits.

A current trivia question making the rounds of the bars goes: "Name the three professional teams—not including soccer— whose nicknames do not end in the letter 'S'?" The answer— White Sox, Red Sox, and New Orleans Jazz—is not nearly as difficult as sorting through the teams on the sports scene. For in the last decade and a half, the number of teams have multiplied faster than the population of a rabbit hutch. Almost all conceivable names have been appropriated, with the possible exception of aardvarks and platypuses.

It was not always thus. Back in the good ol' days, when baseball teams were sixteen and pro football and basketball teams almost the same in number, nicknames were used simply to connote strength and uniform colorations—as in Tigers, the most prevalent college football nickname; or Reds, the first professional sports team. Occasionally, an unusual team nickname would emerge, like the Brooklyn Tip Tops of the Federal Baseball League, named after the owner's bread factory, or the Macon Whoopies of the Southern Hockey League, whose president's favorite song was Gus Kahn's "Makin' Whoopie!" But most names were simple, direct, and possessed strength.

Then something like the World Football League came on the scene, and the landscape was littered with names like the Southern California Sun, the Philadelphia Bell, the Chicago Fire, and the Portland Storm. The league blessedly died. And with it the names. Still, there were more teams than names to go around.

Added to the problem of team identification is the problem of changing a team's name. Today, the changing of a team's name is the first act of a struggling franchise. Closing up shop is next. But it isn't always so. Sometimes the reason for the original name undergoes change, or the owners change or even the franchise city changes.

When the San Diego Padres were on the brink of moving to Washington, Peter Bavasi faced the problem of renaming the team. Several Washington writers started submitting new names to him, including the Washington Waterbuggers and the D.C. Nine. One enterprising scribe, Morrie Siegel, twisted the old name and tweaked the town, calling it the Washington Madres.

Now there was a need to name the Toronto No-Names. And what could be better promotion than a Name the Team Contest? The grand prize for naming the yet-undesignated team would be, fittingly enough, an all-expense paid trip to the yet-undesignated spring training camp the following year with nine runner-up prizes of season tickets for the inaugural year.

Napoleon Lajoie was the first great promotion of the fledgling American League, founded on the premise of "clean baseball, beer, and plenty of 25¢ seats." Enticed to jump from the National League Philadelphia team to the junior circuit by American League president Ban Johnson for a mere $50 more a season in 1901, he promptly paid back the investment by hitting .426 and becoming the American League's first batting champion, Triple Crown winner, and superstar. At the start of the 1902 season, the Philadelphia Nationals got an injunction prohibiting him from playing for the Philadelphia Athletics of the rival league, and Johnson engineered a deal that sent him to Cleveland. There, Lajoie enjoyed such popularity that the team was named after him. Throughout his thirteen years in a Cleveland uniform as player and manager, the Cleveland club was known as the Napoleons or "Naps."

When Lajoie was sold back to the Athletics in 1915, Cleveland was left only with fond remembrances of their departed superstar and a nickname that now seemed out of place. So a local newspaper sponsored a contest to rename the team. The winner was Indians, a name submitted to honor American Indian Louis "Chief" Sockalexis, who had played for Cleveland before the turn of the century and had died the previous year. Ever since, pick-the-name contests have served as great promotions and publicity gimmicks.

Sometimes contests have been used as camouflage to enable the owners to choose the team name they wanted from the start. Poet Marianne Moore once exhausted her *Thesaurus* to come up with suggestions for Ford after it commissioned her to name a new car and they choose the name they had wanted all along: Edsel. So too had the Richmond (Virginia) hockey team in the

American Hockey League, who conducted a name-the-team contest to provide the new franchise with a fitting name. The winner was the Robins and the prize of a motorboat was awarded to the winner by the owner of the team, Claiborne Robins, Jr.

Having decided early on to jettison Maple Leafs—the name of the former minor league club and imitative of the hockey team— McDougall and Metro Baseball Ltd. looked for a new name. The ideal team nickname, it was suggested, "is one that provides instant identification and that works against a name like Maple Leafs. It helps if it is colorful, or pertains to something local and preferably it should be short."

The predominant coloration was blue; the Maple Leafs wore blue and white, and the CFL Argonauts were known as the Double Blue. More importantly, from Labatt's viewpoint, was the fact that they had a product called Labatt's Blue and the incorporation of that primary color in the team's name would make good sense—and good marketing.

Somehow the message got across as more than one hundred eighty-five different variations on a blue theme came in among the twenty-five thousand entries and four thousand different names. There were so many blues you would have thought it was a Billie Holiday revival: Blue Caps, Blue Stockings, Blue Vulcans, Blue Bats—which in French reads Les Battes Bleues—and even Blue Balls. But somehow there were a few who just didn't seem to catch the full importance of Labatt's association with the team and submitted the names Blue Ribbons and Buds.

Then, on August 13, 1976, the name was announced: the Blue Jays. Howie Starkman, the public relations director for the newly named team, proclaimed that the name was unique to major league baseball. But it had been used before, when Robert Carpenter purchased the Phillies in 1944. The very first thing he did was to name his son club president. The second was to initiate a contest to rename the perennial losers. The name selected to replace Phillies was Bluejays, but after another typical Philadelphia last-place finish, the name Bluejays was retired—until Toronto came into baseball and picked it up.

Meanwhile, Peter Bavasi made one of his first public pronounciamentos to welcome the new nickname: "We wanted a name that would endure and was unique. We wanted to stay away from any commercial connection."

Now Bavasi had just nine months, the proper gestation period, to build and field a team. His first act was to appoint Roy Hartsfield manager.

Bavasi had first come to know Hartsfield in his first year of organized ball, in Albuquerque, where he served as business manager and Hartsfield had served as field manager. The dynamic duo had brought Albuquerque in first, the only time Bavasi was to taste first place but one of the first of many for Hartsfield. Hartsfield went on to finish in front four times in seven years in the Pacific Coast League, the last two as manager of Hawaii, a San Diego farm club. In fact, the much-traveled Hartsfield was a perfect choice for the new expansion team in Toronto, having played in eight former minor league cities that have turned "major" in the last two decades: Milwaukee, Baltimore, Los Angeles, St. Paul, Atlanta, Dallas, Fort Worth, and Montreal. More important to Bavasi than the number of travel stickers on his suitcase was his ability to "relate to younger players."

Working around the clock, Bavasi entered the open market for players. His first acquisition was journeyman Phil Roof, a catcher in the White Sox organization. He was, according to Bavasi, necessary because "We intend to draft young players, especially young pitchers. Therefore, we figure a veteran catcher will be a helpful instructor for a young staff and be able to provide game leadership." Some fourteen years before, catcher Hobie Landrith had become the first New York Met. Casey Stengel had said the same thing as Bavasi, only in simpler, less business-like tones: "You gotta start with a catcher or you'll have all passed balls."

A steady stream of announcements flowed out of the Blue Jays' offices: outfielder John Scott . . . third baseman Dave Hilton . . . infielder-catcher Dave Roberts . . . batting coach Bobby Doerr . . . pitching coach Bob Miller . . . spring training facilities at Dunedin, Florida. The Blue Jays were coming to life.

All was prelude to November 4, 1976, the day the organization had been pointing to since its inception. This was the day of the expansion draft, when the Blue Jays would choose thirty players from the rosters of the twelve established American League clubs. Stengel had expressed it all when, looking at the players available to the Mets in 1961, he said: "I want to thank you all for making these boys possible." Possible and improbable, the raw material for a ball club was there for the taking: untried rookies like Bob Bailor from the Orioles and James Clancy from the Rangers, and seasoned veterans like Rico Carty from the Indians and Bill Singer from the Twins. When the draft was finished the Blue Jays had acquired the contracts of thirty players for their $7,000,000.

Despite the draft and the deals, the Blue Jays were to be the least experienced team in baseball, at times experiencing difficulties discerning the difference between the foul line and the blue line. And their salaries reflected it. They were the lowest in the major leagues, an average of $34,320 for the starting team. But the front office was another story. Bavasi had determined early on that he would not come waltzing into Toronto the same way John McHale had gone from the Braves into Montreal in 1969 with his so-called Hired Guns, looking for all the baseball world like the Atlanta Mafia. Instead, he wanted what he called a home-grown management team, one young enough and aggressive enough to build a dream on. He found them and they were home-grown: out of forty-five on staff, only five were Americans; the rest Canadians.

Their task was to make the seemingly impossible happen and Bavasi saw to it that their efforts were rewarded. Unlike Branch Rickey, whose working premise had been that you could find almost anybody to work in baseball because they were dedicated fans who were paid according to their dedication, Bavasi took pride in the fact that "man for man and woman for woman, they were the highest paid front office in baseball." All forty-five played important roles in the making of the team. The frenzied work of the front office staff was best reflected in a six-panel accordion fold-out brochure which delineated seven special days (promotion department), more than fifty ticket outlets throughout the Metro Toronto area (ticket department), information on how to form special groups for Blue Jays' games (group sales), gift certificate information (ticket department), and a thousand and one other pieces of information, all of which meant thousands of hours of work to put together. The brochure even included the infectious optimism of the Blue Jays' management by including the pie-in-the-sky provision that season ticket holders would gain the so-called benefit of having "Priority on playoff and World Series tickets if the Blue Jays qualify." On Opening Day they were rewarded for their efforts with little keychains adorned with the Blue Jay logo on one side and on the other, the inscription "April 7, 1977. We did it!"

Opening Day, April 7, 1977. A frost-bitten, sell-out crowd of 44,649 stood, sat, and parked themselves everywhere as the Toronto Blue Jays became a reality. An early snowstorm had blanketed the field and wiped out the pregame festivities, but the crowd didn't mind: Big League baseball had arrived. In the top of the first inning former National Leaguer Richie Zisk celebrated his debut in a Chicago White Sox uniform with a two-run homer. White Sox announcer Harry Caray shouted, "Welcome to the American League, Richie Zisk," but for everyone at CNE Stadium, the "Welcome to the American League" could just as easily have been directed at them.

And them, miracle of miracles, the snow stopped and even disappeared from the ground by the end of the fourth inning. An omen? The Blue Jays must have thought so, as Doug Ault hit two home runs and Toronto won the very first game they had ever played, 11–9.

The fans cheered every pitch, every fly ball, every out. They didn't seem to notice that the seats in the ball park were forty-one across without an aisle, necessitating more agility to navigate them than needed by a member of the Flying Wallendas. Nor did they seem to notice another missing amenity: beer. Ironically, the team that beer built was the only one in the major leagues that didn't serve it. That is, the crowd didn't seem to notice until the traditional seventh inning stretch. Just as Philadelphia fans had chanted to President Herbert Hoover at the 1931 World Series, Toronto fans now stood and demanded in unison: "We want beer; we want beer . . . "

A Chicago Cubs official once said, "The hot dog is king. For every dollar we get in paid admissions, our total cost of operating the club is $1.06. If we didn't have extra income from concessions in the ball park, we'd have to lock our gates."

Now, more than ever, astronomical salaries and expenses in sports have forced ball clubs to look for additional sources of revenue. One source is concessions, once mere appendages of the action on the field. According to one veteran concessionaire, "arenas thought of food concessions like bathrooms—you had to have them."

But without concessions and the enormous amounts of moneys they generated, there wouldn't be a baseball team in Milwaukee or a stadium in St. Louis. Certain franchises in other sports wouldn't even exist. Ever since Harry M. Stevens advanced money to Harry Frazee and Louis M. Jacobs—the so-called Godfather of Sports—and lent money to Connie Mack to save their faltering franchises in the 1920s and 1930s, financial aid in the form of advances on long-term concessions contracts has been a way of doing business. In the 1960s, Jacobs' concern, Sportservice, guaranteed $12,000,000 in concession fees to insure that Busch Memorial Stadium would be built in St. Louis. In 1970, the firm advanced the Milwaukee Brewers $3,000,000 for concession rights at Milwaukee County Stadium over a long period, providing them with the financial wherewithal to move the franchise from Seattle.

Concessions today are big business. A sports crowd, like an army, travels on its stomachs. The average big league ball park accounts for a total yearly consumption of more than 800,000 hot dogs, 500,000 slabs of ice cream, and 400,000 bags of peanuts, all washed down with 700,000 soft drinks and 900,000 beers. National Football League crowds—with far fewer occasions to dash to the concession stands—still eat more than 3,500,000 bags of peanuts, 1 million bags of popcorn, and swill down 16,000,000 soft drinks and beer and more than 1 million cups of coffee in a single season.

The sale of concessions has been reduced to a "per capita" working formula, reflecting what every fan who sets foot in the ball park is worth in terms of concession sales. The per capita, depending on the franchise, is between $1.00 and $1.50 and the ball club's "take" from the concessionaire is approximately 25 to 35 percent of all food and drink, higher on souvenirs. The amount of money churned is enormous, averaging $375,000 a year for a team drawing a million fans.

The multimillion dollar concessions business started one hot summer's day back in 1887, in Columbus, Ohio. On that day, Harry Mosley Stevens went out to the ball park to escape the heat and watch the local nine play. Unable to decipher the garbled scorecard he had purchased at the front gate, Stevens walked into the front office and offered the club the princely amount of $700 for the privilege of printing and selling an intelligible scorecard in the park. They accepted and Stevens set to work. Improving the design and selling advertising space in his "newfangled" scorecard, Stevens soon recouped his initial investment and started operating in the black.

Soon afterwards, Harry M. branched out into peanuts and soda pop. He reached the big leagues for good in 1894, when he moved into the old Polo Grounds. One day, during a cold and windy Giant game, he noticed his soft drink sales were lagging. Employing the same spur-of-the-moment hustling that had first gotten him into the business, he sent his vendors out into neighborhood stores to buy up all the frankfurters and rolls they could find. He boiled the franks, split the rolls to form a bed and sold them to the chilled spectators with the slogan that still rings up sales to this very day: "Get 'em while they're red hot." His frankfurter sandwiches proved popular from that first game on and were immortalized when cartoonist Tad Dorgan caricatured the dachshund-shaped delicacies as animated dogs. Despite the whimsical "libel" on the beef sausages, "hot dogs" became baseball's staple as fans consumed them in ever-increasing numbers.

Through the years other concessionaires have copied the hustling methods of Harry M. Stevens, who founded the royal family of sports caterers. Sometimes, as Bill Veeck remembers, when the Wrigley Field concessionaires ran out of beef, they would dip dough-balls in beef blood. When hit with a spatula on the grill, they oozed blood. Placed on rolls, they were sold as "hamburgers."

Throughout the years concession revenue has become increasingly important to the sports business. In fact, one franchise, the Milwaukee Braves, alienated their customers by forbidding them to bring in their own beer and sausages, long a Milwaukee custom. The resulting uproar and boycott of the stadium by fans accustomed to having their sausage and eating it too, was the first serious breach between the fans and the club. It would eventually lead to moving the Milwaukee franchise to Atlanta.

The Toronto Blue Jays were "crying in their beer," so to speak. With 26.2 percent of every food and drink dollar sticking to their ribs, they figured to lose, according to Bavasi, "$110,000 on the basis of what we are going to draw" on beer sales or—more accurately—the lack of beer sales. The progressive city of Toronto still suffers from a severe case of schizophrenia. The temperance movement is surprisingly strong in the province of Ontario, with a vigorous antidrinking lobby applying political pressure wherever and whenever possible. Responsible for the prohibition of dancing, movies, and drinking on Sundays as late as the early 1950s, they have kept Toronto, in what one newspaper, the *Ontario Sentinel-Review*, calls "the dark ages as far as its public attitudes about drinking go." The sale of beer at CNE Stadium had, to mix a metaphor, become a political football. They had, as Shakespeare put it, "made it felony to drink small beer."

But even if there was no beer to be had, there were such staples as hot dogs, colas, popcorn, programs, and peanuts. And these concessions more than made up for the lack of beer. A day of two hot dogs, two colas, popcorn, peanuts, a pennant, and a program would cost $4.15 at Shea Stadium, $4.85 at Yankee Stadium, and $5.10 at Tiger Stadium. In keeping with Toronto's over-all high cost of living, at Canadian National Exhibition Stadium the cost would be $6.20. And that was not even including the services of a gastroenterologist.

As the season wore on, it became obvious that the unavailability of beer at the ball park was merely a minor inconvenience; one which was not even perceived as unnatural by Toronto fans, who had no benchmark with which to compare its absence. They came out for one purpose and one purpose alone—to watch baseball. And they came out in record numbers, more than twenty thousand a game, giving Toronto the all-time attendance record for an expansion team—1,700,000.

Even while the Blue Jays were compiling an expansion team record second only to the hapless original Mets, they were also becoming something of a national phenomenon. They were not only the darlings of the Niagara Peninsula, they were also the favorites of most of English-speaking Canada.

To fully fathom how this happened, an understanding of the complex national problems facing the Confederation of Canada is required. Today, the province of Quebec and its five million French-speaking inhabitants (Francophones) desire their own cultural sovereignty and their own destiny, not as a part of the Confederation of Canada, but as a separate nation. Sparked ten years ago by Charles De Gaulle's inflamatory oratory: *"Vive le Quebec! Vive le Quebec libre!"* the province is now governed by the *Parti Quebecois* (Kay-bay-KWAH), which has made French the official language of Quebec. It is their homeland, their country. They no longer consider themselves Canadians or even French-speaking Canadians; they are Quebecois.

The bulk of the population in Quebec lives in Montreal, a city represented in baseball by the Expos. But the Expos, with a franchise ready-made among the French-speaking population primarily and among all of Canada generally, never did anything to perfect their hold. The Francophones knew the president of the team, John McHale, lived in Florida six months of the year and not only could he not speak French, but he made no attempt to do so. With three-and-a-half million French-speaking fans and three hundred thousand Anglophones, the Expos catered to the latter, sending their ball players to English-speaking areas on outside-the-park promotions.

Moreover, the Expos not only had not signed any of the French-speaking prospects growing up in the area (losing one to the Pirates because they failed to come up with an additional $5,000), but had traded away the one hero they had—Rusty Staub. Staub was a great natural promotion, known to each inhabitant of Montreal as "Le Grande Orange," an obvious and loving reference to his bright orange-red hair. A hero on the field, where he was a legitimate big-leaguer batting .311, he was just as much a hero off the field, where he was learning French, dating a French girl and—indulging in his hobby as an amateur chef—preparing a French gourmet cookbook. His over-all popularity was so great that he outranked Jean Belliveau of the Montreal Canadiens in a poll of sports heroes. Then the Expos traded him. The headlines in the local French papers exclaimed, "Au Revoir, Le Grande Orange!" People openly wept on St. Catherine's Street. The Montreal Expos had repeated the mistake made years before when Harry Frazee of the Red Sox had sold Babe Ruth to the Yankees. They had traded an institution.

If the Expos weren't pulling in Quebec, they weren't appealing to the nine other English-speaking provinces either. Welcomed with hope and anticipation in 1969, they had never had a winning season and, in fact, by 1976, had fallen to their worst record since their inaugural year. Now eight years old, they had not only failed to fulfill any of the dreams and hopes of Canadians—both English and French-speaking—but had sold their only stars, Mack Jones, for whom the fans dubbed the outfield area "Jonesville," and Staub, and had even regressed if that were possible. It was a commentary on their fortunes that one of the most successful promotions in Montreal was by a newspaper which ran a "Who's At Fault" contest, a reverse twist in which the fans were asked who was responsible for the Expos' overall lack of success.

At this low ebb in the Expos' fortunes the Toronto Blue Jays came on the scene. They were a new team, one which had not constantly disappointed their fans over and over again and which, importantly, had an Anglo-Saxon name. Headquartered in the next province west, they cut off the Expos' national appeal geographically and boxed the Expos into Quebec and regions east (approximately one-third of the country's twenty-two million). Conversely, the Blue Jays' geographic position gave them access to fully two-thirds of Canada.

The Expos realized the weakness of their position and admitted as much to insiders. One man who will not acknowledge it, and is careful not to, however, is Peter Bavasi. Having spent much of his formative years in Montreal when his father was general manager of the Dodgers' farm team there, Bavasi is sensitive to the national power struggles going on in Canada.

Already misquoted by *Sports Illustrated* as having said "we view ourselves as a national team," Bavasi feels that if "you're an American operating a company in Canada, you damn well better know your place. And your place is not to talk about the national political scene because there is enough U.S. intervention in

Canadian business already and the Canadians are resentful of it." He adds, "And I don't blame them."

Whether Bavasi acknowledged it or not, it *had* happened. The Blue Jays were last in the American League but first in the hearts of their countrymen. From Nova Scotia to British Columbia they plighted their troth by buying more than one million Blue Jays' caps and thousands of other gimcracks and gew-gaws with Blue Jays written on them. The Blue Jays were *their* team.

The 1977 season mercifully came to an end October 2 with the Blue Jays losing to Cleveland, 5–4. It was their 107th loss against only 54 wins. But those 54 wins not only included a 19–3 drubbing of the American League champion New York Yankees, they amounted to more than the New York Mets, the San Diego Padres or, more importantly, the Montreal Expos had in their first years. There were other bright spots: first draft selection Bob Bailor batted .310, the highest ever for a player on an expansion team; pitcher Dave Lemanczyk won 13 games, tying the most ever won by any pitcher on a first-year expansion team; and several players played well above average, including Otto Velez, who was selected as an American League Player of the Week early in the season.

But the real success of the Blue Jays could not be measured by what transpired on the field. What happened off the field truly measured their success. Both the Blue Jays and the city of Toronto had prospered.

Baseball had been good to Toronto. According to a study commissioned by McDougall and compiled by professor William Schaeffer of the College of Industrial Management of the Georgia Institute of Technology, Toronto's new baseball club had an overall economic impact of $62,000,000 on the community.

But if Metro Toronto benefited, so did the Blue Jays— handsomely. Their gross ticket revenues were almost ten million dollars. To that they added another million from the sales of Blue Jay-related merchandise, which became walking billboard ads for the team throughout Canada. American teams are tied into a central pooling organization, Major League Baseball Corp., which throws off only about $25,000 or so to each of the twenty-four American-based franchises each year. But the Blue Jays realized the full benefit of the added revenue since, unlike their sister franchises south of the border, they are not bound to share their Canadian sales.

The net result of the Blue Jays' first year was far different than what had been envisioned by McDougall and Labatt's.

Even before Bavasi came aboard they had prepared a preliminary profit and loss statement, after researching the books of all the other major league clubs that were available to them. Their *pro forma* showed them losing a half a million to a million dollars their first year. When Bavasi saw the projections, he made his own estimates, knowing that the Padres had drawn less than a million the first year and still made money. "I didn't come up here to lose money," he told McDougall. "I want to make money. That's what drives me . . . to make money and win ball games." His *pro forma* showed a profit of a million and a half dollars. "That's ridiculous!" he was told.

It was indeed ridiculous! By the end of the first year the partnership that owned the Toronto Blue Jays had realized a profit of greater than four million dollars: more than one-half their original investment. And, not incidentally, Labatt's sales once again surpassed Molson's in the Toronto area.

Philip K. Wrigley once said, "Baseball is too much of a business to be a sport and too much of a sport to be a good business." But for Labatt's it was good business too. A very good business. Especially if you're a beer company.

2

"Baseball teams make money, you know..."

With the end of World War I and with the promised millennium of world peace still unfulfilled, disenchanted Americans began feeling that their privations and principles had failed to gain them anything. So they turned from the rigors of problem solving to the rituals of pleasure seeking, embracing in their freewheeling mood any excitement and escapism they could find. From a gigantic laundry list of available diversions, they concentrated on two: the movies and baseball.

Movies had grown from flickering one-reelers issued by fly-by-night operators and shown in neighborhood nickelodeons at the turn of the century into the fifth largest industry in America by 1920, with two-hour extravaganzas shown in lavish showcase theaters. Some thirty-five million Americans were going to the movies at least once a week, mainly to see melodramatic love stories and Westerns, with a few war movies just beginning to surface. They were not only respectable; they were fashionable.

The watershed year for baseball was 1920 also. It was the year when, in the wake of the Black Sox scandal, the owners selected Judge Kenesaw Mountain Landis as the new commissioner, replacing the unwieldy three-man national commission. And it was the year the New York Yankees purchased a 25-year-old pitcher-turned-outfielder from the Boston Red Sox who was to become baseball's greatest all-time promotion: Babe Ruth.

Baseball was described as being in its "infancy" in 1908 by Charles Ebbets, president of the Brooklyn Dodgers. That year the sixteen major league clubs had a combined attendance figure of seven million, a million more than the previous year. But for the next eleven years attendance plateaued and even declined. The figure had sagged to six-and-a-half million by 1919.

The first postwar World Series of 1919—even with its dark hints of evil misdoings—was the harbinger of greater things to come. The Series drew almost a quarter million more dollars than the previous all-time high, the half-million dollar Series of 1912; 1919 was also the year that marked the legalization of Sunday baseball in New York. Finally, the addition of Babe Ruth during the winter of 1919–1920 to the American League's showcase franchise in New York marked the moment of baseball's fiscal maturation.

The owners, sensing that a financial bonanza lay in the newly discovered long ball—446 home runs in 1919, including Ruth's record-breaking 29—made some immediate adjustments to insure the continuation, if not the exploitation, of the home run. First they tightened the construction of the ball itself, reducing the raised stitching and wrapping the yarn tighter. The effect, described by one writer who held the ball between his thumb and forefinger, was like "hearing a rabbit's pulsebeat." Then, they outlawed the spitball, the emery ball, and other "freak" pitches, benevolently allowing those eighteen pitchers still employing these pitches to use them until "the end of their careers."

Even these manmade contributions were dwarfed by the emergence of one man who now stood center stage and gave baseball its greatest show ever. To borrow the title of Irving Berlin's paean, "Along Came Ruth," and with him, the long ball and the crowds. In 1920 the Babe "hit," "clouted," "swatted," and "whacked" 54 home runs, almost double his previous number, as 630 were hit in both leagues and more than nine million fans flocked to the ball parks. Baseball was no longer in its "infancy"; it had emerged with the arrival of Ruth in New York.

Babe Ruth. The very name brings back memories to the dwindling number of fans who saw this Gargantuan figure on toothpick-thin legs boom parabolic shots into the stands time and again, and then mince his way around the bases with catlike steps. To the typical adult, he is a legendary figure who gave color to his age as John L. Sullivan gave color to his. To the younger generation, he is merely a name, spoken in reverential terms by their elders and used as a benchmark for modern ball players like Aaron and Maris.

But Babe Ruth was more than a name. He was an institution, a deity. One prominent Methodist minister even suggested, "If St. Paul were living today, he would know Babe Ruth's batting average." Legions of sportswriters formed a cult, with high priests like Runyon, Lardner, Rice, and Broun spreading the Ruthian gospel. They called him The Sultan of Swat, The Wizard of Whack, The King of Clout, The Behemoth of Biff and, of course, The Bambino. He was The Idol of American Youth, and The Symbol of Baseball The World Over.

As each day brought new accolades and exaggerated stories about the man who had become a legend in his own time, Ruth contributed to the lore by writing and then rewriting the record books with every swing of his size-42 bat. Fans jammed the parks to see him, booing their own pitchers when he was given a base on balls. As Ruth drove ball after ball out of the park and record after record out of the books, baseball tied its tail to Ruth's kite. He became more than a player; he and the long ball became baseball's promotion.

Ruth, the greatest baseball promotion of all time, might never have become a New York Yankee but for some other promotions; promotions which had turned sour for Boston Red Sox owner Harry Frazee. Frazee was an incurable entrepreneur who dabbled in all manner of entertainment: Broadway shows, boxing bouts, even wrestling matches. If Frazee was anything, he was consistent. Almost everything he touched, in a reverse Midas syndrome, turned to dung.

Together with his associate, Jack Curley, he underwrote the Frank Gotch-George Hackenschmidt "World Wrestling Championship" in Chicago in 1911, a bout won by Gotch before wrestling's largest paid crowd. Frazee and Curley attempted to parlay their profits by promoting the Jack Johnson-Jim Flynn heavyweight championship fight in Las Vegas, New Mexico, in 1912, and lost most of it in turn. Not satisfied with disaster, they once again tried to promote a heavyweight championship fight, Johnson-Willard in Havana in 1915. This time Frazee and Curley lost everything they made on the Gotch-Hackenschmidt match. And more—much more. Undaunted, Frazee returned to his home arena and first love, Broadway, and the three theaters he owned, the Frazee and Lyric in New York and the Cort in

Chicago. Between 1915 and 1920, he was to produce no less than five shows. All opened in New Haven—and most of them closed there.

But Frazee had one asset which was, metaphorically speaking, "blue-chip," the Boston Red Sox. Purchased from the owner of the *Boston Globe*, Charles Taylor, in 1917, the Red Sox gave Frazee an immediate return on his investment by winning the American League pennant and World Series in 1918. By 1919, however, even with Ruth hitting 29 homers and winning nine games, the mighty Red Sox had fallen to sixth place. Worse yet, Frazee was in desperate need of money, his other investments looking like Bert Lance's portfolio on a bad day. Frazee needed money. And quickly.

Frazee literally didn't have far to go to find an "angel." The Red Sox offices were located in Frazee's own theatrical offices at 1441 Broadway in New York. The New York Yankees were housed at 226 West 42nd Street, barely a half-block away. The hard-pressed Frazee had already done business with Yankee owner Jacob Ruppert by selling him Carl Mays for life-giving cash during the 1919 season. Now he sought a personal loan.

Frazee got the money he asked for and then some. He borrowed $350,000 from Ruppert to put back into his floundering shows, but he had to mortgage Fenway Park as security. On January 3, 1920, Ruppert called the first installment of his loan, buying the man he called "Baby Root" from the Red Sox and Frazee for $125,000. Frazee continued to search for ways to raise money. On March 17, 1920, he borrowed $36,000 from the Fenway Park concessionaire, Harry M. Stevens, and on May 3, 1920, he borrowed $150,000 from the previous owner of the Red Sox. Still it wasn't enough to cover his losses in the theatrical world.

Now Frazee was reduced to making the Red Sox one gigantic rummage sale. Any player was available. Bring cash! In the next two years one-way tickets were given to Harry Hooper, Stuffy McInnis, Waite Hoyt, Wally Schang, Sam Jones, George Pipgras, Joe Bush, Everett Scott, Herb Pennock, and Joe Dugan. Frazee's motto seemed to be "If it moves, sell it." Red Sox fans, irate when Ruth was sold, were incensed when Hooper was sold to the White Sox and McInnis to the Indians. The rest of Boston's crown jewels went to New York and, with the passing of their best players to the Yankees, Bostonians facetiously said that the only Boston club ever to lose a World Series was the Yankee team of 1921.

On July 11, 1923, Frazee did the only honorable thing left: he sold the by-then Dead Sox to Bob Quinn. Frazee received $100,000 down and $500,000 in notes payable, which he promptly discounted. He left behind him a savaged franchise, wrecked almost beyond repair and consigned to the second division for the next decade.

The words to "There Used to Be a Ballpark" (written by Joe Raposo and sung by Frank Sinatra) sound like a funeral dirge for the world that once was, the baseball world of the early 1920s:

> And there used to be a ballpark where the field
> was warm and green.
> And the people played their crazy game with a
> joy I've never seen.
> And the air was such a wonder from the hot
> dogs and the beer,
> Yes, there used to be a ballpark right here.

And there used to be Forbes Field and Shibe Park. And there used to be Redland Field and Sportsman's Park. And there used to be fourteen ball parks—only four of which, Comiskey and Fenway parks, Tiger Stadium and Wrigley Field, are still standing—that housed the sixteen major league teams in 1922. Sixteen parks whose average seating capacity was 26,756 and whose average age was almost eighteen years.

By 1920, it became painfully obvious that if baseball was about to undergo a metamorphosis and take on the new look of the long ball, then the fourteen venerable ball parks would also have to take on a new look. Some of these parks dated back to the nineteenth century and their dimensions were more conducive to the pitch-and-punch game then in vogue than the long ball. They had to be redesigned—or rebuilt—to accommodate the new game. Failing to do so would condemn the new look baseball was striving to achieve to antique trappings.

The need for a new stadium was most pronounced in the case of the New York Yankees. For the new King of Swat and his Royal Family of Long Ball Hitters were without their own baseball palace. They were the guests of the New York Giants at the Polo Grounds.

Ever since Frank Farrell, Jacob Ruppert's predecessor, had petitioned the Giants for leave to move his Highlanders into the Polo Grounds in 1913, the New York American League team had played at 155th Street and Eighth Avenue. The stadium was more than adequate to the needs of the Highlanders, soon to be rechristened the Yankees. In fact, the 38,000-seat stadium, then the largest in the country, had been hailed by *The Sporting News* as a "monument to baseball," and was called by *Frank Leslie's Illustrated Newspaper* "One of the great show places of New York."

By 1922 the Yankees had overstayed their welcome. Like fish, they had begun to take on the odor of those too long in residence, especially to the nostrils of Giants manager John McGraw, whose salary was based in part on the Giants' attendance. From the day Babe Ruth first appeared in pinstripes, Yankee attendance had doubled and they had outdrawn the Giants. McGraw now wanted them out, and the Yankees wanted a stadium of their own: a promotion in itself to showcase Ruth and Company.

Colonel Ruppert and his elegantly named partner, Colonel Tillinghast L'Hommedieu Huston, started searching for a site for a new stadium. They found it: ten acres just across the Harlem River from the Polo Grounds in the Bronx, formerly known as Jerome Park, owned by Leonard W. Jerome, the grandfather of Winston Churchill.

Colonels Ruppert and Huston hired the Osborn Engineering Company of Cleveland to design "the biggest stadium in baseball," a three-tiered edifice that would take 248 working days and $2,300,000 to build. The partners had intended it to be a lasting monument to themselves. Instead, it would become a monument to Babe Ruth.

From the day it opened, April 18, 1923, it was evident why. In the third inning of the inaugural, with two men on, Ruth straightened out one of Howard Ehmke's off-speed curves and sent it into the friendly confines of the short right field stands, built to accommodate many future Ruthian shots. The Yankees beat the A's 4–1. To the announced 74,200 fans—which the Yankees later admitted they padded—the promotions had merged. Yankee Stadium had become The House that Ruth Built, a tourist attraction that ranked ahead of even the Statue of Liberty.

During the twenties, the home run became the most dominant element in the game. Home run production in the majors climbed from 446 in 1919 to 631 in 1920, a gain of more than 41 percent and to 937 in 1921, another 49 percent. By 1925, the weakest slugging team in the National League, the Boston Braves, had more homers then the heaviest hitting National League team in 1910. Baseball had been sacrificed on the altar of the long ball. To many it was merely a manifestation of the "wham-bam-thank-you-ma'am" decade. To purists, it was an outrage, making baseball the Chinese restaurant of sports—twenty minutes after witnessing a round-tripper, you were hungry for more.

Baseball, which had come to pray at the Shrine of the Long Ball, was now to fall prey to it. In their own mind's eye, the owners had improved the product with the introduction of the long ball. The home run, exemplified by Ruth, and the stadium built to induce even more now begot the next obvious step in the syllogism. Baseball determined that if the crowds came out to see Babe Ruth hit home runs *and* the Yankees won, they were coming out because the Yankees were winning. So baseball set out to construct a bionic team that would be an all-winning team. The *sine qua non* of the home run: the New York Yankees.

The Yankees were to dominate the American League throughout the 1920s more completely than Popeye dominated Bluto, with their own version of spinach, the long ball. During the decade, they hit 1,211 home runs, hit .291 with a slugging average of .438, won 933 games, 6 pennants, and 3 World Series. In making the American League the Yankees and the Seven Dwarfs, baseball helped promote the philosophy that winning was not the most important thing—it was the *only* thing! They had built a dynastic Frankenstein, based on one criterion, winning. If, following Leo Durocher's logic, "Nice guys finish last," then the Yankees were not nice guys and were to be disliked. Even hated.

In devoting its collective attention to the betterment of their overall product, however, baseball soon forgot it was dealing in customer satisfaction. There is a marketing premise that holds people do not buy gasoline; they are buying the right to continue driving their car. Similarly, baseball fans were not merely buying a ticket to a baseball game, they were buying entertainment. And that entertainment was positioned by the Lords of Baseball as being a "winning team." Nonwinning teams had been relegated to the back of the bus. There was nothing so deadly, in terms of customer satisfaction, as a game between have-nots. Fans were denied the small conceit that the game they were watching was important, ergo entertaining. Baseball had taken that away from them by continuing to orient itself towards the product rather than the people who bought it.

In fact, the winning-is-everything theory had begun to bear the only fruit possible by 1927. With the Yankees nineteen games in front of the pack, only ten thousand people came out to

Yankee Stadium to see Ruth hit his sixtieth homer. The next year, 1928, saw only the Yankees and the resurgent Athletics making money in the American League. Even the St. Louis Browns, who finished third in 1928 and fourth in 1929, had difficulty meeting their payroll.

The fact that the fans were not as turned on by the "all-winning" philosophy as much as the baseball establishment can be witnessed by the most telling statistic—attendance. American League attendance hit a high of 5,084,300 fans in 1920, parenthetically a year in which the Yankees finished third despite Ruth's fifty-four home runs. American League attendance would reach five million only three times in the next twenty-five years—1924, 1925, and 1945—three years the Yankees, not incidentally, did *not* win the pennant. Moreover, the National League, which had led the American League in attendance only four times in the nineteen years of coexistence prior to 1920, had, by 1926, surpassed the junior circuit in attendance, a position they would hold until 1934, again a year the Yankees failed to win the pennant.

During the 1920s, an age reminiscent of ancient Roman bread and circuses, the owners gave the fans promotional crumbs. Ban Johnson, president of the American League, stressed his circuit's .400 hitters, backing the wire service scorer's version of a Ty Cobb hit over the official scorer's view of it as an error—a hit that gave Cobb a .4011 average rather than .3992 in 1922. His successor, E. S. Barnard, president of the American League in 1928, sent out a "bulletin" to all member teams exhorting them to reduce their average playing time. Barnard took obvious pleasure in the fact "that every club in the league, except New York, had reduced its playing time." To the product-oriented Lords of Baseball, who sat around listening to their arteries harden, these were what they called "promotions."

Within a few short years baseball had painted itself into a marketing corner. The basic problem was structural. First, the owners had improperly defined their market. Despite the fact that the U.S. Supreme Court had held, in the Federal Baseball case in 1922, that baseball was not subject to the Sherman Antitrust laws because it was basically intrastate in nature, most of the baseball hierarchy misread the decision and spread the misconception that they were a sport, not a business. Nowhere in Justice Holmes' decision does he use such language or such reasoning. But baseball did.

Worst yet, the Lords of Baseball followed that misconception by accepting it as the whole truth. By circumscribing their place in the market as a sport and not as an entertainment, they were to suffer much the same consequences movies did by shortsightedly positioning themselves in the movie business and not the entertainment business. Both industries imperturbably believed there was no effective substitute for their services. Movies would eventually see the errors in their ways when television made gigantic inroads into their base. But baseball was slow in realizing its myopia.

The most important miscalculation made by baseball's powers-that-be was making marketing a stepchild, concentrating on the product rather than on the consumer and his satisfaction. Into that vacuum created by baseball's oversight came a new challenger for the entertainment dollar in a few short years, professional football, which promised the fan that no matter who was playing "on any given Sunday any team can win." The sports entertainment market had been baseball's for the asking—and they had handed it to pro football on a silver platter.

While football minimized the difference between winning and losing "on any given Sunday," baseball unknowingly penalized itself. Most of the truly memorable games were played not between the winning teams, but between the more evenly balanced second-division teams. There the fan saw more remarkable individual performances. No .400 hitter ever played on a pennant winner; of the 59 no-hit games thrown in the American and National leagues during the first thirty years of the twentieth century, second division teams appeared in 49 of them; of the seven unassisted triple plays, only one was made by a member of a pennant-winning club, the rest turned in by players on teams that finished fourth or worse in the standings; and of the 61 batting champions in the two leagues through 1929, only once did both batting champions appear in the same World Series. The action on the field, however, was not reflected either in the underlying market philosophy that baseball had adopted of the all-winning team or in the attendance figures of the have-nots.

Baseball is an orderly sport, sprouting, appropriately enough, in the spring, blooming full-grown in the summer, and fading in the first autumnal chill. It is a game of continuity as well, standing in its own time warp, outside temporal considerations, with an historical method of double-entry bookkeeping which allows for the tying of every player, date, and record into one another.

In just such a continuum, baseball literally passed the torch from one great promotion to the next, all in the space of twenty-four hours. On the night of May 24, 1935, the lights went on at Crosley Field in Cincinnati for the first night baseball game in major league history. Just twenty-four hours before Babe Ruth had hit his last three home runs in what was to be one of the last games he ever played. In a sense, it also marked the all-important change in baseball from a sport concerned solely with the product to one concerned with the customer.

Night baseball had long been a novelty. As far back as 1880, two amateur teams had met at Nantasket Beach, Massachusetts, under arc lights strung along the perimeters of the playing field. Other nineteenth-century exhibitions were held at Fort Wayne, Indiana, in 1883, and Houston, Texas, in 1894.

Even though exhibition games continued at night—including a game between two local Chicago teams, Logan Square and Rogers Park, in Comiskey Park on August 28, 1910, before a crowd of more than twenty thousand, when twenty 137,000-candlepower arc lights "made the diamond bright as day"—organized baseball would do without them.

Then on Thursday, October 24, 1929, the stock market crashed and everything changed. The feverish Twenties had exploded in an economic fever soon to be known as the Great Depression, the Roaring Twenties would become the Troubled Thirties, and the word "unemployed," once a seldom-used adjective, was now to become an oft-used and ominous noun as every fourth worker would lose his job. The American Dream was turning into a nightmare.

As it did, bread lines and bonus armies took the place of the boom and bust atmosphere of the 1920s. The go-go spirit had gone. Everywhere people were out of work, with little money to spend and only despair to look forward to.

Into this era of emotional monotony, one entertainment business, the movie industry, continued to thrive. It coped with the Depression by providing escapism to millions every week. It filled the bellies of those who could barely afford food with hope and created Depression-alleviating songs like "We're in the Money" or "Who's Afraid of the Big Bad Wolf." As Hollywood pumped movie after movie into society's Dream Machine, local theaters attempted to capitalize on the abundance of celluloid offerings with double and even triple features and promotions such as bank night or dish night. The public responded, with eighty-five million people a week paying 25¢ a ticket—10¢ for kids—to go to the movies.

Meanwhile, the movies companionate entertainment industry, baseball, was hard pressed. Several franchises were on the brink of collapse. Connie Mack sold off the great stars of his 1929-1931 pennant-winning teams to pay the bills. The National League had to take over control of the moribund Boston franchise. Bob Quinn, down to his last shoe string attempting to resuscitate the franchise Frazee had left for dead, looked to the American League for financial aid and help in finding a buyer. Banks had repossessed the Cincinnati and Brooklyn franchises. And the minor leagues, if possible, were in worse shape.

Major league attendance, which had reached a high of more than ten million in 1930, plummeted to an anemic six million just three years later, the lowest since the war-shortened 1918 season. Things looked less than promising for the Mudville sixteen by 1933.

In that year, attempting to work itself out of its fiscal bind, baseball began to shed its traditional bonds. Doubleheaders, heretofore scheduled only as part of a make-up contest for a rained-out game, became almost as commonplace as double features at the movies. Then there was the first All-Star game, staged as part of Chicago's Century of Progress. Babe Ruth, an institution almost as large as baseball itself, won the game with a home run, naturally.

E. Lee Keyser, president of the Des Moines team of the Class A Western League, boldly announced at the 1930 National Association winter meeting his intention to be the first team in organized baseball to play a regular league game at night. Investing more than $19,000 in the installation of a system of Little Giant generators, he set the date for the first night game as May 2, 1930. Keyser's idea was soon to take hold throughout the minor leagues. Team after team tried what was then called "a scheme," as odd jewels began shining against the velvet of the night. The *Reach Official Baseball Guide* of 1931 was to note the contribution of night baseball and its effect on the baseball's financial well-being by stating: "The Western League had one of its best financial seasons in history. Electric lights saved the circuit at a time when conditions were quite shaky."

Des Moines was like an illuminated pebble thrown into a pond. Minor league ball parks began to take on the look of fireflies at twilight, as the ripples reached parks in Omaha, Oklahoma City, Topeka, Pueblo, Denver, Houston, San Antonio, Shreveport, Little Rock, Indianapolis, and Buffalo. The Texas League, which had played only 4 night games during the first half of the 1930 season, saw 116 of the final 307 games played under the lights. Every team that experimented with night baseball profited because of it. They had chanced across a heretofore undiscovered marketing verity: 90 percent of all entertainment dollars were spent at night. Before Keyser's innovation, baseball had cleverly cut itself out of the entertainment pie by adhering only to daytime play. Now night baseball changed the very face of the game.

Baseball was on the threshold of finally catering to the fans; but it would take the National League five more years to open the door, the American League nine.

The man who put the baseball fan into the act and raised promotion to the level of an art form was Leland Stanford MacPhail. Known throughout the baseball world as Larry, MacPhail was a brash, gaudy promoter, as enterprising as he was energetic.

Before he assumed a role in baseball's marketing revolution, MacPhail played more roles than Lon Chaney. His circuitous route into baseball included law school, a short playing career in the Michigan-Ontario League; a stint with a Chicago law firm where he quit after six months when he wasn't named a partner; a hitch in the army during World War I during which he attempted to kidnap Kaiser Wilhelm from Holland; an automobile salesman; and a Big Ten football referee. He finally lighted on baseball almost by accident.

In 1931 MacPhail chanced to come across a run-down franchise in Columbus, Ohio, that was there for the taking. The club was out of money, out of contention, and out of sorts. Their ball park was broken-down, their attendance and credit were nil, and their players were, at best, second-rate. It was the perfect situation for someone of MacPhail's talents.

MacPhail obtained an option on the team and immediately went to see his former classmate at Michigan Law School, Wesley Branch Rickey, to peddle it. Rickey was then general manager of the St. Louis Cardinals and in the process of building that superstructure known as a "farm system" out of the bodies of destitute minor league teams which would serve as an incubating system to develop and season talent. The Columbus franchise afforded Rickey the opportunity to add another high minor league team to his roster to operate in tandem with Rochester of the International League.

Rickey bought the idea, the team, MacPhail's option—and MacPhail himself. Soon Rickey was stocking the Columbus

Redbirds with some prize unseasoned talent, players like Paul Dean, Evar Swanson, Nick Cullop, Ival Goodman, Roy Parmelee, Burgess Whitehead, and Ken O'Dea.

MacPhail, who was now president and general manager at a salary of $10,000 a year, started his own renovation program to match the Cardinals' rejuvenation program. He built a new ball park with a complete high-level lighting system, taking full advantage of Depression prices.

By 1932 the Redbirds had taken flight and the fans turned out in droves to see their team, once the doormat of the league, actually flirt with first place as late as August before finishing in second place. They turned out in even larger numbers for night games. MacPhail had turned Columbus into a winner, both in the standings and at the gate.

But a funny thing happened to MacPhail as Columbus drove to the top of the American Association in 1933, winning the pennant in the newly created Eastern Division and the playoff against Minneapolis. He was fired, the result of his extravagance.

No sooner was he "at liberty" than Larry MacPhail executed a neat two-and-a-half gainer and bounced back into baseball, this time further downstate in the Queen City of Cincinnati.

The franchise representing baseball's oldest professional city was in terrible shape, both on and off the field. The smallest of the ten cities in the majors in 1930, with few surrounding towns to draw from, the Reds had compounded their problems by providing their fans with little to cheer about. They had had a succession of overpaid, overaged players like Harry Heilmann, Babe Herman, Edd Roush, Bob Meusel, Jim Bottomley, and Eppa Rixey and a succession of second-division teams. For the past three years the Reds had been mired in last place in the National League with little hope and no prospect of ever climbing out.

The owner of the Cincinnati Reds was Sidney Weil, a gentleman who had owned a Ford agency and a string of garages. He had lost everything in the Depression—his agency, his garages, and now his team. The Reds had been "repossessed" by the Cincinnati Trust Company, which had lent the team a considerable amount of money during the past few years and was now threatening that "unless someone came to the front with some ready money, the franchise would be sold to some other city."

MacPhail, who had heard about the situation from his father, a Michigan banker, quickly assessed the situation and hurried down to Cincinnati to talk to the bank. He correctly assumed that the bank didn't want to risk any more capital and was also able to persuade them that he was the man they needed to protect their sizeable investment and find the right backers. So, with what amounted to an option on another team, as he had done three years before in Columbus, MacPhail went out to peddle the team—and himself—to a worthy investor.

Ever the hustling salesman, MacPhail found the man he was looking for in Powell Crosley, Jr., a Cincinnati executive who controlled radio stations as well as a large radio manufacturing concern. Crosley, who knew next to nothing about baseball, was sold on the idea of buying the team as a civic gesture.

So in January 1934, ownership passed from the grateful hands of the bank into Crosley's who rewarded MacPhail with his "finder's fee"—naming him business manager. MacPhail promptly moved to find one manager, two pitchers, and three fans, wheeling and dealing with anyone who had something to offer. MacPhail bought veteran catcher Bob O'Farrell from the St. Louis Cardinals, installing him in the dual position of catcher and manager. He got pitcher Tony Freitas from the Phillies, outfielder Adam Comorosky from the Pirates, and infielder Tony Piet from the Pirates. Nothing seemed to help and after winning only 26 of the first 84 games, he summarily fired O'Farrell, replacing him with Burt Shotton as interim manager. He then named Charlie Dressen to pilot the Reds. Still they finished last, losing more games than ever before in their history. The fans continued to show their appreciation by failing to show up.

With the returns in from the disastrous 1934 campaign, MacPhail now desperately sought something—anything—that would draw fans to old Redland Field, rechristened Crosley Field in honor of the owner. Obviously it was not going to be the ball club. So MacPhail, like an old tiger, returned to the place of his last remembered beauty—night baseball.

As the leader of the New Turks in the palace of baseball's Old Guard, MacPhail petitioned the National League for permission to play some of his home games at night during the upcoming 1935 season. He got unanticipated support from Sam Breadon, president of the St. Louis Cardinals who had him fired just a year and a half before. As president of the world champion Cardinals, Breadon had a far different problem than MacPhail. He faced competition from a softball league. The league played triple headers at night before as many as 10,000 fans for an admission of only 10¢. Promoted by former great George Sisler, it had become a tremendous success in the St. Louis area, where day games were sometimes played in summer heat of up to 120 degrees.

The National League voted "to permit a maximum of seven night games to each of its member clubs desiring the privilege." The new president of the league, Ford Frick, announced the decision by saying, "I believe that with the restrictions we have placed on night games—no more than seven in any city—we will find them both interesting and profitable. . . . In each city there is a vast number of persons whose working hours and conditions make it impossible for them to see daylight games, except, perhaps on Sunday. Night baseball also will appeal to the fans when daylight games mean sitting out in extreme heat."

One owner, Charles Stoneham of the New York Giants, spoke out against night baseball. Although he voted for the resolution, he announced that the Giants would not play night baseball, either at home or away. It was, he believed, an unsuccessful combination, one in which accidents could occur and the initial outlay of "not less than $40,000" wouldn't warrant the extra fans. Two other teams, Pittsburgh and Brooklyn, announced they had no intention of trying night baseball in their parks either.

But MacPhail had seen it work in the minor leagues and knew that major league fans would respond to the innovation just as minor league fans had—in crowds.

And he was right. On the evening of May 24, 1935, just one day after Babe Ruth's last major league homer had ended baseball's first great promotion, President Franklin D. Roosevelt threw a switch and Crosley Field erupted in the glare of lights. It was the beginning of baseball's second great promotion.

Some 25,000 fans watched as Reds pitcher Paul Derringer retired the Phillies lead-off batter, Lou Chiozza, on a fast ball, and the era of night baseball had begun. The Reds went on to win, 2-1, in a game that produced only ten hits and— amazingly—no errors. There were six other night games that year in Cincinnati, often accompanied by fireworks displays, marching bands, and field meets between the two clubs. The fans loved it. The seven games drew an average of almost 18,000 fans, more than three times the attendance at an average major league game in 1935.

Baseball's dark ages had been enlightened—both on the field and in the front office.

MacPhail filled his dull moments feuding and fighting with the press, his staff, Cincinnati policemen, and the owner of the team. The last was to prove his undoing, as Powell Crosley answered the Redhead's demands for stock in the team by exercising his option on June 30, 1936, and assuming total control. By the end of 1936, with the Reds in fifth place—and their best won-lost record since 1928—MacPhail was gone.

Following what was by now a familiar scenario, MacPhail learned that the Brooklyn Trust Company had taken over the Brooklyn baseball team in hock for more than $1,200,000. Tired of pouring money into the bottomless pit of the floundering franchise, the bank was caught in the middle between the warring factions of the Ebbets and McKeever estates. The directors of the bank wanted none of it. Only out. Now they found a way. They turned to National League president Ford Frick. On his recommendation, they made MacPhail executive vice president and de facto head of the team.

So, on January 20, 1938, after a year's sabbatical, Larry MacPhail again landed on his feet, this time at the head of the once-proud Brooklyn franchise. He brought his own special kind of zaniness with him, a nonstop feast of automobile raffles, track meets, beauty contests, fashion shows, and riots—both on and off the field—as he not only turned the club around but converted a bankrupt property into a gold mine.

He brought in Leo Durocher as his kind of manager, hired Babe Ruth as a coach, persuaded the Brooklyn Trust to ante up $888,100 for fresh talent, and installed lights, petitioning the National League for permission to become the second major league team to offer night baseball.

Brooklyn's inaugural under the floodlights on June 15 drew 40,000 fans, a record for Ebbets Field. MacPhail staged pre-game festivities featuring Olympic gold medal winner Jesse Owens running the bases against the clock. But nothing up-staged the game itself, for Reds' pitcher Johnny VanderMeer picked that night to throw his second consecutive no-hitter, blanking the Dodgers 6–0.

Now assured that night baseball was no longer just a novelty, everyone rushed into the act as day baseball became almost as extinct as the horse and buggy. The American League granted its members the right to play night baseball in 1937 and lighting systems started popping up everywhere. Shibe Park, where both Philadelphia teams played, Municipal Stadium in Cleveland, and Comiskey Park in Chicago first turned on their lights in 1939. The Polo Grounds, Forbes Field in Pittsburgh, and Sportsman's Park in St. Louis joined the illuminated band-wagon in 1940. Washington's Griffith Stadium threw its first switch in 1941. Clark Griffith, the owner of the Senators, who at one time had been night baseball's most violent opponent, was soon petitioning the American League to allow more night games, ostensibly for servicemen, but in reality as the salvation for his struggling franchise. Then, in 1942, it was "Alley, Alley, All in Free" as the major leagues took their seven-game restriction off night games and the number jumped from 77 to 128. Braves Field and Yankee Stadium turned on the lights in 1946, Fenway Park in 1947, and Detroit's Briggs Stadium inaugurated night baseball in 1948. The sole holdout was Philip K. Wrigley, owner of the Chicago Cubs. Night baseball soon threatened to replace sex as the nocturnal national pastime just thirteen years after MacPhail had introduced it in Cincinnati.

MacPhail built a pennant winner in Brooklyn, just as he had in Cincinnati, but after finishing second in 1942 he seemed to lose interest. He sold his Dodger stock and joined the army. Resurfacing in 1946, he headed up a syndicate that bought the Yankees from the Ruppert heirs. MacPhail, who often tightrope-walked the thin line between genius and insanity, sometimes lost his balance with the help of two or three drinks. Celebrating the Yankee victory in the World Series of 1947, he got into a liquid argument with his co-owners, Del Webb and Dan Topping. The next day he sold out and retired, never to return to baseball. His legacies, which included the first stadium club, the old-timers game, season tickets, and the first scoreboard that flashed the scores of other games in the league, would remain as tributes to his entrepreneurial and promotional genius. But his lasting monument was night baseball.

The first major league night baseball game had also been the first event the then-embryonic Mutual Broadcasting Company ever broadcast. The selection of Cincinnati was no coincidence. Larry MacPhail believed, in the words of his first announcer, Walter "Red" Barber, that "radio was his best friend." And it was, too, as MacPhail commandeered fifteen minutes of air time every noon before a home game to publicize that afternoon's game. More importantly, when he convinced Crosley to devote his powerful station, WLW, to broadcast the games in their entirety, he was developing potential ticket sales while teaching the fundamentals of the game to another untapped market, women.

The Lords of Baseball still didn't understand what they had or how to market it. Years before they had welcomed press coverage, believing it helped spread the gospel. Ever since May 1, 1853, when the *New York Sunday Mercury* first mentioned a game played on a barnstorming tour by the National Club of Washington, newspapers were an important part of baseball's marketing makeup. The press was a willing handmaiden in promoting the game.

But radio was viewed differently. Baseball failed to comprehend that all it had to sell was an intangible—entertainment— and that radio could help sell it. Instead, the owners firmly believed that only an imbecile would give away something he was trying to sell. So microphones were barred from the ball parks.

There were some promoters who felt differently. Sports broadcasting was finally able tentatively to stick its nose into the sports tent through foresight. It took its first tottering step with the re-creation of the Dempsey-Carpentier bout on July 2, 1921. A technician repeated the telephonic ringside report of Major J. Andrew White over WJZ, NBC's New York flagship station. The same year station KDKA in Pittsburgh re-created a National League game between the Pirates and the Phillies. This was followed by the broadcast of the all-New York World Series that fall. Phoned in by a reporter from the *Newark Call*, an announcer repeated the play-by-play account over the air. But it wasn't until the 1924 Series that Graham McNamee broadcast the first sporting event direct from the site of the action. Ring Lardner, sitting next to him, wrote: "The Washington Senators and the New York Giants must have played a double-header this afternoon—the game I saw and the game Graham McNamee announced."

Radio was to be every man, woman, and child's ticket to news, information, culture, and entertainment. It was also soon to be their vicarious ticket to baseball. In the words of Will Rogers, "Radio it too big a thing to be out of."

The baseball man who understood this best was William Veeck, president of the Chicago Cubs. Veeck firmly believed that radio would introduce the game to a whole new sector of fans, including that future generation of fans, the kids. It would develop an umbilicus between the second-division Cubs and the millions who might be persuaded to follow them in the two-team city of Chicago. Veeck announced he was going to broadcast some of the Cubs' home games in 1925. The National League, still intent on hiding its head in the sand, give him a resounding "No!" for an answer. They wouldn't approve it. "Fine," said Veeck, "I won't play with the league. I'll play with the local teams around here. But I'm going to broadcast." The bluff worked. The league approved and Veeck pioneered by giving away the Cub's broadcast rights for no fee to seven stations in the Chicago market.

In city after city, announcers took to the air to tell the local fans about their favorite team's on-the-field heroics. Cleveland's Jack Graney, Boston's Fred Hoey, Detroit's Ty Tyson, and St. Louis's Franz Lauz all joined Hal Totten, Quin Ryan, and Johnny O'Hara who, together with Bob Elson, embroidered the Cubbies' exploits.

Sam Breadon, finding his Cardinals in a promotional vacuum, thought that any fan-oriented promotion was better than none. He soon introduced Sunday doubleheaders—"twofer" the price of one—a radical departure from the doubleheaders held on Memorial, Independence, and Labor days, which were really two single games played separately. In fact, Breadon had become so enamored with the ritual of a Sunday doubleheader that, according to Red Smith, then a writer on the *St. Louis Record*, he would call a weekday game off "if he so much as spat."

Breadon was the first to discover that radio could become an effective selling tool, when used properly. Weekday radio broadcasts became merely a means to whet the appetite of the fans for Sunday baseball, which he did *not* broadcast. Breadon determined that most of the fans at the Sunday games came from within a hundred-mile radius of St. Louis, so he "papered" the countryside throughout rural Missouri and southern Illinois with posters that heralded the appearance of "DIZZY DEAN" who, it was announced in much smaller type, would "Pitch against the Giants Sunday." Radio, doubleheaders, and advertising worked together to give the Cardinals large Sunday crowds. In fact, a large proportion of every year's total attendance was accounted for by Sunday's attendance.

Still there were those who tried to stick their finger in the dike to stem the inevitable radio flood. The three New York teams signed a formal five-year pact in 1934 agreeing not to broadcast their games. The very same year the commissioner's office signed its own agreement with the Ford Motor Company to sponsor the World Series for $100,000. Radio had become the "friend" of baseball, thanks to the prescience of William Veeck.

William Louis Veeck, according to the baseball record books, was born in Boonville, Indiana, of Dutch parents on January 20, 1878. Trained as a printer's devil—yesteryear's version of journalism school—Veeck followed the lead of so many before him and became a reporter for the *Louisville Courier-Journal*. He left Louisville to join the staff of the *Chicago Inter Ocean* and later the *Chicago Chronicle*. When that paper suspended publication, he joined the staff of the *Chicago American* as a rewrite man.

He soon ascended to the *American* sports department and to the by-line Bill Bailey. It was an old newspaper custom that even though writers came and went, by-lines stayed to provide reader continuity. "Bill Bailey" was such a pseudonym, much the same as today's Galen Drake and Suzy Knickerbocker.

Veeck was revered by his colleagues. A *Sporting News* piece that appeared in 1921 called him "a prince" and asked "Where could they get a better one than Bill?" He was also respected by his readers, for he wrote as he thought, sparing few feelings when he thought he was right.

On one such occasion Bailey-Veeck wrote so candidly of the Chicago Cub operation that the new owner of the team, William Wrigley, Jr., called him to his office to discuss the column and its ramifications. Wrigley, who wanted the very best for his organization, challenged Veeck: "If you think you can do better, why don't you run the club yourself?" Never one to finesse a challenge, Veeck accepted on the spot, joining the Cubs as vice-president and secretary.

Within a year he had succeeded manager Fred Mitchell as president of the club and started his own program of rejuvenating a team which averaged almost thirty years of age for its starters. He also renovated Cubs Park, a small stadium which seated just 16,000 fans, less than half the capacity of crosstown Comiskey Park.

A kindly man of great moral rectitude, Veeck was also a strict disciplinarian who refused to condone failures. Throughout his thirteen-year tenure as president he had no less than seven field managers. Moreover, he could not tolerate slovenliness in his organization, demanding of himself and those around him the holy trinity of order, discipline, and cleanliness. He continually catered to the fans, refurbishing Cubs Park to the point where *The Sporting News* held that "There was not a better-looking, better-kept baseball park or a cleaner and better-uniformed baseball team than that located at Clark and Addison streets in the City of Chicago."

After several years of experimenting to get the right mix, Veeck finally became convinced that a championship team could not be produced unless money was spent for seasoned players. Backed by Wrigley's millions he went into the open market and spent lavishly, picking up such stars as Rogers Hornsby, Riggs Stephenson, Kiki Cuyler, Charlie Grimm, and Chuck Klein. The result was two pennants and eight straight first-division finishes. Veeck felt all his achievements were overshadowed by the team's inability to win a World Series, a goal that had eluded the Cubs since their 1908 win over the Tigers.

Veeck was not only a champion of the fan, but of baseball as well. He campaigned for interleague play and for Sunday baseball in Pennsylvania and other bastions of the Blue Laws where it was prohibited. His efforts were rewarded there, too, as Pennsylvania became the last state to allow Sunday games on November 7, 1933.

The repeal of the Sunday Blue Laws and yet another chance to win the elusive world's championship were something that William Veeck never lived to see. While watching his beloved Cubs play the first-place Giants in mid-September of 1933, he contracted influenza. Within a month he was dead. The obituaries, glowing in their references to his achievements for the team, the fans, and the city of Chicago, closed with the obligatory note: "A widow and two children survive him."

One of the "two children" of William Veeck was christened William Veeck, Jr. But the second-generation baseball Veeck has always been called just plain Bill or Willie. He has even gone to the trouble of legally changing his name to Bill. Therein lies the difference between the two Veecks: one was formal and reserved, the other informal and flamboyant.

If Larry MacPhail was the first to promote to the fans, employing the old art of salesmanship, then Bill Veeck saw him and raised him plenty, using salesmanship with a capital "S" as he heightened and humanized fan-oriented promotions. He became a one-man laboratory for the discovery of new methods of selling the product to the fans, entertaining them in the process, much like the nineteenth-century patent medicine pitchman who offered a little extra show to attract a crowd for his elixirs and nostrums.

To baseball's Old Guard, shot through with the embalming fluid of tradition, Veeck was akin to a one-man leper colony. For his heresy in attempting to market the Grand Old Game, they at first dismissed him as a "clown"; then they tried to isolate him. Failing that, they attempted to freeze him out of baseball completely.

Baseball's magnates neither understood nor accepted the fact that embroidering the basic product, without losing sight of what you're selling, is a time-honored method of good salesmanship. To them Veeck was a "promoter," and they said it through clenched teeth as if it were something dirty. They refused to accept the fact that baseball was a game played for the enjoyment of the fans, not themselves. The public understood and showed their appreciation the only way they could—by showing up to be counted and courted.

Roy Campanella once said, "You've got to be a lot of little boy to play this game." The man who best understood this and knew the way to market it was Bill Veeck. When he purchased the Cleveland Indians in June 1946, his first interview ended with the comment; "It's got to be fun. That's the only way to have it. Everyone has to have a good time; there can't be any standoffish dignity. There's no dignity in my make-up. I'm 'Bill.'" A man among men and a boy among boys. P. T. Barnum incarnate.

Bill Veeck was born into baseball—and into promotions. Raised in a ball park, his very first "job" was helping his "daddy" mail out free Ladies' Day tickets. It was to be the beginning of a beautiful friendship that was to last for the next half century-plus.

Continuing in the giant footsteps of his father, the younger Veeck took a job in the Cubs' front office the year after his father's death, carrying on both a name and a legacy for promotion. Reporting directly to Philip K. Wrigley, the late William's son, Veeck soon become noted for the idea-a-minute style that would be his trademark. Just as fast as he could generate ideas, P. K. Wrigley would reject them.

In the winter of 1934 he first came forward with the idea for night baseball. "I felt we could be first," he remembers "and discussed it with a fellow by the name of Cliff Westcott who was an engineer at the ball park as well as Charlie Gall from the Henry Newgate Company." But Wrigley "felt that night baseball was a fad" and wasn't interested. MacPhail got there before Veeck and the Cubs. When night baseball turned out to be something more than a passing fancy, Veeck brought it up again. "Then he changed his tune. It became less a fad than defacing the neighborhood." Every time Veeck would bring up the subject of night ball, Wrigley had a different rationalization. Veeck remembers presenting "one proposal a year every year and he had a different reason for rejection" every year.

In answer to Mr. Wrigley's objection that lights would "spoil the appearance of the ball park, which was very dear to him," Veeck went to a company that dealt in hydraulics. They worked out a system whereby the "baskets and the lights would come out of the ground behind the stands, lighted, and you wouldn't see them because when the game was over they would go back down into the ground and not deface anything." Strangely enough, Veeck remembers, now Wrigley had a different reason for not putting them in. Veeck began to sense that the reason Wrigley was so set against night baseball was because he hadn't been able to pioneer in having lights put up, as he had in radio when his father had brought forward the idea.

Ironically, Westcott Engineering put up the lighting system at Comiskey Park in 1939 and the company which had spent all the time and effort designing the hydraulic system was able to salvage its efforts by selling its system to the government to light camouflaged landing fields during World War II. But it fared better than Veeck, who was reduced to following Wrigley's constant orders to beautify Wrigley Field with vines or trees, or tabulating the ticket sales of their prime tenant, the football Bears. He did, however, manage to get one idea through, the installation of a light atop the flagpole in center field to tell the passengers on the elevated railway near the ball park whether the Cubs had won that day or not. The remainder of his ideas were filed away, a bank of promotional ideas all dressed up with no place to go.

The Milwaukee Brewers were in serious financial trouble. Although he had no money himself, Veeck immediately called the president of the American Association, George Trautman, to announce his intention. After clearing his maneuverings for the Milwaukee franchise with Wrigley—even turning down financial assistance, more out of pride than anything else—Veeck took it over on June 23, 1941, leaving the Cub organization with no Veeck for the first time in twenty-four years.

Although the parting was friendly, one observer got the impression that the Cubs might have been happy to finally get rid of this enfant terrible, for as a going-away gift they gave him "three guys on option." His most pressing concern was the raising of $25,000 to cover the immediate debts of the club. Veeck promptly set out to hustle up the money. After striking out several times, he finally made contact with a friend of a friend in Chicago who, as Veeck remembers, "probably doesn't know til this day what he put his money into." But put it in he did, and with someone else's $25,000 check and $11 of his own in his pocket, Bill Veeck descended upon Milwaukee. Nothing has been the same since!

Milwaukee had been a steady—if not sensational—member of the American Association since the team's inaugural year in 1902, the year after Milwaukee's American League franchise moved south to St. Louis. During the succeeding forty years they won just three pennants, the last one in 1936, when they won the play-offs and capped it off with a victory in the Little World Series over Buffalo. But 1936 was to be their zenith. While they won the whole ball of wax and their attendance reached almost half a million, it was to be the last year of a working agreement with the Detroit Tigers, who took back both their working agreement and several star players, including Rudy York and Chet Laabs. In 1937, under a one-year working agreement with the Cleveland Indians, the Brewers dropped to third in the standings and even further in attendance. That year the Indians withdrew their agreement and Kenny Keltner and Bill Zuber among others. Now the Brewers were on their own.

By 1941, they had completed their downhill slide, and on the day Veeck assumed control of the team, they were playing in virtual secrecy with just twenty-two fans at tiny Borchert Field. Three of the crowd were the Boy Scout honor guard celebrating Boy Scout Day. So anemic were the Brewers' promotions that these were the *only* scouts who showed up for Boy Scout Day.

Before Veeck could sweep baseball off its feet, he first had to sweep out Borchert Field. His very first promotion, something you won't find in the classic promotions handbook, was to clean up the park that very night. Old Borchert Field, worthy of the name "band box," hadn't had a fresh coat of paint in more than fifteen years and looked it. Bill turned on the arc lights and brought in cleaning ladies, who swept, scoured, and scrubbed the wooden stands by hand. Veeck looks back on it now and says, "We thought we might discover some fans who had been buried under layers of dirt and grime." But it wasn't funny then. Veeck had learned enough about the drawing powers of "Beautiful Wrigley Field" to know the attraction of what Hemingway called "a clean, well-lighted place." Borchert Field, together with its nine thousand seats, became that overnight.

His second promotion was one he had brought with him from Chicago in the person of Charlie Grimm. Grimm was an outstanding player, a good-hit, better-field first baseman who had played eighteen years in the majors, his last twelve with the Cubs. He had also managed them for parts of seven seasons, never finishing lower than third and winning two pennants.

Veeck selected Charlie for his manager of the Brewers for a reason over and above his managerial acumen. It wasn't, as was reported, because Grimm "put $25,000 into the deal." And it wasn't because of his bona fide credentials as a fun-loving, off-the-field companion, reflected in his nickname Jolly Cholly.

Veeck wanted Charlie Grimm because he fit into the Milwaukee German community; he was one of the family. No player, with the possible exception of slugger Joe Hauser, from nearby Madison, Wisconsin—dubbed Unser Choe by the German Burghers—had as much appeal for Milwaukeeans as Charlie Grimm. He was a walking promotion with portfolio as Hauser had been with his booming home runs. Charlie Grimm was there for all the right reasons: he was a leader, he was a winner, he was a fun-loving, left-handed guitar-strumming promotion in and of himself. The fans identified with him and took to him. What more could a promotion be?

For the remainder of that first year, even though he had inherited a team with the miserable record of 19–43, Veeck went to work with all the assiduousness of a hungry bucket-shop operator. He was finally unleashed and all of his promotional ideas came bubbling to the top.

First he built a solid foundation, walking through the stands introducing himself to get an overall feel of the fan. Bill Veeck has always described himself as a "hustler," not in the way the word has come to be used and disused to mean a "con" man, but in the time-honored sense of giving 110 percent. At that time in his life, the 28-year-old Veeck felt that he had to "hustle" to "make up for the lack of talent." He began to hustle and he hasn't stopped since.

Like a man with twenty-eight balls in the air, two of which were familiar, Veeck kept one eye on the ball club and the other on his wandering minstrel band, the fans, the concession stands, and the steady flow of promotions which included door prizes such as salt blocks, stepladders, and sway-backed horses.

He spent much of the time that first year raising capital to keep his ship afloat. He made constant trips to the banks and took to spinning off players to pay the bills. He sold Dave Koslo to the Giants and Johnny Schmitz and Lou Novikoff to his former employer, the Cubs. It was a year for treading water rather than trying to get into the swim of things. 1942 would be different!

By Opening Day 1942, Veeck was prepared to unleash the heaviest barrage of promotions this side of P. T. Barnum.

Opening Day has traditionally been not only the beginning of the baseball season, but also a signal of the official start of spring, a harbinger as true as the first robin. Baseball has come to celebrate it with a ritual second only to Easter, complete with dignitaries—even presidents—parades, and bands.

In Milwaukee in that war year, the bands tootled, the fans

sang, and the marchers marched. It was Opening Day, 1942, a gorgeous April day. The sun was shining brightly and, more important to Veeck, there were sixteen thousand people on hand to fill the nine thousand seats—and much of the outfield. All was right with the world! Then, in the third inning, the wind came up and the heavens opened up, deluging all sixteen thousand and washing out the game. Rudie Schaefer, who was with the Brewers when Veeck arrived—and has been with .Bill ever since—remembers: "Will and I were standing out in the rain, and you couldn't tell if we were crying or not." He adds, "We were though."

But even though Mother Nature's spigot had washed out his first big promotion, Veeck soon turned on his own, loosing a constant stream of promotions with the intensity of an out-of-control Water Pik. He gave out a thousand pounds of poultry feed, live guinea pigs and burros; a two hundred-pound cake of ice; a thousand cans of Chinese noodles; five hundred jars of iguana meat; and suntan lotion to bleacher fans. He staged Barbershop Quartet Day, Taxicab Drivers Day, and Bartenders Night. He let all mothers in free and presented them with baby zimbidium orchids upon presentation of family pictures. He gave 50,000 assorted screws and nuts and bolts to one fan. Some observers thought *he* had lost his screws—but not the fans, who continued to come out to see what he was going to do next.

Veeck believed that "to give away a thousand cans of beer is, in and of itself, nothing. The fans will drink the beer, smack their lips, and go back to watching the game. But to give a thousand cans of beer *to one person* is something else again. Everyone will talk about it and come out to see it happen again." Added to this was his philosophy of never announcing a promotional giveaway in advance. "They must be spontaneous," he says, and thousands of curiosity-seekers will come out to see what the next day will bring. And .it brought more: strolling minstrels, Max Patkin and Jackie Price with their baseball cutups, live lobsters for a lucky fan, morning "Rosie the Riveter" games for wartime night shifts—complete with wandering minstrels in pajamas and breakfasts. It was a circus, a midway, a fair. And fans fully expected the starting battery to be Barnum and Bailey.

But Veeck was as adverse to a nonwinning team as he was to neckware, and he was not about to make them part of the three-ring act he had going on around Borchert Field. Always cognizant of priorities, he has held that "the greatest promotion in baseball's history was Babe Ruth. Next best is a half-game lead with 26 games to go. After that a game lead, etc." So he entered the player market to acquire the warm bodies he needed to give him the half-game lead. His deal was always "$500 down and the rest when you catch me." Still he was able to beg, borrow, purchase, and almost steal players such as Eddie Stanky, Heinz Becker, and Grey Clarke. And he worked his same magic on them. They played winning ball, acting as if they were part of the promotion. In fact, they were.

In 1942 the Milwaukee Brewers became not only a respectable team, but a winning one; one which finished one-and-a-half games behind the front-running Kansas City Blues. With three of the four leading batters, including champion Stanky, they led the league in batting with a .283 average—fourteen points higher than the second best club. Led by Bill Norman's league-leading 24, they had 95 home runs.

A home run in Milwaukee was never merely a home run. It was a "Wheaties Wallop," just as it would become known as a "Ballantine Blast" in New York or an "Old Goldie" in Brooklyn or a "Chesterfield Satisfier" in Washington. In 1942 General Mills purchased a portion of the Brewers' radio broadcasts to extend its Breakfast of Champions franchise beyond its postpubescent Jack Armstrong image. The team hit more home runs than any major league team with the exceptions of the Yankees and Giants. Norman hit 24, Hal Peck 10, and even little Tedd Gullic contributed another 15 down the short 265-foot left-field line. General Mills celebrated each "Wheaties Wallop" with a free case of breakfast food. The first case of twenty-four boxes was always taken home to feed the player's family. After that they'd let them stack up in Veeck's office. As the home run total grew, the stack grew higher and higher. Finally, at the end of the year, Veeck found himself surrounded by wall-to-wall, floor-to-ceiling cases of Wheaties. Not knowing what to do with the cereal surplus, Veeck decided to take some to his farm in West Bend, Wisconsin. He transported almost sixty cases home in a pickup truck and threw the boxes into the pig pen. The next morning he came out to view a scene that resembled a conveyor belt run amok. The pigs had eaten the boxes. And the glassine overwraps. But they hadn't touched the Breakfast of Champions.

The year 1943 was different. The Brewers went to the front of the pack almost immediately and battled Indianapolis and Columbus throughout the remainder of the year for possession of first place. But Grimm needed another left-handed pitcher to spell his ace Charlie Gassaway. He got him. Veeck gave Grimm a party to celebrate his forty-seventh birthday between games of a doubleheader. He had his ushers carry a fifteen-foot birthday cake out onto the field where it was presented to Charlie along with a $1,000 War Bond. When he cut open the cake, Grimm found a left-handed pitcher inside, one Julie Acosta purchased from Richmond of the Piedmont League, where he had been 17–8. Prevailed upon by Veeck to "go ahead and use him," Grimm started him in the second game, only to see him lose 3–2 in 13 innings despite 17 strikeouts. Acosta went on to win his other three starts and help carry the Brewers to the pennant— only the fourth in their forty years in the American Association.

Acosta wasn't the only surprise that Grimm experienced that day. Like most other businesses, the Brewers had set up their own payroll deduction plan for the purchase of War Bonds. Rudie Schaeffer had purchased a supposed "gift" bond for Grimm out of monies deducted from his salary. In effect, he had paid for his gift himself. A few weeks later, when we went in to see Rudie to pick up his bond, Schaeffer—jokingly described by Mike Veeck as "in and out of the till before you realize he's there. He's so quick, I never met a finer thief with finer hands in my life"—told Grimm "We gave it to you, you've already got it!"

Grimm's plight could have been worse. He could have been given the all-purpose trophy. Operating under the time-honored theory, "Who could afford to spend $25 or $30 all the time?" Veeck and Schaeffer had "a nice beautiful trophy that we used for every possible occasion." It was a trophy for all seasons and all reasons; whether to commemorate special days for Hal Peck or Chet Laabs or announcer Mickey Heath or a visiting dignitary, the trophy always stood at the ready, new inscription plate and all. But unlike Monty Hall on "Let's Make A Deal," Veeck and Schaeffer would always take it back, without necessarily giving anything in return. They even trotted it out to award to the city of Milwaukee for the largest opening day crowd in the American Association in 1942, even after the league had ruled that the washed-out game didn't count. No matter! Have trophy, will travel.

Veeck continued to do his own market research, walking through the stands and talking to any and all fans—the numbers had risen from twenty-two to average more than five thousand. On one of his first tours a fan buttonholed him and asked, "Why, with a 265-foot fence, ain't we got any left-hand power hitters?" A valid question, and Veeck—never a man to leave a stone unturned or a fence untampered with—was galvanized into immediate action. The next day he put chicken wire atop the invitingly naked barrier to discourage the Brewers' opponents from taking advantage of his little oversight. By 1943, he had cured the problem, adding power to the lineup and hydraulic control to the fences that could move in and out between batters. Unfortunately for Veeck, the league soon put a stop to it.

But the final game of the 1943 season was the last Bill Veeck ever saw his beloved Brewers play. Before the 1944 season he enlisted in the Marines and was shipped off to the South Pacific, losing the chance to see them win yet another pennant. He was to lose something else, his right leg, a casualty to jungle rot at Bougainville. As he convalesced, baseball became secondary to him. Early in 1945, the man who had arrived with $11 in his pocket sold the Brewers for $250,000 and left baseball. But only momentarily.

The minor leagues have always served as a proving ground for both players and promotions. In the cauldron of small-city baseball, the entrepreneur needs an instinctive understanding of what everyman seeks in the way of entertainment in order to fulfill it, whether by marketing his inferior brand of baseball or by packaging it more attractively.

Prodded by the Depression, many owners resorted to outrageous promotions-cum-publicity stunts to fill both the stadia and the newspaper columns. Some were old, some were new, and some were borrowed; but with seats as empty as their bank accounts the important criterion was whether or not they "worked."

Many promotions "worked" as promoter after promoter tried the most outrageous promotions imaginable to hype attendance. But no promoter was more colorful, more successful, than Joe Engel, The Barnum of the Bushes. Engel was a former ball player who had compiled a mediocre 17 and 22 record for the less-than-mediocre Washington Senators. He was also a former vaudevillian who had once performed on the Orpheum Circuit. Relying more on his show business smarts than his baseball experience, Engel became the prototypical promoter, continually devising new and imaginative ways of drawing attention to himself and his club—and fans to Chattanooga's Engel Field.

On occasion he would hang huge signs outside the ball park to announce "This Park is Not Quarantined!" On others, he would stage mock fights between two seemingly obstreperous fans atop the stadium roof. After much yelling and hollering, two bodies would come hurtling down. Suddenly, little parachutes would open up above the obvious dummies proclaiming "Double Header Tomorrow!"

Engel staged weddings at home plate, elephant hunts, bank nights, and once even avenged Custer's Last Stand—supposedly "scalping" Indians in teepees set up in the outfield. He gave away tickets at the spin of a "wheel of fortune," reasoning that since most fans came in pairs this gimmick was in actuality a "two-fer."

His favorite and most often used promotion was "The Pot of Gold." It was nothing more than a bucket of coins strewn around the pitcher's mound—mostly pennies and dimes, with a few gold pieces seeded in. The "lucky" fan, selected by program number, would have one minute to retrieve as much as could be carried away on his or her person. As most patrons at the Chattanooga Lookout games rarely wore jackets or coats it was a relatively inexpensive promotion, but it helped fill Engel Field time and again. One day it attracted 24,688 paying customers to the 16,000-seat park, setting a minor league attendance record.

The uninhibited Engel added his flair to the game itself as well. He once signed a woman, Virne Beatrice "Jackie" Mitchell, to pitch against the New York Yankees during a 1931 exhibition game in Chattanooga. Babe Ruth and Lou Gehrig struck out gallantly and even though Tony Lazzeri tried to, he walked. Another time Engel traded shortstop Johnny Jones for a twenty-five pound turkey and invited twenty-five sportswriters in to join him in savoring the spoils of the deal. According to Engel, "I still think I got the worst of that deal. That was a mighty tough turkey!"

Engel's antics were the forerunners of 10¢ Beer Night, Scholarship Night, Teen Night, Baseball Bingo, Strike-O, and a thousand and one other nights that sold baseball across the country on a grass-roots level. But baseball was still the centerpiece. So it came as no great surprise when, a few years back, the Albuquerque Dukes held a No Promotion Night: no gimmicks, no give-aways, and no running gag line—just the centerpiece, baseball.

After his convalescence, Bill Veeck determined to get back into baseball in a big-league way. Two franchises were available right after the war: the Pittsburgh Pirates and the Cleveland Indians. After some informal market research, Veeck decided that the Cleveland franchise offered a better opportunity for an injection of Veeck vaccine. A combination of factors made the Indians a far more appealing opportunity than Pittsburgh: they had two bona fide superstars in Bob Feller and Lou Boudreau; they had an enthusiastic citizenry, which was disillusioned over the team's performance; they had had only one championship team since time immemorial; and, not unimportantly, they had a giant stadium seating over 80,000 that challenged Veeck to fill it.

On June 22, 1946, almost five years to the day since he had taken over the Milwaukee Brewers, Bill Veeck purchased the Cleveland Indians for $2,200,000, making them his own personal reclamation project. He was back in baseball.

Will Harridge, the president of the American League and the head of the Old Guard's Welcoming Committee, greeted Veeck's reentry into the ranks with a touching "But of course, you're going to cut out the gags." The so-called Old Guard, a group of men whose idea of a good time was wearing brown shoes, viewed anything that wasn't 110 percent pure and unadulterated baseball as kippered baseball, unworthy of them.

But Veeck, who believed that "baseball was the best entertainment buy, dollar-for-dollar," was prepared to use "the gags" to sell the product. For in what was less vision than merely common sense, he knew baseball had to be sold like any other product, but from a marketing standpoint it was totally different from most. "You go to a store and buy a chair for $39.95," his casebook reasoning went, "and it doesn't really matter when you're all finished with the transaction and gotten the chair home whether the salesperson was polite, whether you could find a place to park or not, whether the credit manager sneered at you or whatever because," he added, "when you go home with the chair and say 'What a great buy,' you have a tangible product. But although baseball is a product, when you come out of a ball park—or any entertainment—you have only the ephemeral idea that you had fun and a good time. And that's why you want to go back.

"Now that feeling of enjoyment or pleasure could be destroyed even before a person becomes your customer. If they get locked up in traffic on a hot day, if they pull into an unpaid parking lot and it's dusty or muddy. . . . These things can spoil the fun. But more particularly, there are those things you can control: if your ticket sellers are not pleasant; if the gateman hits you in the backside with the stile; if the usher doesn't know where you should be sitting; if the vendor stands in front of you before every important play and then turns around and spills beer on you. . . . All of these things can make happen what didn't happen in the case of the chair. They can spoil the ephemeral idea that you had a good time."

Veeck began almost immediately to raise the selling of the intangible fun to an art. He unveiled a dynamic duo in the coaching boxes: contortionist Max Patkin and comedian Jackie

Price. He gave away hard-to-get nylons, pushed Bob Feller to break the all-time strike-out record, and showered the fans with promotions and the field with fireworks.

With wartime restrictions lifted, attendance in the major leagues—still measured by the 1920 record—soared to 18½ million in 1946, up 69 percent over 1945. But Cleveland's attendance climbed even more. When Veeck took over the team at mid-season, attendance stood at only 289,000. At season's end, attendance figures stood at 1,057,289, up an astonishing 89.4 percent from 1945 and surpassing the previous Cleveland record set in 1920 by 150,000. One Sunday, the second largest crowd in major league history showed up at Municipal Stadium to watch the Indians play a doubleheader against the Yankees. Apparently what had been called "bush" in the bush leagues worked just as well in Cleveland.

The team itself was hardly able to match Veeck's pyrotechnics, finishing sixth, while compiling the lowest batting average and second lowest run production totals in the league.

With the team about to move into large Municipal Stadium from small League Park for all its home games, something would have to be done to shore up the weak Indian team before "the gags" would even take. Veeck's entire marketing premise was based on one factor: "You start with a product." At best the Indians were an inferior product.

One of the first trades Veeck put together to give the team some muscle was the "almost" trade of player-manager Lou Boudreau to the Browns for shortstop Vern Stephens and a cast of thousands. But the Tribe's new chieftain underestimated Louie's popularity. Cleveland fans, especially women, rallied to his defense and Veeck in a *mea culpa* admission of his mistake retained Boudreau and gave him a raise. Instead, he traded Allie Reynolds to the Yankees for Joe Gordon, picked up Gene Bearden in another trade with the Yankees, acquired old Milwaukee Brewer Hal Peck from Philadelphia, bought Bob Kennedy from the White Sox, and added Johnny Berardino and Bob Muncrief from the Brownies. The job of building a creditable team had begun.

The Indians improved their team batting average by 14 points, increased their home run output by 33, and their runs scored by 150 and moved up to fourth in 1947. Attendance, sparked by the team's better play, the use of Municipal Stadium for all the Indians' home games, and more Veeck promotions, climbed almost another half a million—the largest increase in the majors—to 1,521,978. The Veeck method of merchandising the National Pastime was succeeding, in spite of the doubting Thomases, Griffiths, Comiskeys, and Harridges.

The year for Veeck's hat trick was 1948. The Indians captured the pennant, won the World Series, and set the all-time attendance mark as 2,602,627 baseball- and promotion-mad fans flocked into The House that Veeck Promoted Hell Out Of.

Earlier that year Veeck had paid tribute to Kenny Keltner, who had just broken the record for the most games ever played at third base for Cleveland and was finishing up his tenth full year as an Indian. Ironically, it was to be his last full season in the majors. But Veeck staged the night for another less obvious reason: Keltner, so vital to the Indians, was then on the threshold of his biggest year ever, a year which saw him hit more homers, score more runs, and drive in more than ever before. Veeck felt a little bit of psychological encouragement would go a long way.

Keltner responded as Veeck knew he would. One who responded differently, however, was a plant foreman at the Chevrolet plant named Joe Earley. Rudie Schaeffer remembers sitting around the front office one day when someone came in and read a letter to the editor of the *Cleveland Press* asking "Why not honor the guy who pays the freight?" "Boy you could just see the bell ring!" recalls Schaeffer. And so, Good Old Joe Earley Night was held. It had all the trappings of what was to become known as Fan Appreciation Night. Orchids were flown in from Hawaii at a cost of $30,000 for the first 20,000 women entering the park. And more than sixty thousand fans joined in to help commemorate the common man. Earley received an automobile, a refrigerator, a stove, and a "house." Rudie Schaeffer had "a piece of property out in Brecksville, Ohio, halfway between Toledo and Akron. And one of the houses on the thing was an outhouse we really didn't need. So we gave it to him."

It was a time for celebrating—and promoting. Everyone was fair game. Ladies were wooed with an avidity not seen since Clark Gable burned holes in the screen and in their hearts. They were given gifts, provided with baby-sitters, and generally made to feel at home in Municipal Stadium. Clowns, fireworks, giveaways, and a great team provided the rest of the inducement. Every game was a "happening" and Veeck had made it all happen!

But Cleveland was not about to do it again. 1949 saw the Tribe fall to third, far off the pace set by the Yankees and Red Sox.

Even that begot promotions. Charlie Lupica, the owner of a small Mom & Pop novelty store, who was a flagpole sitter at state fairs, had hoisted himself up a flagpole, determined not to come down til Cleveland regained first place. Veeck finally enticed Lupica down after the Indians were mathematically eliminated and, moving the whole apparatus to Municipal Stadium, rewarded him for his deed and dedication by giving him a gift of a bathtub. After 117 days atop a flagpole, he used it before going home to greet his wife.

One of the few promotions Veeck ever staged that raised howls of indignation was a decent burial of the Indian pennant. The ceremony took place at the stadium, complete with coffin and hearse and a procession made up of a "grieving" cortège of Cleveland players. While Veeck thought it was humorous, many thought it made a mockery of losing, a travesty of baseball.

The flag burial is one of the few promotions that have come to "grieve" Veeck. He has had many he felt "didn't work, because they were ill-conceived or ill-developed or couldn't be sold to anybody" like having Morton Salt sponsor the rain tarpaulin with their slogan "When It Rains, It Pours," written on it. But few have gone so far awry as to anger fans. However, even Veeck occasionally makes miscalculations, like the time he gave Ohio Hall of Famer Cy Young a Day and presented him with a car. Just as he handed Young the keys to the car, Young advised him he didn't know how to drive. Veeck recovered quickly and announced that, as part of the gift, he was throwing in a left-handed chauffeur.

The Indians drew 2,600,000 fans in 1949, a year that could have been called a success were it not for the loss of the pennant—and for Veeck's constant headaches and dizzy spells. The headaches continued with increasing regularity and, in November, Veeck sold out and retired. Again, momentarily.

Within two years, Bill Veeck was back in baseball. Or at least it looked like baseball. It was the St. Louis Browns, for most of their history a nearly invisible team and now almost totally so. Veeck acquired the team for approximately $2,000,000. After taking control on July 5, he summed up the patently obvious situation: "The Browns are unable to beat their way out of a paper bag with a crowbar."

That came as no great surprise to their fans, of whom there were few. For years their chore in following the team had been relatively simple. All they had to do was look at the bottom of

68

the standings in their morning papers and there they were. And July 5, 1951, was no different—the Browns were two full games out of seventh and driving.

The Browns had ambushed the league to win the only pennant in their futile history in 1944, a wartime year that still saw them finish dead last in attendance. They had had the ill fortune to meet their crosstown rivals, the Cardinals, in the World Series. They lost it in six games. The following year they finished third. Since then, they had been no higher than sixth.

In this, their fiftieth year in the American League, the Browns and their fans could look back on few golden memories, having finished in the first division only twelve times. The 1951 edition of the team was destined to have the lowest batting and fielding averages in the league and the highest earned run average. Their own bona fide major leaguer was Ned Garver, who would become the fourth pitcher in major league history ever to win twenty games for a last-place club. Unlike the Boston ditty that had gone "Spahn and Sain and two days rain" three years before, the Browns' chant might well have been "Garver, Ned, After that we're dead!"

Added to that bleak performance on the field was the Browns' equally dismal showing in the stands. They had drawn just 247,131 fans in 1950, the lowest in the majors, lower even than any club in the Pacific Coast League. If familiarity breeds contempt, unfamiliarity breeds inattention, even neglect. John Lardner, upon hearing of Veeck's purchase, wrote in amazement, "Many critics were surprised to know that the Browns could be bought because they didn't know the Browns were owned."

The Browns were, in short, what a gambler might call a guaranteed loser. They had become merely a bad joke. Veeck, however, thought the price was a bargain. Based upon what he had done in Cleveland and Milwaukee, he thought he could turn the situation around. After all, he had had destitute clubs before, particularly in Milwaukee. But this was ridiculous!

Veeck immediately went to work, hoping to kindle a spark that would set off St. Louis. He dug into his bag of surefire tricks, hiring Max Patkin as contortionist-coach. He signed up Satchel Paige, the ageless wonder who had helped pitch the Indians to the pennant three years earlier, and immediately installed him in the bullpen with a rocking chair.

Veeck added new wrinkles, including Grandstand Manager Day, where the crowd was called upon to give the signals in response to signs asking questions such as "Shall We Move the

Infield Back?" "They defeated Connie Mack's Philadelphia A's. Hell, I'm the only owner in the majors who has 3,700 undefeated managers to his credit." He capitalized on the Browns' position as the "poor relation" of St. Louis baseball by signing former Cardinal heroes like Marty Marion and Harry Brecheen to coach and Dizzy Dean to announce.

But it wasn't his normal antics that were to gain him national attention so much as one particular gimmick. The idea was no vagrant inspiration. Veeck has always believed that promotional stimulants are transferable, "you just change the gag line." Rudie Schaeffer states if even more trenchantly: "We've never said that we're not above stealing or copying somebody."

Now Veeck borrowed from everyone to come up with the one big promotion that would put the St. Louis Browns on the baseball map and fans in the stands. He started with one birthday party and a big birthday cake with someone in it, a la the party he had thrown for Charlie Grimm ten years before in Milwaukee; tossed in one midget engendered by his use of midgets four years earlier in Cleveland; stirred it up with the midget actually playing, prompted by his remembrance of John McGraw's little hunchbacked mascot, Eddie Bennett, whom McGraw had insisted he would send to the plate before he retired. Mixed them all together—and *voilà!* A promotion!

Wherever the idea came from—McGraw or Thurber's short story, "You Could Look it Up"—it was sheer genius. It was also calculated lunacy rubbing the establishment's nose in some of its long-cherished traditions. But it didn't matter. Something was needed. And this looked like it could be it!

A number of preliminary steps were necessary to set up the gag so that it would work. First there was the problem of getting some semblance of a crowd into Sportsman's Park for the game, always a challenge. It was not only the American League's fiftieth birthday, but Falstaff, the beer stuck with the sponsorship of those God-awful Browns, was celebrating some birthday. Veeck went to the Griesediecks, who owned the brewery, claiming that he had "something terrific" lined up for a doubleheader a couple of Sundays hence—although he still wasn't quite certain what the hell it was. He proposed a joint birthday party for the Brownies and the beer. They bought it and Falstaff salesmen were put to work pushing tickets—almost as difficult as pushing beer uphill.

Next he called a theatrical booking agent in Chicago, Marty Caine, who had supplied him with the midgets in Cleveland a few years back. Then he had to get the midget, one Eddie

Gaedel, into town unnoticed and sign him to a contract, calling for the standard equity salary of $100 a day. He pilfered a uniform bearing the number ⅛ from the small son of vice president Bill DeWitt to give him the verisimilitude of a real-life Brownie. Now all was in readiness for the big day!

Sunday, August 19, 1951, broke bright and clear. True to form, the Browns lost the first game of the doubleheader to the Tigers. But nothing could dampen the spirit or the enthusiasm of the Browns' staff as they bustled about the Veeck office-apartment high atop Sportsman's Park to make sure all was in order for the second game. Gaedel's contract had been sent in to the American League headquarters. The programs had been printed with the number ⅛ on them. The cake and the little elf's shoes had arrived. The Falstaff birthday party was about to begin.

After some old cars and two couples in Gay Nineties dress had bicycled around the field and Satchel Paige and the wandering troubadors had serenaded the 18,369 fans—the largest Brownie crowd at Sportsman's Park in many a year—a seven-foot cake was wheeled onto the field. The occupant of the cake had had some second thoughts, proving that even the little feet of midgets can get cold. Veeck had to force him into the cake.

When the cake was opened and a midget popped out, the Falstaff execs failed to see the humor. "A goddam midget, what's so goddam big about that?" said one, who had been promised "something special" for their birthday. But Veeck, sitting next to them in his roof aerie, merely gave them his old Mona Lisa smile.

The second game started while the Falstaff contingent fidgeted in their seats, unsure of what they had seen or of what was so "special" about it. Stricken by the strange sickness that often afflicted visiting clubs in Sportsman's Park, the Tigers went down in order in the top of the first.

As the public address announcer intoned "Now batting, Numbrrrr one-eighth, Gay-dell, batting for Sauce-ier" and the three foot, seven-inch elf strutted up to home plate carrying a toy bat, the Falstaff execs began to get the idea. When Saucier, the man for whom he was batting looked up at Veeck's box and shook his fist, Veeck waved back and so did all the Griesediecks, now sure of what Veeck had meant when he promised "something special."

As Gaedel took his one-eighth of a place in the batter's box, Umpire Ed Hurley called time. Enough was enough. The between-the-games promotion was now leaking into the game itself. "Get him out of there," he told St. Louis manager Zack Taylor. But Taylor had been well-prepped and waved a legitimate American League contract under Hurley's nose. Hurley, seldom at a loss for words, was stricken speechless and waved for Tiger pitcher Bob Cain to get on with the game.

As Detroit catcher Bob Swift shifted out of his normal position and got down on both knees, Cain stared increduously at the batter, looking for something resembling a strike zone. It was there somewhere, about one-third the size of the ordinary one; a target from knees to armpits, the size of a milk bottle. While cameras clicked gleefully away, he threw in a high hard one. And then another. The strike zone seemed to be getting even smaller. As a third, and then a fourth ball sailed over Gaedel's head, he threw his miniature bat away and strutted to first. It was the biggest moment of his career and he wanted to milk it for all it was worth. When Jim Delsing came out to run for him, he patted him avuncularly on the rump. Instead of leaving at once, he strolled around the infield waving his cap to the cheers of the delighted fans and the now-appreciative Falstaff executives.

It was a moment to be remembered by Eddie Gaedel, by Falstaff, by Bill Veeck—who now envisioned that his tombstone would read: "The Man Who Helped the Little Man"—and, not incidentally, by baseball's establishment who, the very next day, barred the further use of midgets as inimical to the "best interests of the game" and sought to expunge from the record books the one at-bat of the smallest man ever to play in the majors. Without either a decent burial or an asterisk.

But while that one moment represented the high-water mark of Veeck's efforts to resuscitate the comatose Browns, he did have others.

One day in 1952, a salesman, knowing Veeck's off-the-wall reputation and having something unusual to sell, called on Veeck and Rudie Schaeffer. "You have no idea how many peddlers come to the door every day just trying to peddle something," says Schaeffer. "And the reason they come to us is because by now we had established a reputation. We were the nuts." The "something" this peddler was trying to sell was the remnants of an out-of-business bat company. "If you have something like unfinished bats, pieces of wood and logs to hustle, are you going to go to a sane guy?" Schaeffer asks rhetorically.

Almost as surprising as the merchandise was the offer the salesman got from the Browns to buy it, stock, lock, and barrel handles, at approximately a thousand dollars, or 20¢ a unit. But a unit of what? "Half this stuff—I say half, but I really don't know the exact equation—but most of them were unfinished. There were some that needed the ends sawed off; they had been turned but the end hadn't been sawed off. Some had been sanded, but weren't varnished. Some were still a length of wood," remembers Schaeffer. But they bought "the whole damn schmear," according to Schaeffer. It was the germination of one of Veeck's greatest promotions.

It was the beginning of Bat Day, a promotion that has grown like wildfire. Today almost every club—with the notable exception of the Dodgers, who are afraid the constant pounding on the cement floor of the stands would create a "structural problem," and the Montreal Expos, who are afraid of pounding on other things, like windshields in the parking lot—has a Bat Day.

Ironically, after Veeck introduced Bat Day in St. Louis, no other major league team picked up on it until he reentered baseball again in 1959. The very name Veeck was anathema to baseball's establishment, those stout-headed men who look like the faces on Mt. Rushmore. To them, everything he touched was diseased.

After two more futile years in St. Louis, Veeck was ready to give up the ghost. He wanted to move the franchise. But the other owners, using the excuse that it was too close to opening day to reprint schedules, refused him permission to move to Baltimore. Even though he had raised attendance up to the almost respectable level of 518,796 in 1952, he was stymied. Frozen out of Milwaukee by the Boston Braves' move in 1953, he was then frozen out of baseball completely by the end of the year. The franchise was sold and moved to Baltimore, and Veeck himself moved to the eastern shore of Maryland.

But Veeck had left two lasting legacies: Eddie Gaedel and Bat Day. One, loved by triviots and fact-filberts, the other loved by baseball itself, even if That Man had introduced it. That Man would be back to introduce many more things, but it was to be a long six-year wait.

Special Days date back to 1889, when the owner of the Cincinnati Reds first discovered that when handsome Tony Mullane, known as the Apollo of the Box, was scheduled to take his pitching turn the stands were filled with hundreds of females who had flocked to the park to see their idol. Soon the local newspapers were carrying small ads which read: "Mullane will

Pitch for Cincinnati Today!" and in small print added the hooker "Women accompanied by male escorts will be admitted free." It was the unofficial start of Ladies' Day.

The Washington Senators (then of the National League) soon picked up on the idea, having a handsome pitcher of their own, Win Mercer. Mercer was on his way to winning twenty games in 1897 when the management named one day each week Ladies Day, females to be allowed in free of charge. During one of his last appearances that year, Mercer took exception to the umpire's calls of balls and strikes. He walked in from the mound and handed the official a pair of eyeglasses. The ladies in the stands shrieked with delight. But the umpire was not amused. He handed the glasses back to Mercer and forthrightly ejected him from the game. Now that the reason for their attendance had been removed, the ladies unleashed all the fury they normally saved for Christmas shopping on the unfortunate umpire, who compounded his felony by calling a Washington player out on a close play in the ninth inning to end the game. That did it! Hundreds of infuriated females surged out of the stands intent upon nothing less than inflicting physical mutilation on the ump. Seeing the sea of parasol-wielding females descending on him, the umpire made a mad dash for the business offices of the Washington club. Once inside, the front office staff shuttered the windows to save him from the stones and bricks that filled the air. Several of the ladies guarded the exits with clubs and bricks lest the umpire try to make his way out, while the office staff secretly ferreted him out a rear door to a team of fast horses. The female mob hung around for hours afterwards, brandishing their weaponry in hopes of catching a glimpse of the defiler of their hero.

Thus Ladies' Day began and almost ended. It would be another twenty years or so until William Veeck, Sr., was to brave the obvious and advertise Ladies' Day again. Now an institution, they have come almost full circle, with some minor league clubs offering Women's Lib Days where the woman pays and her companion gets in free!

But team-sponsored promotions remained few and far between in the early Days. Most were generated from outside, by the fans, who—true to their roots and their root word "fanatics"—constantly sponsored Days for their favorite player.

Sometimes they took the form of spontaneous collections from the player's personal following in the stands, like the time Yankee center fielder Earle Combs was asked to come to the center field bleachers for a presentation. "I was presented with a beautiful watch bought with nickels, dimes, and quarters contributed by fans in the bleachers—fans of all races and colors." And sometimes they were held to celebrate a birthday or some feat that merited some reward. When Jay "Nig" Clarke hit eight homers in eight times at bat one afternoon for Corsicana of the Texas League, the delirious fans passed the hat for him—eight times—and collected $200, more than his yearly salary. And when little Miller Huggins, then the second baseman for the St. Louis Cardinals, hit a home run off Christy Mathewson one day back in 1907—the only one he hit that year and only one of nine in his career—the grateful fans celebrated his performance by presenting him with a pair of shoes, the traditional gold watch, a five-pound box of chocolates, a scarf pin, a silk scarf, and a Morris chair.

Many of the so-called Boys of Summer were given their Days at Ebbets Field in the late 1940s and 1950s. One such day was given a local Brooklyn boy named Hank Behrman, a "Herky-jerky" relief pitcher who won 21 games and saved 19 more for the Dodgers from 1946 through 1948. Behrman, a cross between Mortimer Snerd and pitcher Billy Loes, was one of those who would more than occasionally "tip a glass of kindness for auld lang syne." So it was only fitting that his friends placed little "push-keys" on the bar in neighborhood saloons to raise funds for a gift to be presented on Hank Behrman Day. On the day of the presentation, a fan came out of the stands and presented Behrman with an envelope. He intoned "Hank Behrman, your friends and neighbors want to pay tribute to you . . . " Behrman suspiciously looked at the envelope and said, "What's in it?" The presenter, momentarily taken aback, could only reply "A $100 Savings Bond." "For Christ' sakes," said the infuriated Behrman, "Campanella got a car, Roe gets a cabin cruiser, and all I get is a $100 bond? Shove it up your ass!" And with that he threw the envelope down on home plate and walked away showing none of the appreciation Yogi Berra had shown at his Day when he thanked everyone "for making this day necessary." Writer Tom Meany, knowing Behrman had potential paternity problems, was heard to mutter, "He's lucky it's not a subpoena."

Other celebratory Days have been given returning heroes after they left the city in which they gained their fame. Frank Chance Day was one. The Peerless Leader, who had been with the Cubs both as player and manager for fifteen years, was honored on his first trip back to Chicago after becoming manager of the Yankees. Another such Day was given Willie Mays upon his return to New York as a member of the Mets in 1972. Mays, who had started his illustrious career twenty-one years before with the Giants, had demanded a Day for himself. He also demanded that his former boss, Horace Stoneham, present him with a car. Stoneham, strapped for funds, worked out a deal with a local Rolls-Royce dealer for a new car. But when Mays heard about his gift-to-be, he remarked, "Jesus Christ, that'll fuck up my deal with Pontiac." After receiving all of his gifts, Willie immediately left the ball park without waiting around for the game to be played.

Now Days for ball players are filled with pomp, pageantry, and presents, including cars, dolls that wet and even, in the case of Norm Cash Day, a bat with an inch-and-a-half hole in it to commemorate the man who struck out more than anyone in Tiger history.

There were other promotions that even took in the game of baseball as well. The thirties saw the emergence in places like St. Louis and Brooklyn of something called the Knothole Gang, a name evocative of the days when kids stood outside ball parks and stared through a hole in the fence. In the heyday of membership cards for everything from Little Orphan Annie's Secret Society to Uncle Don's Club, it provided kids with cards signed by pseudo-celebrities like radio announcer Happy Felton. For a nominal 50¢, kids were allowed into a weekend game to root for this year's heroes and build an affiliation for tomorrow's teams.

And then there were the field contests, including foot races and pitching, batting, and distance-throwing contests. Some of the first of these were races between ball players. Billy Sunday won one of the first on record before he retired to become an evangelist. His time was later eclipsed by Hans Lobert, a third baseman who played fourteen years in the National League, the last three for the Giants. It was during his last year, 1917, that the new Giant owner Charles Stoneham and Giant Manager John McGraw, who had a mutual interest in the Oriente Race-track in Cuba, pitted their speedster against a car and a horse down at the track. Lobert was to run a quarter mile, the car a mile, and the horse a mile and a quarter. Even though the manager of the track added sixty yards to Lobert's distance, he still won.

During World War II, when bond drives were in vogue, there were several such contests. In one at the Polo Grounds, Debs Garms was matched against the clock in the 60-yard dash. The emcee, Milton Berle ("There's Boris Karloff . . . oh, sorry, madame!") announced Garms' time was a "new world record," but after much deliberation and a remeasurement, it was determined that Garms had only run 52 yards.

In Washington, Junior Wooten threw a baseball for a distance record, Sam Snead hit golf balls out of Griffith Stadium and Bob Feller threw his fast ball into an apparatus that measured its velocity. Washington owner Clark Griffith advertised the promotion, but had neglected to tell Feller, who refused to do it. Less than fifteen minutes before game time, Griffith agreed to pay Feller $100 and it went off as advertised.

There were home run hitting contests galore. The most famous was held in 1942 at Yankee Stadium, a nostalgic smorgasbord that featured Walter Johnson pitching to Babe Ruth. By the 1950s they were everywhere and seemingly all won by a husky itinerant first baseman named Steve Bilko, with whom writer Harold Rosenthal readily identified "because both he and I have varicose veins." For their efforts the winning players were usually given about $150 in merchandise which the local merchants wanted to get rid of.

One baseball promotion that worked when it was first introduced and still does is Old-Timers' Day. Larry MacPhail and the Yankees started it officially in 1946, but it really began in 1939 when first the Yankees honored the dying Lou Gehrig and the Philadelphia Athletics presented the 1911 A's against the 1929 A's as part of the celebration for baseball's centennial. It has been so successful that no less than a dozen clubs now have Old-Timers' Day, including the Mets, who staged one in their very first year. The scenario is always the same. The same old-timers are dusted off year after year and trotted out in slow motion to the roars of an appreciative and nostalgic crowd. In what has become a cast of thousands resembling the old barnstorming tours of yore, the Fellers, the Mantles, the Vernons, the Musials, the Kuenns, the Fords, and other recognizable names and faces appear—but never Ted Williams or Hank Greenberg, who won't accept.

Everyone seems to share in this tribute to yesteryear, overweight and shortness of breath with few exceptions. One of the exceptions was Hoyt Wilhelm. When asked what he thought of Old Timers' Day after pitching in his first after twenty-three years on the mound, he could only answer "Crap!" The cost of this inexpensive promotion is the participants' air fare, living expenses for the weekend, parties in their honor, and gifts costing approximately $100 a man. As one player said, "Because we played in 1934, they think they should pay us 1934 wages."

But these are as nothing compared to the gift days that now dot the baseball schedule with more frequency than doubleheaders. The first Bat Day in St. Louis begat more offspring than Jesse, with Cap Day, Jacket Day, Batting Helmet Day, T-Shirt Day, Tote Bag Day, and any other piece of baseball-oriented *chatzkah* Day following in its wake.

Baseball's great giveaway game costs major league teams more than a million dollars a year, and the results are such that the teams are coming back with more. The Atlanta Braves, who haven't had a bona fide promotional vehicle since Hank Aaron broke Babe Ruth's record, actually saw their attendance increase 52 percent in the face of a last place finish in 1976. Bob Hope, the Braves' director of promotions and public relations, admits that "We must and do remember that our main product is baseball, but right now, we're trying to win the all-time award for shooting the bull until we have more quality to offer on the field."

Many promotion directors count the billboard effect of having kids walk around with their team's T-shirt or cap or jacket on as a plus. But Rudie Schaeffer, now business manager of the White Sox, feels that this is like trying to sell nickel Cokes for four cents and hoping to make it up on the volume. "Actually, I don't view it from the standpoint of residual benefits at all. That's just extra meat on the bone, and that I expect anyway. I have to stay within an economic framework in order to justify it. As far as I'm concerned, they have to pay their own way *today*."

But how do they "pay their way"? One recent introduction is the cosponsored or co-op promotion, with a sponsor picking up part of the tab. In this day of rising costs it is often necessary. Milwaukee looked to Grafs Beverage to cosponsor their expensive jacket giveaway; the Blue Jays looked to Coca-Cola to help underwrite their Cap Day, and a local merchant, Shopsy's to underwrite their T-shirt promotion; and the California Angels were aided by J.C. Penney in defraying the costs of their team jersey.

But still most promotions work, regardless of whether they're held on good days or "dog" days, against good teams or also-rans. In spite of the fact they drew almost three million people to Chavez Ravine, the Los Angeles Dodgers still employ promotions. And heavily. The Dodgers opened their 1976 season with three consecutive jacket giveaway nights, all three weeknight games. Fred Claire, vice president-promotions and public relations for the Dodgers, attributes their success to "the advantage of using the spring training period to promote the jackets on radio and television." And with 40,000 at the opening game, and 52,000 the next two nights, they more than served their purpose. In fact, special giveaways have proved so successful that one press box wag even suggested that the Baltimore Orioles sponsor the first World Series Bat Day to fill the yawning chasm of empty seats at the 1971 Series.

Not all promotions work out as planned. A few years ago, the Angels gave away an inflatable beach ball bearing the Angels logo and simulated seam stitching to give it the appearance of a baseball with a pituitary problem. In its deflated form, however, the beach ball not only moved like hotcakes, it looked like a pancake and as such made a rather unglamorous package. The alternative would have been to distribute them inflated, but that would have taken a trainload of cartons and a windless evening.

Sometimes promotions get out of control. A few years back the Indians sponsored a 10¢ Beer Night and the beasties that go bump in the night consumed their fill of Old Sweatsock and turned on the visiting Texas Rangers and the umpires. The umpires had their fill too and, after watching the sufficiently sloshed fans cavort on the field, forfeited the game to the Rangers, only one of ten forfeits in major league history.

And sometimes the affinity to baseball is lost altogether, as in Pantyhose Day. Or Halter Day, such as the ones the Minnesota Twins staged in 1978, giving away halters emblazoned with the name "Twins" on the giveaway two-baggers. Or Hot Pants Night, first introduced in 1971 by Charlie Finley. Any woman wearing the then-fashionable G-strings gone legit was admitted free. Finley thought that those wearing the brief garments would have to be lured onto the field with free pairs of tickets and held 500 in readiness. But even he wasn't prepared for what happened. As soon as the public address system bellowed: "All right, it's time for hot pants, ladies . . . " five thousand gals in abbreviated shorts hopped the railings to join in a scheduled parade on the field. The A's honored all who wrote in and told them they "were on the field," a minor planning mix-up that cost them almost ten thousand tickets.

But the Wretched Excess Award for all time belongs to former Washington Senators owner Bob Short and his promotional "genius," Oscar Molomot, who celebrated Mother's Day by giving out cans of Right Guard deodorant to all mothers in attendance.

Maybe the best promotion of all is that admitted to by Bob Hope of the Atlanta Braves: "Our idea of a good promotion is to get them home from the park safely!"

Nineteen fifty-nine marked the hundredth anniversary of Charles Darwin's theory of natural selection and also the resurfacing of Bill Veeck in baseball, proving not only the correctness of Darwin's theory that the fittest survive but that Veeck was as unsinkable as Molly Brown after his St. Louis blues. God knows the establishment wanted to keep him out! The owners were still miffed at the man who had spoofed their fine old marinated traditions. Some, unhappy with his wildly successful promotions, were doubly irked that he was constantly stealing newspaper space from them. After all, if you rob the same bank four or five times, people are bound to get angry at you!

They all rallied behind, in front of, and even underneath that great executive, Ford Frick, who led his minions with directions and courage, even, it has been noted, in meetings. At one interleague meeting he adjourned the assemblage with the stirring "Gentlemen, I want to congratulate you. This has been our finest meeting. We finished everything in seven minutes." Frick, whose name today is synonymous with asterisks, had led the fight to squeeze Veeck out in the first place. Still commissioner of baseball, he didn't want him back in the second place, or the third, or in Chicago.

But that's where they got him, for Veeck had reemerged with the Chicago White Sox, a team which had been in the American League since 1901 and in the hands of the Comiskey family equally as long. While the Comiskey heirs were locked in an internecine war, Veeck marched in with all deliberate speed and walked out with a majority of the stock.

This time the team he bought was no run-down-at-the-heels contingent, but a team which had finished in the first division every year since 1951 and in second place the last two. They were a scrappy team, one which, in the true Veeck mold, promoted wins. A walk and a stolen base usually signaled the start of a rally. Veeck, who is happy to be at the card table with any hand knowing the cards will eventually be redealt, had dealt himself a winner.

But if the team wasn't down-at-the-heels, the ball park was. Comiskey Park, built in 1910 and the oldest park in the American League, had seen its great moments. But it was beginning to show its age. Veeck immediately went in with a bucket brigade and scrubbed and painted the park until it almost came to resemble its crosstown competition, Wrigley Field, The World's Most Beautiful Ball Park. He built an Isle of Light to safely convey the fans to the park, and he set out to renovate the parts of the stadium that were sorely in need of repair.

It was while the refurbishing of Comiskey Park was going on that Veeck performed an act of misdirection worthy of Houdini. The master plan called for the laying of new sod as well as for the installation of a new gate behind the right field stands. Things were not moving apace and the plan was woefully behind schedule. Workmen wheeled in wheelbarrow after wheelbarrow filled with sod from trucks parked outside the fence. Something more drastic was needed to expedite the operation.

Veeck—who confesses to having occasionally planted barricades around the stadium reading "Under improvement" even though "I don't know what the improvement was, but it looked nice"—now decided to turn the renovation to his advantage and make it part of a promotion. In what he called a "planned disaster," Veeck simply tore down the gate and part of the wall as well, enabling the sod-ladden trucks to drive right into the ball park. He camouflaged the tearing down of the gate and wall with a coverup he entitled Fox. Besides being the most popular of all White Sox, Nelson Fox was well on his way to the Most Valuable Player award and as deserving as anyone Veeck could think of for a Day. Needing a raison d'être for tearing down the wall, he came up with the most outrageous one he could. Fox, a native of the landlocked central portion of Pennsylvania, would be a natural for a massive yacht. The yacht—borrowed, naturally—was brought into the park and instead of "losing points" Veeck made them. The fans stared at the imitation of postwar Berlin and exclaimed in amazement, "Hey, this guy had to tear down the whole right field stands to get the boat in!"

The White Sox rewarded Veeck's efforts and the devotion of the long-suffering by winning their first pennant in forty years. Ranking no better than sixth in the league in batting with a .250 average and last in home runs, the Go-Go Sox more than adequately made up for their lack of power with hustle—leading the league in stolen bases, fielding, saves, earned run average, and one-run victories. True to their 1906 ancestors, the Hitless Wonders, the Sox alchemistically blended one hit, one hit batsman, ten walks, and three Kansas City errors to mold an 11-run inning in one game that year.

Veeck, the Minor League Executive of the Year in 1942 and

Major League Executive of the Year in 1948, had done it again, becoming the first American League owner to win a pennant in his inaugural year since Jim McAleer's Red Sox did it in 1912. And, in the process, broken the all-time White Sox attendance mark with 1,423,144.

As the White Sox rested and prepared to host the National League champion Los Angeles Dodgers, Veeck himself was preparing to go all out hosting the visiting press. His greatest commodity has always been his acceptance by the fans and the press, if not the owners. And the 1959 World Series gave him a ready-made forum.

Harold Rosenthal, then of the *New York Herald-Tribune* recalls the occasion: "It has always been World Series practice for the Commissioner, whoever he is, to allot X thousands of dollars to each of the competing clubs to run their press headquarters, which is always pretty heavily patronized by club officials and their chums. 'Press' is just a figure of speech, mostly.

"The allotments have always been considered fairly sufficient, but no one can ever run a Roman orgy on say thirty-thousand dollars worth of expense money to cover four days of big hotel food and drink entertaining a thousand people nightly. The shameful part of it is that some very big owners in their day have actually come out of this with a profit. In other words, what you don't spend you keep!

"Not Veeck. He took the thirty big ones and stuck them into petty cash. Then he called for the sommelier and his finest wine list. Ah, the wine! It came out of fountains. Not one fountain, but a whole string of them. Some kind of machinery pumped the grape in a continual flow so that all you had to do was hold your glass under a spigot. A year later, at the Pirates-Yankees World Series headquarters, there were still some hangover headaches.

"The eating department offered double the entrees of most World Series pressrooms. And no lights were blinked at 12:05, either. That's because Veeck was in the joint. He'd have brained any employee fooling around with the light switch while he was in the middle of a good story. Ditto for 1:05, 2:05, and 3:05. When there were lights to be turned off, it was Veeck who would be doing the turning."

But, sad to relate, the 1959 White Sox didn't hit the giant quiniela, going down to defeat at the hands of the Dodgers in six games. It seems that promotions, even great promotions, are no substitutes for great ball clubs. Still, Veeck could point with pride to another achievement on the field: the New York Yankees were stopped in their annual drive to the top of the American League only three times between 1947 and 1964, a span of eighteen years. All three were at the hands of teams developed or headed by Veeck: the 1948 and 1954 Indians and the 1959 White Sox.

The next year Veeck introduced two promotional ideas that were to become a permanent part of the sports scene.

The first was the introduction of the names of players on the backs of uniforms. Veeck, who believes that "traditions are things that are around to be broken," never could comprehend why the fan at the park was entitled to know less than the guy watching the game on TV. They were at least entitled to know the names—as well as the numbers—of players. To Veeck, "it was like announcing them." But the traditionalists, who had once railed at the Yankees when they first put numbers on the backs of players because it would hurt scorecard sales, howled bloody murder. Next, they said, he would be putting "Joe's Bar & Grill" on the backs of the uniforms. A delighted Veeck, who had struck yet another nerve, could only chuckle, "I sure would if it would help any."

To introduce the hardly revolutionary idea and "to get everyone to realize what I was doing," Veeck purposely misspelled Ted Kluszewski's name. The name Kluszewski was spelled more incorrectly than correctly, anyway, and most writers wouldn't have noticed that the only back broad enough to carry the ten characters in his name also carried it incorrectly spelled if Veeck hadn't accentuated the mistake by reversing the "Z", so that it read "KLUSƧEWSKI." Then to call further attention to it, Veeck let the photographers in on the idea and, suddenly, to the collective chant of "bush" from other owners, the picture and the idea were spread across sports pages throughout the country. And Veeck's program sales? They increased the next year, despite the Cassandra cries of the owners.

Nineteen sixty was also the year the American Football League began. One day soon after the picture ran in the New York papers, Milt Woodward, the assistant commissioner of the AFL, called Veeck and asked "Can we put the names on the backs of players? We want to adopt it as a league rule." "Of course," volunteered Veeck, "It's not copyrighted or anything. But I'm flattered you took the trouble to call and that you remembered who started it." With Veeck's permission the American Football League put names on the backs of all its jerseys, more as an aid to television than for the fans, who were few and very far between in the early years.*

Veeck had long been fascinated by the exploding pinball machine that stood at the end of the bar in William Saroyan's *Time of Your Life.* But he had never been able to translate it successfully into the baseball idiom, primarily because of the cost. Finally, he was able to interest Charlie Gibbs, president of Spencer Advertising, a national firm which represented a network of programs for advertising purposes, in his concept of an exploding scoreboard. Veeck knew that he wasn't able to afford it without advertising. Only after Gibbs was able to find advertisers who were willing to enter into long-term contracts for space on the scoreboard was he able to finance its construction by "banking" the contracts.

In keeping with the Veeck axiom of "never announcing your gags in advance," the new gimmick was unveiled without fanfare. The scoreboard consisted of ten pylon mortars extending from the top housing Roman candles or rockets, a flip-top mechanism, colored "strobe" lights, and background music to provide instant celebration for each and every White Sox home run, all at a cost of $104.98 a home run for the "works."

At that, it was a bargain. The Sox, who hit only 97 homers—lowest in the majors—when they won the pennant, responded to the "do-it-yourself" party by hitting 112 in 1960. From the very first one hit that year by Roy Sievers through the last one by Minnie Minoso, it was a "blast." Even more, it proved to be a bonanza for Veeck. It became one of those "happenings" that everyone had to see for themselves. This meant that fans had to come back any number of times before actually seeing it go off, the Sox' outpouring of homers being, in reality, a constant drizzle. And everyone who saw it go off would tell the world about it and the world would come beating to the door of Comiskey Park. Bill Veeck had built a better mousetrap and everyone appreciated it. Well, almost everyone. Some opposing ball players found it more than a little disconcerting. Jimmy Piersall, then with the Cleveland Indians, once picked up the

---

*When the football leagues finally merged in 1966, the AFL agreed to waive its two-point conversion if the National League would put names on the players' backs. The merged entity now requires the names of all players on their uniforms, but not baseball, where many of the teams still refuse to defile their uniforms.

ball after a White Sox homer had kicked back on the field and threw it up against the scoreboard—to no avail.

It has always been one of Bill Veeck's Articles of Faith that the best promotions are those you don't advertise. "We could get more people coming to see what was going to happen." One of these that did happen with some frequency, not every night, mind you, but often enough to "merely illustrate that you couldn't count on it," was fireworks.

It seemed to many that Bill Veeck was a member of the Fireworks Auxiliary. Fireworks held the same fascination for Bill Veeck that the tar baby held for Br'er Rabbit. He couldn't get enough of them. He was his own market research sample, and he was right: "Fireworks are something that everybody likes. I know because I like them." But he had empirical evidence, too. Between 85 and 90 percent of the people stayed with Veeck to watch the rockets' red glare. And, just as importantly, bought more at the concession stands in the afterglow. Every day was the Fourth of July. Or so it seemed.

Veeck had more days than leap year. He had a Smith Day, admitting all persons named Smith, Smythe, Schmidt, or anything that resembled the root name to help slumping outfielder Al Smith celebrate something or other. This provided him with a cheering section of namesakes to help pull him out of his batting and mental funk. Veeck gave out 1,000 cupcakes and 1,000 cans of beer as door prizes. He had tickets printed with the pictures of different players on the back of different days; a promotion that had fans constantly calling up and asking to go on Jim Rivera Day, so they could complete their set. He had Dairy Farm Day and Little League Day and Honor Student Day and S&H Green Stamp Day and just about any day imaginable.

He had other gimmicks at the ready, too. One was something he called the Pitch-O-Meter. It was built into the scoreboard complete with what he described as "the most marvelous siren I guess at that time in the country." The Pitch-O-Meter's function was to enforce the twenty second rule for pitchers then in the rule book by loudly calling attention to an opposing pitcher's dalliance on the mound.

Veeck was prepared, knowing that he could "only use it once and they'd declare it illegal, even though it was in the rule book." Veeck even had the right pitcher already picked out. It was to be Oriole knuckleballer Hoyt Wilhelm. Wilhelm's fame rested on several factors: he had hit a home run in his first time up in the majors and would never hit another; he was to become the last World War II veteran in organized ball; and, most importantly, he was notoriously slow. It was this last piece of trivia that interested Veeck. This and the fact that Wilhelm combined his slowness of hand with a quick temper and would be upset by such a little thing as a bellowing siren in the middle of his windup.

The Pitch-O-Meter was never used. But it wasn't Frick or the rules committee that prevented it. It was the Mayo Clinic. The headaches and dizzy spells had returned and the doctors advised Veeck to exit as quickly as possible. By July 1961, Bill Veeck had returned to his retreat in Easton, Maryland. This time voluntarily retired, not frozen out as before.

Veeck stayed retired from the sporting scene for nearly fifteen years, except for a brief fling as president of Suffolk Downs Race Track in Massachusetts. By the mid-seventies, he had the old itch again.

His antennae told him the days of the sixties—when the watchwords were speed, action, violence, and mugging—were gone. There had been a change of mood. One which sought less turbulence. And Veeck believed they could find it in baseball, the "only thing besides the paper clip that hadn't changed." He felt that baseball, full of eloquent pauses allowed for the game "to be savored rather than taken in gulps." In short, he found "baseball had once again arrived."

And when Bill Veeck arrived back in Chicago in 1976 he brought along a fifteen-inch file chock-full with more than fifteen hundred promotional ideas he had conceived while awaiting the right moment. Some thought he was burned out. One owner, who asked not to be identified, said, "There's a problem with Bill. It's the stuff that sold in 1930 and 1940 and 1950 for him. Now he's doing it in 1970 and it doesn't have the same impact. Giving away lobsters and all that other shit doesn't do it today."

Veeck was given two weeks by the critics. He fooled 'em all. He took the door off his office to make himself accessible to the only people that really mattered, the fans, rolled up the sleeves on his tieless shirt, and went to work the only way he knew how, promoting. He unveiled the greatest baseball family act since all three Alou brothers started in the same outfield. With his lovely wife Mary Frances and son Mike running downfield interference for him and occasionally extricating him from his own thoughts, he pulled out all stops. At first his ideas merely took the form of returning to those wonderful days of yesteryear, appealing to White Sox nostalgia buffs. He removed the artificial turf that had covered the infield only, replacing it with natural grass. He changed the name White Sox Park back to Comiskey Park and dressed up his players in the uniform colors worn by the White Sox of the Hitless Wonders era, navy blue. He installed Paul Richards, manager of the Go-Go Sox of the early fifties to lead the team and hired Minnie Minoso as a coach. One of his first gimmicks to infuriate the Old Guard, was his introduction of an abbreviated version of the navy blue uniform, complete with short pants. He initiated some simple promotions, including a Non-Smoking Section and a shower in the bleachers for the comfort of the fans. Then, there were the exploding scoreboard, fireworks, a wandering minstrel band, clowns to greet the fans as they walked in, and walls chock-a-block with drawings from school kids from the Chicago public schools. And giveaways and more giveaways. Comiskey Park began to take on the free form of a Fellini movie.

And it worked. It worked so well that the man they said wouldn't last two weeks was back—960,000 fans worth! Bill Veeck was, in the words of the title song from "Hello Dolly," back where he belonged.

About the only thing that hadn't worked from that Pandora's file drawer was an idea Bill had borrowed from his son Mike, who is a rock fan. Mike had been intrigued by the use of laser beams by a rock group called Blue Oyster Cult. Bearing in mind that Bill Veeck is not a rock fan, he still knows a good idea when he sees one—or steals one. He intended to construct a screen of lasers shot down the foul lines to check the umpires' calls on balls hit foul. But this was one Veeck idea that died aborning, not because the establishment wouldn't let him use it so much as the cost, which was ridiculously expensive.

It was about the only thing that didn't work. By 1977, even the team was working. The financial success was an artistic one as well. The White Sox—picked to finish last in the American League's West Division by most, and even last in the *American Association* by some—led the American League West for two thirds of the season and wound up with the most wins by a Sox team since 1965 and the most fans in their history, 1,657,135. Sometimes it wasn't quite clear, however, whether the fans had come out to watch the players or the players had come out to watch the fans.

Former Yankee President Mike Burke once said, "The marketing men don't wear uniforms, but it may be that they'll mean more to the future of baseball than the home run hitters and the twenty-game winners."

Bill Veeck, the man already known as The Man Who Helped The Little Man, has proved that they already *have* meant more! Much more.

3

With apologies to Grantland Rice, there is more to football than "how you played the game"

On Saturday, November 6, 1869, Rutgers and Princeton met in a contest that resembled organized King of the Mountain. With twenty-five men a side, students of the two New Jersey institutions kicked an object resembling a pregnant goat bladder up and down the field until Rutgers had scored six goals and won 6–4. There was no running game. It was Americanized soccer, although later it would be remembered as the first game of something called "football."

Throughout the succeeding years, this throwback to the Vandals, who tossed around a skull for sport, would become refined. Rules changed, styles of play changed and gradually the game we know today emerged.

One phenomenon that was apparent from that very first game was football's enormous spectator appeal. The students encircling the field that beautiful autumn afternoon in New Brunswick gave football its real reason for being. As school after school picked up the game, their followers also picked it up as a social event. By the 1890s, when Yale met Princeton in their annual Thanksgiving game, at New York's Polo Grounds, the game had arrived as a major happening. In what had become the most glamorous outdoor social event in the country, collegians and alumni wearing greatcoats and carrying banners and canes wrapped in ribbons formed a procession up Fifth Avenue to the game.

The baseball fan has traditionally been the beer drinker

exploited by the early interests of the game. These blue-collar workers formed the very backbone of baseball, identifying with their city's team as if it were a personal extension of themselves. Conversely, the football crowd at a very early date was, by definition, a more affluent group, having attended or been associated with a college at a time when college was beyond the expectations—let alone the means—of the majority of Americans. They were the "carriage trade," later to become the martini-drinking crowd. And they brought to college football the same specialized quality they brought to everything they touched: a touch of class, with banners, bunting, and star-spangled pizzazz.

After baseball had said its World Series valedictory, college football strutted on the scene, complete with cheering sections, bands, banners, and floats. It was an obsession for students and alumni—real and imagined—alike.

From its birthplace in the Northeast, college football rolled out across the country, in ever-increasing swirls, capturing first the Midwest, then the South, and finally the Far West.

By 1925, when twelve million fans paid to see teams in twenty-six recognized baseball leagues play, twenty million jammed their way into stadia, bowls, and fields throughout the country to watch two hundred and ten leading colleges play football.

College football's fabulous success was partially attributable to a subtle change. The emphasis was shifting imperceptibly from the social aspect to the financial—to the tune of $50,000,000 a year; a shift that started when admission prices for the Harvard-Yale game of 1875 "soared" from 25 to 50 cents per ticket.

Across the country, colleges began to awaken to the realization that football meant money. Granted that academia's official stance had always been that college football was an amateur sport open to undergrads who maintained an acceptable scholastic standing and that it helped to build character, the subtext was that football begat money. For some schools, this meant a profit of as much as half a million dollars a year. With this in mind, colleges busied themselves marketing their overlooked product. They built large stadia to cash in on customers foolish enough to spend four Coolidge dollars each to sit and watch the antics of twenty-two young men in cold and rain, sleet and snow. Soon large lunar craters began to fill with stadia. Physical plants were built at Yale, Ohio State, Notre Dame, Kansas, Purdue, California, Iowa State, Tulsa, Utah, and all points north, east, west, and south to house the thousands who flocked to the Saturday rituals. All were built on the come, debt financed and, in most cases, secured by gate receipts.

The most unique offering for funds was made by the University of Michigan, whose 1926 prospectus had a provision not found in any other school's offerings. Each $500 3-percent bond carried the privilege of purchasing two seats between the 30-yard lines for a period of ten years or for life of the bond. The circular carried a seating plan leaving little to the imagination. Arrows indicated "You might sit here" for an end zone seat; "If you are lucky you might be here" for a seat on the twenty; and one reading "You might even be here," pointing to an area just outside the stadium. But in bold type was the legend "Stadium Bond Owners will sit here," indicating two midfield sections. The come-on proved so popular that many investors refused to cash in their bonds at maturity, preferring to hold them in order to retain their seats.

As the giant erector set bowls started pockmarking college campuses, officials sought a way of filling them. And paying for them. The surest way to fill the colossal new stadia was to have a winning football team. And the surest way of having a winning football team was to recruit the best players—regardless of their scholastic potential or ability to pay for school.

The body academe was so shot through with football fever that when Yale alumni were called upon to honor the late Walter Camp in 1925, they responded with $180,000 for a memorial gateway leading to the Yale Bowl. Admirers of the great Yale mathematician and physicist Josiah Willard Gibbs were unable to come up with $12,000 for a far more modest tribute.

Unlike baseball, no one man was ever credited with creating the game of football. Like baseball, it developed from English antecedents. But one man, more than anyone else, caused its transformation into an American game.

Known as The Father of American Football, Walter Camp was the primary architect of the game. As a former Yale captain and one of the founders of the Intercollegiate Football Association—the forerunner of today's Ivy League—and its rules committee, he wrote the first rule book ever published and introduced many of the basic concepts of the game as we know it today: the eleven-man team, the substitution of the line of scrimmage for rugby's "scrummage," the quarterback position, the adoption of downs and yards-to-go, signal calling, and the scoring system.

But the anchor of Camp's fame was his All-America selections, which he started in 1889. In the days before everyone got into the act, he was recognized as the arbiter. His list of the eleven greatest men on the gridiron was considered the "official" team.

True to his Ivy League heritage, his first selections consisted of five Princetonians, three Yalies, and three Harvardians. In 1891, a center from the University of Pennsylvania sneaked in and in 1895 a Cornell quarterback entered the *sanctum sanctorum*. But it was to remain an Ivy League monopoly until Clarence Hershberger of the University of Chicago was selected in 1898. Then, with a stunning show of begrudging ecumenism, he selected a Carlisle halfback in 1899 and two Army players in 1901. In 1904 he named two midwesterners, Willie Heston of Michigan and Walter Eckersall of Chicago, but still the team had eight Ivy Leaguers and nine easterners. It was not until 1915 that he named his first player from west of the Mississippi, Bert Baston, a Minnesota end. The 1916 All-America team was the first to have a majority of non-Ivy Leaguers. From there it was only a short forward pass to Camp's first West Coast selection in 1917—and his first Southern selection in 1918.

Death was to come to Walter Camp, fittingly, at the age of 65 while attending a rules committee meeting in 1924. His mantle passed on to sportswriter Grantland Rice, who made the "official" selections for *Collier's* magazine, beginning in 1925. The following year, Rice's dream eleven was comprised of representatives of teams from Alabama to Southern California, with *no* Ivy Leaguers. Football's heroes reigned from sea to shining sea, emblematic of a truly national game.

The personalities of the twenties burned more brightly than those of other eras. Made larger than life by flamboyant, get-the-story newsmen, immortalized by Ben Hecht and Charles MacArthur in *The Front Page*, they became rapid-fire sensations in deadly circulation wars. Some who were blown out of proportion by writers fanning the flames of fame included a flagpole sitter named Shipwreck Kelly and an evangelist named Aimee Semple McPherson. But even in that colorful era, they all took a rumble seat to the sports figure. And no sports figures were made to sound more colorful than those who performed on the gridiron: George Gipp of Notre Dame, Harold "Brick" Muller of California, Bo McMillan and his Praying Colonels from Kentucky's tiny Centre College, Chris "Red" Cagle of Army, Ernie Nevers of Stanford, and the aptly named Bronco Nagurski of Minnesota.

They epitomized the sights and sounds of the upbeat sport of football.

Myth making reached its heights at the 1924 Army-Notre Dame game when Grantland Rice etched this metaphoric marzipan into the nation's consciousness: "Outlined against a blue-gray October sky The Four Horsemen rode again. In dramatic lore they were known as famine, pestilence, destruction and death. These are only aliases. Their real names are Stuhldreher, Miller, Crowley and Layden." Although another writer was to ask, "I wonder where Granny was watching the game from?" it made no difference, as the catch phrase took hold immediately. The art of ballyhoo had encompassed football.

But if ballyhoo started with The Four Horsemen, it arrived with Harold "Red" Grange. Grange was to receive more "gee-whiz" adulation from the press and public than all the other glamorous names of that Golden Age of Sports combined. He was, to quote one writer, "Jack Dempsey, Babe Ruth, Al Jolson, Paavo Nurmi, and Man O' War rolled into one." Grange became the only football player known to people who had never seen a game. His name became synonymous with the game of college football and the catalyst for the then struggling entity called professional football.

Red Grange was half-man, half-myth. The problem was, which half was myth? In an age surfeit with heroes, Red Grange stood taller than most and ran faster than all. In the true tradition of Frank Merriwell, he made the impossible look possible and the possible very probable. The epic grandeur of this man with a football cradled under his arm evoked flavorful nicknames like The Wheaton Iceman, The Galloping Ghost, The Flying Terror, and just plain old Red, because of his shock of flaming hair. Grange was to focus the nation's attention on a sport which had, until his arrival, been considered a newspaper filler between baseball seasons.

Harold Grange was born in the little town of Forksville, Pennsylvania, in the Hemlock part of the state near Williamsport, on June 13, 1903. The third of four children, his father was the foreman of three lumber camps around Forksville, a tough man whom Grange recalled as being "quick as a cat. He had over a hundred lumberjacks working under him and he had to be able to lick any one of them." When he was five, his mother died and his father packed up the family and moved to Wheaton, Illinois, a small prairie town twenty-five miles west of Chicago.

At Wheaton High, the boy who had been Wheaton's best street game player blossomed into a 5-foot 10-inch, 172-pound man-boy whose stylish freedom of movement enabled him to evade oncoming tacklers and amass 75 touchdowns in 3 years of varsity football. Added to this were 82 points-after-touchdown for an incredible record of 532 points scored. He also starred in basketball, baseball, and track for a total of 16 high school letters.

In those days before athletic scholarships were handed out with all the abandon of latter-day flyers for a bank opening, this high school phenomenon was without one when it came time to enroll in college. This despite the fact that only that previous spring, while participating in the state interscholastic track meet at Champaign, Illinois, football coach Bob Zuppke had introduced himself to Grange (whom, with a Teutonic accent, he addressed as "Grainch" being unable to pronounce the soft "G") and told him, "You may have a chance to make the team here." Grange had entered Illinois in the fall of 1922 because "all the kids in the state wanted to play for Zuppke" and also because "it was the cheapest place for me to go."

The boy who had worked summers on an ice truck in Wheaton to earn the munificent sum of $38.50 for a six-day week, came to Champaign, sure of only two things: he wanted to study "a general business course" and go out for basketball and track. But all that changed when, as a fraternity pledge, he was lined up against the wall with his fellow pledges and told he was to "go out for football" as his extracurricular activity.

He made the freshman team, scoring two touchdowns in its very first game against the varsity after only one week of practice. From that time on, Zuppke paid particular attention to the freshman squad—and especially to the 18-year-old boy he called "Grainch."

At practice the following spring, Grange—now 6 feet tall and weighing 185 pounds—was given the number that he would carry to fame, 77. It was a number thought by many to be doubly lucky, but when coach Zuppke was asked how Grange chanced to come by it, he replied, "Well he was in the lineup as a sophmore behind the guy that got 76 and he was ahead of the guy that got 78. That's about it!"

Grange started making the number famous in his very first game as a sophomore, against a strong Nebraska team. In the first quarter, he sprinted for a 35-yard touchdown; in the second he added a 60-yard scamper, starting wide, cutting back, then cutting back again, leaving eleven frustrated Cornhusker tacklers on the ground. He added still another TD in the third quarter on a 12-yard burst. By the end of the season, running behind the blocking of Earl Britten, Grange had scored twelve touchdowns—more than half Illinois' total points—gained 1,296 yards, been named to Grantland Rice's All-America team, and led the Illini to an undefeated season and the National Collegiate Championship.

The day that would stamp Grange as the greatest open-field runner of all time and make him a living legend occurred the next year on October 18, 1924. On that day the University of Illinois dedicated its new $1,700,000 Memorial Stadium, playing host to the previous year's co-champion, Michigan. The Wolverines had gone twenty straight games without a loss under the guidance of the legendary Fielding "Hurry Up" Yost and were favored to make it twenty-one against the Illini.

Yost, who had only that year stepped down as Michigan's head coach on doctor's orders, was still the athletic director and chief spokesman for the self-proclaimed Champions of the West. Before the game he indulged in a little psychological warfare against his opposite number. He proclaimed "Zuppke can't even pronounce this fellow's name, calling him 'Grainch.' We hear he can run the ball a bit, but my men will take care of him. If there's some sort of myth about Mr. 'Grainch' this'll end it!"

Following Knute Rockne's trenchant observation that he couldn't swap remarks with Yost because "my father taught me never to interrupt," Zuppke waited until the game itself to answer Yost. When the orange-and-blue clad Illini came spurting out of the tunnel to the ovation of 67,000 fans, they emerged sans socks. Yost immediately left his seat in the stands and ran on the field screaming at the officials, "Zuppke's cheating! It's illegal and we won't play." But try as they might, the officials found no admonition in the rules book against not wearing socks. Now Yost was beside himself. Before he returned to his seat, he ordered the opening kick off aimed directly at 'Grainch.'

He had barely settled back when the opening kick off was taken by Grange on his own five-yard line. Grange, who had once said that he tried to envision where his teammates were and what they were doing as he ran, now used that uncanny ability to sight tacklers. First he cut to his left, then reversed his field and then, cutting back once again, cut a large swath that resembled an oversized version of Zorro's stylized "Z." He weaved his way past the eleven Michigan tacklers at least twice each. Finally, after one last change of pace, he raced into the end zone unmolested. Two minutes later, with Illinois once again in possession of the ball, Grange took it on his own 33-yard line, burst through the line with his quick start, eluded two tacklers with his excellent balance, and was off on another 67-yard scoring scamper. Two more times he touched the ball in the first twelve minutes of the game, and he swivel-hipped and straight-armed his way to two more touchdowns, one for 56 and one for 44 yards. Before Zuppke mercifully took him out of the game Grange had handled the ball four times, run for 262 yards, and scored four times against a Michigan team that hadn't allowed four touchdowns in one game in five years.

But Yost wasn't through yet. He scrambled down to the bench and berated his players. Stirred by Yost's call to battle, they rallied and scored 14 points to narrow the score to 27–14. But Zuppke put Grange back in in the second half, and he ghosted his way to yet another touchdown on a 15-yard sprint. Then, for good measure, he capped off the day by throwing a pass for Illinois' sixth touchdown. On that day, Red Grange amassed a total of 402 yards, scored five times, threw for one more, and earned the sobriquet The Galloping Ghost from disbelieving sportswriters. Amos Alonzo Stagg was to call it "the most spectacular single-handed performance ever delivered in a major game."

Now most newsmen were singing the praises of "The young Lochinvar come out of the West," even hard-boiled Eastern sportswriters who believed that the only brand of football worth watching or writing about was displayed on Ivy League playing fields. Grange had opened their eyes and changed their minds.

Grange came East on October 31, 1925, with a thrice-beaten, injury-riddled Illinois team for the first and only time in his three-year varsity career to play the University of Pennsylvania, the Eastern champions. He had one last opportunity to impress the still-incredulous Eastern writing establishment. He made the most of it. On a rain-drenched Franklin Field, Grange went 55 yards the first time he carried the ball, zig-zagging through the entire Quaker team. The next time he handled the ball he went 55 yards again, down to the Penn 25-yard line. In the second period, he swiveled his way 12 yards for another score and in the third period he twisted 20 yards for still another. Illinois won, 24–2, Grange scoring three times, setting up a fourth TD and gaining 363 yards in thirty-six attempts.

As soon as the game was over, newspapermen took the covers off their typewriters and started banging out paeans of praise for the legend they had just seen in action. Damon Runyan was to write "What a football player—this man Red Grange. He is melody and symphony. He is crashing sound. He is brute force."

Grantland Rice and Ford Frick also responded with journalistic Pavlovian reflexes, if not as eloquently. And on one side of the press box, Laurence Stallings, author of *What Price Glory* and famed World War I correspondent who had covered many events of earth-shaking importance, was alternately pacing the floor and shaking his head in despair. When one of his colleagues asked him what was the matter, he lamented, "I just can't write about it!" Stallings cried. "The story's too big for me."

The Grange story was "too big" for many of them. During that decade of sensationalism, only Lindbergh, Ruth, Valentino, and possibly Dempsey were to bear the same crushing load of fame that The Galloping Ghost had to shoulder. He was turned into a touchdown king to rival Ruth as the home run king. For Grange, like Ruth, was the stuff heroes were made of. Ruth had earned his legendary status by making famed beau gestures, taking huge dramatic risks, and turning it to his advantage in a reverse of "Casey at the Bat." Grange had taken an entirely different route to his stardom, seemingly alone against eleven men bent on his destruction—like Lindbergh on his epochal flight or Robinson Crusoe on his island—and succeeded in spite of isolation.

Such bare-bones recapping only hints at Grange's glistening achievements and immense contributions. But he made one more. The star system—long the special province of the movies, had come to football. And Red Grange was the star. During the frantic final month of his collegiate career—a career that spanned 20 games and saw him gain 2071 yards in 388 carries for a 5.3 average, amass 4085 total yards, and score 31 touchdowns—his name became a daily staple in the press dispatches. Everything he did was news.

On November 22, Grange turned professional, signing with agent, Charles C. Pyle. It signalled the true start of professional football, a game that had been struggling for almost thirty years. With one sweep of the pen it would change its entire course by enrolling into its much-ignored ranks the most famous name in football, the *Good Housekeeping* seal it desperately needed.

The antediluvian beginnings of the game of professional football can be traced back to the year 1892. In an era when men liked their mustaches long and their beers tall, a tall, raw-boned freshman from Minnesota named William Walter "Pudge" Hefflefinger, played right end for a Yale team that won all fourteen of its games, scoring 698 points to none for its opponents. For the succeeding three years, this Paul Bunyanesque lineman with a blue "Y" on his chest was to leave his mark on the still-embryonic game. He revolutionized line play, becoming the very first guard to pull out to lead interference for the ballcarrier. He was a member of Walter Camp's first team and the first three-time All-America. After his last game for Yale, Hefflefinger accepted an offer of $500 to play in a game for the "Pittsburg" Athletic Club against a club from nearby Oakmont. Pudge—who was to play in pick-up professional games for another forty-two years, finally hanging up his cleats a few days before his sixty-sixth birthday—brought three other collegians with him, all of whom were paid "twice railroad fare" to play. In a game devoid of finesse, Hefflefinger picked up a fumble and rumbled with the ball for the game's only touchdown, pro football's first of thousands.

Pro football waited until 1895 to take its tentative first steps as a full-fledged professional sport. In what has been called the first recorded professional football game, the Latrobe (Pennsylvania) YMCA beat Greensburg four goals to none on November 30, 1895. Although earlier that year a Canton, Ohio, team had beaten a team called the West Enders, the Latrobe game was accredited as the first pro football game largely because of the news dispatches which committed the event to history.

New teams began to sprout up throughout the heartland of America, dotting the landscape like billboards along an interstate throughway. The more successful teams represented athletic clubs such as the Olympics of McKeesport, Pennsylvania; the Duquesnes of Pittsburgh; the Orange Athletic Club of Newark; and the Morgan Athletic Club of Chicago; the forerunner of today's St. Louis Cardinals.

The pro game had gained enough of a foothold by 1898 to warrant the attention and support of some professional baseball operators. Barney Dreyfuss, owner of both the Pittsburgh Pirates and Exposition Park, pioneered in an early version of what marketing men know today as "product extension" by forming a team to compete with Latrobe and Greenburg in the regional league surrounding Pittsburgh. The team, appropriately enough, was called the Pittsburgh Pirates. Stocked with such former collegiate stars as Poe of Princeton, Randolph of Penn State, and Richardson of Brown, Dreyfuss' team won the league title and provided him with another attraction for his stadium.

Within four years, Dreyfuss' idea of extending his season and his profits with a nonbaseball attraction had gained a disciple, Connie Mack. Mack formed a team of his own, known as the

Philadelphia Athletics, and numbered among his squad several outstanding collegians as well as a few athletes already under contract to the baseball A's, including Carlisle great Chief Bender and screwball pitcher Rube Waddell. Fully one year before the two warring baseball leagues were to play for a world's championship, Mack challenged and beat Dreyfuss' Pittsburgh team—which now starred former Bucknell great Christy Mathewson at fullback—12–6, to lay claim to the A's first world championship, that of professional football.

Three years later, in 1905, the two most famous teams in the early history of pro football were formed—the Canton Bulldogs and the Massillon Tigers. Both took on a patchwork quilt pattern of several previous pro teams as well as the colleges then playing big-time football. Massillon's team was comprised of no less than seven members of the 1902 Pittsburgh club together with Drake of Cornell and Salmon of Notre Dame. Canton's team, on the other hand, took on the look of a University of Michigan alumni squad; it included three-time All-America back Willie Heston and teammates Graver and James, as well as Bulldog manager Will Day, who had once played for Yost at Michigan. Massillon not only beat the Canton contingent 14–4, but also broke Heston's leg in a pile-up on the first play, ending the professional career of the most famous pro football conscriptee up to that time, and providing pro ball with a reputation for violence.

The growth of the game was stunted. Instead of offering an alternative to college football, it merely offered an inferior extension of the game on another day of the week, Sunday. Pro football suffered from an inferiority complex it had rightfully earned. There was no attempt to build a pattern of allegiance to a team with identifiable players appearing in one uniform for more than one game. It was a time when an itinerate group of players traveled the countryside, like the troubadours of old, ready and willing to play pick-up football for money whenever a game could be found. Not easy money—many a midwestern collegian gained extra employment on Sunday as a hired Hessian playing for one of the many pro teams, using fictive aliases to hide their identity and protect their eligibility.

But at this low point in its maturation, the game of pro football inadvertently struck upon the strategy that was ultimately to make it a marketing success.

Nineteen fifteen was the watershed year. Until then professional football was a game played on Sundays in a little island in

Mid-America by local and regional players whose presence was far more important than their names. Occasionally a name player might pause and stop, gazing more than grazing, but his name would have only regional appeal to followers of his particular school's exploits.

But in 1915 professional football began to take form, to come of age. In that year, the Canton Bulldogs signed football's first superstar to a contract guaranteeing him $250 a game. The player was the legendary Jim Thorpe, the Indian who was part Black Hawk, part Sac and Fox—and all football player. Twice All-American at Carlisle, he now played baseball for the most famous team in the world, the New York Giants. But his claim to lasting fame as an athlete had come three years before at Olympiad V where he had won both the pentathlon and decathlon gold medals and was proclaimed by Sweden's King Gustav to be "the greatest athlete in the world."

Now he was coming to play professional football for one team, Canton. The 29-year-old Thorpe acquitted himself well on the gridiron that first year, leading Canton over archrival Massillon in their final game by drop-kicking field goals from the 45- and 38-yard lines. But it was not his kicking but his style of play that the fans came out to see. And they came out in droves. Whereas before there were only 1,200 fans at an average Canton game, Thorpe's very presence brought 8,000 out to his first game.

Thorpe extended professional football's turf almost as far as his own. He was to expand its horizons beyond its insularity, give it its first real gate attraction, and serve as the beginning of the star system in pro football.

With the coming of Thorpe, franchises began popping up like dandelions. Teams like the Akron Indians, the Youngstown Patricians, and the Dayton Triangles all joined the Canton Bulldogs, the Columbus Panhandles, and the Massillon Tigers to form a free-lance league of sorts, one that had no formal schedule or records, merely a desire to keep alive.

Professional football needed to make order out of chaos and put together a skeletal government to exploit the obvious market for their product. The incubation period was over.

If the 1920s were to be The Golden Age of Sports, the decade also was The Golden Age of the Automobile. The appearance of this single device wrought the greatest revolution in the American way of life, changing everything from courtship customs and working habits to living patterns. It deeply touched our national psyche, becoming the major fabric of the American dream. Sinclair Lewis, in describing the protagonist of his Middle American novel *Babbitt*, wrote, "To George F. Babbitt, as to most prosperous citizens of Zenith, his motor car was poetry and tragedy, love and heroism."

As "automobilitis" swept the country, every car manufacturer tried to shoehorn its way into the act by romanticizing its car's virtues. The Stutz motor car was advertised as "the greatest car ever built"; the Packard had "Superior performance, maximum comfort, combined with a minimum of operating cost"; and the Lincoln was found "where fine cars congregate." There were more than six hundred manufacturers of automobiles screaming for attention. But one of those that didn't need to scream, only to pucker up and whistle, was the Hupmobile which, in the words of one historian, "made a perfect portable saloon or a four-wheeled sofa for youth to flame on."

One Hupmobile agency was located in Canton, Ohio, and belonged to Ralph Hay, a longtime football fan and the manager of the Canton Bulldogs. On the evening of September 17, 1920, he graciously offered his entire showroom, including the running boards of his new series "R" Hupmobile, for an organizational meeting called by two backers of the Akron Steels. He threw in growlers of free beer hanging from the fenders of one of the cars as an added inducement.

Eleven clubs sent representatives to the meeting, many with no team yet formed or nickname yet selected. But all believed that a professional football league was an idea whose time had come.

Among those in attendance—according to the minutes, the meeting included representatives of the "Canton Bulldogs, Cleveland Indians, Dayton Triangles, Akron Professionals, Massillon Tigers, Rochester, N.Y., Rock Island, Ill., Muncie, Ind., Staley A.C., Decatur, Ill., Racine Cardinals, Wisconsin and Hammond, Ind."—was a 25-year-old football player-turned-baseball player-born again-football player named George S. Halas.

The son of Bohemian immigrants who settled in Chicago, Halas attended the University of Illinois where he studied civil engineering and played end on one of Robert Zuppke's Western Conference champions. He also played outfield on the Illini baseball team in the spring. After graduation, he entered the navy. Assigned to nearby Great Lakes Naval Training Station, he led its football team to the 1919 Rose Bowl game where he scored one touchdown in Great Lakes 17–0 win over the Mare

Island Marine base. Mustered out of the service shortly thereafter, Halas turned to baseball, signing with the New York Yankees as a switch-hitting outfielder.

It was while the team was coming north on an exhibition tour against the Brooklyn Dodgers that Halas' future was decided. Trying to stretch a double off Rube Marquard into a triple, Halas tore the ligaments in his leg. He never regained his speed or his form, getting only two singles in twenty-two times at bat as a Yankee, and was sent down to St. Paul soon after the 1919 season started. That right field position that Halas had tried so valiantly to fill was more than amply filled the following season by the large figure of a man acquired from the Red Sox named Babe Ruth.

After one season playing for St. Paul, Halas went back home to Chicago and took a job as an engineer in the bridge department of the Chicago, Burlington & Quincy Railroad, playing for the Hammond (Indiana) Pros on Sundays.

The A. E. Staley Company, founded by A. E. Staley, Sr., in Baltimore, Maryland, in 1906, had moved to Decatur, Illinois, in 1912. "Old Man" Staley, an avid sports fan, sought ways both to improve employee relations and morale and to further the name of the company. Staley's first venture into sports in 1919 was a baseball team managed by 48-year-old "Iron Man" Joe McGinnity, the second winningest pitcher of all time with 482 total victories, 247 in the majors and 235 in the minors.

That same year Staley organized football and basketball teams made up entirely of local athletes. The first Staley football team won the Central Illinois Championship. It was led by Charlie Dressen—later of Brooklyn Dodger fame—as football's first T-formation quarterback.

Now Staley conducted a search for the right man to take over the football team, a man as qualified to lead the team as McGinnity was the baseball team. In January 1920 he heard that a young bridge engineer, then employed in the Chicago area might be the man he was looking for; one who could, in his words, "recruit, reorganize, play, and coach the team." That man was Halas.

After an interview, the two men agreed to a combination deal: Halas was to learn the starch business, play on the company baseball team, and recruit, reorganize, play, and coach the 1920 Staley Starch football team.

Halas' first team was handpicked and included Guy Chamberlin, an All-American from Nebraska; Jimmy Conzelman, famous Missouri star; Edward "Dutch" Sternaman and Burt Ingwersen of the University of Illinois; and George Trafton, all-time great Notre Dame center. Most of these men had played with Halas either on the Great Lakes Naval Training Station team or professionally.

Halas' first team trotted onto Staley Field, adjacent to the plant, on Sunday, October 3, 1920, to play the Moline (Illinois) Tractors, before two thousand curious onlookers. They defeated them 20–0 for their first victory. Playing 13 games, they won 10, lost 2, and tied 1, scoring 166 points to their opponents' 28. Each regular on the team received $2,200 for three months' work. Staley Starch was not so fortunate. The auditing department records showed a net loss of $14,406.36.

For 1921 Halas added All-American Chic Harley and his Ohio State teammate Tarzan Taylor. The team won nine, tied one, and lost one while winning the championship of the new league.

But something more important was happening off the gridiron. A. E. Staley decided that the losses, coupled with the inadequacies of the Decatur area for attracting prospective fans, made the team a risky venture. So, a few days after the Staleys second game on October 10, 1921, the team moved to Chicago and Cubs Park for the remainder of the year. Staley gave Halas $5,000 not only to insure the completion of the season, but also to maintain the name "Staleys" throughout the campaign.

By the end of the 1921 season, Staley's financial acumen had overcome his football avidity and he cut the umbilicus, telling Halas "Here's the team. You can have it; do what you want with it. We won't finance it anymore." So it was that the most successful team in the history of the National Football League was launched by a commercial venture.

It was while Halas was serving as the athletic director of the Staley Starch Company that he first began to envision a wider canvas for the game of football as played by his own team and by others in the Midwest area. And so, while Frank Nied and A. F. Ranney of the Akron Steels were simultaneously moving for a meeting to give substance and muscularity to just such an organization, Halas was himself addressing Ralph Hay to suggest the structuring of a league.

The meeting itself was relatively short, all parties being of a like mind—to form a government of some sort, a league. After old business had been disposed of and Massillon withdrew from professional football for the 1920 season, a name was chosen: the pretentious "American Professional Football Association." Pretentious because the eleven teams represented only four states, three contiguous Midwest states and New York. They then selected the most prestigious player in pro football history as their figurehead, naming Jim Thorpe president of the new league. As the third order of business "it was moved and seconded that a fee of $100 be charged for membership in the Association." Halas remembers, "there wasn't $100 in the room but still each of us put up a hundred dollars for the privilege of losing money." Other business included such administrative details as appointing a committee to work out by-laws and rules for the association, sending in a list of previously used players, and printing on all clubs' stationery "Member of American Professional Football Association." But nowhere was a formal schedule mentioned.

The meeting ended, fittingly enough, with the tire division of the Brunswick-Balke Collender Company offering a silver loving cup to the champion team of the association, the first promotional tie-in with industry by the new league.

And so, that very first year, with a mythical schedule, thirteen franchises sallied out to do battle on a catch-as-catch-can basis. In the absence of any schedule, each club had to arrange its own schedule against both league and nonleague opponents, and records were virtually nonexistent. Soon teams began to become nonexistent too, as franchises opened and closed with the frequency of the blossoms of a day lily. Massillon and Muncie had not even bothered to suit up, folding before the first kickoff. Others who hadn't even shared the *gemütlichkeit* of the Hupmobile showroom showed up with enough regularity to be considered bona fide members of the league.

Those teams who came to play were the Akron Steels, Buffalo All Americans, Chicago Cardinals, Chicago Tigers, Canton Bulldogs, Cleveland Panthers, Columbus Panhandles, Dayton Triangles, Decatur Staleys, Detroit Heralds, Hammond Pros, Rochester Jeffersons, and the Rock Island Independents.

Three teams claimed the championship: the Canton Bulldogs, where Jim Thorpe provided far more articulate direction by his on-the-field exploits than his off-the-field administrative leadership, together with Fats Henry and Indian Joe Guyon; the undefeated Akron Steels, led by two blacks, Fritz Pollard, the great All-American from Brown, and Paul Robeson, the equally distinguished end from Rutgers; and Buffalo, led by Army's Elmer Olipant. A three-team round-robin tournament was decided upon to determine the winner of the Brunswick silver loving cup. Buffalo ground out a 7–3 win over Canton in the first round before 15,000 spectators in New York's Polo Grounds and played Akron to a scoreless tie the next day, leaving the issue undecided and the silver loving cup unclaimed.

But artistic and territorial accomplishments aside, the association's first year was an unmitigated economic disaster, aided by the postwar recession which had paralyzed the country as a whole and the Midwest in particular. Without any attendant fanfare, the American Professional Football Association expired from natural causes at the end of its first year.

The one man who wasn't disheartened by the disaster was Joe Carr, manager of the Columbus Panhandles. Then 41 years of age, Carr had a long background in sports. Starting as a sportswriter for the *Ohio State Journal,* he had become at age 24 the secretary of baseball's Ohio State League and later its president. He had aided in the organization of the Tri-State League and acted as its chief executive officer. After adding managerial experience as the pilot of the Newark (Ohio) baseball club, he became president of the Columbus franchise in the American Association. Ever the busy administrator he proved the old adage that "when you want something done, give it to the busiest man," by also becoming the chief executive of the Columbus football team. Then he went on to become an administrative three-letter man, organizing one of the very first professional basketball leagues, the American Basketball League and serving as its president for three years. He also distinguished himself by later becoming the promotional director for the National Association of Professional Baseball Leagues.

But for the moment, the triple-threat administrator's main concern was the resuscitation of the stillborn American Professional Football Association. Carr saw that professional football had a place in sports, especially among fans who couldn't get enough of their collegiate heroes during the three or four years they played.

The bespectacled administrator called the demoralized team owners to a meeting at the La Salle Hotel in Chicago to discuss the revival of the league. Elected president of the association, Carr turned out to be a super-administrator, issuing a set of get-tough rules to insure that the debacle of 1920 wouldn't happen again. He lowered the entry fee to $50, this time making sure each member-club anted up. And, believing that the future of the professional game rested upon a détente with the colleges, he pushed through a rule forbidding tampering with college players. Any violations would be met with expulsion from the league. The association was alive and drop-kicking again. With direction from the top.

Teams lined up with their hat and $50 in hand. Seventeen clubs wanted in to the new association, including a newcomer from the small town of Green Bay, Wisconsin.

If you believe the natives of Green Bay today, you'd think Lewis and Clarke had come across Green Bay with three guides, a supply of salt, and eleven footballs. But in reality, the franchise had been born in the dingy editorial room of the *Green Bay Press Gazette* on August 11, 1919. The guiding force behind the new semipro team was Earl L. "Curly" Lambeau, a former player for Notre Dame whose greatest claim to fame was that he had been a substitute for George Gipp. Now an employee of the Indian Packing Company in Green Bay, he had persuaded his employer to form a team, purchase the equipment, and allow the use of its athletic fields for practices and games. In return, the Indian Packing Company was to gain the benefit of having the nickname Packers affixed to the Green Bay Club.

The first year the fledgling team played other semipro teams in the Wisconsin and Upper Michigan areas on open fields, passing the hat among the few curiosity seekers who lined the field for remuneration. With a 10-1 record in its first two years, Lambeau persuaded his employer, J. E. Clair of the Acme Packing Company, which had taken over Indian Packing, to underwrite the cost of entering the revitalized professional league. Clair's outlay was rewarded by a team which went 6-2-2 and took the field in jerseys proclaiming them to be the Acme Packers.

Without a formal schedule, the 1921 season proved to be another guerilla warfare year. Four clubs folded in football interruptus, their won-lost records expunged forever from the league's standings. When it was done, the Chicago Staleys, nee the Decatur Staleys, emerged as the champions on the basis of a 10-1-1 record. But their toughest foe continued to be money.

In his new incarnation in Chicago, George Halas had made halfback Dutch Sternaman his partner in an effort to cut losses. Despite winning the championship, the partnership lost $71.63. Halas was reduced to taking extra employment as an auto salesman and Sternaman as a gas station attendant to provide enough money to continue fueling the champions.

Fighting a lack of private money and public ennui, the 1922 season was noteworthy primarily because of some off-the-field manuevers. Association president Joe Carr found that the Green Bay franchise had openly recruited and used college players under assumed names the previous season. He withdrew the franchise from the Acme Packing Company and returned its $50. But Green Bay would remain in the league. Curly Lambeau raised the requisite $50 by persuading a friend and professional fan to sell his car. In return, Lambeau promised his friend the Walter Mittyesque experience of performing one play in Green Bay's opening game.

The Staleys, however, ceased to exist after 1921. Taking a long-term lease at Cubs Park, Halas changed the name to Bears in order to exploit whatever associative benefits his new club could derive from its more famous landlords. He also rechristened the league, suggesting the more straightforward name National Football League to supplant the somewhat tarnished Association name.

The newly named National Football League struggled along for the next two years, with revolving-door franchises showing up and then melting away again in such places as Muncie, Evansville, Marion, Hammond, Duluth, Racine, Toledo, Louisville, and Kenosha. By 1925 a total of twenty-eight cities had come and gone, and there were those who thought that professional football was no closer to becoming a physical and fiscal reality than it had some four years before when the founders met at the Hupmobile agency in Canton. But all of that would be changed with one stroke of a pen, the signing of one man.

On the night of October 25, 1925, a group of University of Illinois football players were taking in Rudolph Valentino's latest potboiler, *The Eagle*, at the Virginia Theatre in Champaign. An usher came down the aisle and paused at the row where the football players were seated. Finding who he was looking for, he said, "Mr. Grange, Mr. Pyle would like to see you in his office."

The "Mr. Grange" in this scenario was, of course, Red Grange, the famed Illini football star. The "Mr. Pyle" was the owner of the Virginia Theatre, one of a string he owned throughout Illinois and Indiana. Pyle had always provided free tickets to team members for his two theaters, but neither Grange nor any of the other members of the team ever "paid any attention who they came from." Until that day, they never knew him or had ever heard of him.

Grange followed the usher up the aisle and through the baroque lobby into the front office. Seated behind a desk was a florid man with a smartly trimmed mustache and graying hair—a fashion blueplate with two side dishes, spats, and a walking cane. The "best dressed man I ever met in my life," remembers Grange. He introduced himself as "Charles Pyle" and without any overtures immediately got to the point. "Red, how would you like to make a million dollars?"

More than somewhat taken aback, Grange would only say, half in jest and half in surprise, "I don't do those things. I can't kill anybody."

The dapper theater owner went on, "No, I have in mind your becoming professional. I think we can set it up. I'll go to Chicago and talk to George Halas and the Bears and we'll set up a tour around the U.S." To emphasize his point, he added "I think we can do right well."

Pyle and Grange came to a tentative agreement. Pyle was to act as Red's manager for two years—the first conventional agent-principal relationship in sports history—and receive one-third of the money he would earn playing football, appearing in motion pictures, and "other ventures." Pyle immediately set to work, contacting Halas and Sternaman.

And so, one month later, not twenty-four hours after he had led Illinois to a 14–9 victory over Ohio State in the last game of his illustrious college career, Grange signed a contract negotiated by Pyle with the Chicago Bears.

Grange's first professional game was played only four days later, on Thanksgiving Day 1925, in Cubs Park against the Chicago Cardinals.

The atmosphere was totally different from any Grange had experienced. At Illinois he had always had the crowd behind him as he raced into the open, wriggling his hips here and changing his pace there. Now the crowd's spirited attitude was replaced by an unemotional one, one that was cynical and skeptical with an aura of "show-me."

Nonetheless they showed up, thousands upon thousands of rubber-neckers intent upon seeing this man advertised as The Galloping Ghost. One man who was there was Bill Veeck, who served that day as an 11-year-old soft-drink salesman.

"Nobody knows how many people came in that day," remembers Veeck. "They came in over the wall, through the wall." The crowd was so thick that he sold the wooden soft-drink cases to fans without seats. "I sold the cases and saved the pop and sold that later." The even-then entrepreneurial Veeck had what he called his "best day ever" as a concession salesman because "if you sold one to a guy, or more accurately rented it to him, then the guy standing behind him had to get two of them . . . and so on."

Grange reaped $12,000 for his first game. Then he and his

supporting cast of football minstrels, better known as the Chicago Bears, took their show on the road. They attracted 36,000 to Philadelphia's Shibe Park on December 5, as Grange scored two touchdowns, both on one-yard plunges.

The very next day the Flying Circus came to New York. Seventy thousand more jammed into the Polo Grounds to see Grange. Thousands of others coming out of the subways were told over a loudspeaker that the game was sold out. He scored on an interception and the crowd, which came to see him and no one else, chanted everytime he was taken out "We want Grange! We Want Grange!" In Detroit, the injured Grange sat out the game and $18,000 was returned to fans who wanted to see Grange. And nothing but Grange.

They continued their tour: eight games in eleven days through Boston, Washington, Pittsburgh, and any city which had a team or a stadium. The barnstorming binge began to draw something equally as important as crowds; they began to draw press coverage. "Up to that time most of the papers would take the scores of the pro leagues and they'd put them on the third or fourth page. They didn't mean anything. Nobody paid much attention," remembers Grange. All that changed as four writers joined them in New York: Damon Runyon, Grantland Rice, Westbrook Pegler, and Ford Frick. Grange told Halas, "Well, if these guys are going to pay attention to pro football, we've got it made!"

Grange and professional football found that the fans, like Alice, were "curiouser and curiouser" to see a living legend in action. They also found a marketing verity that would soon become professional football's *raison d'être*. As football fans found it hard to work up much identification with clean-cut youngsters who, in a here-today-gone-tomorrow world can only spend four years at the most on the college gridiron, they began to seek longer-term identification. Pro football offered that. Stars would perform in an open-ended career that could last as long as their talents lasted. Thorpe had given them the first hint of a casual connection between a star and the game's drawing power. Grange would cement the relationship.

The Svengali to Grange's touchdown Trilby was Charles C. "C.C." Pyle. Dubbed "Cash and Carry" Pyle by Westbrook Pegler—"Don't worry what I write, Charley, just so I keep your name in the singular"—he was to Grange's career and professional football what yeast was to bread.

As a youngster on the Orpheum Circuit, Pyle started as a

magician's assistant. From there he turned to selling organs to silent movie houses. Then he entered theater management and owned a chain the night he sent his usher in search of Grange—and his fortune.

Like any showman, Pyle loved acclaim. He would sponsor $100 sprints during Six-Day Bike Races "just to hear his name come over the loudspeaker," remembers Grange. During rides on the Twentieth Century from Chicago to New York, he would leave a $10 tip when recognized by a redcap or a waiter. If they didn't recognize him or call him by name, he left nothing.

Now, with a two-year agreement with the hottest property in the nation in his pocket, he was going to ride it for all it was worth, particularly with an agent's commission of 33⅓ percent. Believing that pro football could thrive if it had a real gate attraction and that he had that real attraction under contract, Pyle turned his attention immediately to the Chicago Bears. Grange recalls Pyle and Halas going into "a suite of rooms at Chicago's Morrison Hotel and staying in there for two days because they couldn't agree and wanted to see who could wear who out." Finally, it was agreed. Grange would play what amounted to an eighteen-game tour for the Bears and would be guaranteed half the gross gate receipts.

But the Bears were merely one component of Pyle's master plan. According to Grange, "He didn't just sit back and make my deal with the league. He went out and got me contracts with movies and different products and things." And so, in rapid fashion, endorsement deals were struck with a soft-drink company and for a meat loaf, a football doll, socks, clothing, and even a Red Grange Candy Bar produced by the Shotwell Candy Company. "Football," according to Grange, "was just one part of it."

In one such deal, Pyle contracted with Joseph Kennedy and the Film Booking Office, later to become RKO, for two movies, *One Minute to Play* and *Racing Romeo*. At the time of his signing, Grange had said, "I don't want to play a sheik part. This business of lollygagging around with a girl most of the time is not in my line. I can do all the rough work on the gridiron, but I want to do very little in the parlor."

This was quite alright with Kennedy and FBO, which had bought Grange's drawing power more than his acting prowess, and he was cast in a part he was comfortable with, that of a football hero. One scene in the so-called "grid thriller," *One Minute to Play*, called for a football sequence, complete with crowd shots. Grange recalled that "to get crowd shots you had to hire extras and pay them $15 a day." With thousands of extras needed and money involved, Pyle's imagination started earning its keep.

The script called for a game "played in the Northeast." In order to fill the stands with unpaid-for extras, Pyle advertised an exhibition game at the Rose Bowl between Red Grange's All-Stars and those of Wildcat Wilson, the great University of Washington All-American halfback. Pyle placed ads in all the Los Angeles papers announcing that anyone wearing an overcoat and a hat would be let in free. Despite the fact that the "All-Star" teams were, in reality, made up of members of the USC and California teams and that it was hotter than 100 degrees in the shade on that July day, more than twelve thousand spectators showed up. The only extras Pyle had to pay were the so-called "All-Stars" who received, according to Grange, "something like twenty-five dollars apiece."

Pyle's hyperthyroidal imagination kept churning out ideas. "I don't know how he got a lot of ideas, but he always did; he always had ideas," remembers Grange. One was for the construction of a supermodern stadium back in 1926, nearly forty years before the Houston Astrodome. The stadium was only to be a means to an end because Pyle, in Grange's words, "didn't only want to build a stadium. He wanted to control sports, and he figured anyone who got three or four of these would control sports in America."

The stadium, which got to the blueprint stage, looked like it came straight out of a Flash Gordon comic strip. The roof was designed to be retractable, with a landing pad for autogyros, the precursors of helicopters. All aisles were gigantic conveyor belts. The moment the game ended, they would start moving and every spectator would be transported outside the stadium in minutes. The fans in the cheaper seats would have windshields, in reality gigantic magnifying glasses, with hand cranks to roll them up or down. The further back the seat, the higher the magnification. Finally, in the completely mechanized stadium, the entire field could be changed over from football field to ice hockey rink in less than two hours. Pyle finally jettisoned the whole project when he realized it would cost him more than two million dollars to build one stadium, let alone three or four.

One of Pyle's ideas which did get off the drawing board was a new football league. He fondly remembered the overflow crowd of 70,000 which had jammed into the Polo Grounds to witness the New York debut of Red Grange. Seeing that as merely the tip of the iceberg, Pyle petitioned the National Football League for a New York franchise.

But the New York franchise already belonged to a professional bookmaker named Timothy Mara. Mara stoutly refused to share his newly allocated turf with anyone.

Pyle retaliated by setting up his own league, appropriately called the American Football League—the same name other disgruntled men of means would take some thirty-four years later when they were refused admission to the closed corporation known as the National Football League. Pyle's new league consisted of clubs in New York, Philadelphia, Cleveland, Chicago, Boston, Brooklyn, Newark, Rock Island, and a nominal road team representing Los Angeles. Even though he had a few bona fide stars like Wildcat Wilson in Los Angeles and Harry Stuhldreher in Brooklyn, the real drawing card of the new league was Red Grange. In fact, it could be said that the entire league merely served as a showcase for Grange and the New York Yankee franchise, playing, fittingly enough, in New York's new stately pleasure palace, Yankee Stadium.

The NFL responded in kind. It increased its 1926 membership to twenty-two, putting franchises into territories Pyle had staked out, including Brooklyn and another vagabond club playing "out of" Los Angeles. The "shoot-out" was a disaster for both sides. Escalated bidding for talent and an ornery weatherman who caused it to rain almost every Sunday took their collective toll. American Football League teams in Cleveland, Boston, Brooklyn, and Newark all disbanded during the season, forcing the remaining five clubs to fold and fade into football history.

The casualties from the first professional football war littered the battlefield. Eight of the nine American Football League franchises had sunk from sight. And no less than twelve of those in the NFL, including first-year entrants Brooklyn, Hartford, and Racine, inoculated with the professional football virus after having seen Grange on tour, also went the way of all football flesh.

The one American Football League franchise that survived was C.C. Pyle's creation, the New York Yankees, which petitioned and gained admission to the hallowed halls of the NFL. "That was the only thing he wanted anyway," said Grange.

It was a Pyrrhic victory for Pyle. Piled atop his many losses now came another, one he was ill-prepared for—the loss of Grange. Early in the Yankees' third game of the 1927 season against the Bears in Wrigley Field, Grange leaped high for a pass and came down on a muddy field, catching his cleats in the mud and George Trafton on his knee. He spent the remainder of the season on crutches.

Although Pyle's Grange-less Yankee franchise was to limp along for one more year, his star possession limped out of the picture. After making one more motion picture, *Racing Romeo*, in October 1927, the two years of the Pyle-Grange arrangement were up, and Grange went his own way, thinking he would "never play again."

It was estimated that Grange, who made $12,000 in his very first pro game and $100,000 during his 1925 tour, together with movies and product endorsements earned $300,000 during his two years under Pyle's guidance.

Pyle's appetite had been whetted by serving up a superstar. He now reasoned that there were other untapped sports where the same formula would work: a substantial amount of money as an inducement, an outstanding international superstar, and a tour.

He chose tennis. Although there had been professionals in tennis before, most prominent amateur tennis players reaped only the social prestige attached to the sport. And that didn't pay the bills. So Pyle looked for that one standout, that one charismatic name, who could draw the way Grange had.

He found one: Suzanne Lenglen, six-times Wimbledon champion. "La Grande Lenglen" had been playing tennis from the time she was eleven. Between sixteen and thirty, she was unbeaten as a tennis player, once sweeping through an entire Wimbledon tournament without losing a single game.

Pyle offered the incomparable Lenglen $50,000 for a proposed professional tour. This was half the amount P. T. Barnum had used to lure the last great European female sensation, Jenny Lind, seventy-five years before. Lenglen accepted.

Despite Mlle. Lenglen's glamourous reputation, Pyle felt fans would demand the faster, harder-hitting game played by the men so he signed up Vinnie Richards and three other male players.

The time was ripe for the tour. American crowds flocked to see the newly minted professionals. A crowd of 25,000 packed Madison Square Garden for the first stop on the tour. The players welcomed it, too. Before Pyle, the leading tournament winners, playing for fun and at their own expense, could gain nothing for their efforts but free clothing and housing. And there was precious little time for another job to pay the bills. Now Pyle had made it respectable to play for pay. And the next year Vinnie Richards organized a professional association and tour.

By then Pyle was gone from the tennis scene. He was now putting together another kind of tour; totally different from any ever conducted.

The twenties were epitomized by zany fads, and there was none crazier than the one which had couples dancing endlessly to the frenzied jazz tempo that was sweeping the country. Everywhere people were trying to outdance—or outlive—other couples in endurance marathons for prizes of as much as several thousand dollars. Now Pyle tried to capitalize on the marathon fad.

On the morning of March 4, 1928, C.C. Pyle unveiled a coast-to-coast marathon race which he called "the toughest athletic event ever conjured up," but which the newsmen promptly dubbed The Bunion Derby.

Some 275 contestants of all ages, from 16 to 63, paid $100 a head for the privilege of running the 3,422 miles from Los Angeles to New York, for prizes totaling $48,500. Each man was to run from a given spot every day. Elapsed times were totaled up at the end of the marathon.

Starting out in a specially built bus, Pyle and Red Grange preceded the runners to set up a sideshow in advance in each town. Grange was literally along for the ride. No longer under contract to Pyle, he "came back with them as just an observer with no financial connection whatsoever."

Pyle steered his plodding charges through the highways and the byways of America—for a price. He charged towns for the privilege of housing his runners overnight. The U.S. 66 Highway Association pledged $60,000 for Pyle to route his band down its highway. Manufacturers of shoes, foot ointments, suntan oils, and what-have-you contracted for sponsorship. Pyle had 500,000 programs printed to sell along the route at 75¢ apiece.

But problems started erupting like boils in the hot sun from Day One. On that day the 275 contestants dwindled down to 199. One of them was struck by a hit-and-run motorist. Another 75 deserted. The concessionaire hired to feed the athletes at $2 a head a day demanded more money and was fired somewhere west of the Mojave. Town after town reneged on its promised money. So did the Highway Association. And the expected crowds, ergo the program sales, failed to materialize.

Finally, as the remaining 55 runners limped into New York's Madison Square Garden 84 days after the start of the race—19 days late—only 4,000 people awaited their arrival. The winner was an 18-year-old Oklahoma farm boy named Andy Payne with a cumulative 16-hour lead over John Salo of New Jersey. Payne won $25,000 for averaging almost 41 miles a day. Pyle was less fortunate.

For his efforts, C.C. Pyle (the C.C. had come to mean "Corn and Callous" in the press) lost more than $100,000. As a postscript to the event he could only add, "There has been a lot of talk about how much these boys suffered. There is not one of them who has suffered more than I did." A glutton for financial punishment, Pyle tried to recoup the following year, running the derby from New York to Los Angeles. Like any derivative, it did half as well as the first and sealed his financial fate.

That was to be the last time C.C. Pyle's name ever graced the national sports pages. But for three meteoric years he had fired the public's imagination with his innovative promotions.

The star system introduced by Pyle had now pervaded all of pro football. Ernie Nevers played for Duluth and then the Chicago Cardinals, Wildcat Wilson with Providence, Benny Friedman with Cleveland and New York, and George Halas brought back Red Grange to play for the Bears.

But the real change in pro football, as it headed into its second decade, was not as readily discernible. It happened not on the field, but in the front office.

Even before the Depression pro football was a guaranteed big loser. The Depression only brought the rest of the country back into step. So football needed the direction of men who had the stomachs and the bankrolls to stay with it. If there was one common denominator among those known as the Founding Fathers of Football—the Maras, the Rooneys, and the Bells—it was their desire to take a gamble on football, as well as a gamble on anything else. For these men who sought to make eight—the hard way—were gamblers all.

Tim Mara was a professional bookmaker who bought his franchise which was to become the New York Giants for $500 only because "any franchise in New York is worth $500." Bert Bell and Art Rooney bought theirs in Philadelphia and Pittsburgh in 1933 only because the state of Pennsylvania was repealing its Sunday Blue Laws—Rooney reputedly from his winnings at Saratoga Racetrack and Bell, a reformed gambler, from his family war chest.

But none of these swashbucklers who approached pro football less as a business than as a real sporting venture was the equal of the owner of the Washington Redskins, George Preston

Marshall, for whom all of life was a promotion and all of promotion was a sporting venture.

George Preston Marshall had even more callings than names. A frustrated thespian, he insinuated himself into the exalted position of publisher of the *Washington Times*, and was the producer of many shows and extravaganzas including those for the Dallas Pan-American Exposition. He owned a string of laundries which he ultimately sold because "I couldn't get my shirts back." He also owned a professional basketball team and, like Rooney, was president at one time of Roosevelt Raceway. George Marshall was a man who liked to put his finger in the pot and keep stirring. And nothing gave him more of an opportunity than a professional football franchise.

One of four partners who purchased the new Boston franchise in the floating crap game known as the National Football League in 1932 for $7,500 apiece, the 36-year-old entrepreneur installed himself as president. By the end of the year he was the sole owner of the Boston Braves. The other three had washed their hands after the franchise lost $46,000.

In the tradition of a Catskill resort *toomler*, Marshall performed in every capacity. When a precious football would go into the stands, Marshall, in his raccoon coat, would appear immediately at the rail waving his arms, asking for its return. When the team picture was taken, with the team completely bedecked in warbonnets and war paint, he'd be there, front and center. And he oversaw all promotions—of which there were many—including the team name.

By 1933 he had changed the club's venue from Braves Field to Fenway Park, changed the name to Redskins, and hired a fullblooded Indian, William "Long Star" Dietz, former Carlisle teammate of Jim Thorpe, as the head coach. Not content to leave well enough alone, Marshall also seeded the team's roster with Indians, including Chief Johnson and Orien Crow. Unfortunately, none of them could play like Jim Thorpe.

Despite Dietz's winning record as a college coach at Washington State, Purdue, and Wyoming, among others, Marshall felt compelled to tell him how to coach. Commingled with legitimate plays, which had greats like Cliff Battles going around end, were some Marshall fantasy plays like the "broken-shoelace" and "fake-fumble" plays.

Marshall's fertilizing effect was soon to extend far beyond his own franchise. Before he had entered pro football in 1932, the game was an anachronism that bore more resemblance to its nineteenth-century forebears than to the modern counterpart we know as professional football; a grunt-and-groan game. By comparison, the product was in much the same stage of development as baseball had been in 1899. The games were low scoring contests. Power backs disdained protective padding, having been born with it. And Nagurski of the Bears and Nevers of the Cardinals were the dominant figures in a game in which three-yards-and-a-cloud-of-dust was the rule. It was still organized King of the Mountain. Added to this lack of activity on the field was the structure of the league; it looked like a crazy jigsaw puzzle pieced together by drunken carpenters, with a sliding number of clubs scheduling their own "patsies" when they needed to win. Something would have to be done—and quickly—before professional football became a dinosaur.

George Preston Marshall changed all that. Teaming up with the man who had been one of the first to offer any structure to the league, George Halas, Marshall led the other clubs in adopting innovations which brought professional football kicking and bellowing into the twentieth century. He introduced three resolutions that would open the game up and one which would increase interest in the game itself: moving the ball in ten yards from the sideline on every play; legalizing the forward pass from any point behind the line of scrimmage and, finally, moving the goalposts up to the goal line, making field goals easier. Marshall also proposed splitting the league into two divisions, Eastern and Western, thus creating two championship races and a natural championship game, as well as the splitting of the gate proceeds on a guaranteed 60–40 partition.

The National Football League had arrived. And if it weren't immediately evident during the regular season of 1933, then the first championship game in the history of the NFL would prove the wisdom of Marshall's innovations.

Twenty-five thousand fans crowded into Wrigley Field on a perfect day in the middle of December, as the Western Division champion Bears hosted the Eastern champion Giants. In a championship game that was everything a championship should be, the lead changed hands six times. The Bears' Jack "Automatic" Manders kicked three field goals through the newly relocated goalposts and both teams engaged in an aerial circus from anywhere behind the line of scrimmage, with Giant quarterback Harry Newman hitting on twelve of seventeen throws.

The outcome was decided in a storybook ending. With the Bears ahead 23–21 and seconds remaining, Newman threw up the middle to halfback Dale Burnett for 28 yards. Only one man stood between Burnett and the goal line, Red Grange. Sensing that Burnett intended to lateral to Mel Hein, who trailed him by only a step, Grange tackled Burnett high, pinioning his arms and saving the game for the Bears.

Pro football was on the move, thanks in no small measure to George Preston Marshall. And so was Marshall.

The 1936 Redskins won the Eastern Division title with an unimpressive 7–5 record, playing to less than four thousand fans a game. Marshall knew it was time to move. "When Princeton and Harvard drew 20,000 at Cambridge the same day 40,000 watched the horses run at Narragansett, I knew it marked the end of football in Boston," Marshall lamented.

With that pronunciamento, Marshall moved his entire team south to the nation's capital, with a brief stopover in New York to play the 1936 championship game against the Packers. It was the first—and last—time an NFL championship game would be played on neutral grounds, until the Super Bowl came into being.

Stopping in at the "21" Club to toast his team's fortunes in the upcoming game with the Packers, Marshall spotted Grantland Rice. Holding aloft his burgundy-and-gold goblet, Marshall bellowed across the room, "Who's the best player in the country?" The dean of American sportswriters answered, "Sammy Baugh or Dixie Howell. But for your purpose, Baugh of TCU." Then Rice threw in a gratuitous "But take my advice. If you sign him, insure his right arm for a million dollars. Those big pros will tear it off."

Arriving on the banks of the Potomac with but 916 season tickets sold, Marshall set out to convert the nation's capital into a football town, sweeping through Washington as none had since the British in 1812. His vehicle was to be the strong right arm of Samuel Adrian Baugh. Confiding to newsmen the night before Baugh was to arrive to sign his contract—calling for anywhere from $10,000 to $25,000—that "This is the Baugh Era," Marshall meant to milk it for all it was worth.

Marshall had ordered his new, slightly scrawny 6-foot 2-inch quarterback to outfit himself like a "true Texan," with "Texas boots and a ten-gallon hat." So when the DC-3 taxied to a halt at Washington's National Airport on the first day of June, 1937, the crowd of reporters and photographers was treated to the unusual sight of an apparently tipsy cowboy careening down the ramp, in high-heel boots and chaps. Francis Stann, there to cover the happening for the *Washington Evening Star*, remembers Baugh "walking like a drunk. He could hardly walk and was having a helluva time negotiating the ramp." Marshall, in his desire to get the best pictures possible, had never considered the possibility that Baugh hadn't worn cowboy boots before.

But that didn't stop Marshall. Little did. He took the wrappings off "Slingin' Sammy" on the night of September 15, 1937. In the first night game in NFL history, Secretary of Commerce Jessee Jones threw out the first ball—white with black stripes—and 24,500 fans watched Washington's debut as they beat the Giants, 13–3.

One other significant thing happened that year as the Redskins scalped the opposition on their way to another NFL championship. A local company's employee band asked permission to parade and play at the Redskin home games. Marshall was equal to the idea, even though it had come in over the transom, and transformed the group into the Redskin Marching Band, 110 strong. With $25,000 worth of colorful Indian costumes and headdresses, the band performed before the games, during halftimes, and even on out-of-town trips. Marshall saw the band as instilling the same spirit into professional games that colleges had cornered long ago. With the added entertainment, the NFL began, in his words, to "make a he-man sport interesting to women and children and lure new customers into pro football." It was all part of Marshall's theory that "if you get women and kids steamed up over a football game, you have papa hooked."

By the following year, Marshall had a dance band perched in a teepee high atop the temporary stands; halftime entertainment which included live elephants, monkeys, and bears and headline stars; and even a fight song. For the annual Christmas game he brought Santa into Griffith Stadium by dogsled and helicopter, even by parachute, although a substitute Santa had to be brought in at the last moment one time when the original Santa parachuted into a neighbor's wash.

The Chicago Bears had been the first pro club to have their own fight song, the never-to-be-forgotten "Bear Down, Chicago Bears." But it was the Redskin fight song "Hail to the Redskins" that brought the spirit and verve of college football to the pro stadium. Reminiscent of "Onward Christian Soldiers" played to an upbeat tempo, the song exhorts the Redskins to "Fight on, fight on, 'til you have won, sons of Wash-ing-ton." And as if that weren't enough, the 'Skins were to "read 'em, weep 'em, touchdown, We want more . . . " whatever the hell that meant! The song was written by orchestra leader Barnee Breeskin and Marshall's wife, Corinne Griffith, the former Orchid of the Silent Screen.

Many thought his best promotion was marrying the former screen star. In fact, when Alexis Thompson, then owner of the Eagles, dated a noted Hollywood celebrity, Marshall called him and rather emphatically suggested that he "Marry her! Think of all the publicity it will give the league."

As his lasting legacy, George Marshall changed the face of pro football, investing it with order, entertainment, and color. Unfortunately, however, one of those colors wasn't black. George Marshall is remembered for something else: he was the last owner to integrate his team, answering one reporter who commented that the "Redskins' colors seem to be burgundy and Caucasian" with the retort, "I'll integrate my team when Abe Saperstein integrates his." He finally threw in with the times—the times he had once led and which had passed him by—and in 1962 traded his first-round draft choice to the Cleveland Browns for Bobby Mitchell.

But the man who was the last to accept the changing times and tides had led the National Football League into its greatest period.

In a few short years from 1935, when Jay Berwanger, first winner of the Heisman Trophy, had eschewed an offer to turn professional, the entire picture had changed. The pro ranks were now able to tap the rich college market and entice former stars like Byron "Whizzer" White of Colorado, Davey O'Brien of TCU, and Sid Luckman of Columbia. In signing Sammy Baugh, George Preston Marshall had become the C. C. Pyle of the 1930s.

Professional football was never to take another look back after the entry of George Preston Marshall. From a league which had had more than fifty franchises in many places only a professional cartographer would know, it settled down to a league represented only by big-time cities. Attendance steadily grew from an average of 8,200 a game in 1934 to 25,400 a game in 1945.

Twice in the Thirties and early Forties the National Football League fought off the incursions of upstart professional leagues trying to horn in on its action. Then it staggered through the lean years of World War II, losing first players, then fans, and finally teams. One makeshift wartime entry was the combination Philadelphia Eagles/Pittsburgh Steelers of 1943, known by the curious amalgam Steagles. Just as the NFL emerged into the sunshine of an eagerly awaited postwar boom, it looked as if it would have to share that prosperity with yet another league.

It's a marketing truism that every successful venture begets imitative ones attempting to siphon off some of the profits. It is the same in sports. Baseball faced a competitive threat in 1914, when the Federal League challenged the supremacy of the established American and National leagues. It raided the older leagues for players and raised salaries—the primary cost of doing business—to the point where the only solution was a merger. After two years of attempting to gain equality, both on the field and at the box office—and after a plaintive call for a series to determine the "real" world's champion was ignored— the Federal League made peace with the majors. Except for two owners who bought their way into the established leagues, it disappeared from the sports scene forever, leaving few ripples and little history.

Now professional football had reached the point in its maturation where it stood on the threshold of success with an unlimited potential market. This appealed to several claim jumpers who now sought to tap the rich vein the NFL owners had carefully been mining for so long.

Leagues started sprouting up in every corner of the country. Wherever there was talk of football, there was talk of forming a league competitive to the NFL. On the West Coast, a circuit known as the Pacific Coast League began to play. Red Grange headed up a group representing six cities which called itself the United States Football League.

But the league which had done the most spadework and planning was a group that called itself the All-American Conference. It sprung from the fertile mind of the same man who had given the sports world the All-Star games in both baseball and football, Arch Ward, sports editor of the *Chicago Tribune*. Originally conceived prior to the outbreak of World War II, the interested parties had postponed their expansionist dreams until those of the Axis had been destroyed. With the end of the war in sight, they reformed and reformulated their plans. An eight— perhaps ten—team league was envisioned with franchises in NFL cities which once had been part of professional football, like Buffalo and Cleveland, recently deserted by the Rams; and non-NFL cities like San Francisco, Miami, and Baltimore. With "Sleepy" Jim Crowley, as commissioner—faithfully mirroring the older NFL, which had Elmer Layden, another of the legendary Four Horseman of Notre Dame as its commissioner—the All-American promoters sought major league status. But the NFL brushed off their bid for recognition with a derisive suggestion that they "get a football first." And so they went to work, getting several footballs and bankrupting the Green Bay

Packers in the process who, even with their eleven footballs, were no match for the ruinous game of financial football.

The first step was a traditional one, as the AAC raided the NFL for players. Almost a hundred established players were signed immediately. Others were pursued and wooed. Every member of the world champion Cleveland—soon to be Los Angeles—Rams received phone calls the night before the championship game with Washington from Ray Flaherty, the coach of the upstart New York Yankees, attempting to sign them. Ace Parker, Angelo Bertelli, Frankie Sinkwich, Wee Willie Wilken, and others accepted. But few first-line players signed, though some were sorely tempted, like Bob Waterfield, Sid Luckman, and Charley Trippi.

Others were jumping too. In what may have been the first recorded incident of an owner of an established franchise jumping to an embryonic league, Dan Topping, part-owner of the New York baseball Yankees, left the NFL and his Brooklyn Dodger franchise behind to take over the fittingly named New York Yankees in the AAC. This created another precedent as well. He became the first baseball owner since the early days when Connie Mack and Barney Dreyfus had fielded pick-up football teams to enter the world of professional football. Heretofore, football teams had taken nourishment and even names from the older baseball teams, but never ownership. But it was a natural product extension, not dissimilar to that to Coca-Cola, which found itself to be in the beverage business, not just the soft-drink business, and had bought coffee and orange juice companies.

From a financial standpoint, it made little sense. For the All-American Conference—as well as all of professional football—was almost a guaranteed loser. The high cost of the financial warfare accounted for that and the markets where teams battled head-to-head for fan acceptance would take care of the rest. Yet there were several clubs which would do well, both on and off the field. The Cleveland Browns, filling the vacuum left by the newly departed champion Rams, had the kind of year in 1946 that could best be described as fantastic by anyone's standards. Averaging more than 57,000 a game, they ran through their schedule like Patton's army through France, losing only two of fourteen games. Structured in the mold of the team's namesake Paul Brown and stocked with unknowns—with the exception of Otto Graham who had been drafted by the Detroit Lions—the Browns made their owner, taxi fleet entrepreneur Mickey McBride, extremely pleased. Business never being far removed from sports, McBride's commercial pursuit became subtly intertwined with his professional pursuit, as extra players were assigned to work for his cab company, forming the first "taxi squad."

Other teams which did well in the AAC were the San Francisco 49ers, the Buffalo Bills (née Bisons) and, occasionally, the New York Yankees. The rest of the franchises either took a financial bath or a financial bleeding, depending upon the magnitude and duration of their losses. The Miami Seahawks failed the first year and moved to Baltimore, where the Colts couldn't meet their payroll. The Chicago Rockets changed coaches and owners and even their nickname—Hornets—but in four years they won only eleven games and couldn't hold their own in a city dominated by the Bears and Cardinals, who were strangely winning championships. The Brooklyn Dodgers ran through a flock of owners as well, finally coming to rest in the hands of Branch Rickey, who tried his own sort of magic, even bringing in baseball's Pepper Martin to serve as a kicker. But it was to no avail, as the fans who supported the Boys of Summer would not support the Boys of *Tsouris*. Rickey returned the franchise to the league after one season, to merge it with the rival Yankees. The Los Angeles Dons, although backed by the millions of racetrack owner Ben Lindheimer and Don Ameche's telephone bills, couldn't continue to underwrite their losses plus the rest of the league's as well.

For the first time an entire league had not failed, merely parts of it. Some clubs survived and prospered in spite of the weak underpinnings of the league. After four years of tenuous existence, the AAC sued for peace and got it on the NFL's terms. A merger was consummated which had the NFL opening up its door just a crack, allowing in the Cleveland Browns, the San Francisco 49ers, and the Baltimore Colts. Then, after picking those three ripe franchises from the AAC family tree, they slammed the door shut again, consigning the remaining franchises to that scrap heap especially reserved for former teams.

The man who saw the National Football League through its war with the AAC was De Benneville "Bert" Bell, who had taken Elmer Layden's place as commissioner soon after the new league's formation had been announced. Bell's place in NFL history was assured by his manipulation of circumstances vastly more important than victory in the war with the AAC.

For Bell had seen something on the afternoon of October 22, 1939, that would change the entire face of pro sports—

particularly pro football. On that afternoon Bell's Eagles had lost to the Brooklyn Dodgers, 23–14, at Ebbets Field. But it wasn't the score that stood out in Bell's mind, as the Eagles won only one game that year—their usual quota. What made that game different from any other beating Bell's team ever took was that it was televised by the National Broadcasting Company. It was the birth of a new era, and Bert Bell had been there to witness its raw beginnings.

With an innate sense of the future, Bell saw what television could mean to the game he had labored so hard and long to make popular. More people could see a player like Doak Walker in a single game than had watched Red Grange in his entire career. A whole generation could be proselytized by the proper use of the medium. And to insure its proper use, as commissioner he issued perhaps the most important edict in the history of professional sports: no NFL home games would be televised in the host city, only away games. In so doing, Bell shaped the future of professional football, making television its handmaiden rather than the other way around; a policy perpetuated by his successor, Pete Rozelle.

Television and professional football were made for each other. In a symbiotic relationship, both were to prosper. Pro football offered an almost made-for-television format and television offered football an entire new group of fans and fans-to-be. With the notable exception of boxing, football was the only game tailored to the dimensions of the TV tube: played on a rectangular field, fully within the range of TV coverage, it allowed for slow digestion and even, when necessary, regurgitation in such innovative techniques as slow-motion and isolation shots. Unlike a baseball, a football was relatively easy to follow and the game was offered in a tidy time capsule—three hours on Sundays— when the competition was grass growing and ghetto programming.

Coupled with its discovery by television, professional football was soon to be discovered by the tastemakers of Madison Avenue. The exact date might not be as simple to find as the date of the first televised game, but it seemed to have been sometime during the 1958 season, as the New York Giants were clawing their way hand-over-raw-knuckle back from the edge of extinction to the Eastern Division title. As the Giants clung to life, week-after-week, first beating the defending champion Detroit Lions on a blocked field goal attempt with seconds left and then beating the Cleveland Browns in the last game of the season, precipitating a play-off with the Browns, New York and its style makers were becoming excited about this "new" game in town. It was fast becoming the "in" thing among those who set the trends.

Just two years before, as the Most Valuable Player in the NFL, Frank Gifford had signed in on "What's My Line" as "F. Newton Gifford" and it had taken the unblindfolded panel fully eight guesses to decipher who was sitting in front of them. Now there was no guessing!

Now Gifford, Conerly, Huff, Patton, Modzelewski, Webster, Rote, Chandler, and the rest of the men in blue were known. The Giants were "in"! Pro football was "in"! And if reassurance was needed, it came two games later. After beating the Browns in the play-off, the Giants lost 23–17 to the Colts in what has been called The Greatest Game Ever Played, complete with a post-prandial period, seen by millions of now football-crazed fans on television.

Professional football took off like a Sputnik as it entered the 1960s. In a decade given to fast-paced action and violence, pro football became even more popular. True to form, there was soon another league, the American Football League; then there was war between the leagues, this time underwritten by the television networks.

The American Football League was as much a cotillion as a consortium. When the NFL denied a few petitioners admission, momentarily depriving them of their prospective toys, they did the only thing any red-blooded little rich boys would do: they went out and bought a league of their own.

The three prime movers behind the new league were Texas-rich Lamar Hunt, oil-rich Bud Adams, and hotel and charge card-rich Barron Hilton; hence the names of three of the new entries—Texans, Oilers, and Chargers. They then set out to flesh out the rest of a new league with warm bodies: Ralph Wilson, Detroit trucking magnate was given a choice between Buffalo and Miami; Billy Sullivan, a New England impresario and publicist was given a crack at the warmed-over province of Boston; Max Winters was given the rights to Minneapolis; and the Phipps Brothers were conscripted for Denver. When the NFL expanded into the Dallas and Minneapolis areas, Hunt chose to stick it out in Dallas and make a battle of it; the Minneapolis backers leaped at the chance and joined the NFL, and the AFL franchise moved on to Oakland. One thing still was missing: a New York franchise.

Failing to find one of their own to head up the all-important

New York franchise, they turned instead to a New York sportsman and sportscaster named Harry Wismer. Despite an obvious
lack of capital, Wismer might have been just what they needed
in their formative stage. They needed a team in New York and
they also needed a team that would make noise. Wismer certainly would provide noise.

Wismer was, in the words of one of his few fans, always "Well,
Harry . . . " He had married Henry Ford's "favorite niece,"
insinuated himself into broadcasting the ABC football games of
the week, and ultimately became ABC's sports director. Now he
was on the threshold of entrepreneurial greatness with his New
York Titans. It was a threshold he was never to cross, because
he continued to be "Well, Harry . . . "

The nickname Titans was derived from that of a missile
housed at Cape Canaveral. It was also Wismer's tongue-in-cheek
take-off on the name of the established pro team in New York,
the Giants. But the joke soon became not the name, but the
team. The small fraternity of sportswriters and football mavens
who frequent watering holes like Mike Manuche's began to call
them "The Miss-iles." Titan stories spread like Polish jokes.
When one newspaper wrote to the Titan offices requesting
publicity pictures, they received fifty glossies of Wismer.

Then there were the fans. Or more correctly, there was the
lack of fans. Playing in the dilapidated Polo Grounds, they had
to compete with the Giants across the river in Yankee Stadium.
When the NFL club was on the road, football fans preferred to
stay at home and watch them on TV. The second year Wismer
chose to play head-to-head against the Giants, who were packing
the stadium week after week. But with the television blackout of
the Giants' home games, Wismer invited fans to come to the Polo
Grounds with their portable radios to watch the Titans and
listen to the Giants. Still his attendance bordered on the nonexistent. Things were so bad that once, when "paid attendance"
was announced, sportswriter Dick Young of the *New York Daily
News* quipped, "Wismer must be counting fingers instead of
noses."

Even the fabrication of attendance figures was not enough to
save Wismer. The walls were crumbling in around him, literally. His deluxe apartment house at 247 Park Avenue was razed,
so he moved himself and the club offices to Manhattan's Cha-
tham Hotel. But that, too, was now destined for the wrecker's
ball. Even as physical plants were coming down around him,
Wismer's substantial stock holdings in Brunswick Corporation
were tumbling almost as fast in the bear market which followed

Kennedy's get-tough policies with the steel companies. On the brink of financial ruin, he sought help from Hunt, Adams, and Hilton. None would even return his calls. One November night, in what would turn out to be his last year at the helm, Wismer cried into his drink at the Waldorf-Astoria's Bull and Bear, "What a shame it is. I've been spending my own money while these guys that I helped when they needed help have been spending dad's money." And then reflecting on the proposed new stadium going up in Flushing Meadows, he added, even more sorrowfully, "and now I just want to get through the season."

But it was not to be. The Titans had to run faster to the bank than down the field, hoping to catch their bouncing paychecks. The Titans and Wismer were broke. The league stepped in and took over the franchise for the rest of the 1962 season to preserve both its image and its New York franchise. Then, in March 1963, with the franchise on the verge of being canceled, the team was sold to a group of five men led by David "Sonny" Werblin for one million dollars.

The American Football League, which had overcome such difficulties as an acute talent shortage, public ennui, and advertiser indifference to its TV telecasts, had somehow managed to pull through its first three years. The league's average attendance had slowly built from 16,538 a game in 1960 to 20,487 a game in 1962. It had put a reasonable product on national television, culminating in its exciting six-quarter championship game between the Houston Oilers and the Dallas Texans, the longest afternoon in football history. More importantly, it had weeded out the unprofitable franchises, shifting Los Angeles to San Diego in 1961, the Dallas Texans to Kansas City in 1963, and finally substituting Sonny Werblin for Harry Wismer in New York. The AFL had come of age, turning a laughable league into a laudable one.

The man who replaced Wismer at the head of the AFL's New York franchise was David A. Werblin. Better known as "Sonny—Just Like in Money," as he was heralded in an article in *Variety*, Werblin was vice-president of MCA, Inc., and president of MCA TV, a subsidiary. *Variety* called him "the world's greatest agent" and the man who had shaped broadcasting "perhaps more than anyone else" in America. In fact, *Variety* effusively went on, "if he were not broadcasting's greatest showman, he certainly was its greatest promoter and salesman."

Werblin first packaged the American Football League into a neat five-year plan and sold the entire league's television rights to NBC for more than $42,000,000. With one million guaranteed each club each year, it was assured of its continued existence and its ability to sign high draft picks. Then, with one swipe of his pen, Werblin performed the single act that assured the AFL's credibility and put it on an equal footing with its older rival. The one swipe was the signing of a quarterback from Alabama named Joe Willie Namath.

Werblin, who had spent a lifetime selling the star system, firmly believed it could be translated from the silver screen to the sports scene. "It's the only thing that sells tickets. . . . The star system is what you put on the stage or playing field that draws people." And so, cracking to Namath, "I don't know whether you'll play on our team or make a picture for Universal," Sonny Werblin signed him to a contract calling for a reported $400,000 bonus—including the salaries of three of Namath's relatives on the newly renamed Jets' payroll, a bonus for signing, a three-year contract, an annuity, an insurance policy, and a new car.

Werblin's antennae were correct. The Jets' season ticket sales soared from 11,000 to more than 35,000 on the strength of Namath's signing. The Jets now played to full houses at new Shea Stadium, setting AFL attendance records almost every game and bringing believability to the new league, both in the press and in the minds of the public. AFL Commissioner Joe Foss commented, "People have now stopped asking me *if* we are going to make it." They would. And the man who had done it singlehandedly was Sonny Werblin, not only the shaper of the AFL, but its savior as well.

But Namath's signing was not an isolated instance. The AFL had long made a practice of signing many of the top-flight college stars right off their campuses—and in the case of some, like Fred Biletnikoff, right between the goalposts of their last collegiate game. Stars like Billy Cannon, Johnny Robinson, Bobby Bell, Mike Garrett, John Huarte, Matt Snell, John Hadl, Lance Alworth, Larry Eisenhauer, and hundreds of others soon began wearing the uniforms of the eight AFL clubs. The bidding was becoming ruinous to all pro clubs. And when the AFL appointed Al Davis commissioner early in 1966 and made a raid on NFL stars—especially quarterbacks like Roman Gabriel, Craig Morton, and John Brodie—both leagues decided they had had enough and sued for peace. The settlement was announced on June 8, 1966. For the first time the National Football League had been forced to take on and absorb another league to preserve its territorial and financial prerogatives.

By the Super Bowl of 1972, a specially commissioned Gallup Poll showed what everyone had come to believe, that football had become America's Number One Spectator Sport. Granted that the poll was taken during the football season, it still showed that 36 percent of those who answered "What is your favorite sport to watch?" had responded "football," as compared to only 21 percent answering "baseball."

Pro football, which had prospered at the hands of television, had become the Number One Sport in the country. It was storming of the Bastille, the Changing of the Guard. Long live the new king, Pro Football!

Everything the National Football League touched turned to gold. In 1963 it established a subsidiary, funded by $7,500 from every member club, called National Football League Properties, Inc., with the stated intent of promoting "the NFL as broadly as possible through association of the League name and its member clubs with acceptable and reasonably standardized products . . . to increase female awareness of NFL football . . . and to promote the image of the League and its member clubs." The only "products" at the time were quaint bobbin' head dolls that looked like moronic Munchkins and Topps bubble gum cards—which paid in the first $50,000. Still, NFL Properties grossed more than $124,000 in the fiscal year ending January 31, 1964.

As revenues and licensed products continued to grow like Topsy, NFL Properties looked for new horizons to conquer. In a confidential study prepared by Fry Consultants in 1969, they investigated the possibilities of entering into other allied fields, such as publishing, boys' camps, employment placement bureaus for player personnel, ownership of a sporting goods manufacturer, "executive health spas," and a multiple-line insurance company.

One of the few suggestions acted upon was the extension of their publishing venture from game programs into "other expansion ventures." Those expansion ventures included the joint publication of books to "create and maintain increasingly favorable exposure of the NFL." In line with that recommendation, the creative staff of National Football League Properties produced several books which were deemed to reflect well on the NFL, including a table-top book issued in 1969 called *The First Fifty Years: A Celebration of the National Football League in its Fiftieth Season*.

The party line of the NFL, as reflected in the foreword, "A Game for Our Time," went thusly: "The field is an artificial plain, flat and spare, the focal point of a monumental stadium of concrete and steel. It is an area for war, with the rules and unwritten ethics of classic warring places, and on any autumn Sunday, the field is occupied by two dedicated and disciplined armies. . . . Professional football is basically a physical assault by one team upon another in a desperate fight for land."

But while the NFL was concerned with "physical assults" and "wars," the temper of the country was changing, seemingly unbeknownst to pro football. We were pulling out of Vietnam and blocking it out of our memories while the NFL, which had associated itself with patriotic overload—even to the point of having a squadron of air force planes "flyover" during a Super Bowl game to accentuate the Star-Spangled Banner as sung by such super patriots as Anita Bryant—had tied itself to an anachronism.

Professional games were taking on all the appearances of a battle zone, with hired headhunters bent on nothing short of total annihilation. The battlefield was littered with casualty cases and the injury reports began to take on the semblance of a body count in a gory battle, as the list of the walking wounded and the basket cases often took up more space in the daily papers than the results of the game. Professional football seemed intent on leaving no survivors, as players became perishable commodities and coaches confused "head-up" aggressiveness with legalized muggings. To many pro football seemed to symbolize all that was wrong with the 1960s.

Writers given to analyzing football from a sociological standpoint now found nourishment in the war-oriented language of "bombs," "blitzes," and "shotguns," in the numbering of Super Bowls as if they were world wars, and in the obvious symbolism of warriors resplendent in the colors of the tribes they were going out to represent in battle. Whether the analogy was correct or not was unimportant, for professional football characterized itself in these terms and had marketed its product as such. Even while the halftime drummer was beginning to beat out a different tune.

Being bypassed by its times was not pro football's only problem. Another potential area of concern was oversaturation.

Oversaturation didn't come all at once; it built slowly. Starting with the American Football League's entry in 1960, it gained momentum with the amoebic expansion of the existing leagues into twenty-six teams by the end of the sixties. Then came the spinning off of a game on Monday nights and even televised doubleheaders. Soon it became impossible to sample football as an hors d'oeuvre. It became a feast, a banquet, and finally a *grande bouffe*, an orgy. And then came the World Football League.

The World Football League was the creation of Gary Davidson, a sports version of Johnny Appleseed who went around the country seeding franchises in several sports like Colonel Sanders and his chicken takeouts. Here a Winnipeg and an Edmonton in the World Hockey Association. There an Anaheim and an Indiana in the American Basketball League. And now came his *Götterdämmerung*, the World Football League with twelve teams sporting imaginative and singular nicknames in twelve cities at a single blow. It was an instant league—all one had to do was add money.

Like the old-time snake-oil salesman, Davidson backed up his covered wagon, dropped the tailgate, and waited for the customers to come running, cash in hand. His spiel, superficially sound, was "Why pay $16,000,000 for an NFL franchise when you can get one for only $2,000,000, or $1,000,000 or whatever you have; this is investment spending and through television and press exposure you'll make a profit before . . . " And he stood back and watched them flock in. He sold franchises on a sliding scale, for whatever the market would bear. They came from Memphis, New York, Chicago, Anaheim, Philadelphia, Detroit, Orlando, Birmingham, Washington, and all points where money could be found.

Soon after the first draft meeting in the winter of 1974, the World Football League began to take on the appearance of a Monopoly game for high stakes as franchises were swapped, moved, and discarded with a dizzying rapidity. It was hard to tell the franchises without a scorecard. The Boston Bulls became the New York Stars; the New York No Names became the Portland Storm; the Washington Ambassadors became the Norfolk Something-or-Others and finally settled in Orlando as the Florida Blazers. And that was only the first time around.

In an effort to get his "baby" off the ground, Davidson was criss-crossing the country, almost lapping himself, looking for franchise owners, television contracts, and sponsor commitments. Locked out of the three major networks, all committed to the NFL, he negotiated a deal with TVS, an independent sports packager, to broadcast the games Wednesday nights starting July 25, 1974, over 125 stations. He met with major advertisers, such as Chevrolet, which was excluded from sponsoring professional football by Ford's sponsorship on CBS and ABC and

Chrysler's on NBC, and sold them three minutes a game. With full sponsorship, it was anticipated that the WFL teams could realize between $550,000 and $700,000 a year. And Davidson, ever the wheeler-dealer, reserved 10 percent of all television revenues for himself. This, plus "finder's fees" for new franchises, the legal work for the league, and a $100,000-a-year position as commissioner, insured his future. The future of the league was another matter.

Nothing was too small for Davidson to attend to. He negotiated a deal with Spalding to produce a gold-and blue football called the Globemaster, with the League getting 5 percent plus on royalties. He implemented new rules, which he hoped would publicize the wide openness of the WFL game. He had an interpreter translate the WFL rules into Russian in hopes the Soviets might want a franchise. He even concocted some ball-breaking promotions to call attention to the league and get them in the *Guinness Book of World Records*, like having strong-armed Greg Barton throw a football all the way from Honolulu to New York aboard a 747—1,600 completions in all, culminating in the Big Throw at Randalls Island before the New York Stars' first game.

Slowly the WFL began to gain credibility, as first Daryle Lamonica, then Calvin Hill, Larry Csonka, Jim Kiick, and Paul Warfield in one day, and Kenny Stabler and Ted Kwalick all signed on the "come," packaged for delivery in the second season. But the younger draft choices continued to elude the upstart leagues as they all signed with the NFL, from David Jaynes, the first choice, down through the entire roster of draftees.

Meanwhile, the NFL was in dire jeopardy of losing its season to a strike. The WFL, which had anticipated getting out of the starting blocks earlier by converting meaningless exhibition games into regular season games, was now the only game in town. When the season opened on July 10, 1974, football-hungry fans flocked John F. Kennedy Stadium in Philadelphia, the Gator Bowl in Jacksonville, everywhere. It seemed that Gary Davidson's dream had become a reality.

But within three weeks the dream had become a Kafkaesque nightmare. The first indication that the emperor had no clothes was the report that the Philadelphia Bell had inflated their attendance figures by "papering the house" with free tickets while failing to differentiate between paid and actual attendance. The WFL had lost its credibility three weeks into the first season.

As the air slowly leaked out of the balloon with an audible hiss, other problems began to crop up. First it was attendance figures, then stories of unpaid bills in places like Detroit and Jacksonville began reaching the papers. The rout was on. Sheriffs repossessed uniforms for unpaid laundry bills. Clubs filed for bankruptcy. Then the second round of transfers from city to city began as frantic franchises began looking for a port, any port, in the storm—or the Sun, or the Fire.

Finally, after trying to interest some oil-rich Arabs in bailing them out, the WFL owners abruptly closed up shop in the middle of the second year and quietly went away. A product which had tried to roll out nationally without adequate test-marketing was found wanting.

But even though the WFL sunk beneath a sea of red ink—like Atlantis, never to be seen again—it did leave the football fan with the distinct impression that enough was enough. Pro football was literally "flooding" its own secondary. The man who paid the freight was being pro football-ed to death.

Assuredly professional football had come a long way from the Paleolithic days when Red Grange had traveled into the hinterlands of America and told "them that pro football was a good game, that the pros blocked hard and tackled hard, and they'd laugh at you."

Gone were the days when Tim Mara would stand on street corners and buttonhole everyone and anyone to come to see his Giants play; when teams and players played in almost total obscurity. Now they played to almost 59,000 a game. Television ratings and revenues climbed to more than thirty-seven million TV homes every weekend watching the 26 NFL teams, which, starting in 1978, will get TV revenue of almost $162,000,000 a year *more than* Ed Sullivan and Milton Berle during their salad days combined.

But pro football possesses a weak underbelly with signs of stress and weaknesses. Its stands are often populated not by real fans but by blocks of large corporations using tickets as tax writeoffs. Not only do these fair-weather fans freeze the real fans out of the stadia, but they stay home in the face of the increasing showing of sold-out games on local television on less than balmy days. Possibly because of these specialty spectators, despite the increase in television ratings and revenues, pro football crowds have plateaued—even dropped—from their high point in 1972. And to many of those who remain in the stands, pro football has become "stereotyped and dull."

Less evident than the quality of the fans is the specie. According to the U.S. Census and latter-day sociologists, the potential growth of the country is now centered in an area called the Sunbelt, which cuts across the United States in a wide swath from its southernmost states to the West Coast. Professional football's franchises are grouped almost exclusively in the old-line industrial crescent—from the Atlantic Coast states out to the Midwest—an area whose population and growth has stagnated. Only the more recent franchises are in the Sunbelt. The rest of this fertile land of exploitation is College Football Country, the land of the Southeast, Southwest, and Big 8 conferences.

College football is pro football's country cousin. Over the years the pros have viewed the colleges with much the same affection as wealthy manufacturers lavish on the farmlands, looking to them for their raw material and little more.

And as pro football went hunting for big names and big cities to conquer, college football continued to punt, pass and kick its way along, all the while providing great teams, great theater, and great tradition. Only at the college level were the spirited rivalries of yore possible—USC and UCLA often outdrawing the Los Angeles Rams, Michigan-Michigan State the Detroit Lions, and so on. A successful season for some schools is determined not by the overall record but by victory over a hated archrival. An All-American or Heisman Trophy candidate enjoys celebrity status far beyond the ivied walls of his own school, often becoming the darling of an entire region or section of the country. To many (including the legendary sports editor of the *New York Herald-Tribune*, Stanley Woodward, who once admonished a cub reporter, "Now, when I say football, I mean college football, son. The pros are bald-headed. We also cover soccer. They're equally important.") the *only* football game in town was the 125-play-per-contest, bottled-in-bond college game.

College football has always been the bastion of traditions, wearing them comfortably and warmly like old felt slippers. One of its greatest traditions is the Rose Bowl. Curiously enough, the granddaddy of all postseason games began as an offshoot of a promotion for the city of Pasadena.

A transplant from the East, Dr. Charles Frederick Holder, was originally responsible. Long a fancier of flowers and an admirer of the many flower festivals of European cities, Holder proposed that his adopted city stage a gigantic display to herald the new year and celebrate the ripening of California fruits and flowers. It would also serve notice to the rest of the world that

California weather was balmy and the landscape verdant, in sharp contrast to the rest of the country's freezing weather. The first Tournament of Roses was held in 1890. A parade was added in 1891, and then chariot races, bands, and floats with their frameworks of flowers.

But something was missing: a sporting event. So in 1902, the tournament addressed two prominent football teams, one from the Far West and one from east of the Mississippi, to play in something later-to-be-called the Rose Bowl. Played before a thousand fans at a small outdoor bowl called Tournament Park, the University of Michigan's point-a-minute team—which that year had been undefeated, untied and unscored upon while amassing 501 points in 10 games for new coach Fielding Yost—completely swamped the pride of the West, Stanford, 49–0, in a game foreshortened at the entreaty of Stanford. Then the game was shelved for another fourteen years. It only began as an annual event on New Year's Day 1916, when Washington State beat Brown, 14–0.

This is the stuff traditions are built on, for the Rose begat the Orange in 1933, the Orange begat the Sugar in 1935, the Sugar begat the Sun in 1936, and the Sun begat the Cotton in 1937, and so on and so forth, ad nauseum. The land was filled to overflowing with more bowls than Tidy Bowl ever cleaned, including the Glass Bowl, the Vulcan Bowl, the Oil Bowl, the Aloha Bowl, the Derby Bowl, the Yam Bowl, the Pineapple Bowl, the Cigar Bowl, The Bamboo Bowl, the Alamo Bowl, the Lily Bowl, and any other bowl you can possibly name.

But even with all its traditions—or maybe because of them—by the late 1950s and early 1960s, as the country had turned its back on its traditional past with ever-increasing velocity, college football seemed to suffer almost as much as did baseball. It became a poor stepbrother of pro football, while still continuing to outdraw it 4–1.

For college football has had its troubles. Faced with lagging support and skyrocketing costs, many schools dropped their football programs completely, among them such former stellar teams as Fordham, Carnegie Tech, Georgetown, George Washington, and Manhattan. In the East, the former citadel of collegiate football, the void was quickly filled by professional ball. More recently, other schools have de-escalated their programs to the point of invisibility. Stephen Horn, president of Long Beach State, says "only four college football teams will be left by the 1980s." The rest, he says, will have been "driven out of the game because of increasing costs, leaving super powers such as Texas and Ohio State playing each other twice a year to pad their schedules."

But even with all its problems, college football seems to have become the biggest beneficiary of the recent re-emergence of tradition, nostalgia, and the turning back of the clock. And now has come forward with at least one champion to take on the pros at their own game: promotion.

Dating from its first intercollegiate game against Racine in White Stockings Park in Chicago in 1879, which it won one goal to none, the University of Michigan has now won more football games than any other non-Ivy League college. The Wolverines won the first Rose Bowl game; they are the only college to hold an edge in competition against Notre Dame and they possess the largest college stadium in the country. In short, they have a great winning tradition—and a history of successful merchandising of that tradition.

The man responsible for merchandising tradition at UM is Athletic Director cum Marketing Director Don Canham. In his nine years at the helm, Michigan has returned to the ranks of the nation's powerhouses. Previously, Canham headed his own firm which did a multimillion dollar business supplying sweat socks and athletic gear to colleges throughout the country.

Canham brought his promotorial skills into Ann Arbor, and in his own words "hustled like a whore on Main Street." His efforts have paid off handsomely as he has managed to attract an average of 104,000 bodies every game to a plant which seats 101,701, every year for the past five, generating enough monies to defray some of the costs of other athletic programs which sup at the table of football.

Stealing several pages from professional football's promotional booklet, Canham has gone out to do battle with the pros on their own turf. With all the moxie of a Professor Harold Hill, he has advertised everywhere: on billboards, in newspapers, and even on airplane trailers. One which flew over Pontiac Stadium during a Lions' game had this message: "62,000 Youths Watched Michigan Football Last Fall—Were Your Students There?"

As his piece de résistance, Canham publishes a lavish brochure possessing all the surface slickness of a Christmas catalog designed by a Madison Avenue ad agency which offers a line of maize-and-blue gewgaws and gimcracks to more than one million Wolverine alumni and well-wishers.

This master promoter, who brought Bo Schembechler to Michigan and big-time football back to Ann Arbor and then packaged that attractive product with all the maize-and-blue trimming he could find, was compared by *Sports Illustrated* to "The best in the business, going all the way back to Cash and Carry Pyle, right along with Bill Veeck . . . " His approach to salesmanship is not unlike theirs, which is to "understand that sports is primarily just a game, fun, and that their hustle is a game, too."

Don Canham may well be the forerunner to many like him in college football, a plain, old-time "hustler" in the best sense of the word, taking it to the big boys on the block and beating pro football on its own turf. That's what promotion is all about. This might be the wave of the future as college football flexes its collective muscles for the next round to see just who is the biggest jock on the football block.

4

Boxing: "It ain't the number of seats you got, it's the number of asses that are in 'em"

Throughout history writers and artists have been drawn to prizefighting. To the likes of Homer, Hogarth, Byron, Dickens, London, Odets, Saroyan, Schulberg, Hemingway, and Mailer the boxer is a fellow artist, expressing himself with his fists and body. To them the motions of fighters serve as instinctive metaphors, their skills phrase manly similes and their strategy punctuates their psychological plot line. The Sweet Science transcends mere physical battle. It is combat elevated to the level of a morality play.

But boxers also express themselves in other, less physical ways. They have contributed their own rough but unforgettable expressions to the lore of the sport, with such phrases as Bob Fitzsimmons' "The bigger they are, the harder they fall," and Joe Louis' "He can run, but he can't hide." But manager George Gainford summed it all up, not for boxing, but for all sports, when he said, "It ain't the number of seats you got, it's the number of asses that are in 'em."

Ever since the early annals of time, dating back to the very first mention of a promoter, "The great Thydides," in the twenty-third book of Homer's *Iliad*, promoters have been concerned with the problem of placing "asses" in "seats." If the two fighters stand alone, stripped to the skin and prepared to do battle, so too does the promoter, in one of the classic *ménage à trois* in all of sports and in all of business. For the word "promoter" almost singularly belongs to the boxing arena, being the sole example in the definition cited in *The American Heritage Dictionary of the English Language*—"Promoter . . . A finance and publicity organizer, as of a boxing match."

The first American worthy of the name "boxing promoter" was neither an American nor a promoter of boxing. He was an Irishman who used the sport as a promotion to sell his publication.

Richard Kyle Fox was a penniless 29-year-old who came to the United States from Dublin in 1874 and found work with a New York newspaper. In two years he had saved a couple of hundred dollars. Adding this to a few more hundred he was able to borrow, he purchased a moribund publication called The *National Police Gazette*. Once a vital weekly dedicated to scandal and sensation, the *Gazette* was now more weakly than weekly. It needed more than an infusion of capital. It needed a first-class publisher with the talents for promotion.

Fox proved himself to be a promotional genius, giving away more than a quarter of a million dollars in cash prizes, medals, belts, and trophies to boost the *Gazette*'s circulation and to promote himself. Using the word "champion" to describe anything and everything that moved, as long as it moved the *Gazette*'s circulation, Fox's mustachioed face adorned various cups and medals he sponsored as he commemorated men who allowed their craniums to be sledgehammered through blocks of iron, strong men who lifted the *Police Gazette* Ferris wheel on their chest, bartenders who could make a *pousse-café* with the most layers, barbers who clipped hair the fastest, and champion rat-catching dogs. Under Fox's direction, his publication was less journalism than an early-day *Guinness Book of World Records*.

But even with his promotions bombarding the American public like misdirected buckshot, it was the targeting of his 10¢ weekly to the wants of the American people that was to earn him a place in history. The first thing Fox did when he took over was to add his name, "Richard K. Fox, Editor and Proprietor," to the masthead. The second was to add a sports section to the pink pages of the *Gazette*, bringing—in the absence of any such feature in the daily newspapers—accounts of races and prizefights to the thousands of Americans who were fascinated by such news.

Although prizefighting was illegal in every one of the thirty-eight states in 1880, Fox believed that many people were interested—interested enough to buy the *Gazette* to read about it.

Following this intuitive belief, he assigned several artists and reporters to cover a championship fight between England's Joe Goss and America's Paddy Ryan in Collier Station, on the West Virginia-Pennsylvania border. The 42-year-old Goss was the ex-champion. The dearth of good American heavyweights was attested to by Goss' opponent, 27-year-old Paddy Ryan, The Trojan Giant from Troy, New York, who had only had one professional fight—and lost it.

Goss' experience gave him an edge of the fighting for 60 rounds, but slowly Ryan wore down his older opponent by squeezing and tripping him, finally landing an awkward round-house right in the 86th round and then tossing him to the ground and landing on top of him for good measure. When Goss couldn't "come to scratch" for the 87th round, Paddy Ryan was declared winner and new American Champion. Immediately after the battle, the *Gazette* issued a special edition, complete with a full account of the fight as well as an artist's ringside renderings. For weeks the *Gazette* presses kept rolling to fill the demand of the sports-starved public, and circulation ran well into the tens of thousands as the magazine reached every barbershop, pool hall, saloon, police station, and fire hall in the land.

The astonishing success of the *Police Gazette* and its sports section attracted the attention of other papers, now aware of the circulation value of sports coverage. First they merely assigned general reporters to cover sporting events. Then, as the publishers gained expertise in the field and circulation rose, they assigned reporters to sports exclusively and soon began to feature separate sports sections. Seeking readers for his penny *New York Herald*, James Gordon Bennett began to publish the results of races and fights, and so did Benjamin Day in the *New York Sun*.

But it wasn't the fact that he had unwittingly spawned the sports pages that would serve as the anchor of Fox's fame. Rather it was because Fox, motivated only by his enormous ego, was to set the course for boxing in this country and serve unofficially as America's first boxing promoter, all because of a slight he suffered at the hands of John L. Sullivan.

While Paddy Ryan proudly wore both his mantle as American champion and the *Police Gazette* belt—"Presented by Richard K. Fox, Proprietor"—a new claimant was gradually making his name known, first in the Boston area and then nationally. That claimant was a 23-year-old bully, braggart, and boozer named John Lawrence Sullivan. Knowing little about the niceties of boxing, he had taken on all comers at the Dudley Street Opera House, Boston Music Hall, and the Howard Athenaeum in what were called "sparring exhibitions" in order to stay inside the law and outside the grasp of the Boston constabulary. Knocking out most of his opponents and several off the stage, John L. Sullivan gained the reputation of a knockout puncher. One opponent likened the impact of Sullivan's punch to "a telephone pole," which "had been shoved against me endwise." "It was like being kicked in the head by a runaway horse," said another.

As his reputation grew, so did the clamor to see him in action. Sullivan toured the vaudeville circuit, offering $50 to any comer who could last four rounds, building his reputation and his growing list of victims in Cincinnati, Philadelphia, Chicago, and finally New York. During his stopover in New York, late in March 1881, Sullivan dropped into a public house known as Harry Hill's Dance Hall and Boxing Emporium. Harry Hill's was a group of two-story buildings on Houston Street at the edge of New York's famed Bowery, where wrestling and boxing exhibitions were offered as a divertissement for the many stage and sports personalities who frequented the place, including its landlord P.T. Barnum, Diamond Jim Brady, Lillian Russell, James Gordon Bennett and, of course, the most influential sports figure in the country, Richard K. Fox.

Sullivan had just beaten one Steve Taylor in two rounds on Hill's oversized stage, saving himself $50 which he was reinvesting in drinks for friends and hangers-on, when Fox, seated just two tables away, beckoned his waiter over and told him to instruct Sullivan "Mr. Fox would like a word with him." But Sullivan was not up to being granted audiences, even by so influential a man as Fox, and bellowed back at the waiter—loud enough for Fox and everyone else in the place to hear—"You tell Fox that if he's got anything to say to me he can Gahd-damn well come over to my table and say it!" No one had ever addressed him like that before. And Fox never forgot it.

This affront caused Fox to crusade against Sullivan. It was to keep John L's name in the limelight for the next dozen years. After Sullivan had disposed of John Flood, a New Yorker gang leader who had never failed to "get his man," Fox started a search for a boxer who could "get" Sullivan.

The perfect man was the holder of his belt, Paddy Ryan. Ryan had kept the belt and the title for a little over a year, but showed no proclivity for risking it in the ring, especially against so formidable an opponent as the Boston Strongboy. Finally, with Fox as his backer and operating as the *de facto* promoter,

Ryan agreed to the bout, $5,000 a side. But here a hitch developed. After $500 of the stake money was deposited with Harry Hill in New York, Sullivan's backers had difficulty coming up with the remainder of the $5,000. It was Ryan who saved the bout, by appealing to Fox to reduce the stakes by half because Sullivan could not obtain sufficient funds.

The reluctance of Sullivan money was rooted in the unsettled state of boxing at that time in the United States. While most fights were then fought under the old London Prize Ring Rules—bare knuckles and rounds ending when a man was knocked, tripped, or thrown to the ground, having thirty seconds to come "to scratch"—Sullivan was an ardent advocate of the new Marquis of Queensberry Rules. Sullivan had begun a crusade against the use of bare fists in his travels around the country and had started to popularize the use of gloves, called "pillows" by their detractors. While Ryan had established himself as a bare-knuckle fighter, Sullivan's ability as one was practically unknown. Stimulated by the relative merits of both fighters, talk of the match filled the land—and the *Police Gazette*.

The fight itself was anticlimatic. On the morning of February 7, 1882, Sullivan and Ryan met in a ring pitched in front of the veranda of the Barnes Hotel in the Gulf resort town of Mississippi City, Mississippi. The two men approached the ring and threw their hats inside, indicating they were ready for combat. With a frustrated Fox vainly screaming to the champion to inflict damage on his sworn enemy, Sullivan took the fight from Ryan in just ten minutes and thirty seconds under London Prize Ring Rules. He had captured the championship, leaving Ryan insensible and Fox incoherent.

The newly crowned American champion immediately set out to merchandise himself, barnstorming across the country on a knockout trip that made boxing popular and John L. well-to-do. The going price was now $1,000 for anyone who could last four rounds under Queensberry Rules with the heavyweight champion. Boasting "I can beat any son-of-a-bitch in the house," he would totter out nightly to center stage so drunk that his handlers had to help him into his tights and push him in the direction of the curtain. But he backed up his *defi* by meeting and beating a collection of local barkeeps, bullyboys, and blacksmiths, with an occasional "professional" fighter thrown in for good measure.

The only one of the hundreds of challengers who stayed the four rounds was an experienced British heavyweight, Joe Wilson. Fighting under the name "Tug" Collins, he was backed by none other than Sullivan's *bête noir*, Richard K. Fox. Persuading Sullivan to agree to revert to the old London Prize Rules, Wilson fought Sullivan at Madison Square Garden on the night of July 17, 1882, in a four-round exhibition hypocritically allowed by Mayor Grace, although prizefighting was "illegal." According to the *Ring Record Book*, " 'Tug' Collins (Joe Wilson) stayed by hugging and falling to the floor," thus providing Fox with some small satisfaction and Wilson with $1,000 in prize money.

Fox was now aligned with Sullivan's former manager, Billy Madden, who had had a falling out with Sully. Knowing of Sullivan's pride in everything American, Madden sought to humiliate John L. by bringing over an Englishman to beat him. Madden advertised in the *London Sporting Life* for warm bodies to fight in a heavyweight elimination contest. But unlike a similar ad that ran some eighty years later for a firm called Kid Galahad, Inc., which begat them nothing more than a 7-foot, 2-inch reluctant giant named James J. Beatty, Madden found himself a live one in Charlie Mitchell. Mitchell, a sturdy 158-pounder, beat the same Tug Wilson that Sullivan had had problems with and was proclaimed by Madden to be Boxing Champion of England. He was now matched with Sullivan.

The international fight brought a crowd of more than ten thousand to Madison Square Garden. And they weren't disappointed. Fighting with gloves under the Queensberry rules, the lighter Mitchell took the fight to Sullivan and in the very first round, to everyone's surprise, delivered a short right which knocked Sullivan down for the first time in his career. In the third round, after Sullivan had knocked the Englishman through the ropes in the second and out of the ring in the third, the police jumped into the ring. The master of ceremonies— there being no referee—gave Sullivan "a decision," although it was a "no-decision" bout. Fox had part of his pound of flesh.

Fox continued his search for the elusive Golden Fleece, a man who could best John L. He imported Herbert A. Slade, a giant Maori, supposedly the best fighter in the Antilles. He lasted three rounds. Next he brought over Alf Greenfield, one of England's finest. He went two.

But Fox was far from through. There now hove onto the scene a native of Long Island christened John J. Killion, who fought under the name Jake Kilrain. During the early 1880s Kilrain fought, and beat, some of the best of the heavies, including Jack Burke, Jack Ashton, Frank Herald, and Joe Godfrey among others, and had fought a four-round draw with Mitchell. The undefeated Kilrain, with Fox and the *Gazette* noisily urging him on, repeatedly challenged Sullivan to battle. When the champion failed to respond, Fox declared Kilrain the champion and gave him a belt as the American Champion with the understanding that he would 'fight Jem Smith, then champion of England, with $5,000 a side and the belt going to the winner. Fox, of course, put up Kilrain's $5,000.

The match against Smith took place in des Souverains, France, and after 106 rounds of no-holds-barred fighting, the battle was declared a draw. Kilrain returned to the United States with a claim to the world title and the belt.

Now with a legitimate claimant on his hands, Fox's campaign against Sullivan picked up momentum and viciousness. Sullivan's fans in Boston took up a collection and presented him with a belt of his own, fancier, if possible, than Fox's. Sullivan, who had no use for either Fox or Kilrain, contemptuously sneered, "I wouldn't put Kilrain's belt around the neck of a Gahd-damned dog," and made plans to go to England to take on the best there. When asked by a reporter why he was going abroad when the most worthy challenger for his crown was here in America, Sullivan took off the wraps and verbally took off after Fox: "I've been abused in the papers. I've been lied about and condemned by men who, for commercial reasons, wanted to see some true American, a son of the Stars and Stripes, whipped by a foreigner. So now I'm intending to get even by unfurling Uncle Sam's victorious flag in the land from which my enemies brought men they hoped would conquer me."

With few worlds left to conquer after a victorious six-month tour of England and the continent, Sullivan returned to the United States in April, 1888, and immediately took refuge in the only other world he ever knew: the bottle. After several bouts with a far more formidable opponent than any he had ever met in the ring, Sullivan was finally rendered senseless for the first time in his life. For four months, he was confined to bed, suffering from delirium tremens combined with physical collapse, cirrhosis of the liver, and a touch of typhoid fever, thrown in for good measure.

The time seemed ripe for Fox to pluck the crown away. The weekly pink pages of the *Gazette* beat out a monotonous one-note story—that the once-proud physical specimen was now a physical wreck. There was a question whether John L. would in fact survive and, if he did, would he ever fight again? Everywhere, the *Gazette* went—livery stables, barber shops, saloons, fire halls, police stations—controversy was sure to follow. Was the sick Sullivan refusing to meet the "real champion?"

Within a month of leaving his sickbed, Sullivan accepted the long-standing challenge of Kilrain and Fox and posted $5,000 in New York to fight Kilrain, $10,000 a side, for the championship and possession of the belt, "the ring to be pitched within 200 miles of New Orleans."

Almost before the ink was dry on the contract, John L. took off on another prolonged bender. With the bout only months away, the champion was informing all present in any bar he entered that he would win easily. But his bloated 240 pounds gave lie to his braggadocio. Sensing their hero was beyond the realm of self-discipline, Sullivan's backers hired William Muldoon, the wrestling champion and physical fitness fanatic, to wrestle John L. back into shape. Finding Sullivan quaffing down a stein of straight bourbon in one of his normal hangouts, Muldoon physically dragged him from the premises to his health farm at Belfast, New York, for a period of rest and rehabilitation.

In a scant six months Muldoon did the impossible. It almost equaled resuscitating Lazarus. First Sullivan's eyes cleared, then he regained his wind, and finally he recaptured his style and power. Under Muldoon's watchful eyes, the flabby 240 pounds turned into a fighting 207 pounds. John L. was ready for "any son-of-a-bitch-in-the-house" again. But particularly Fox and his hand-picked gladiator Kilrain.

As the date for what was to be the last bare-knuckle fight in the history of boxing drew closer, thousands of the faithful were drawn to New Orleans. A robust, rollicking town, the New Orleans of 1889 was renowned for its jetties, its Cotton Centennial Exposition, and its infamous Storyville section. Because "prizefighting" was illegal in Louisiana, as it was in all the other 37 states, great secrecy surrounded the movements of the principals and their backers. Only the promoter of the fight, a New Orleans sportsman named Bud Reneau, and a few others, knew the exact location of the fight. So, when, just after midnight on July 8, 1889, the special fight train pulled out of the Queen and Crescent Yards, filled to overflowing with fans from every walk of life, few knew the exact destination.

Not until daylight after a slow and tedious all-night ride did the passengers know where they were bound for. Finally, around 8 A.M., the train lumbered into Richburg, Mississippi, a lumber camp some 104 miles north of New Orleans, where a ring was set up in full view on the thirty thousand-acre estate of pines

146

owned by Colonel Charles W. Rich. As it came to a stop, the train disgorged its human freight, all of whom made a dash to the specially constructed wooden arena.

A few minutes before ten Kilrain and his cornermen, Charlie Mitchell and Mike Donovan, together with their timekeeper, Bat Masterson, pushed their way down the aisle. After tossing his hat into the ring, Kilrain entered, wearing green trunks anchored with an American flag which served as a belt. Then, to the roars of the crowd, Sullivan appeared and, after the ceremonial toss of his hat, entered wearing a green robe. Discarding it immediately, he stood resplendent in emerald green knee breeches, flesh-colored long stockings and high-topped black fighting boots. His waist was also encircled with an American flag, together with his own colors, green and white.

Sullivan hardly looked like the man the *Police Gazette* had been depicting for the past several months. He appeared quite fit except for a small protuberance in the lower belly. But the unanswered question was how long could he go, especially against a wrestler like Kilrain? Pulitzer's *New York World* had ventured an opinion: "According to all such drunkards as he, his legs ought to fail him after twenty minutes of fighting." Still, Sullivan was the betting favorite at ringside.

At exactly ten minutes after ten, referee John Fitzpatrick of New Orleans hollered "Time!" and the two adversaries advanced to the mark. They circled quickly. Kilrain threw a long left, grabbed Sullivan by the shoulders, and threw him over his heel to the ground. The first round had taken exactly five seconds. The pattern of the fight began to take shape in the second, as the enraged Sullivan chased Kilrain, who kept his distance and employed the defensive tactics of his cornerman Charlie Mitchell, jabbing, holding, and wrestling. By the fourth round, which took 15 minutes and 21 seconds, a frustrated Sullivan could only stop momentarily to snarl, "Why don't you fight, you son-of-a-bitch? You're the champion, huh? Champion of what?" But Kilrain didn't take the bait. He only laughed and went back into his shell. All the while Kilrain's corner, especially Mitchell, kept up a steady stream of abuse, trying to goad Sullivan into anger. Kilrain's strategy was obvious: wear down the bigger man and exhaust his energies, no matter how.

It seemed to be working. In the seventh, Kilrain landed a roundhouse right to Sullivan's ear and tore it open. "First blood, Kilrain," announced Fitzpatrick, and an exchange of bills accompanied the announcement of first claret. But this was to be the last time the supporters of Kilrain were to take heart, as the champion, not John L., began to wilt in the 104-degree heat. Sullivan's determination and condition were attested to by the fact that he refused to sit down between rounds: "Why should I? I only have to stand back up again." After the twelfth round, when Muldoon asked him how much longer he could "stay," Sullivan snarled, "'Til tomorrow morning, if necessary."

As the fight wore on, the result became more and more apparent. The question was no longer whether John L. could survive Kilrain's attacks or even if he could win, but *when*. By the end of the seventy-fifth round, Kilrain's head was rolling loosely on his shoulders as if his neck were broken, his back was covered with beet-red blisters, and he could no longer stand up, let alone throw a punch. A physician took his second, Mike Donovan, aside and advised him that "Kilrain will die if you keep sending him in there." As Kilrain uncertainly made his way back out to the center of the ring to toe the mark for the seventy-sixth round, Donovan tossed in the sponge.

The last championship bare-knuckle fight was over. The proud line of champions that had begun in 1719 on a wooden stage at James Figg's Amphitheatre ended in a clearing on a lumber estate in Mississippi some one hundred seventy years later. John L. Sullivan was still the champion. And the possessor of the *Police Gazette* belt, "Presented by Richard K. Fox, Proprietor."

For the next year and a half Sullivan toured the country appearing in a play called *Honest Hearts and Willing Hands*. Finally, after almost two years of performing all over the world, *Honest Hearts* either ran out of villains or Sullivan ran out of patience with his critics—Fox, as always, in the forefront. Sullivan issued one of his famous proclamations in the papers to quiet those who were taking off pieces of his hide in public:

> I hereby challenge any and all bluffers to fight me for a purse of $25,000 and a bet of $10,000. The winner of the fight to take the entire purse. I am ready to put up the first $10,000 now. First come, first served. I give preference in this challenge to Frank P. Slavin of Australia, as he and his backers have done the greatest amount of blowing. My second preference is that bombastic sprinter, Charles Mitchell of England, whom I would rather whip than any man in the world. My third preference is James J. Corbett, who has uttered his share of bombast. But in this challenge I include all fighters. The Marquis of Queensberry must govern this contest, as I want fighting, not footracing, and I intend to keep the championship of the world.

> Yours truly,
> John L. Sullivan
> CHAMPION OF THE WORLD

For once Fox did not have to go out and manufacture opponents. Thoroughly piqued at the many shafts thrown at him by the Lilliputians who still savaged him in the papers, John L. had taken care of that himself. The first to come forward was a bank clerk from San Francisco, James J. Corbett, whom Sullivan had sparred with only the previous June.

The fight was signed, sealed and delivered for September 1892, in New Orleans—under a new state law allowing club "prize fights," Marquis of Queensberry rules. It would cap a three-day boxing carnival that featured a lightweight championship bout, a featherweight title fight and, on the third night, the heavyweight match between Corbett and Sullivan.

On the night of September 7, 1892, almost nine out of every ten who entered the Olympic Club carried the Sullivan colors, a broad band of green silk with an American eagle in the center. But more than their sentiments went with the Boston Strongboy; they also made Sullivan a prohibitive 4–1 favorite.

But it was soon obvious that although he outweighed Corbett by some thirty-four pounds, Sullivan was no match for the dancing stylist, who thwarted every rush with a sidestep and slipped every roundhouse right. Sullivan couldn't land a punch for twenty rounds. When he went down, head first in the twenty-first, the gallery got rid of its Sullivan colors as quickly as possible, throwing their green bands toward the fallen gladiator. They fluttered down on the stricken exchampion in clouds, covering him like a shroud. When he finally groped his way out from under his own colors, he asked Jack McAuliffe, his second and the winner in the first fight two nights before, "What happened, Jack? What happened?" With tears in his eyes McAuliffe told him the awful truth. Some staunch friends helped him make his way unsteadily to the ropes. He grasped the top rope and spoke to the crowd: "The old man went up against it just once too often. He was beaten—but by an American. Yours truly, John L. Sullivan."

And the belt? Although Fox now had a champion he could back, he never gave him the championship belt. For Sullivan had entrusted the one he had won from Kilrain to a friend for safekeeping. The "friend" had left it in a pawnshop in New York City, and that was the last time the belt emblematic of boxing's most cherished prize was ever seen.

In the world of the 1900s, still awash with Victorian gentility and doily-type embroidery on everything from manners and modes to conversation and literary tastes, the individualistic style of Jack London stood out starkly.

A forerunner of Hemingway, London eulogized rugged indi-
vidualism in the face of ruthless and oppressive circumstances,
whether they be man-made or creatures of nature. He was the
chronicler of the Yukon Territory in books for and about "men
with the bark on."

London wrote about Alaska and the Yukon because he had
been there. So had thousands of other independent spirits, all
chasing the illusion of getting rich quick in the halycon days of
the Yukon gold rush. They walked on and off stage like so many
cameo bit-part players. There could be found celebrities-to-be
London and Rex Beach, best-selling authors; Alexander Pan-
tages and Sid Grauman, motion picture entrepreneurs; Miss
Marjorie Rambeau, one of the greatest of all Broadway beauties;
Key Pitman, fabled United States Senator from Nevada; Wilson
Mizner, promoter, publicist, playwright, and consummate con
man who followed the action from the Guatemalan jungles to the
Klondike gold fields to the Florida land booms to the Hollywood
fantasy factories with the philosophical belief "Always be pleasant to the people you meet on the way up, because they are
always the very same people you meet on the way down." And
there could also be found George Lewis "Tex" Rickard.

One of London's works, *Burning Daylight*, the story of an
intrepid wanderer, might well have been about Tex Rickard.
For Rickard had fought his way through the snows of the Yukon
in the dead of winter, arriving before gold was even a glint in its
finder's eye, out of money, out of supplies, and out of sorts.
Before he left he was to amass a list of occupational credentials
including miner, faro dealer, saloon owner, professional
gambler, hotel owner, and a universal reputation for honesty.
All would serve him in his next life as a boxing promoter. But
none more so than his reputation for honesty.

Rickard was born on January 2, 1871, in Clay County, Missouri. Six years after peace had been signed at Appomattox,
Southern sympathizers in Clay County were still "at war."
Nightly lynchings, bushwhackings, shootings, and bank robber-
ies took place, aided and abetted by no less than the James Boys
and the Younger Brothers. The Rickard farm was next door to
that of Mrs. Zerelda Samuels, mother of Frank and Jesse James,
and young George Lewis "Tex" Rickard's sleep was often disturbed by the gunshots and hoofbeats of nightly visitations from
posses looking for her famous sons.

In 1880, the year Paddy Ryan won the heavyweight championship, the Rickard family finally decided it had had "enough"
and moved to Henrietta, Texas, a whistle-stop on the Fort Worth

& Denver Railroad. Fatherless at the age of 11, young Rickard became a prodigy trail cowboy, catching, containing, branding, and calming meandering longhorns that had been loose on the range during the Civil War while their owners went off to do battle. By 1894, the still-young cowpoke, now as experienced at bucking the tiger at faro as he was at riding the trail, ran for town marshal—and won. He was paid on a fee basis: $2.50 for each person arrested and $1 for every animal impounded. To make ends meet, Tex hired local boys to find dogs with wanderlust at 25¢ a head, turning a profit on every contribution to the city pound.

In 1895, after losing his wife, Rickard made a decision. He had heard about a far-off place called Alaska, where whatever streets there were were literally paved in gold; and it was all there for the taking. So he handed in his badge and headed north, two years before the rest of the world started beating a path to its door. It was a normal head start for Rickard!

After experiencing many of the travails of the hero in *Burning Daylight*, Rickard finally made his way to a desolate mining camp on the Yukon River known as Circle City—and equally known as the only purveyor of fun and amusement miners could find for miles around. Without funds or friends, he found the local gambling shack, where the proprietor, Sam Bonnifield, gave him a job as barkeep and faro dealer. Within a month, Bonnifield had amassed enough gold dust to buy the fanciest saloon in Circle City and, with a gesture known only to professional gamblers, turned his place over to the newcomer from Texas—now called "Tex"—who had brought him luck.

While he was a gambling man, Rickard wasn't a professional gambler. In just a few short weeks he lost the gambling house to a sourdough with a run of luck. Shaking his hand, Rickard walked down the street to find employment, again with Bonnifield in his new pleasure palace. Then, in what was to become a familiar scenario, word reached Circle City that gold had been found in the Klondike. So, along with hundreds of other prospectors, Rickard took off for a tent city called Bonanza Creek in the dead of winter. Staking out a claim and taking out their pickaxes, Rickard and a partner worked the ground during the grueling winter months. But this sort of work wasn't for Tex, and with the coming of spring he sold out his claims to a British investor for $60,000.

In the spring of 1896 Rickard wandered into Dawson, a boom town filled with gold-seekers already twice the size of Circle City and growing. With his Bonanza-strike money, he opened up a gambling house and saloon called The Northern. Once again, he lost it to prospectors who ran their gold dust and luck at the roulette table into house and Rickard's temporary home.

Now broke, Rickard spent the next fifteen months as a twenty-dollar-a-day faro dealer, barkeep, and front man for other Dawson gambling houses. It was an incubation period for Rickard, the boom-and-bust entrepreneur. He lived in an unreal man's world where gold dust was plentiful and amusements few. News finally reached the United States that a magical "ton of gold" could be found on the streets of Dawson. Imaginations stirred and men moved as the exciting news brought the depression of 1897 to a screeching halt. It was the beginning of the second greatest gold rush in history, a rush that would see almost one million starry-eyed dreamers descend on the Yukon.

One of those million was Wilson Mizner, scion of a wealthy San Francisco family. A unique combination of con man, hustler, faro dealer, and supesalesman, Mizner would influence Tex Rickard's life greatly. Mizner, who later managed Stanley Ketchel and Jack Kearns, who in turn managed Jack Dempsey, was equal to any task, often uttering memorable witticisms. When told of the death of Stanley Ketchel in a lovers' quarrel, Mizner incredulously murmured, "Boys, start counting ten over him. He'll get up at nine."

Wandering around the Yukon, Mizner had selected the boom town of Dawson as a momentary resting place, supporting himself as a professional gambler. While serving temporarily as a bartender at the Monte Carlo Saloon, the 21-year-old Mizner found himself working next to the 26-year-old Rickard. The two of them became fast friends, one a great talker, the other, Rickard—who, according to one friend, "didn't have two sentences to rub together"—a great listener. Together they would share many stories, most of them Mizner's. And many experiences.

The Klondike was a man's world, not because of chauvinism, but because there literally were no women to be found. Men were reduced to making their own entertainment, whether it was dancing with the house girls at the saloons or each other, bellying up to the bar night after night, or seeking out stage shows and other amusements. One such popular amusement was boxing. Wilson Mizner was the first to put a card together, staging his free-lance entertainment at the Monte Carlo.

The use of a boxing card to promote business was a lesson not lost on the still-impressionable Rickard. When he pulled up stakes to move on to Rampart to set up yet another saloon called The Northern, the first thing he did was hang up signs which read: "Grand Opening—THE NORTHERN—Featuring a Grand Ball and Prize Fight." Its success was the first of many for Rickard.

But Rampart proved to be more a bust than boom town, and soon Rickard was moving again, this time to Nome, where he established still another saloon called The Northern, scant days before Nome became the center of the latest gold rush. And Rickard, who had gone into The Northern with but $21, had soon parlayed his grubstake into a half-ownership which netted him $100,000 the first year and almost half a million in four years.

In that buy-now, pay-later atmosphere that always characterizes towns on the "come," Rickard opened the Northern's portals to familiar faces and strangers alike, trusting them for drinks, debts, and gold dust. With money scarce, the negotiable currency of Nome quickly became gold dust. As each sourdough came into his fortune, he would bank it at The Northern, trusting Rickard, as he had them. For Nome, as in all boom cities of the North Country, honesty was as hard to find as the precious metal itself. Soon Tex's was not only the largest saloon in Nome, but the only totally honest one, the only one where dishonest gamblers never tried to ply their trade.

In 1902, after seven years in Alaska, Rickard decided it was time to move along. He cashed in his chips and took with him $65,000 to look for something else. That "something else" included a side trip to Africa to look for diamonds and another to San Francisco in an attempt to catch a glimpse of the man Rickard called "my idol . . . 'Gentleman Jim' Corbett." Rickard was to make one last excursion back to Nome and The Northern. This brief pass lasted less than a year, and Rickard left Alaska for good in 1904, having heard of a new gold strike in Nevada.

The Nevada strike was but one of a string in a state rich in precious metals. Created by the discovery of the rich Comstock Lode in 1859, a strike that produced almost four hundred million dollars in silver, the state of Nevada was admitted to the Union in 1864 because it possessed enough silver to provide much of the funding for the Civil War. Fourteen years after its first strike, the Comstock Lode produced another, The Big Bonanza. Nineteen hundred saw a strike of rich silver ores in the southwestern part of the state, near Tonopah. And four years later and forty miles further south, the discovery of gold in the vicinity of the aptly named town of Goldfield precipitated yet another rush.

One of those who migrated into Goldfield in 1904 was Rickard. Except for the temperature, Goldfield was not unlike the mining towns of Nome and Dawson. Population was sparse, topography barren, and foliage nil. But it mainlined on the excitement boom towns generate. And that was the place for Rickard. He opened a new saloon and gambling house predictably named The Northern.

Everyone seemed drawn to Goldfield. A group of high-powered press agents pumped sensational story after sensational story out to a nation suffering through its second major depression in ten years. The good news—one mine produced more than five million dollars of gold-bearing ore in three months—worked the same magic as a carnival barker attracting thousands to the tent city pretentiously called "the greatest mining camp ever known." With their first taste of self-promotion the town fathers sought new and more spectacular ways to draw the world's attention to their dusty little Golconda. A meeting of the local chamber-of-commerce types was called. One merchant pitched unsteadily to his feet and suggested that a manmade lake be constructed on Main Street to be filled with beer every morning. A mine owner wanted the town to hire a hot-air balloon to circle the city with a basket filled with ten-dollar gold pieces which would be tossed overboard to reinforce the belief that there was gold on Goldfield's streets. Another wanted a racetrack stocked with camels imported from the Sahara. And so on. Rickard suggested a prizefight.

Stimulated by Rickard's suggestion, the men formed the Goldfield Athletic Club on the spot and raised $50,000 to back a fight in less than an hour. Then they began jockeying for the most prestigious titles.

As one man after another, all bursting with pride like pouter-pigeons, jumped up and offered himself for one exalted position after another, only one man in the room hadn't volunteered. That was the man who had put forward the idea, Tex Rickard. With no one desiring to have anything resembling work get in the way of his honorary title, Rickard was appointed the positions of treasurer, "promoter," and number one honcho. He would see to it that the fighters were found, contracts negotiated, and an arena erected. In short, Rickard was to do all the work.

But he was to have the last laugh. As The Promoter, his name would become known far and wide. Equally important, he was to learn how to use "other people's money"—O.P.M.—something any promoter worth his calling must do.

First Rickard wired the managers of Jimmy Britt, claimant to

154

the lightweight crown, and "Terrible" Terry McGovern, former bantamweight and featherweight champion, offering "Fifteen thousand dollars for a fight to the finish." In those days of fighting for a percentage of the gate, such an offer was unheard of. So was Tex Rickard. The managers remained silent. Thinking he had to increase the ante, Rickard turned his sights to the newest claimant and sensation, Battling Nelson, who had just beaten Britt for "the white lightweight championship of the world," and wired him an offer of $20,000 for a "finish fight" against the recognized titleholder, the black great, Joe Gans. Again no answer.

But Rickard wouldn't take "no" for an answer. Unable to ferret out Nelson, he turned his attention to the champion Gans. Locating him in San Francisco, where he had just knocked out "Twin" Sullivan, Rickard wired him with the offer of $20,000. Gans was destitute and immediately wired back his acceptance, agreeing to any terms Nelson demanded.

With Gans in the fold, Rickard felt reasonably assured of the fight and entrained to Reno to purchase the needed lumber for construction of an arena. There he heard that although his offer of $20,000 was the largest guarantee ever offered, an emissary from Sunny Jim Coffroth's famed San Francisco Fight Trust—the number one fight promoter in the country who got his nickname not for ruddy coloring, but for his fabled luck with the weather for his outdoor fights—was heading east to meet Battling Nelson and offer him even more. Realizing he was fast becoming the almost-promoter of an almost fight, Rickard increased his offer to $30,000. That did it! When he returned to Goldfield a telegram awaited him. It was from Nelson's manager accepting the bid, with his man to get two-thirds of the guarantee.

Rickard had his match. He immediately went to the bank adjacent to The Northern and had them array the total purse, $30,000 in all, in tall stacks of newly minted double-eagle gold pieces in its window. Rickard's display was big news, calling attention to the largest guarantee ever given for a fight. Anyone could talk money; Rickard had produced it. The sight of gold excited everyone, especially cynical newsmen. Pictures of the bank window were circulated around the world, bringing momentary fame to Goldfield. But Tex Rickard was half the news. In those days of con men, connivers, and cheats, Rickard stood alone as a man of his word. That alone was newsworthy!

Prophetically christened Oscar Battling Matthew Nelson, the man more simply known as "Bat" or "The Durable Dane" had amassed both a record and a reputation. Using the time-worn cliché, he came to fight, taking few survivors and usually three punches—preferably to the head, where it was said he was invulnerable—to every one he landed. His favorite shot was a vicious punch to the kidneys. Time and again, Nelson would take everything his opponent had to offer, then pick up the tempo, resorting to continued and often dirty in-fighting, and then knock out the thoroughly dispirited and discouraged fighter.

Joe Gans, on the other hand, was one of the classic boxers of all time, called—even today—the greatest boxer pound-for-pound and punch-for-punch of all time. In 144 fights before Goldfield, Gans had scored 49 knockouts and lost just 5 times. Three of those losses were tainted, supposedly to satisfy the betting whims of a crooked manager, since departed. But without his manager, the impoverished "master" was having trouble getting fights. For this reason, he agreed to each new division of the guarantee Nelson's manager demanded, finally settling for $10,000 to Nelson's $23,000.

As the fight date approached—Labor Day, 1906—the ballyhoo increased in decibels and Rickard's plans increased in deliberateness. The streets of Goldfield began taking on the look of a midway, with every exhibitionist for hundreds of miles around descending on the town to offer his specialty, whether it was a cakewalk and watermelon dance, or bull-sticking. They were all there. And so were thousands of fans of the Gentlemanly Art of Self-Defense spilling out of hotels, bars, and brothels, all searching vainly for a place to eat and sleep.

Rickard pressed ahead on his crash program for erecting the arena a half mile outside of town. He purchased 214,667 feet of green lumber for $50 per thousand feet, more than $10,000, four-fifths of which was refundable if the lumber was returned after the fight. Then, he oversaw the construction of a 7,926-seat arena, in only ten days at a cost of $13,000. He established a policy to prevent ringside cash customers from being physically preempted from their seats by toughs from the cheap seats, guaranteeing "a seat for every customer." To insure this departure from the typical "free-for-all" that traditionally accompanied every opening of the doors, Rickard hired a band of courteous but brawny ushers and paid them well not only to establish but to maintain order and decorum at ringside.

Perhaps Rickard's greatest contribution was in making the fight an attraction for both sexes. Rickard meant to make the Gans-Nelson championship the first fight attended not only by society "swells," whose support he desperately sought, but by the ladies. He held afternoon training sessions at Nelson's camp for the ladies and constructed a special section with screened boxes for them far from the ring. Rickard told newsmen anxiously awaiting each and every tidbit on the fight, "nearly every society woman in Goldfield would see the fight."

The day of the fight burst forth bright and typically Nevada hot. After the prefight preliminaries that usually took place in any small fight town—including rock-drilling and races between humans and burros—almost eight thousand fans of all stripes and stations, among them 300 women, made their way into the newly constructed arena.

Gans, seriously weakened by having to make the weight just minutes before the fight at the insistence of Nelson's manager, was the first to enter the ring, just after three o'clock. He was clutching a poignant telegram he had just received from his mother in Baltimore: "Joe, the eyes of the world are upon you. . . . Bring home the bacon!" Then, it was Battling Nelson's turn to enter the eighteen-foot ring. This was yet another concession to Nelson's manager, who was positive the smaller-than-regulation ring would help his boxer.

Referee George Siler, a Chicago newspaperman, called the contestants together and the fight was on. For the first ten rounds, his lithe black body glistening under the boiling Nevada sun, Gans stuck and hit, stuck and hit, pummeling Nelson in a masterful display of boxing skill. In the eleventh, Bat gained control with his stylized roughhousing, which consisted of a steady diet of butting, cuffing, and gouging. Nelson's fight plan included using every bone in his body.

By the forty-first round, it was obvious even to Nelson that his fouling technique wasn't working. He was desperate. In the forty-second, while Gans smothered Nelson's infighting in a clinch, the challenger began raining blows somewhere south of Gans' beltline. As referee Siler issued a warning, Nelson drove his right hand into Gans' groin with everything he had left. Gans fell to the ground, rolling over, and shivering convulsively. Siler pushed Nelson to his corner, returned to the stricken champion, and raised his arm. Gans was the winner on a foul in the forty-second round.

Gans returned to his dressing room, still the champ, and composed a wire to his mother: "Mammy, your boy bringing home the bacon with lots of gravy on it." For Rickard and the merchants of Goldfield, there was lots of gravy, too. The gate receipts were $69,715, all tax-free in those pre-IRS days. After paying the fighters their $33,000 and another $23,000 in expenses, Rickard netted $13,715 for himself and his partners in the Goldfield Athletic Club. The town of Goldfield had profited mightily by generating almost a million dollars' worth of free publicity, to say nothing of the additional business they had drawn to their budding community.

Before another year was out, the gold had given out and so had Goldfield. And Rickard was on his way to other gold fields. But the fight between Gans and Nelson—the first of 234 Rickard would promote during the next twenty-two years, bringing in more than twenty million dollars in gate receipts—would prove to be the most important one he would ever promote. For it provided him with experience and a platform from which he would ultimately launch himself toward becoming the premier boxing promoter in the world.

On the day after Christmas in 1908—Boxing Day—a large black cat played with a small white mouse in a boxing match-cum-race war, less for nourishment than for sadistic pleasure. The winner not only took the heavyweight championship of the world, but unleashed a damned-up wall of hatred. For on that day in Sydney, Australia, The Galveston Giant, Jack Johnson, outweighed, outpunched, and outgunned little Tommy Burns to take the heavyweight championship of the world.

This wasn't merely a changing of the guard in the manner of Corbett beating Sullivan or Fitzsimmons dethroning Corbett or Jeffries knocking out Fitzsimmons. This was a black man beating a white man. Judgment Day had come. The White Man's Burden had become his master.

Johnson underlined the importance of his victory by the manner in which he achieved it. He rubbed the collective Caucasian noses in the resin. He talked to the audience and taunted his foe from the opening bell. ("Come on leedle Tahmmy!" bam-bam-bam; "Come right here where I want you" bam-bam-bam; "No good, Tahmmy! I'll teach you," bam-bam-bam.) Between rounds he expectorated with unerring accuracy over the heads of his seconds onto a vacant space at ringside the size of a handkerchief between members of the disbelieving white press. And throughout he grinned, smiling at the twenty thousand white faces in the Sydney stadium, teeth agleam. He was insufferable.

The helpless Burns was knocked down in the very first round and unable to land a blow throughout. By the fourteenth, he was hanging onto the ropes with his jaw dangling open, drooling. The local police stopped the fight. Jack Johnson had become the world's heavyweight champion. And the rallying point for a great white crusade.

Seated at ringside in Sydney, Jack London sounded the initial call to arms in the final paragraph of his story in the *New York Herald:* " . . . one thing remains. Jeffries must emerge from his alfalfa farm and remove that smile from Johnson's face. Jeff, it's up to you!" The call went out, from public and press alike, for the unbeaten James J. Jeffries to return and avenge the defiling of the white Desdemona by putting this black Othello back in his place.

But Jeffries, who had not fought since 1904, had gone to bloat sitting on his farm in California. He saw no reason to leave it now. He refused to fight Johnson, invoking his right as an American citizen to "draw the color line." Hatred crescendoed as Johnson marched through the land disposing with equal ease of brave plowboys, willing white women, and tall glasses of rum. Only the invincible Jeff, the chosen representative of the white race, could answer for the real and imagined slights the Caucasian psyche was suffering at the hands of this black who was living life to the fullest and flaunting his color in the white man's face.

Jeffries finally succumbed. Whether it was because he heard the call for a standard-bearer, the tinkle of money, or the skin-pricking jibes of the devil-may-care Johnson, who had disposed of Jeffries' brother in five rounds in Los Angeles some eight years before and now mocked "I've got Jim's number," is not known. One thing is: the first so-called Battle of the Century was about to take place.

The free-lance world of boxing has one enormous plus going for it: its matchmakers are able to structure their offerings so as to offer comedy, melodrama, even a morality play within the confines of four ring posts. The early club fights in New York always seemed to pit an Italian against an Irishman or a Jew, as when Benny Leonard would take on Frankie Conifrey to determine territorial rights. Sometimes it would take the form of a battle for bragging rights, as when Leonard Delgenio slugged it out with Baby Salvy Sabin—one of the participants acknowledging the semi-race war conditions that existed in boxing by confiding to ring announcer Sam Taub and several hundred thousand radio listeners: "I guess the Jews had a good time watching a couple of Dagos kill each other." And sometimes, in a world of point and counterpoint, a boxer would fight a slugger in a battle of style.

159

But none of these classic match-ups would measure in drama the bout between the black champion and the former white champion. It was more than a morality play. It was an allegory. Black versus white. Invader versus avenger.

No one grasped the marketing potential of the match better than Tex Rickard. And he eagerly sought to become its architect. But he was not alone. Others saw its inherent drama and profit. Representatives of Johnson and Jeffries met and agreed to a bout to be held in July, 1910. They stipulated that all bids for the bout must be submitted to them on December 1, 1909, in New York. And the "promoters" came out of the proverbial woodwork. There was Sunny Jim Coffroth and his Fight Trust from San Francisco; there was Hugh D. "Huge Deal" McIntosh of Sydney, who had promoted Johnson-Burns; there was Eddie Graney, premier referee with promotional aspirations; there was Uncle Tom McCarey of Los Angeles; and, of course, there was George Lewis "Tex" Rickard.

Believing that whoever had the champion had the fight, Rickard made his way to Pittsburgh to catch up with Johnson. There he found the champion, whose big spending had left him broke, taking his turn on the vaudeville circuit, skipping rope, punching the bag, regaling the audience with stories, and playing a bull fiddle. When Rickard aproached him backstage, Johnson greeted him with "This is the situation, Mr. Tex. No matter what the papers say about the big money for the fight, nothin' is set. Now, what would be helpful to me is about twenty-five hundred to settle up some bills and damn all." Seeing his opening, Rickard reached into his greatcoat and peeled two thousand-dollar bills and a five hundred from his roll and handed them to the wide-eyed champion, whose face broke into the golden smile London had referred to. There was no signature, no handshake. But from that moment on Rickard had the champion—and the fight.

With his roll of bills in one pocket and Johnson in the other, Rickard proceeded to Hoboken, New Jersey. Because the state of New York threatened to arrest anyone who talked or "conspired" to fight anywhere within its jurisdiction, the auction for the rights to the fight was scheduled to take place at Meyer's Hotel in Hoboken. Rickard believed $100,000 would secure the rights. He was prepared to see that and, in gamblers' jargon, raise it one.

More than twenty-five promoters, participants, press, and predatory hangers-on crowded into the room at Meyer's, sipping the free champagne provided them. Sealed envelopes with bids quickly made their way to the head table. Eddie Graney offered a guarantee of $70,000 plus all film rights; Fat Jack Gleason, speaking for the San Francisco Fight Trust, offered a Chinese menu of choices, either $125,000 with no film rights or $75,000 plus two-thirds of the film rights; the Australian, Hugh McIntosh, offered $55,000 for the fight if it was staged in America or $100,000 and a fourth of the film rights if held in Australia; and Uncle Tom McCarey offered "on behalf of the Pacific Club of Los Angeles" the entire gate receipts and fifty percent of the movie rights or a guarantee of $100,000 with fifty percent of the film rights.

Finally it was Rickard's turn. Like a good poker player, he had patiently waited. Now he came forward and dropped a bulky envelope on the table, cautioning the stakeholder to "Be careful with this one, it's got real money in it." When it was opened, the contents spilled out: fifteen $1,000 bills, a certified check for $5,000 more, and a piece of paper which read: "We offer the fighters the price guarantee of $101,000 with 66⅔ percent of the movie rights. The bout will be staged on July 4 in California, Nevada, or Utah. In addition to the $20,000 contained in the envelope, $20,000 will be deposited sixty days before the fight and an additional $50,000 forty-eight hours before the encounter." The reading of the offer was superfluous. Jack Johnson kept staring at the bills and asked permission to touch them. "Those checks may be all right," he said, "but they don't look so good to this baby as those bills with big numbers on them." Everyone had talked big money. Only Rickard had produced it. The Battle of the Century was his for $101,000— plus $10,000 bonuses for each fighter under the table.

In 1910 reform was on the move. State after state promulgated legislation forbidding drinking, prizefighting, and just about anything else that smacked of fun. Reform had seen to it that each state west of the Mississippi, with the exception of two, had legislation on its books banning prizefighting. The two exceptions were Nevada, which had passed legislation to allow the staging of the Corbett-Fitzsimmons fight in 1897, and California, which allowed "sparring exhibitions."

Now the reformers had a cause—Jack Johnson. White against black was unnatural, so the reasoning went. And this particular black was the most unnatural of all. Intimating that no white woman was safe in her own boudoir, intermingling choice words like "miscegenation" and "mongrelization," the reformers set upon California's Governor James J. Gillett to ban the fight with a steady staccato of letters, telegrams, and veiled threats.

Coupled with the invasion of their borders by the black champion was something equally pernicious—the rumor of a fixed fight. The betting crowd was convinced that the "fix was in." It had supposedly been arranged for Jeffries to win, with the black champion to take a "dive." As rumors of fix and the rumbles of the reformers reached his ears with an ever-increasing din, the governor saw political wisdom in throwing the fight scheduled for San Francisco out of his state. Less than a month before it was to take place, he puffed up his chest and poured out his greatest campaign rhetoric, proclaiming to the press: "If Tex Rickard is looking for a fight with me he will get a bigger one than he has advertised for the Fourth of July. We've had enough of prizefights and prizefight promoters. They've been breaking the law long enough and we'll have no more of it. When the fighters can lick the state of California, they can go ahead and lick each other. But not before."

If California didn't want him, his old home state of Nevada did. He received offers from Goldfield, Reno, and Ely. As he left San Francisco, the man whom the *San Francisco Examiner* held had "taken the hardest blow since boxing gloves were invented," could only look back and reflect on what-might-have-been. "I'm leaving $250,000 in cash behind, and at least a couple of hundred thousand more, and I'm damned glad to get away from here with my hide," he stated.

Rickard now proceeded to Nevada to hear the three towns make their presentations. Each of the delegations had brass bands out to meet Rickard when he disembarked at Reno station. Adjourning to the nearby Golden Hotel for the presentations, he emerged within the hour to announce his decision: "Boys, its gotta be Reno because more railroads junction here."

It wasn't the train service alone that influenced his thinking. Reno had promised to build a twenty-thousand-seat stadium to accommodate the fans who would turn out for the Battle of the Century.

With less than three weeks to go, Rickard had to convert more than $110,000 in advance orders into tickets for the fight in Reno—which ranged up to $50 ringside—and refund the monies of those who had originally made plans to go to San Francisco, but had since cancelled plans to attend. He also had to minister to the needs of his fighters, who both had their own peculiar problems.

With the bout no longer in California, Johnson sent word that he was no longer bound by the *sub-rosa* agreement to "go in the tank," an arrangement worked out between the advisors of the two combatants which guaranteed a 60–40 split of the purse to the winner rather than the 80–20 Jeffries wanted. Jeffries, on the other hand, was holding to the fine print in the articles of agreement which specifically called for the fight to be held in California. In point of fact, Jeffries was reluctant to return to Nevada because more than $25,000 in his unpaid markers were held by gamblers. Tex approached the operators as a member of the family. He appealed to their sportsmanship and settled Jeff's debts for fifty cents on the dollar.

Still, problems vaulted the Sierras and vexed Rickard. Rumors of a fix continued to grow in intensity. So did the reformers. The governor personally visited Rickard to set his mind at ease. "They can do whatever they please," he told Rickard. "Nevada state law provides for the licensing of fights, and you have more than complied with the requirements. I have nothing more to say on the matter." Then, as he was leaving, a nagging doubt caused him to wheel around. "The only thing I want is to have you tell me, man-to-man, that the fight's on the level. I know you, Tex, and your word's good enough for me." Rickard shot straight from the hip, "It will be the squarest fight ever pulled off," he promised.

With all bets and fixes off after the change of venue, Johnson wanted a neutral referee, one he could count on not to favor his white rival. In his mind's eye, there was only one, the man who had promised him in Pittsburgh that he'd see to it "that no one takes advantage of you"—Tex Rickard. Jeffries agreed. Rickard had wanted Sir Arthur Conan Doyle, creator of Sherlock Holmes, to referee. But Doyle had turned him down. Reluctantly, he now took on yet another chore.

For the moment, he was concentrating his efforts on more pressing matters. One was the completion of the twenty-thousand-seat arena in the two weeks left to him. Another was the recurrent theme in all Rickard promotions: the accommodation of women in what formerly had been a man's sport. Announcing "We are going to make it possible for women—good women—to see the fight," he oversaw the construction of a number of curtained boxes, removed from the public view, each with its own private entrance where "good women" and their duennas could witness the fight, much like Spanish ladies at the theater in days of old.

Prefight entertainment has long been a staple of boxing. Now, in the only major bout in modern ring history without preliminaries, Rickard introduced yet another promotional prefight stunt: the introduction of great former champions before the fight. It was the first time boxing had honored, rather than eaten, its venerable old warriors and it added to the overall gala atmosphere of the occasion. Brought to Reno, all expenses paid, they would all be there to be seen: John L. Sullivan, Jim Corbett, Tom Sharkey, Joe Choynski, as well as many current greats, like Stanley Ketchel. It was boxing smorgasbord. And the beginning of a long-standing tradition.

Everyone who was anyone descended on Reno that Independence Day in 1910: writers, miners, land and cattle barons, swells and sports, pickpockets, society ladies and ladies of the street, promoters, thieves, millionaires, boxers, beggars, butchers, bakers, and Indian chiefs. It was a clan meeting of the great, near-great, and not-so-great. And all came bearing Jeffries money. How could The Boilermaker, the man who had entered the ring twenty-three times and never lost, lose to a black man? The odds climbed to two-and-a-half to one, with no Johnson money to be found anywhere.

A hopeful crowd of 15,760 crowded into the stadium, chanting "Jeff, It's Up to You." This would be their day, the white man's day, in the Armageddon between the forces of good and evil. In those innocent days before World War I, the outcome was foreordained. It was as simple as black and white.

But as a gleeful Johnson strode into the ring, a haggard and seemingly unnerved Jeffries slowly moved up the aisle. Some at ringside sensed that the hoped-for miracle might not take place. Maybe some of the fighters who had been criticizing Jeffries' training methods had been right. Maybe their prejudice and emotionalism had blinded them to the fact that the once-great symbol of white supremacy had been robbed of his skills by the enforced loss of seventy pounds and a six-year absence. Still, he was the invincible Jeff. Or so the miracle workers hoped.

As the scheduled 45-round bout began, all of their misgivings took form. The huge black man played with the thirty-five-year-old former champion and mouth-fought with those in his corner. For fourteen rounds Johnson muffled everything Jeffries threw, playing pattycake with him. He picked off every blow and drew the frustrated white champion-turned-challenger into clinches, all the while taunting him with "Now stop lovin' me like that, Mr. Jeff" and "How do you like this jab, Mr. Jeff?"

In the fifteenth round Johnson did the unthinkable. Springing at the shambling form in front of him, the panther-like Johnson sent Jeffries reeling to the ropes with a quick series of blows. Then he drove the dazed hulk in front of him to the canvas with a series of short, snappy punches to the head. For the first time in his career, Jeffries was down. He staggered to his feet only to be hit by two more jolts to the jaw and knocked down again. As the obviously beaten Jeffries fell to his knees, the crowd screamed "Stop it! Stop it! Don't let him be knocked out!" hoping to save themselves and the Caucasian race the embarrassment of having their standard-bearer so evidently disposed of. But Rickard waved the two fighters together again, oblivious of the pleadings of the stricken crowd. As Johnson landed unanswered blow after unanswered blow on Jeffries' vulnerable Nordic jaw, he sank to the canvas for yet a third time, one arm wearily hanging over the middle strand of rope. One of Jeffries' cornermen started climbing into the ring. Without finishing his count, Rickard walked over to Johnson and placed his hand on the champion's shoulder. The black man had won. The crusade had failed.

Rickard, who had grossed $270,715 from the Battle of the Century—far below his original expectations of a half-million gate in the thirty-thousand-seat bowl he had originally constructed in San Francisco—was now hailed as the King of the Sport Promoters. Tex, who never kept books and never knew until he had tabulated the gate receipts how he fared, never disclosed his profit. Johnson collected $120,000—$70,000 from Rickard—and Jeffries retired back to his alfalfa farm with $117,000—$50,000 of it Rickard's.

But Rickard's promotional victory was bittersweet in the face of his idol Jeffries' downfall. He swore he would never again promote a fight between a black man and a white man.

Bulging as they were that first weekend in July with people, motorcars, and excitement, the streets of Reno also sported another addition which made it different from any other town that weekend. For that matter, different from any other fight town before the Johnson-Jeffries fight—a portent of things to come. For festooned over downtown Reno, its hotels, and even the training sites were large banners, proclaiming proudly "James E. Pepper Whiskey/Born with the Republic."

It was the beginning of a natural tie-in between boxing and business; the start of a love affair that would see many strange things done in its name. Once the commercial camel had stuck its nose into the boxing ring, it appeared everywhere—ring posts, robes, trunks. Nino Benevenuti climbed into Roman rings wearing a robe sporting an ad for Desportive, a local laxative. Ring posts throughout Europe have been emblazoned with the name Cinzano. It was almost as if the time reference had been reversed, and the movie *Rocky* with Sylvester Stallone walking down the aisle with a robe displaying the colors and the name Shamrock Meats had come first and these were takeoffs on that cinematic spoof.

This not-so-subtle association between big business and big bouts finally reached its natural—as well as its unnatural—consummation with the trunks worn by Joe Frazier during his ill-fated title defense against George Foreman. The commercial chain of events started with a British promoter who went by the uncharacteristically meek name of David Maybe. Maybe made his money selling advertising on everything from the sides of sheep for Highland Springs Scotch to the back walls of zoo cages for Kodak, so that all snapshots of animals carried an ad for film. Now Maybe approached the camps of both participants with an offer to wear trunks emblazoned with his clients' logos. Yank Durham, Frazier's manager, was receptive for a price—$2,000 in cash. Foreman's business manager, Le Roy Jackson, was also receptive, but held out for more, suggesting he could do better elsewhere.

Promoter Hank Schwartz of Video Techniques was in Jamaica with his wife, Claire, who had a dream the night before the fight which forewarned that a fighter in white trunks would go to the canvas six times. Schwartz ridiculed her noctural premonition, having already seen the trunks of each participant: green for Frazier and red for Foreman. But unbeknownst to Schwartz, Maybe had handed Durham the pair of promotional trunks just minutes before Frazier stepped in the ring. They were white with a stylized black "W" for Woolco. And that night they went to the canvas six times, together with Frazier, as both Claire Schwartz's and David Maybe's dream came true.

After the Johnson-Jeffries bout, Tex Rickard had a fling at raising cattle in Paraguay. In his absence, much had changed. Jack Johnson—the high-flying black who flouted the rules and respectabilities of the white establishment with fast-paced racing cars, shocking marriages to three white women, and ownership of the free-wheeling café de Champion which served all comers and none of society's mores—had been brought to earth by his own personal profligacies and the passage of the Mann, or White Slavery, Act. Defending his championship just one more time in the United States, Johnson was harassed into fleeing the country and spent the next three years wandering Europe and its prize rings. Finally enticed back to the Western Hemisphere to defend his crown, he lost it in April 1915, to a Kansan by the name of Jess Willard.

Willard was a 6-foot 6-inch hulk of a man who had emerged from a grizzled ancestry of miners, cowpokes, gandy dancers, oil men, lumberjacks, and plowboys to lay claim to the ersatz title of Great White Hope, a distinction given to any fighter of more than 175 pounds and the right complexion. Nicknamed The Pottawatomie Giant, the cowboy-turned-fighter had established a respectable record in the ring and an aura of invincibility outside it, having killed another of the White Hopes, Bull Young, with one punch. Matched with an out-of-shape and mentally weary 37-year-old Johnson in Havana in 1915, Willard wore him down in the Havana sun. In the longest heavyweight championship fight in Queensberry history, Willard knocked him out in the twenty-sixth round, a result Johnson later was to merchandise to any magazine that would pay him as having been "thrown."

With the title safely ensconced under his enormous arm, Willard hit the obligatory vaudeville circuit, and then extended his triumphant tour by joining a Wild West show. With the crown all but invisible, boxing fans—particularly those in the East who had not seen a heavyweight championship fight since 1900—began clamoring for a championship bout. Jack Curley, who had promoted the Havana Johnson-Willard fight in tandem with Harry Frazee and had taken a financial bath, had an option on Willard's services through February, 1916. But February came and went. And with it Curley's option.

Promoters everywhere started bidding for services of the new heavyweight champion against one of a trio of contenders: Fred Fulton, an awkward, 6-foot 4½-inch former plasterer from Minneapolis who had boxed an exhibition against Willard two years before; Jack Dillon, a 5-foot 7-inch battler who weighed but 158 pounds and regularly fought middleweights—but had knocked out enough heavier men to be known as Jack the Giant Killer; and Frank Moran, a red-headed ex-sailor who lived the life of a playboy, regularly squiring around such leading ladies as Pearl White of *Perils of Pauline* fame. Of the three, Willard immediately dismissed Dillon and then opted for Moran, who had lost to Johnson in Paris two years before. Willard also opted for an offer made by former cattle rancher Tex Rickard to pay a guaranteed $60,000 for the fight—two-thirds to the champion, one-third to the challenger.

Now that Rickard had the fight, he needed a site. Rickard had long harbored a desire to stage a fight in New York's famed

Madison Square Garden. Then as now the doyen of all indoor arenas, the "old") Garden stood proudly at Madison Avenue between 25th and 26th Streets.

Madison Square Garden is at once a building and a symbol. But it had not always been thus. Originally a New York, New Haven & Hartford Railroad freight yard and depot, the structure had been converted in 1874 by none other than P. T. Barnum into a magnificent hall that measured 425 feet by 200 feet with an elliptical arena some 270 feet long in the center surrounded by a tier of seats. On April 27, 1874, Barnum opened for public display his new and grandiose Great Roman Hippodrome or, in Barnum's grandiloquent manner of puffery, Barnum's Monster Classical and Geological Hippodrome.

That first night the fifteen thousand curiosity seekers who crammed into the Hippodrome were treated to a veritable Circus Maximus: Arabian horses, waltzing elephants, cowboys and Indians, tattooed men, chariots driven by women drivers, fire-eaters, and just about everything else imaginable.

But then winter came and Barnum went, finding the former depot building too drafty for his menagerie. And so, Commodore Cornelius Vanderbilt, owner of the railroad, auctioned off the building to a new leaseholder, Patrick Gilmore, the popular bandmaster, who promptly redubbed it Gilmore's Gardens.

When Gilmore's lease expired in 1878, the Commodore's son William reclaimed the former railroad property and began staging social entertainment that appealed to the glittering crowds of society—horse shows, dog shows, and even one entitled the First Annual Show of Horses, Ponies, Mules and Donkeys. And with the new bill of fare came a new name: Madison Square Garden.

But on those nights when society wasn't turned out, the Garden wasn't turned on. And in 1889, Vanderbilt decided to raze what *Harper's Weekly* called "the patched-up, grimy, drafty, combustible old shell" and construct "a palace of pleasure" in its place.

Putting together a syndicate of Ward McAllister's fabled Four Hundred—including John Pierpont Morgan, Hiram Hitchcock, and William F. Wharton—Vanderbilt raised $1,500,000 to replace the razed building. To design the magnificent amphitheater of his dreams, Vanderbilt commissioned noted architect Stanford White, paying $75,000 for the design of the building and another $450,000 for the design of a majestic 300-foot tower, complete with a revolving statue of a nude Diana.

White designed an awe-inspiring edifice by any standards, but especially those of the 1890s: 200 feet by 465 feet with an exterior of white Pompeian terra-cotta and yellow brick, complete with the largest auditorium then in existence, with accommodations for 8,000 seats and floor space for several thousands more; a 1,200-seat theater; a 1,500-seat concert hall; a roof-garden; and a restaurant. Surely, this was the "pleasure palace" Vanderbilt had in mind.

And when the complex opened its doors on June 16, 1890, with Eduard Strauss of Vienna conducting a concert and two ballets before a well turned-out crowd of seventeen thousand of society's finest, who had paid up to fifty dollars for the inaugural event, not only Vanderbilt, but all of New York knew that Madison Square Garden had, according to the *New York Times*, "one of the great institutions of the town, to be mentioned along with Central Park and the bridge of Brooklyn."

But almost as quickly as Madison Square Garden had gone up, the white terra-cotta building became a white elephant. And a white elephant with a past, at that. For in 1906, the architect who had designed the building, Stanford White, was shot and killed in its rooftop aerie by the demented Harry K. Thaw in the most sensational murder of the early twentieth century. But that was the most attention the Garden got and, as the sensation subsided, so too did much of the business inside White's creation.

Finally, after twenty years of underwriting their "pleasure palace," the directors of the syndicate tired of their folly and decided to divest themselves of their expensive playtoy. Purchased in 1911 by a realty firm for a price that fell far short of the asked-for $3,500,000, they too soon found that the Garden couldn't support even the payments of the scaled down purchase price. When the real estate corporation declared bankruptcy in 1916, the Garden reverted to the mortgagee, the New York Life Insurance Company, which had plans to tear it down to make way for a skyscraper.

But regardless of its financial footing, Tex Rickard now sought to gain his own foothold in what had become known not only as New York's, but the world's, most famous arena.

In spite of the fact that New York allowed only no-decision fights in those days, Rickard felt the Garden offered important peripheral perks: it was the most prestigious arena in the United States and, situated in the midst of the crowd Rickard most coveted, it offered that touch of class provided by millionaires and society people who frequented the "pleasure palace."

But to get the Garden, Rickard had to deal with Jimmy Johnston, the man who held the boxing rights. The going rate for one-night stands was anywhere between $1,000 and $1,500, but the man known as The Boy Bandit, for obvious reasons, lived up to his name by demanding—and getting—25 percent of the receipts, although he had leased the building for only $1,000. This amounted to $15,000 in rent plus another $400 for the use of the concessions.

The fight itself, held on the night of Saturday, March 25, 1916, was noteworthy only from the standpoint that it afforded Rickard a showcase in New York. It went the full ten rounds to a "no decision" with only one punch of any consequence, a vicious left to the head by Willard in the seventh round. Moran's vaunted Mary Ann haymaker was strangely quiescent and so was a packed house which anted up $152,000, the largest indoor gate in boxing history. Despite Johnston's pound of flesh, Rickard cleared more than $42,000 and, more importantly, had first call on Willard's services for his next title defense.

At the time Willard disposed of Moran there were no other bona-fide challengers on the horizon. But just below the horizon and rising like the morning sun was a man named William Harrison Dempsey. Together, Dempsey and Rickard would combine to give color to the Twenties as The Golden Age of Sports, making the million-dollar gate a common occurrence.

Dempsey—originally fighting under the name Kid Blackie, in testimony to his penetratingly dark features, and then under the adoptive name of Jack, taken from the former middleweight "Nonpareil" Jack Dempsey—had blazed a path across the West with a string of one-round knockouts. Fighting out of a bobbing crouch that would become legendary, he approached every bout as a war. From his very first fight, against One-Punch Hancock in Salt Lake City in 1915, whom he prophetically dispatched with his first left hook following a feint, through his first four years of boxing, Dempsey had scored more first-round knockouts than any fighter in history—26. Only once had the favor been returned, when the semi-starved slugger had been taken out in the first round by Fireman Jim Flynn.

The boy-man who once had ridden the rails and lived in the hobo camps of the West now had a future and a manager, Jack "Doc" Kearns. Dempsey and Kearns emerged on the scene in 1918 to challenge the giant Willard, who had gone underground after his defense against Moran, surfacing only three times in two years for exhibitions.

Together they had stepped over the prone bodies of up-and-coming—as well as down-and-going—heavyweights up the ladder to the heavyweight title, while Kearns invested the pronoun "I" with imperial importance, inserting himself into every situation, as in "I knocked out Gunboat Smith in two rounds." Carl Morris went in four rounds, six rounds, and then in 14 seconds; Fireman Jim Flynn was returned the favor in kind in one round; Bill Brennan was disposed of in six; Fred Fulton was dispatched in 23 or 18 seconds depending upon which paper you read; Battling Levinsky went in three; and so on. Now there remained only one challenger, and Doc Kearns had him.

Kearns had long harbored a grudge against Rickard for supposedly "stealing" a promising fighter from him, middleweight Les Darcy of Australia. Even though the man he contemptuously called Rube had merely one-upped him, Kearns waited for an opportunity to get his harpoon into Rickard. Now the chance had come.

Rickard had signed the champion to defend his crown for a guaranteed $100,000 against any warm body the promoter produced. There was none warmer than Dempsey. Rickard knew it. Kearns knew it. And both knew each other knew it. But Kearns played his hand carefully, making noises to the effect that his tiger would fight for nothing, or expense money, or even $15,000. Just get "me" Willard! So without bothering to reduce Kearns' pleas and "please" to writing, Rickard announced the match. The next day Kearns sprung the trap: "Okay, sucker, now you can pay me $50,000." When Rickard threatened to renounce the match, Kearns threw in another zinger: "You ain't gonna go back on your word now, are you?" "Why not?" demanded Rickard. "Cause, I never prance around posing like some honest John," retorted the pint-sized wheeler-dealer, who knew he had hit Tex in a very vulnerable spot—his carefully built reputation for honesty. The matter went to arbitration and although a group of newsmen ultimately decided on a guarantee of $27,500 for the challenger, both men thereafter were to swear less by each other than at each other.

The fight was set for July 4, 1919. The site was set for Toledo, Ohio. Toledo had been selected because it not only was "near the center of population," one of Rickard's underlying principles of promotion, but also because Ohio Governor James M. Cox guaranteed that, in the absence of any adverse boxing laws on the books of the Buckeye State, the fight would take place as promised.

The Dempsey-Willard bout generated more interest than any fight since Rickard's previous outdoor promotion, the Jeffries-Johnson match, nine years before to the day. Buoyed by the postwar economy and the close proximity of Toledo to the major population centers of the East and Midwest, all linked to Toledo by the network of railroads that honeycombed the area, Rickard foresaw a million-dollar gate. To house the expected throng, he commissioned what one reporter called "the most remarkable structure of wood ever erected for a sporting event," an eighty-thousand-seat stadium, with additional room for another twenty thousand standees. The giant stadium, which made the Reno bowl look like a teacup by comparison, was built from more than one and three-quarter million feet of lumber at a cost of $100,000. It stood proudly just outside the city limits on the shores of Maumee Bay.

The million-dollar gate never materialized. The railroads, which had been "Hooverized" during the war, had not yet been returned to private hands, and accommodations, especially Pull-mans, were in short supply. Those who made it to Toledo were gouged by local merchants. For thousands of others, there was literally no room at the inn. Coupled with these problems was the statement released by Rickard's press agent that "seats were going fast," an old carney come-on that backfired and kept many hopefuls away.

As the day of the fight approached, everything was in a constant state of confusion. Most particularly the concessions. Rickard had sold these profitable ancillary sidelines to "Professor" Billy McCarney, who, in turn, farmed out peanuts, opera glasses, cigarettes, candy, cushions, chewing gum, and condiments to willing sub-concessionaires. Through some oversight, he assigned the lemonade franchise to two different subcontractors. When they confronted him, he bulled through the obvious double sale by saying: "Look, I sold you the *pink* lemonade concession, and I distinctly remember telling you that you were buying the rights to the *yellow* lemonade."

Battling Nelson arrived, complete with ghostwriter, to cover the fight for the *Chicago Daily News*. Seeking respite from the 100 degree heat, he took a running dive in his underwear into a mirage that resembled a swimming pool. Unfortunately Nelson, in his overheated state of mind, had mistaken the pink lemonade tank for the swimming pool of his dreams. Upon hearing about Nelson's "tank job," Rickard paid the pink lemonade concessionaire to dump the contaminated contents of his vat into Maumee Bay. But the concessionaire, already the subject of a double cross, pulled one himself and doled out the pink *eau de* Battling Nelson, making a double profit on his concession.

He was one of the few who did make a profit, as the ice cream vendor's stock melted, the sandwich concessionaire's inventory fell apart, and the peanut purveyor's possessions were worthless in the heat, which soared to 112 degrees on the day of the fight.

With the thermometer at the breaking point, so were Rickard's nerves. His whole future depended on the show's success. He found Dempsey alone in his dressing room, minutes before he was to depart for the ring. Pushing his straw hat back on his head and puzzling about how to begin, he dove in with "Jack, this Willard's a big and tough fighter. He just might kill you. Remember what he did with a single punch of his to Bull Young." Dempsey broke into Rickard's soliloquy to say, "I know he did, Tex." Encouraged that Dempsey was paying attention, Tex took another puff on his two-dollar cigar and hurried on, "Take my advice. If he hits you a good shot and hurts you, go down and stay down before he kills you. I don't want you killed." Wishing Dempsey good luck, he turned and walked quickly out of the room.

After a steady procession of preliminaries a half-hour apart, blimps and biplanes flying overhead and a bayonet and dagger fighting exhibition, the two fighters came down the aisles more than thirty minutes late.

Standing opposite each other to get the referee's instructions, the fighters' height differential was exaggerated. Willard looked even larger than his 6 feet 6 inches and 245 pounds because of his obvious flab and Dempsey looked smaller than his 6 feet 1 inch, 180 pounds, because of his tanned, intense look, magnified by a two-day growth of beard. Then, the bell and the fight started. With the first punch, Dempsey's right to the heart, followed by a devasting left hook to the jaw, the fight was all but over. As Willard fell for the first time, his jaw had been broken. He staggered upright to face Dempsey, who stood above him like an avenging angel, ignoring all niceties. Dempsey dropped him again. Again he struggled upright and again Dempsey floored him. This was repeated again and again, with metronomic repetition, until finally the giant fell for the seventh and last time in the round, sitting in the corner like he was relaxing after a swim, his arms extended along the lower strands of rope supporting his huge body, which heaved and shook. The referee's arm swung down in rhythmic motion as those in the crowd who could—many were pinioned to their seats by the oozing green sap of the wood—stood and roared. It was all over! Willard's jaw had been broken in seven places and Kearns, who had wagered $10,000 to $100,000 that Dempsey would add yet another one-round knockout to his record, danced around the ring, hugging his warrior. Dempsey put on his sweater and made his way down the aisle, while all was confusion in the ring.

But unbelievably the fight was *not* over! The bell had rung while Willard was reposing in the corner, the turnbuckle as his backrest, the count unfinished. Willard was dragged back to his corner—his jaw broken, four teeth missing, his eyes closed, his nose smashed, and two ribs cracked—to do battle again. And Dempsey had now to fight his way back up the aisle to take his place in the corner for another round. But it was only a matter of time now, and when, after the third round, Willard sat on his stool unable to continue and sobbed "I have a farm in Kansas and $100,000 . . . I have a farm in Kansas and $100,000 . . . I have a farm . . . ," it became official. Jack Dempsey was the new heavyweight champion.

Although the fight did not fail to meet expectations, the attendance and gate did. The hoped-for million-dollar gate fell far short, with less than twenty thousand in the stadium that Tex built. Even with the $60 ringside seats, the gross receipts amounted to under one-half million, $496,310. With expenses of more than $310,000 and another $76,680 for federal and state taxes, and yet another 7 percent of gross receipts going to the Toledo Charity Fund, plus the necessary gratuities to the local politicians, Rickard emerged with little to show for his efforts. Still, Tex Rickard now stood on the threshold of becoming the greatest promoter in the greatest era sports has ever seen.

What had been called The Manly Art of Self Defense in simpler times now became known as The Manly Art of Modified Murder in the hands of zestful and imaginative sportswriters, as the world and the sport both turned the corner into that sensational era known as The Roaring Twenties.

In the first year of that zany decade, two events took place which propelled boxing to the forefront of the sports pages and the nation's consciousness. The first was the acquisition of a ten-year lease on Madison Square Garden by Tex Rickard.

Rickard now envisioned a great postwar revitalization of interest in all sports, and boxing in particular. Wanting to exploit that revival, Rickard had been like the inventor of a universal solvent who had nothing to keep his potential product in. That was until now. With the backing of John Ringling North, who desperately needed a New York hindquarters and a headquarters for his traveling circus, Rickard negotiated a ten-year lease for the Garden at $350,000 a year, saving the landmark from the wrecker's ball.

The second event to shape the future of boxing was the passage of the Walker Act and the establishment of a boxing commission. When the New York State Boxing Commission first assumed its duties on September 1, 1920, the first license issued was to Madison Square Garden Sporting Club. Then it issued licenses to nine boxers: Jack Dempsey, Andy Chaney, Tommy Noble, Pete Hartley, Sammy Nable, Robert Hansen, Joe Welling, Joe Benjamin, and Johnny Dundee. Sixteen days later eight of those nine licenses were put to use in the first legal fight card in New York under the new law. The Rickard Era had started.

Eleven days before Rickard's first Garden card, the man who would become his meal ticket, Jack Dempsey, had defended his title for the first time. It was the first of only two times Dempsey would fight for someone else than Rickard. He fought what was in essence a benefit for his opponent Billy Miske, who suffered from Bright's Disease. The fight drew a gate of $134,904 in little Benton Harbor, Michigan. Dempsey quickly dispatched the seriously ill Miske, knocking him out in the third round. Miske received $25,000 for his troubles; the champion $55,000.

On December 14, Rickard finally got Dempsey into a New York ring to fight Bill Brennan for the championship. A capacity crowd of fifteen thousand paid $162,760 for the privilege of witnessing the first heavyweight title bout to a decision in New York since Jeffries fought Corbett twenty years before. Dempsey received a guarantee of $100,000 and the surprise of his life. For eleven rounds, the champion was outpunched and outpointed. Then, in the twelfth, his head cleared, Dempsey caught up with the elusive challenger, and knocked him out. But the disappointing showing by the supposed maneater was to set the stage for Rickard's biggest conquest.

Although postwar America was hell-bent on pleasure-seeking, it still prided itself on its patriotic efforts in the recent conflict. It was the stated belief of many that the war had "knit us together," and an aroused America demanded conformity from its citizens. More than six thousand persons were arrested for criticizing the government, the Constitution, and the flag. Americans paraded with signs identifying themselves as "100 percent patriots," and super-Americanism was in vogue. One thing that could not be tolerated by a proud and victorious America was anyone who had not "pulled his weight" during the war effort.

In February, 1920, Jack Dempsey was indicted by a federal

grand jury in San Francisco for draft evasion. He stood accused of violation of the Selective Service Act and making false statements to the district draft board in San Francisco. His first wife, Maxine Cates—a self-confessed "lady of loose morals"—initially testified against him. When she recanted, the jury brought in a verdict dismissing the charge. Nevertheless, the taint remained. Jack Dempsey had been a "slacker."

The charge and the resultant stigma together with Dempsey's lackluster defense of his crown against Brennan provided Rickard with a matchmaker's dream and the opportunity to attain his goal of a million-dollar gate.

Rickard's announced philosophy was "Give the people what they want, the way they want it, and not the way you think best." Now he was prepared to give them what they wanted: a fight between Georges Carpentier and Jack Dempsey. Few professional judges of fighters agreed that it would be the best, but Rickard wasn't counting on them to buy many tickets.

At that moment in time, the light-heavyweight champion and one of the leading boxers in the world was a handsome French war hero named "Gorgeous" Georges Carpentier. Carpentier had been a professional boxer for fourteen years, fighting in every division from bantamweight up as he matured. He had won all his six postwar fights by knockouts and had captured the light-heavyweight crown by knocking out Battling Levinsky in four rounds in October 1920. But what made Carpentier a "natural" opponent for Dempsey was not his ring record but his war record. While Dempsey was labeled a "slacker," Carpentier was a bona fide hero, having spent eighteen months at the front flying a two-seater observation plane. He had been wounded twice and received the Croix de Guerre and Médaille Militaire. Rickard saw the fight not as an overgrown middleweight challenging for the heavyweight title but as a "hero" against a "villain." It was a classic matchup. A draw with a potential million-dollar gate.

Rickard put together a loose-fitting international consortium with British theatrical impresario Charles B. Cochran, who had an option on Carpentier's services and the money for the bout as well. Associated with Cochran was his American representative, William A. Brady, who had formerly managed both Corbett and Jeffries and had been associated with Cochran in some of his across-the-sea theatrical productions.

Still Rickard was not prepared for the demands from the two participants. Doc Kearns demanded $300,000 and 25 percent of the film rights for the champion Dempsey. Carpentier, speaking through his French-speaking manager, François Descamps who, in turn, spoke through his interpreter, crafty Jack Curley, demanded $200,000 plus one-quarter of the movie rights. Together the two fighters were demanding more money than any fight had ever grossed.

Bluff and counterbluff followed, as each side played their hands for all they were worth. But Kearns' high-handed treatment of Cochran, Rickard, and Brady soon incited the wrath of the press. Kearns tried one more bluff, trotting out two waiters posing as "Cuban millionaires" to go through a ritualistic contract signing. It worked. The promoters gave in, hot on the scent of the elusive million-dollar gate.

The final articles of incorporation were signed November 5, 1920, fully one month before Dempsey stepped into the ring against Carpentier. Three days before, the country had had its first postwar election and, yearning to return to a nebulous state called Normalcy, it had swept out the Democrats. In the Harding landslide, New York State had elected Republican Nathan Miller governor. The new governor banned the Dempsey-Carpentier fight on the grounds that half a million dollars was too much to pay a pair of prizefighters for a few minutes work at a time when thousands of men were out of work. That was enough for Cochran and Brady. Feigning headaches like an unwilling wife, they retired from the scene, leaving Rickard alone.

Rickard decided to do what came naturally: gamble. Short of funds—but not friends—Rickard posted the $100,000 promoter's bond and officially announced that he had taken over all other interests. The money came from a ticket speculator named Mike Jacobs, who had organized the leading Broadway ticket brokers for the purchase of preferred seats. They provided Rickard with $160,000, a sufficient grubstake to carry out his promotional plans.

With the money—and bout—in hand, Rickard searched for a site for the match close to the New York area. He found one on a desolate lot near Jersey City owned by a paper box manufacturer named Boyle and contracted for a massive bowl which would house over ninety thousand. The press quickly named the site Boyle's Thirty Acres.

Rickard had the right "mix": a handsome war hero, the darling of society who had led a charmed life and was called The Orchid Man (the title of his movie then making the rounds) versus a forboding animalistic former hobo with a dark stubble of beard, who possessed no charm and had been labeled a "slacker" by a federal grand jury. It was a classic matchup for hero and villain and Rickard ballyhooed it for all it was worth. Plenty.

The excitement was contagious. The first truly international fight in more than a decade attracted global attention. David Sarnoff arranged with Rickard to broadcast the fight on radio, the first major sporting event ever to grace the airwaves. Society in general—and ladies in particular—were planning to attend, lending tone, glamor, and the all-important element of celebrity to the event. Newspapers from around the world were sending correspondents. What was in actuality a mismatch between a second-rate fighter and a first-rate heavyweight champion was transcending the level of mere sporting event; it was now an international event. Everything about the fight, even Carpentier's little poodle, Flip, was news. Weeks before the fight, Rickard was guaranteed his dream—a million-dollar gate.

On the afternoon of Saturday, July 2, 1921, eighty thousand fans crammed their "asses" into the rickety stadium just outside Jersey City, paying a still-record $1,789,238. Rickard was not only amazed at the success of the ballyhoo, but at the appearance of so many of society's finest. "Did you ever see so many millionaires?" the impressionable Rickard asked everyone within earshot, looking at the $50 ringside seats which contained more money per square foot than any event in the history of sports. And way out "there," somewhere east of Newark, the cheaper seats began to sway precariously under the excited movement of thousands of fans.

As the appointed time of 3:30 approached and the last two preliminary fighters—A.E.F. champion Gene Tunney and Soldier Jones—had left the ring, the sweatered Dempsey and the robed Carpentier began to make their way into the vast amphitheater. There they were greeted by the full-throated roars of the 80,000-plus spectators and the sounds of trumpets blaring forth *"La Marseillaise."* The far more popular Carpentier received the adulation of the crowd, while Dempsey merely got the ovation due a champion—commingled with more than a few shouts of "slacker."

A few prefight words from Rickard admonishing Dempsey not "to spoil it," and the fight was on. At the bell, the challenger, looking smaller than his announced 172 pounds, came out jabbing. The champion answered with a left hook to the body followed by a straight right to the nose. In the second, the challenger attacked and nailed Dempsey with a hard right high on the head. He pursued his advantage, driving Dempsey to the

Doubleheader

6:30 P.M.

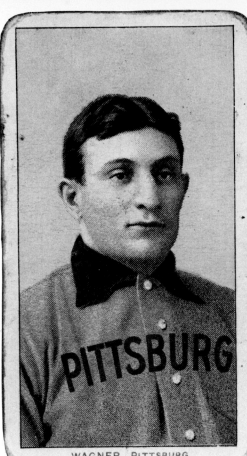

WAGNER, PITTSBURG

MAJOR LEAGUE BASEBALL
PITCH, HIT & RUN COMPETITION

NATIONAL RECREATION
AND PARK ASSOCIATION

Radio TV Reports

41 East 42nd Street New York N.Y. 10017

(212) 697-5100

PRODUCT: MILLER LITE BEER

PROGRAM: BASEBALL
WNBC—TV

6/26/76
(NEW YORK)

767822
30 SEC.
2:43 PM

1. MARV THRONEBERRY: You know it used to take forty three Marv Throneberry baseball cards to get one Carl Parelli.

2. So I was surprised when the Lite Beer people called me to do this commercial.

3. I mean, I do drink Lite Beer.

4. And it tastes great.

5. It's got a third less calories than their regular beer. And it's less filling.

6. But you know I'm kinda worried.

7. Because if I do for Lite Beer what I did for baseball I'm afraid their sales might go down.

8. ANNCR: Lite Beer from Miller. Everything you always wanted in a beer and less.

ROY WHITE

Cohen's FAMOUS

Knishes

THE ORIGINAL "ROUND" KNISH

K

COHEN'S FAMOUS FROZEN FOODS, INC.
NEWARK, N. J. 07114

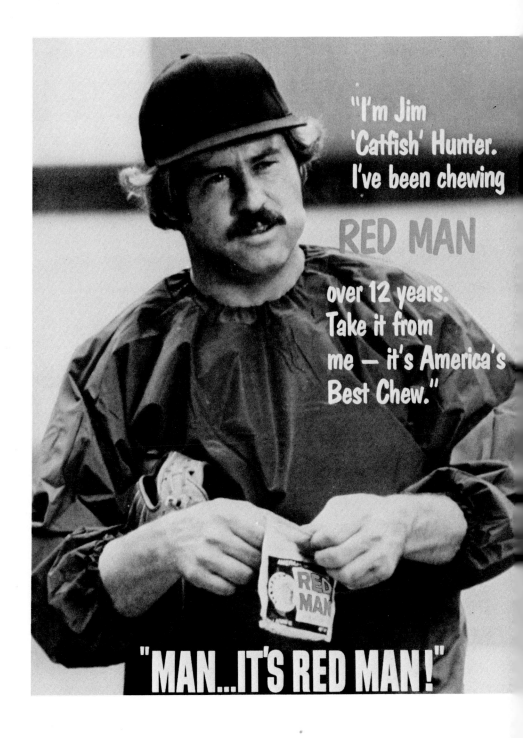

MR. PEANUT'S GUIDE TO TENNIS

FREE!
FROM
Brylcreem®

MICKEY MANTLE'S
W⚾RLD SERIES FACT B⚾⚾K

BUY A TUBE OF BRYLCREEM
and get Mickey's guide to the exciting
highlights of the World Series games
FREE inside every specially marked
tube of BRYLCREEM

ENTER NOW—FILL OUT AND MAIL

ENTER Brylcreem's
BASEBALL
SWEEPSTAKES
WIN ONE OF 3 GRAND PRIZES
SEASON BOX FOR 4
**FOR ALL THE HOME GAMES OF YOUR
MAJOR LEAGUE BASEBALL TEAM**

NO PURCHASE NECESSARY

SORRY

If this store is out of ENTRY FORMS,
send a self-addressed, stamped envelope to 1976 Brylcreem Baseball
Sweepstakes, P.O. Box 3488, Grand
Central Station, New York, New York
10017

What makes him the
basketball player's basketball player
makes us the
Scotch drinker's Scotch.

Black & White.
The Scotch drinker's Scotch.

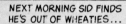

 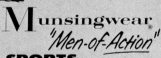

WHEATIES

now come to you

BETTER, CRISPER, FRESHER

More Delicious Than Ever!

- Solid nourishment for folks of all ages in these crisp, toasted whole wheat flakes. And now—because of improved packaging protection, Wheaties flakes come to you crisper, *fresher than ever before!*

- Wheaties, with milk and fruit, a famous training dish. Eaten and recommended by top-flight coaches and athletes. (Jackie Robinson, Bud Wilkinson, Sam Snead—many more!)

- 100% whole wheat flakes! Provide 3 B-Vitamins; also minerals, food energy, protein.

- Famous for flavor, Wheaties are the whole wheat flakes America likes best of all. *More families eat Wheaties than any other whole wheat cereal!*

- Had *your* Wheaties today?

General Mills

WHEATIES

Breakfast of Champions

General Mills

"*Breakfast of Champions*"

Jackie Robinson won National League's Most Valuable Player award last season. Dodger star also voted *Baseball Champion of the Year* by nationwide audience of "Jack Armstrong—All-American." And—he's a Wheaties man! "A lot of us ball players go for milk, fruit and Wheaties," says Robinson. "Nourishing and swell eating he year around."

"Wheaties" and "Breakfast of Champions" are registered trade marks of General Mills

"Merlyn made these pancakes <u>in seconds!</u>"

SAYS MICKEY MANTLE

"Just seconds—that's all it takes my wife Merlyn to make these man-sized pancakes," says Mickey Mantle. "Just take Batter-Up from the refrigerator . . . pour out on a sizzling hot griddle—*that's it!*

"And delicious! You get light golden-brown pancakes every time. Sure puts muscle on a man, too. Yes, making pancakes with Batter-Up is so easy, you'll want to serve your family pancakes *any time!"*

C&C ®

Batter Up

READY-TO-POUR

PANCAKE BATTER

Shake Vigorously

C&C

Batter Up

instant
PANCAKE BATTER

EXCLUSIVE LEVENING PROCESS

Keep Refrigerated C&C SUPER FOODS

MANUFACTURED BY C&C SUPER FOODS COR

"Ever shave with a blade of Golden Swedish Steel?

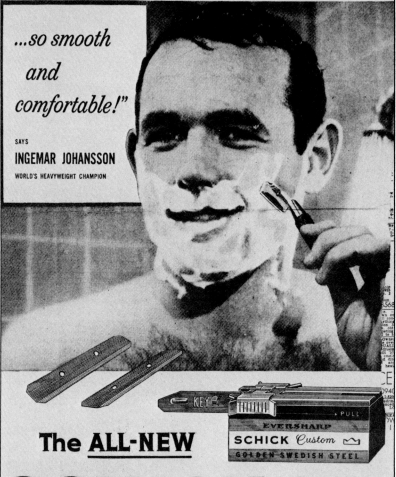

...so smooth and comfortable!"

SAYS

INGEMAR JOHANSSON

WORLD'S HEAVYWEIGHT CHAMPION

The ALL-NEW
SCHICK *Custom*
INJECTOR BLADE

Now, from steel-famous Sweden, comes golden Swedish steel, for new SCHICK Custom Injector Blades—world's smoothest shaving blades. This fine-quality Swedish steel takes and holds a keen, sharp edge—actually a thousand times thinner than a human hair! Here's a blade that even the toughest beard can't dull or slow down. For quality, luxury, performance... try the new SCHICK Custom Injector Blade—custom-honed for the smoothest, most effortless shaves of your life. Fits all Injector and Hydro-magic razors. Try one tomorrow morning.

20 INJECTOR BLADES... ONLY $1.29

SCHICK QUALITY AROUND THE WORLD. Factories in Holmstad, Sweden; Toronto, Canada; New York-Los Angeles, U. S. A.

PLUS

PUT USED BLADES HERE

HANDY COMPARTMENT FOR USED BLADES

MODERN SCHICK SAFETY RAZOR SHIELDS BLADE CORNERS SO THEY CAN'T NICK YOU. IT'S THE RAZOR SO SAFE YOU CAN SHAVE IN THE SHOWER

THIS

NOT THIS

For a treat instead
of a treatment ... I recommend
Old Gold Cigarettes.
Jackie Robinson

MADISON SQUARE GARDEN
49th and 50th Sts. and Eighth Ave., N. Y. C.
Friday Eve'g, AUGUST 4, 1944

MICHAEL S. JACOBS, Promoter

WAR BOND BOUT
SPONSORED BY
GILLETTE SAFETY RAZOR CO.
AND
WAR BOND SPORTS COMMITTEE

BOB MONTGOMERY
VS
BEAU JACK
10 ROUNDS

2

This ticket is issued without charge, admission
only by purchase of U. S. War Bonds, in
maturing denomination of

$100.00
MEZZANINE

SECTION	ROW	SEAT
219	E	8

MADISON SQUARE GARDEN
49th and 50th Sts. and Eighth Ave., N. Y. C.
Friday Eve'g, AUGUST 4, 1944

WAR BOND BOUT
MONTGOMERY vs JACK
MEZZANINE

SECTION	ROW	SEAT
219	E	8

TED'S
CREAMY
ROOT BEER
TED'S
Ted's
TED'S
Delicious
CREAMY
ROOT BEER

WHEATIES CHAMPIONS 1942

BOB FELLER, Baseball's greatest pitcher, now in the United States Navy.

for the tough days ahead!

WHEATIES

"Breakfast of Champions"

WITH MILK AND FRUIT

2 PKGS.

¢

Barry Halper

RED SOX READY TO DO BATTLE FOR WORLD'S CHAMPIONSHIP

(Above) "Nap" Lajoie and Ty Cobb in a Chalmers automobile.

(Below) Football players in the Universal film *All America:* (Line, left to right) Daly, Linehan, Baker, Yarr, Munn, Quatse, Orsi. (Backfield, left to right) Cagle, Nevers, Cain, Schwartz.

World's Championship Battle July 4, 1910
Round 2

(Below) The *Police Gazette* belt.

Belmont Park

The Marlboro Cup ®

Thoroughbred Race of the Year.
October 2, 1976

Official program, compliments of Marlboro.

(Top and bottom) A promotional foul-up: Virginia Squires toy giveaway (American Basketball Assn.)

1977 Gillette All-Star Balloting

TOP TEN VOTE GETTERS

Name	Position	Club	Total Votes
Rod Carew	1st Base	Minnesota Twins	4,292,740
Steve Garvey	1st Base	Los Angeles Dodgers	4,277,735
Carlton Fisk	Catcher	Boston Red Sox	3,476,028
Thurman Munson	Catcher	New York Yankees	3,362,177
Joe Morgan	2nd Base	Cincinnati Reds	3,309,754
Carl Yastrzemski	Outfield	Boston Red Sox	3,297,854
Johnny Bench	Catcher	Cincinnati Reds	3,262,680
Ron Cey	3rd Base	Los Angeles Dodgers	3,102,186
Dave Concepcion	Shortstop	Cincinnati Reds	3,098,750
George Brett	3rd Base	Kansas City Royals	3,058,453

DONOVAN of Detroit   CHANCE of Chicago   KLING of Chicago   WAGNER of Pittsburg   JENNINGS of Detroit

The men who uphold the standards of American sport today are clean men—clean of action and clean of face. Your baseball star takes thought of his personal appearance—it's a part of his team ethics. He starts the day with a clean shave—and, like all self-reliant men, he shaves himself.

Wagner, Jennings, Kling, Donovan, Chance—each of the headliners owns a Gillette Safety Razor *and uses it.* The Gillette is typical of the American spirit. It is used by capitalists, professional men, business men—by men of action all over this country—*three million of them.*

Its use starts habits of energy—of initiative. And men who *do* for themselves are men who *think* for themselves.

Be master of your own time. Buy a Gillette and use it.

You can shave with it the first time you try. The one perfectly *safe* razor and the only safety razor that shaves on the correct hollow ground shaving principle.

No stropping, no honing.

Send your name on a post card for our new Baseball book. Schedule of all League games batting records. 24 pages of interesting facts and figures. Every fan should have it. It is free.

King C Gillette

GILLETTE AND BASEBALL
A Marketing Combination Since 1910

The Gillette Company . . . Safety Razor Division
Gillette Park . . . Boston, Mass. 02106

ropes where he landed several more hard punches to the head of the obviously disturbed champion. As the bell sounded for the third round the real possibility existed that not only would Carpentier "make a fight of it," but that the championship might actually change hands. Dempsey decided he had had enough. Rickard and the crowd had gotten their money's worth. Now it was Carpentier's turn in the barrel. The 3-to-1 favorite landed punch after punch on the almost-defenseless Frenchman as he swayed in front of the oncoming champion in cadence with the swaying stands that rimmed the stadium. A full three minutes of pummeling closed one of the challenger's eyes and caused his body to turn lobster red. Only the bell staved off the inevitable as the wounded Frenchman barely made it back to his corner. At the bell signaling the fourth round, the now tiger-like Dempsey sprang from his corner. Two short lefts accompanied by a crushing right put the challenger down. He dragged himself up, barely beating the count, and was met by yet another flurry of punches. He went down again and curled up womb-like on the canvas. Major Andrew White screamed into his ringside microphone: "The Frenchman is down! . . . three . . . four . . . Carpentier makes no effort to rise . . . six . . . seven . . . he's lying there . . . nine, ten. . . . He's out. The fight is over! Jack Dempsey remains the heavyweight champion of the world."

Although one writer was to call it "an afternoon waltz," the Rickard flair for matchmaking and promotion had made boxing history. He was now indeed The King of Promoters.

There will never be another period for boxing like the twenties or another man like Tex Rickard. In the next eight years, the man called the Napoleon of Promoters continued to bring boxing to the fans, including four more million-dollar gates, all of which featured Dempsey. He built a new Madison Square Garden at 50th Street and Broadway, underwritten by "six hundred millionaires," where the new hockey team was named Rangers in his honor. And he contributed more to the sport of boxing than any other promoter—before or since.

But it wasn't the Garden or the many fights he promoted there that would secure his fame. It was Jack Dempsey. As promoter of all of Dempsey's championship fights—with the notable exceptions of the Miske fight in Benton Harbor and an ill-fated Tommy Gibbons match in Shelby, Montana, in 1923, where Kearns and Dempsey financially sacked that ambitious oil-rich burg—Rickard paid Dempsey more than $2,300,000 in purses. And, like any good promoter, he enjoyed his promotions; and his promotee. After Dempsey was beaten twice by Gene Tunney and the Dempsey era had passed, Rickard began to lose interest. The night of the Tunney-Tom Heeney fight in Yankee Stadium in 1928, a bout in which Rickard lost over half-a-million dollars, he said, "I had fun with Dempsey in the ring. With him out, this is just a business."

Rickard promoted only thirteen fights after the Tunney-Heeney fiasco. He died on January 6, 1929. But just before he cashed in his chips, this gambler-promoter began to count them and wrote his own epitaph—as well as that of promoters everywhere. Trying to assess his "worth" as a promoter, Rickard viewed the "millionaires" who had helped him finance the new Garden and wondered aloud: "How is it that I get all the publicity and those respectable, church-going business fellers end up with the profits?"

With the death of Rickard and the retirement of Dempsey and Tunney, boxing languished in a state of suspended animation. Every year or so some new warm body would appear from nowhere only to fall back into obscurity almost as fast. Between 1930 and 1935, the world was given a flea market of heavyweight champions: Max Schmeling, Jack Sharkey, Primo Carnera, Max Baer, and Jimmy Braddock, in chronological order, if not in order of distinction.

If the stature of the boxers suffered, so too did the sport. Nineteen thirty-three saw the country in the depths of the Depression. Not incidentally, it was the worst of all years for boxing as well. Attendance and gate receipts hit an all-time low and the heavyweight champion—Carnera—was a clown and a joke. If boxing had been a wake, it would have been an insult to the deceased. There was no place to go but up.

The man who maneuvered heavyweight titleholder Jack Sharkey into the ring for his date with destiny and Carnera was the same Jimmy Johnston who had held up Rickard seventeen years before when he wanted the Garden for the Willard-Moran fight. Johnston, whose promotional star had waned during Rickard's reign, now rose again to the exalted position of boxing promoter at Madison Square Garden.

Johnston vainly attempted to create chicken salad out of boxing's current crop of chicken droppings, even resuscitating the inert figure of "Phainting" Phil Scott. Perhaps his greatest coup was in giving shape to the heavyweight division. After Schmeling won Tunney's vacated title by resting on his elbow and crying "foul" at one of Sharkey's errant lefts, he refused to give Sharkey a rematch. Instead, he carried the crown home with him to Germany, defending it just once in two years. Meanwhile, Johnston, who had the ear of New York State Boxing Commissioner James A. Farley, was pressing for a showdown fight between Schmeling and Sharkey. He gained a decision from the commission vacating Schmeling's throne unless he gave Sharkey a rematch for the championship. Sharkey was under Johnston's control—insiders intimating that Johnston had dealt himself in for a 10 percent interest in Sharkey's purses before he became Garden promoter. Johnston got his fight and Sharkey got his championship on a fifteen-round disputed decision.

Now Johnston spun his magic again, steering his new champion into the ring to defend it against the Ambling Alp, Primo Carnera, who just as magically won the championship in the sixth round in what one reporter called "an unsatisfactory affair." Johnston had first call on Carnera's services and this set up an organized procession to the championship under the aegis of Jimmy Johnston and Madison Square Garden.

But even though the Garden and Johnston had a series of exclusive service contracts with the heavyweight champion and champions-to-be, the Garden continued to lose money on boxing. The thirty-two weekly bouts in Rickard's last year had drawn an average "house" of 13,224 fans and $51,807. Under Johnston those numbers shriveled to only nineteen shows in 1933, drawing an average of 9,687 fans and $16,095 per show.

Mrs. William Randolph Hearst's pet charity was The Free Milk Fund. Dedicated to providing "helpless infants" with the primary necessity of life, it was underwritten by Hearst's *New York American* and took its own fund-raising nourishment from an annual boxing bout. Starting with a 1922 match between Harry Greb and Tommy Gibbons—which drew $118,000, with $75,999 of the proceeds going to the Milk Fund—the annual fight benefited the charity by an estimated $1,500,000 over the next twelve years.

By 1933 even the "helpless infants" were caught in the crossfire of one of boxing's perennial wars. Johnston's glaring deficiencies as a promoter as well as his devious dealings with boxers came under the scrutiny of several newspaper columnists. But none were more savage than Bill Farnsworth and Damon Runyon of Hearst's *Journal-American*, the unofficial matchmakers for the Milk Fund boxing shows. Their attacks brought a swift reprisal, but not from Johnston. The counterattack came instead from Colonel John Reed Kilpatrick, the president of Madison Square Garden. He announced that the rental for the next Milk Fund boxing show would be increased.

Farnsworth and Runyon—joined in their crusade by sports editor Ed Frayne—not only wrote righteously that the Garden was depriving "helpless infants" of milk, but they sought out ticket broker Mike Jacobs to join them in promoting the next Milk Fund show. Together they formed the 20th Century Sporting Club.

And so, on January 24, 1934, Mike Jacobs, long a behind-the-scenes promoter, came out of the closet to promote the 13th annual Milk Fund fight, an over-the-weight match between lightweight champion Barney Ross and the Fargo Express, Billy Petrolle, at the old New York Coliseum in the Bronx. Fifteen thousand crowded into the Coliseum—another ten thousand were turned away—as Jacobs' 20th Century Sporting Club answered its first bell.

Better known as "Uncle Mike," Michael Strauss Jacobs was the son of an immigrant who hustled other immigrants right off the boat, procuring jobs for them for a fee. True to form, his son was a hustler in the best traditions of New York's West Side. He started on the piers, first selling newspapers, then souvenirs, and then graduating to the concessions on pleasure cruises. Known as Steamboat Mike, he parlayed one small concession into a fleet of seven boats running to and from two amusement parks he also owned. Jacobs got his customer coming and going.

But building a fleet of pleasure boats was not Jacobs' ticket into the boxing arena. As a hustling young man, he had supplemented his entrepreneurial education by working for David Belasco as office boy and shill. He would round up entire cheering sections to applaud and laugh enthusiastically in the right places, thus turning potential box office flops into Broadway hits.

From there it was just a short step to becoming a ticket broker, who scalped tickets for shows, sporting events, and just about anything else that came down the Great White Way. He met Tex Rickard just prior to the Dempsey-Carpentier fight in 1921 when Rickard was scrounging for backing. From that day on, Jacobs served as the behind-the-scenes consultant for Rickard, advising him on the salability of matches. On those few occasions when Rickard chose to ignore Uncle Mike's advice, such as staging the Tunney-Heeney fight on which he lost $500,000, he suffered for his failure to do so.

Now Jacobs and his new 20th Century Sporting Club moved

into the old Hippodrome Theatre. An entertainment palace that took up the entire block between 44th and 45th streets and Sixth and Seventh avenues, The Hipp was once called "the pride of New York City." And to anyone even remotely associated with show biz, it was! Built in 1905, for the then-heady cost of more than two million dollars, it was a brick, marble and steel edifice 72 feet high in front, rising to 110 feet in the rear. This magnificent old 5,200-seat structure, once host to such great acts as Annette Kellerman performing in a thirty-foot tank right on the stage and Harry Houdini making a ten thousand-pound elephant disappear, now was to be the "home" of the 20th Century Sporting Club with its own elephantine boxers performing their own "tank" exploits.

While in Miami promoting the Barney Ross-Frankie Klick junior welterweight title fight in January 1935, one of Jacobs' many contacts informed him of a black heavyweight fighting out of Detroit who deserved his attention. He immediately sent emissaries to Pittsburgh where the new phenom was to make his second start inside of a week. When they returned, they convinced Jacobs that the black heavyweight, known as Joe Louis, was all that he was cracked up to be—and more.

That was all Jacobs had to hear. Within a month he negotiated a contract which gave the 20th Century Sporting Club exclusive promotional rights for all future bouts involving the Brown Bomber. Mike Jacobs now had his ticket to the top of the heap, but this was one he wasn't going to scalp.

Jacobs took a press party of twenty-five New York newsmen out to Detroit to see Louis fight Natie Brown in March, 1935. Their glowing reports about this unbeatable phenomenon who had now won seventeen fights in a row, thirteen by knockouts, created public demand for a look-see at the new heavyweight hope. When Louis debuted in New York on June 25, 1935, against Primo Carnera, some 62,000 crowded into Yankee Stadium—paying more than $328,000—to see the Brown Bomber destroy the hulking ex-champion, hitting him so hard in the sixth round that he broke his ankle. With a house almost twice as large as that which had watched Braddock beat Baer in Madison Square Garden's Long Island Bowl just two weeks before, Jacobs realized he had found black gold in this man who spoke only with his fists—eloquently. After a side trip to Chicago's Comiskey Park, where Louis disposed of King Levinsky in one round before another 39,000 fans who contributed yet another $193,000 to 20th Century's overflowing coffers, Jacobs brought Louis back to New York to face Max Baer.

The ex-champion was many things: awesome puncher, cutup, playboy, and exciting fighter; an irresponsible whacko who trained on bleached blondes and beached bottles. But there was one thing Baer never had been—and that was knocked out. Now he faced a man who had knocked out his last seven opponents. He had KO'd twenty in twenty-four fights and his punch was being compared to Fitzsimmons', Jeffries', and Dempsey's. Could Baer stand up under the onslaughts of this seemingly superhuman slugger? A crowd of 88,150 jammed Yankee Stadium to see this new superman of boxing while thousands more were turned away, as Mike Jacobs entered into the inner circle of promoters with his first million-dollar gate, the sixth richest of all time; the other five tricks having been turned by Tex Rickard. In four rounds Louis answered all questions. After absorbing some of Louis' best shots, Baer sat down in the fourth round fully resigned to his fate and made no attempt to get up.

Jacobs did indeed have a Superman, one who could generate million-dollar gates for him just as Dempsey had for Rickard. And just as Dempsey had been the catalyst for five million-dollar gates—Carpentier, Firpo, Tunney I, Sharkey, and Tunney II—Louis would produce three for Jacobs: Baer, Schmeling II, and the second richest live gate of all time, Conn II.

But a funny thing happened to Louis on his path to the richest prize in all of sportsdom. He was beaten. On June 19, 1936, he met another of those former heavyweight champions he had been eating up and spitting out with regularity. This one, Max Schmeling, had "See'd something," a propensity by the young Brown Bomber to lower his left hand after he hooked. Schmeling proceeded to exploit the weakness he had "see'd" and caught Louis time and again on the left side of the jaw with an overhand right, sending him to the canvas in the fourth round and out altogether in the twelfth.

The defeat of the supposedly invincible Brown Bomber was the most stunning reversal since Corbett had beaten Sullivan almost a half-century before. But in a year and two days Joe Louis was to gain the heavyweight title and Mike Jacobs would be the top boxing promoter in the land.

Jacobs' year was consumed with Louis, his personal reclamation project. He brought him back just two months after the Schmeling debacle to face another former heavyweight champion, the enigmatic Jack Sharkey. Louis made quick work of Sharkey, leaving him both prone and with a special niche in the boxing trivia hall of fame—the only man to face both Dempsey and Louis and be knocked out by both. Louis then faced Eddie

Simms in Cleveland. With the bout eighteen seconds gone he pulled the trigger on a devastating left hook. Simms went down and rolled over. Apparently listening to the count, he was up at eight. Instead of facing his opponent, Simms turned to referee Arthur Donovan. "Let's take a walk up to the roof," he said less than coherently. Ten minutes later, back in his dressing room, Simms was still incoherent. Jacobs had guided Louis back to the top of the ranks of challengers for Jimmy Braddock's heavyweight crown.

Not everyone thought so. Especially not Max Schmeling, who had destroyed the Black Destroyer less than a year before. Now rated the logical contender in some quarters, including those of Madison Square Garden and Jimmy Johnston, Schmeling signed to fight Braddock for the title on June 3, 1937, at Madison Square Garden Bowl in Long Island City. Tired of their bath in red ink, the directors of the Garden tried to protect their flanks by making Mike Jacobs a partner in the promotion, hoping not only that Jacobs' promotorial prowess would insure success but also that his association with the Garden—no matter how tenuous—would assure them of future successes, mostly with the fighter under Jacobs' control, Louis.

Jacobs, however, had plans of his own. He completely outflanked the Garden. Approaching Braddock's manager, Joe Gould, he offered him a best-of-all-worlds contract for a Braddock-Louis fight. Jacobs not only bettered the guarantee offered by Johnston, but offered Gould 20 percent of all Louis' earnings as champion for ten years should Louis prevail. That was all Gould had to hear. He signed a contract calling for Braddock to defend his title against Louis on June 22 in Chicago, sidestepping the Garden, Johnston, and Schmeling completely.

When Louis knocked out Braddock in the eighth round, he accomplished in less than twenty-four minutes what Jacobs had been attempting to do for the previous forty-one months: make Mike Jacobs king of the boxing mountain. For it has always been a boxing bromide that whoever controls the heavyweight champion controls boxing. And Mike Jacobs controlled the champion.

Still he did not control boxing, at least not Madison Square Garden boxing, where Jimmy Johnston still tenaciously held onto the promoter's chair. As the 1937 indoor boxing season came to an end, one boxing publication, *Bang*, felt compelled to shout: "AND SO GOES BY ANOTHER INDOOR SEASON AND JIMMY JOHNSTON IS STILL IN THE GARDEN."

But the handwriting was on the wall. Garden President John Reed Kilpatrick relieved Johnston of his duties and the Garden of a terrific headache by terminating his contract after his 113th Garden boxing show on September 16. While Johnston's cards had averaged 9,916 fans per show and a gate of $23,779 going back to 1931, his last year drew just $18,800 and 9,121 fans. Trying to stem the tide of red ink, the Garden worked out a deal with the 20th Century Sporting Club giving Jacobs all boxing rights at Madison Square Garden. Tex Rickard's mantle had fallen on the likely shoulders of Michael Strauss Jacobs.

Starting with the October 29 fight between Henry Armstrong and Petey Sarron, Jacobs' first fourteen fights grossed a total of $618,000 and 170,342 fans, an average of $44,142 and 12,167 per show. Added to the best numbers posted by the Garden since the year Rickard died was an additional $56,000 for radio rights.

King C. Gillette was a man of genius and vision. As a struggling salesman in the Boston of the late 1890s, his exploring spirit discerned the need for a razor that would allow men to shave at home every day. Working backwards from what was actually a marketing premise, Gillette began sketching designs for a safety razor, although he had never invented anything before in his life.

Obtaining a patent in 1895, Gillette began selling his invention door-to-door. It was not an instant success, for turn-of-the-century America included among its quaint institutions the local barbershop or tonsorial parlor, where the works—"Shave and a haircut, two bits"—was available in a world of mustache cups, barbershop quartets, and the custom of "dropping in" to pass the time of day. Those who did shave at home were wedded to the time-tested straight razor. It was a tough make. Gillette sold only fifteen hundred razors and grossed $600 in his first few years in business.

On the brink of going out of business, Gillette hit upon another revolutionary marketing concept: give away the holders and create a vacuum for the blades. It worked. In 1901 he established the Gillette Sales Company to handle the demand for his blades. The new firm's advertising read: "If you are still depending upon the barber or old-fashioned razor, you are in the same category as the man who climbs ten flights of stairs when there is an elevator in the building. . . . With the Gillette, the most inexperienced man can remove, without cut or scratch, in three or five minutes, any beard that ever grew."

In 1910, Gillette decided to tie into baseball, the self-proclaimed National Pastime, running an ad with the endorsements of four personalities who had played in the 1909 and 1910 World Series. But while Gillette had aligned his company with four creditable stars, their endorsements were somewhat less than believable. John McGraw, the crusty manager of the 1910 National League Champion Giants supposedly gushed, "I wouldn't be without my Gillette, especially when I am on the road with the team. It makes shaving all to the merry."

Still sales of the Gillette safety razor were not "all to the merry." It took two masterful marketing strokes to make it so. The first was the sampling of the Gillette safety razor to four- and one-half million A.E.F troops in France during World War I. They returned to the United States converted to its use. The second vehicle employed by Gillette was sports.

In 1929, Gillette decided to test tentatively the sports waters, sponsoring a half-hour network radio show with Graham McNamee. It took the full plunge in 1935 when it sponsored its first fight, the championship bout between heavyweight champ Max Baer and challenger Jimmy Braddock. Gillette banked heavily on the swashbuckling Adonis from Livermore, California, retaining his crown.

Regarding Baer as a "sure" winner, a belief shared by the bookmakers who made him a prohibitive 15-1 favorite, Gillette signed him to a thirteen-week radio contract for a program called "Lucky Smith, Detective." Baer came into the fight with forty-one victories, including thirty knockouts over the likes of Max Schmeling, Tom Heeney, and Dolph Camilli's brother Frankie Campbell, whom he killed in the ring. He had KO'd Primo Carnera just 364 days before for the title. The 26-year-old champ looked like he could go on for years. But the screwball Baer trained too lightly and underestimated the former dock-walloper and welfare recipient. When the fifteen-round dance-athon was over, Braddock had won the title and the sobriquet The Cinderella Man. Afterwards Baer quipped, "Braddock can use the title. He had five kids . . . I don't know how many I have." All Gillette had was six more weeks of "Lucky Smith, Detective."

Stuck with something as old as yesterday's newspaper, an ex-champion, Gillette tried to extract some mileage out of the tie-in by sponsoring a contest. They asked listeners to name "Max Baer's wiry little he-dog" for a $1,000 prize. More than a quarter of a million entries came in during the four weeks the contest ran, all with proofs of purchase. After counting and discarding all the Princes, Pals, and Trays, they selected Livermore Gay

Blade, a hopelessly mixed metaphor combining Baer's birthplace and his style of training on the nightclub circuit with a cherished reference to the product.

The program itself did not enjoy quite the success of the contest and was cancelled. But Gillette took note of the quarter million contest entries and believed that the way to their target audience was through sports.

Gillette was fast becoming the leader in a crowded market with 16 percent in a field that included more than three thousand brands of blades, most of them the penny variety. The company's managers looked for a property to carry their advertising message to the men of America. They found it in the 1939 World Series. It would become the prototype for all sports programming as we know it today. Gillette allocated one-fifth of its annual advertising budget, $203,000, for the acquisition of radio rights, air time, and lines and talent for the fall classic between the New York Yankees and the Cincinnati Reds. The total expenditure was just a little more than what a one-minute commercial on a World Series telecast costs today. Although the Series went just four games, with the Yankees romping over the Reds, it nearly trebled sales for a "special" Gillette razor set that was a duplicate of the regular one with a special baseball overwrap.

Gillette's gamble had paid off. Now they sought other properties as part of a package that was to begin: "The Gillette Cavalcade of Sports is on the air." They bought the rights to the Orange Bowl, the Sugar Bowl, the East-West football game, the Kentucky Derby, and the NFL Championship. Sports was the launching pad for its marketing success, even though sometimes it had to overlook the gaffes of athletes in those days of live commercials, such as the time Billy Southworth was asked if he used Gillette Blue Blades. The Cardinal manager answered, "You're bloody right I do!"

But Gillette needed a year-round program that could be scheduled on a regular basis. The answer was the weekly fight card presented by Mike Jacobs' 20th Century Sporting Club. Gillette came to terms with Jacobs to assume the exclusive sponsorship of the fights on NBC, starting with the Joe Louis-Billy Conn fight on June 18, 1941.

Radio had been a novelty when Tex Rickard granted NBC the rights to broadcast the Dempsey-Carpentier fight in 1921. Now it became an integral part of boxing's fabric. And Mike Jacobs was already thinking ahead to the day when even radio would be supplanted by television. "I remember back in 1942," recalls former welterweight champion, Fritzie Zivic, "Mike and I were flying to a fight. 'Fritzie,' he said, 'you'll see the day when two thousand people will see a fight in a studio and twenty million will watch it on television in their homes.' I thought he was nuts," remembers Zivic. "But he was right!"

Jacobs was so sure he was "right" that he sold Gillette on the next logical step in the marketing equation. And on September 26, 1944, he signed a contract with the razor company to televise the Willie Pep-Calky Wright world featherweight championship three days later as well as the next fifty boxing shows at Madison Square Garden and St. Nicholas Arena. It was, as Humphrey Bogart said to Claude Raines at the final of *Casablanca*, "the beginning of a beautiful friendship."

During the next nineteen years Gillette continued to sponsor the Friday Night Fights as an integral part of its Cavalcade of Sports, introducing knowns and unknowns who quickly slid down the razor blade of life, plus a little bird named Sharpie, an animated parrot who sounded like Donald Duck with a herniated vocal chord. Accompanied by the familiar three-chime slogan—"Look Sharp, Feel Sharp, Be Sharp," in F#, A#, and C#—Sharpie announced proudly to the millions of faithful who tuned in each and every Friday night that "The Gillette Cavalcade of Sports [was] On the Air."

While Rickard had given away his money to just about anyone who approached him for a handout, Jacobs judiciously loaned his money to fighters and managers, obligating them to give him first call on their talents. He controlled the boxers. And he continued to spew out fight card after fight card between fighters who remain as unknown as the soldier under the tombstone at Arlington National Cemetery.

Added to this, he controlled the big arenas. In an advertisement on the back cover of the 1938 *Boxing News Record Book*, headlined with an air of self-importance "Boxing's Wheel of Fortune," no less than eleven arenas and stadia were listed as connected with Jacobs, "the hub of the wheel that holds the destiny of boxing": Madison Square Garden; the Polo Grounds; Yankee Stadium; the New York Hippodrome; Municipal Stadium, Miami; Sesqui-Centennial Stadium, Philadelphia; Kansas City Auditorium; Comiskey Park, Chicago; Cleveland Auditorium; Soldier Field, Chicago; and the Madison Square Garden Bowl.

And what of his meal ticket, Joe Louis? The fourteen men who had held the heavyweight title under Queensberry rules since James J. Corbett had held their title an average of three years and made three-plus defenses of their crown. Louis ran through the contenders dished up to him like fatted calves on the average of one every three months for the next decade.

One led to slaughter was Max Schmeling. The bout was a natural, pitting the champion against the Number One contender and the only man ever to beat him. But it was also fraught with political implications. Schmeling was the symbol of Aryan supremacy, Hitler's favorite fighter. Only moments before the fight he received a trans-Atlantic call from his Führer wishing him good luck. Louis bore the colors of Americans of all colors. And Jacobs had the match between warriors of warring ideologies and his second million-dollar gate.

Whatever Schmeling stood for, he didn't stand for long. Louis—who later gave voice to his crusade, stating "We're gonna . . . win, because we're on God's side"—battered the left side of the German's body again and again with powerful rights. His stricken foe fell twice in just 2:04 of the opening stanza, leaving him a prime candidate for the Home for the German Bewildered. Louis now stood alone as king of the heavyweight mountain. And Mike Jacobs stood with him, hand-in-hand or, at least, hand-in-pocket.

Louis began to take on all comers, disposing of contenders in every city with a Jacobs connection. Although the steady procession of challengers was dubbed The Bum of the Month Club by the press, in truth, few if any were—unless it was Tony Galento, who called everyone else a "bum." Most were, in the words of ring announcer Harry Balough, "highly regarded contenders," who were not allowed by Jacobs to fight each other; saving both themselves and their best efforts for Louis. But it made no "never mind" to Louis, as the cream-skinned destroyer in the black satin trunks with the JL monogram on the left thigh took them all apart, including two of Jimmy Johnston's fighters, Bob Pastor and Abe Simon, light-heavyweight champion John Henry Lewis, and a raft of others that sounded like a medley from one of Cab Calloway's scat songs: Galento, McCoy, and Godoy.

Then came Louis' fight with Billy Conn, hardly a "bum" in any month and assuredly not in the month of June, 1941. Conn, the classy light heavyweight posing as a heavyweight, looked like the heavyweight champion for twelve rounds, but he grew impatient under the accumulating weight of his crown-to-be and tried to trade punches with that most deadly of cornered animals, a champion in danger of losing his title. It was popgun versus howitzer. Instead of becoming the sixteenth heavyweight champion of the world, Billy Conn merely became Louis' sixteenth knockout victim in defense of his crown; his eighteenth victim altogether.

Louis fought twice in 1942, easily defeating two contenders who had previously extended him, Buddy Baer in one and Abe Simon in six. But neither Baer nor Simon came out of their fights any worse off than Louis. For Louis, now an army sergeant, had donated the purses to the Navy Relief Society and the Army Emergency Relief and was reduced to submitting a Statement of Financial Condition to the Internal Revenue Service which averred that his sergeant's pay was "barely enough to support wife and parents." IRS agents began pulling straws to see who would handle his case.

Louis' money problems antedated both his induction in the army and his donation of the purses. The government had been a 60 percent partner in all his earnings the previous year when he had made an estimated $471,892. But out of this seemingly lush half-a-million came the commissions paid to his managers, Julian A. Black and John Roxborough, in accordance with their contracts for $106,715.03 each. He paid another $20,780.81 to his trainer, Jack Blackburn. There was another $58,000 in fight-related expenses, including $11,000 for that catch-all called "publicity and promotion." Louis faced a predicament endemic to boxers—including Max Baer who once sold 110 percent of himself, believing he was dealing with a universe of 1,000 percent instead of 100 percent. He was in the hole and beholden to 20th Century Sporting Club and Mike Jacobs from the start. And to the IRS right to the end.

Sandwiched between the Conn fight and the 1942 bouts in the name of charity was one against the master of the Cosmic Punch, Lou Nova. Nova, more concerned with his potential at the box office than his potential in the ring, brayed, "I shall insist upon the return of the million-dollar gate." But while the fight produced the second-largest gate for any Louis title defense to date, ranking only behind his annihilation of Schmeling, it fell far short of the hoped-for million-dollar gate. Some 56,500 fans paid $584,000 to see Louis dismantle Nova in six rounds, Cosmic Punch or no.

But it wasn't the Nova fight that Jacobs envisioned as his next million-dollar fight. Instead, it was a return bout between Louis and Conn.

Jacobs began orchestrating the planning and publicity for the rematch. Without bothering to fully explain to Louis how a fight with the entire proceeds going to Army Emergency Relief would help defray his $117,000 tax liability—except to pay off a "loan" he had taken from Jacobs—Jacobs scheduled the bout between "Sgt. Joe Louis" and "Pvt. Billy Conn" for Columbus Day 1942, at Yankee Stadium. Placards decorating the five boroughs read "Entire Profits for Army Emergency Relief."

In the face of mounting concern emanating from Secretary of War Henry Stimson's office that the bout was not in "the national interest," sportscasters Bill Corum and Grantland Rice flew to Washington to plead Jacobs' cause. Stimson was flabbergasted by the excitement the fight was generating. During the meeting he exclaimed, "I never heard of anything like this fight's going to be." In a whispered aside, Corum said to Rice, "Watch out, somebody'll tell him there's a war going on." Despite the personal visitation by two of sportsdom's most respected spokesmen, on September 25 Stimson ruled against the fight, just 17 days before it was scheduled to take place.

For the first time in his promotorial career, Jacobs had been bested. He was forced to call it off. For four years.

In 1946, with the war over, the dream bout materialized, this time between citizen Louis and citizen Conn. Jacobs allowed neither a tune-up fight, lest his promotion lose its glamour, and recruited so-called "experts" to visit the training camps and plant newspaper stories. Louis was supposedly "dull" and Conn "sharp." Everything was in place and working toward a million-dollar gate.

But nothing worked better than an idea Jacobs had long cherished: charging the elitist price of $100 for a ringside ticket. Only twice before—Jackson versus Corbett and Corbett versus Sullivan—had $100 been charged and both times for front row seats only. Now, with the first flush of the postwar boom at hand, Jacobs wanted $100 for *all* ringside seats. During an interview with a "friendly" reporter Jacobs floated a trial balloon. When asked what the top price would be, he off-handedly responded, "Oh, I don't know. . . . Maybe I'll charge one hundred bucks for ringside."

The balloon took off. Although the planted comment had been made less to see what the traffic would bear than to emphasize, as Rickard always had, the bigness of the project, the response indicated that the traffic would bear the highest priced ticket in the history of boxing. Jacobs sold 10,574 ringside tickets, enough alone to make the magic million-dollar mark. The total gate was $1,925,564, the second-richest take in boxing history as each fan spent an all-time high average of $42.50 per ticket.

The fight itself was hardly as rewarding, with Conn succumbing to rust and Louis in the eighth round.

The Louis-Conn fight was Jacobs' third million-dollar fight. Rickard had had five. By the end of 1946, the 56-year-old Jacobs had fallen ill. Like Rickard before him, Jacobs was a one-man *bumpas*, delegating few, if any, responsibilities to underlings. As a consequence, while he lay ill the 20th Century Sporting Club languished. After several years of illness, he was forced to retire. In 1949, the same year Joe Louis announced his retirement as heavyweight champion, Jacobs sold his boxing holdings to James D. Norris.

Mike Jacobs was once described as "the greatest dictator boxing ever knew, and the ablest promoter." He now passed the torch he had picked up at Rickard's death to a man who would add much to the dictator designation and little to the promoter's appellation.

James D. Norris was a member of the baronial Norris family, inheriting a grain fortune from his multimillionaire father, with whom he owned the Detroit Red Wings. In 1946 he joined with his father's partner, Arthur Wirtz, to buy the Chicago Black Hawks, giving him two of the existing six NHL franchises. A sportsman and promoter who had his hand in hockey, ice shows, and horse racing, Norris had first entered the boxing arena by setting up the Tournament of Champions shortly after the war. Seeking to compete with the 20th Century Sporting Club but lacking an adequate arena, all of which belonged to the Jacobs syndicate, Norris had to bide his time until he could buy out Jacobs. Then he amalgamated Jacobs' holdings and the Tournament of Champions to form the International Boxing Club.

The IBC soon had a stranglehold over not only Madison Square Garden but also the Detroit Olympia and sports arenas in St. Louis, Chicago, Indianapolis, Omaha, and Washington. The mortar that held it all together was home television. Norris began packaging the Wednesday night fights for Pabst and the Friday night fights for Gillette, frequently dishing up such fighters as Holly Mims and Ralph "Tiger" Jones more often than fish.

But Norris wasn't content merely to serve up matches; he served them up garnished with sprigs of Frankie "Mr Gray" Carbo and Blinky Palermo. Dan Parker, the noted writer for the *New York Mirror*, smelled the redolent fragrance and was moved to write "There's always been larceny in boxing, and when I've seen it, I've written it. But it's worse now than ever before." Norris put his shows on the road, but featured them in cities such as Washington, D.C., where it was still possible for members of the press to smell them out. One time a writer for the *Washington Daily News* was standing in the dressing room at Washington's Uline Arena when local impresario Goldie Ahearn came running in to tell the two featured fighters, Alex Miteff and his current sparring partner, "It's going too fast. We've been having too many knockouts. Carry each other!"

But if Norris wanted to run with the hares and hounds, hoping to use Carbo and Palermo to strengthen his hold over boxing—a hold which won for the IBC the nickname of Octopus, Inc.—he also was running with the new boy in town, television. Norris not only understood the new medium, he "used" it as he used Palermo and Carbo to further his grip on the smaller clubs throughout the country. And on the other side of the coin, he kept many of his more lucrative bouts off home television, including the Sugar Ray Robinson-Randy Turpin and Rocky Marciano-Roland LaStarza fights, which he put on another medium he pioneered, closed-circuit television piped into theaters.

Norris' downfall came with the Senate Committee Hearings on Organized Crime in Interstate Commerce, chaired by Estes Kefauver, with bit parts played by the most outrageous characters this side of Damon Runyon, such as Hymie "The Mink" Wolman. When asked by counsel "Do you know Frankie Carbo?" he answered, "Yeah, I knew him on Ellis Island when he was known as Jimmy the Wop." Kefauver, who hadn't been paying attention to the line of questioning, looked up and asked, "What was that?" Wolman answered, "Wop, Senator, You know W-o-p."

The Kefauver Committee found that Norris had openly consorted with known hoodlums like Frankie Carbo and Blinky Palermo, both of whom were charged with "fixing" fights, including several with name fighters like Billy Fox, Jake LaMotta, and Don Jordan.

Within months the antitrust division of the Justice Department picked up the beat and found Norris and the IBC guilty of monopolistic practices and ordered Norris to divest himself of more than $2,500,000 in Madison Square Garden stock and dissolve the New York and Chicago divisions of the IBC. An appeal softened the blow somewhat, allowing the IBC two championship fights a year, but upholding the basic 1957 antitrust decision.

And so Norris was forced to sell his holdings, dissolve the IBC, and retire from boxing. Boxing was on the ropes. Dan Parker wrote, "I've been at its bedside waiting 40 years for boxing to die." Now expiration seemed imminent, brought on by the very men who had sought to promote it.

Aside from the fact that the inmates were running the asylum, the greatest problem afflicting boxing was television.

Having been lured by the kleig lights of television as early as 1944, boxing now tried to fly as close to the flame as it dared. By 1952 it had been all but consumed. It was now a staple on the home screen, appearing more hours than variety shows, old movies, and even news. Prime time was a veritable gymnasium: Monday night the DuMont network carried the fights from St. Nicholas and Eastern Parkway arenas; Tuesday the fights emanated from New York's Sunnyside Gardens; Wednesday Pabst Blue Ribbon Beer beamed fights from throughout the country over CBS; Thursday the Newark fights were carried live over a network extending from Schenectady to Washington; Friday was Gillette's night out on NBC; and, to cap off a long week, on Saturday nights ABC carried Ray Arcel's fights.

In the homeopathic discipline of medicine, minute quantities of a substance are administered, which if dosed in massive amounts would have produced effects similar to the disease being treated. Boxing's equivalent was Chuck Davey. If boxing was suffering from overexposure, its excesses were no more apparent than in Davey's case. A college-educated white south-paw out of Detroit, he became TV boxing's "glamour boy." In 1952 alone, he appeared seven times on the Wednesday night fights, becoming as familiar as Bill "The Bartender" Nimo, who poured glasses of Pabst between rounds.

Boxing seemingly existed for one purpose and one purpose alone: to make sponsors happy. Gillette was happy although hardly ecstatic, having paid $250,000 for the second Marciano-Walcott fight in 1953, when Jersey Joe looked for, and found, a comfortable resting place after 2:25 of the first round, forcing them to run their commercials like a string of pearls. Pabst was delighted, even if Chuck Davey was the permanent condiment for its brew. In fact, the only unhappy sponsor seemed to be Buick, which sponsored the 1957 heavyweight championship bout between Floyd Patterson and Tommy "Hurricane" Jackson over NBC. When the network cut late to a commercial between the ninth and tenth rounds and deprived viewers of the fight being stopped, Buick staged its own "Hurricane" and blew its ad agency out of the water.

John Crosby, writing in the *New York Herald-Tribune*, may have discovered why the sponsors were so happy. One CBS executive, Crosby recounted, decided to try a little experiment one night. Watching the Pabst Wednesday night fights over his own network, he determined to follow the advice of the between-rounds announcer who sternly advocated that he visit his refrigerator and repay the kindness of the beer company for bringing him the fights for free. Gulping furiously, he managed to stay abreast of the announcer, getting a new bottle every time he was told to. The result: the losing fighter was knocked out in the tenth; the executive was flat on his back by the end of the ninth.

But while the fans at home were enjoying the fights for free, the grass roots of boxings, the small clubs, were drying up. By 1952, there was only one for every ten that had existed in the postwar boom year of 1946.

Just as importantly, the IBC, which had a contract calling for the production of some eighty-plus matches on Wednesday and Friday nights for $1,500,000, was to lose more than that amount in live gates. Thirty-three dates in 1946 at Madison Square Garden yielded a total of 406,681 fans and a gross of $2,062,000. Twenty fights in 1952 pulled only 137,381 fans and $435,450, a total loss in revenues of more than $1,600,000. Boxing was not only eating its young; it was devouring itself.

By the end of the decade boxing was among the walking wounded. Its promoters were tainted, its product was diminished by overexposure, its "farm system"—the small clubs—had been undermined and its fans were staying away in droves, unwilling to pay for what they could get free.

But an even more important cause for boxing's sorry state was its own variation of Gresham's Law: that bad boxers will drive out good promoters. There were no Jack Dempseys or Joe Louises or even Rocky Marcianos to attract promoters like Rickard, Jacobs, and Norris. The fighters who ruled the eight weight classes in 1959 were relatively nondescript battlers, with the exception of two all-time greats, Sugar Ray Robinson and Archie Moore, both of whom were getting long in the tooth and more than a little wearisome to the National Boxing Association, which was in the process of stripping them of their crowns for inactivity. The others were in the process of retiring on their own.

But if the names of the divisional champions—with the notable exception of featherweight king Davey Moore—were hardly household names, even in their own household, the name of the heavyweight champion, Floyd Patterson, inspired even more ennui. Patterson, who had been skillfully maneuvered to the heavyweight crown by his manager, Cus D' Amato, and just as skillfully kept out of the clutches of the IBC, was the titular successor to Marciano as heavyweight champ. But he was scarcely the successor to his popularity. Floyd remembers only too well the many times he would stand outside the old Garden talking with D'Amato and remain unrecognized by the denizens of what had become known as Jacobs Beach.

Patterson did little for his image, fighting has-been and never-wases. Between the time he won the championship in an elimination contest against Archie Moore and the first Ingemar Johansson fight, his title defenses included fights with Tommy "Hurricane" Jackson, amateur champ Pete Rademacher in his first professional start, Roy "Cut and Shoot" Harris, and Brian London in such non-IBC places as Seattle, Los Angeles, and Indianapolis.

And each of Patterson's whistle-stop title defenses had a different promoter as well. In Seattle it was Jack Curley, in Indianapolis Cecil Rhodes, in New York Bill Fugazy and Roy Cohn, and in Los Angeles it was a young vice president of TelePrompter named Bill Rosensohn, who hustled up $75,000 when Marciano's former manager, Al Weill, was turned down because of suspected underworld associations.

Rosensohn sold the fight as if he were "promoting a bar of soap." This latter-day snake-oil salesman sent direct-mail pieces advertising the fight to the one hundred twenty thousand members of the Diners' Club of Southern California, who responded to the guaranteed seats in "preferential locations" with more than $30,000 in orders the first week. Rosensohn extended point-of-purchase advertising to neighborhood bars, getting the salesmen for a local liquor distributor to hang up fight posters in taverns. And he decked out the training camps with massive outdoor advertising signs. With a $210,000 guarantee from the closed-circuit telecast pledged by his former employer, Tele-Prompter, Rosensohn's innovative marketing yielded a live gate of $234,000 and a total of more than $444,000, the largest since Marciano had beaten Moore three years earlier. But Rosensohn was soon gone from the scene, his grubstake having been discovered to be "tainted" by associations with hoodlums.

Patterson himself was also dethroned soon thereafter by Johansson. And then, in an instant replay of the mid-1930s, the heavyweight championship seemed to change hands almost every year. Patterson regained it only to lose it to Sonny Liston, who in turn lost it to a brash young upstart named Cassius Clay.

Boxing had once again fallen to its nadir, but it was on the threshold of a new era wrought this time by one man who, although not a promoter in the strictest sense of the word, was to become the greatest promotional genius in boxing history.

Cassius Clay, a/k/a Muhammad Ali, is the "only fighter I know who can bullshit himself," wrote José Torres, former light heavyweight champion and co-author of . . . *Sting Like a Bee.* More importantly, Ali is one of the few fighters who bullshits patrons and promoters as well.

Cassius Clay was an amalgam of a strutting fighter cocksure of his skills and of Gorgeous George, the outrageous wrestler. Clay began predicting the outcome of his bouts "after watching Gorgeous George. I hear this white fellow say, 'I am the World's Greatest Wrestler. I cannot be defeated. I am The Greatest! I am the King! If that sucker whups me, I gonna get the next jet to Russia. I cannot be defeated. I am the prettiest. I am the greatest!' When he was in the ring, everybody booooooed. Oh, everybody just boooooooooed. And I was mad. I looked around and saw everybody was mad." An idea struck Clay. "I saw fifteen thousand people coming to see this man get beat. And his talking did it. And, I said, this is a g-o-o-o-o-o-o-o-d idea!"

And so, young Cassius began talking himself up, forecasting the exact round in which he would dispose of his next opponent: "Archie [Moore] had been living off the fat of the land/I'm here to give him his pension plan/When you come to the fight don't block aisle or door,/'Cause ya all going home after round four."

This braggadocio was too much for the traditional, bottled-in-bond fight fan. They came out in droves to see Clay beaten. But it was fruitless. In a scenario repeated time after time, Clay belted out his opponent in the prescribed number of rounds and then strutted around the ring like a conquering hero while the fans fumed.

In March, 1963, the unbeaten Clay was brought to New York to fight another up-and-coming contender, Doug Jones, right in the middle of a ninety-five-day newspaper strike. "This is unfair to the many boxing fans New York City has. Now they won't be able to read about the great Cassius Clay," ballyhooed the immodest boxer. Clay made it his personal crusade to provide Madison Square Garden with its first capacity crowd in thirteen years, appearing on every radio and television station in the city. "Clay did everything," Johnny Condon, Madison Square Garden's publicity director, remembered. "He went around town. He talked to the people. And he filled the place." Even "the pigeons in the rafters had to make room" for the newest promoter in boxing; a self-promoter at that. He soon added punches, like the "Anchor Punch" and the "Ghetto Whallop" and his own patented soft-shoe, the "Ali Shuffle"—all in the name of promotion, of course.

Within a year, Clay had promoted himself into a shot at the heavyweight championship against Charles "Sonny" Liston. And when Liston retired on his stool between the sixth and seventh rounds, the world found itself with a new heavyweight champion with a new name—Muhammad Ali.

Ali was beholden to no one; especially no promoter. His title defenses took place under the flags of almost as many promoters and countries as there were fights. Starting with his first defense under the auspices of Sonny Liston's own promotional firm in a high school skating rink in Lewiston, Maine, down to the last before he was defrocked as heavyweight champion, his odyssey took him to Houston's Astrodome, London's Arsenal Stadium, and West Germany's Frankfurt Stadium, all for different promoters. But Muhammad Ali needed no promoter—he was his own, in and out of the ring.

But if he marched to a different drummer than other champions had, the unfamiliar beat was to prove his undoing. His refusal to play the hero's role the way the public demanded—standing for induction into the army and behaving as "a credit to his race"—became unbearable. Unable to see him beaten in the ring, boxing's Babbitts did the next best thing—they took his title away from him.

With Ali down and apparently out, the qualified and the unqualified queued up to assume the mantle of "promoter," boxing licenses in hand, seeking in futility to fill the vacuum left by his enforced departure. The World Boxing Association conducted a heavyweight elimination tournament. Madison Square Garden held its own sweepstakes, pitting Joe Frazier against the man New York State Boxing Commissioner Ed Dooley called "Buddy" Mathis for New York's split portion of the championship. It was "Ali-Ali, All in free!" Frazier won, but who cared? The fans weren't interested in fractional heavyweight champions. Until the triumphant return of the prodigal son, Muhammad Ali, interest in the heavyweight championship lay dormant.

With his return, all signals were off; everything was changed. The presence of the former champion, who had been dethroned not in the ring but in the anterooms of those political bodies known as state boxing commissions and was now coming back—

courtesy of the courts—gave a different coloration to everything. No longer were fights between Manuel Ramos and Joe Frazier meaningful. There was only one fight that would make any sense: Frazier versus Ali. It would be the *sine qua non* of all fights. Never before had two unbeaten heavyweight champions met. It would not be merely another in a long line of Fights of the Century. In the words of columnist Barney Nagler, it would be The Fight. Promoters immediately began jockeying for position, hoping to light their candles from Ali's torch.

The first match after Ali's enforced exile was against Jerry Quarry. He wanted Frazier immediately. But Frazier's manager, Yank Durham, a black version of Everett Dirksen, was skeptical of the ex-champion's chances against his charge after a three-and-a-half year layoff. "Prove you're ready for us, then we'll fight you," he said, speaking in the colorful pluralism of boxing managers everywhere. He also doubted that Ali would "get his license." He did, but after many false alarms—and in Atlanta, of all places. A strange pastiche of promoters and political-types put together an *ad hoc* company which they called House of Spice. Two of them, Hal Conrad and Mike Malitz, offered Ali Jerry Quarry instead of Frazier. Part matchmaker and all promoter, Ali leaped at the chance: "Great! You got it! Nigger and draft-dodger against the Great White Hope. . . . That'll sell a lot of tickets."

It did. In October, 1970, big-time boxing made its reentry into Atlanta after almost twenty-five years in front of a small gathering of dudes and sports. But the real audience were the hundreds of thousands who crowded into theaters all across the country to see Ali stop Quarry on cuts in three rounds. Ali's next "comeback" fight was held in Madison Square Garden on December 7. He kayoed Oscar Bonavena in the fifteenth round on a day the American Legion pickets who paraded outside the Garden reminded us will always "live in infamy."

Now only Joe Frazier stood between Ali and his coveted crown. Ali-Frazier! A fight to resolve all claims to the heavyweight championship. But even more important for the boxing business, it was a fight for promoters to exploit. Within a week of Ali's knockout of Bonavena and just two and a half weeks after Frazier's devastating knockout of light-heavyweight champion Bob Foster, the lines were forming. Madison Square Garden wanted The Fight. So did the Houston Astrodome. So did Senator Leroy Johnson of Georgia, whose political influence had cleared away the thick underbrush of red tape for Ali's return in Atlanta. So did Tommy Roberts and Fred Hofheinz and Bob Arum. And many more names familiar to the boxing world as promoters.

One name that wasn't on anybody's lips or list was that of Jerry Perenchio, a second-generation Hollywood talent agent with ancestral ties to Budd Schulberg's Sammy Glick. Perenchio's firm, Chartwell Artists, handled Andy Williams, Sonny and Cher, Elizabeth Taylor and Richard Burton, Henry Mancini, and Sergio Mendes among hundreds of others. But he had never had anything to do with the likes of Muhammad Ali. In fact, he had never seen a fight live.

One phone call was to change all that. On the afternoon of December 15, one week after Ali had dispensed with Bonavena, Perenchio received a call from Frank Fried, one of the country's largest concert promoters and a personal friend of Ali's manager, Herbert Muhammad. Fried had found Perenchio in London and called to tell him that he had just left a meeting with Herbert and Ali's lawyer, Bob Arum. Would Perenchio "be interested in bidding for the fight" between Ali and Frazier?

Does a promoter promote? "Of course," replied Perenchio, now hooked on the idea. "They want $6,000,000—$3,000,000 each—plus a million option on a rematch," said Fried. Perenchio told him he'd have to get the numbers together and get back to him.

Perenchio did his homework, and got back to Fried. "I think it's worth $4,000,000, but somebody else will probably think the same. So I'm prepared to offer $5,000,000 flat for the outright purchase of *all* the rights to the fight—down to the trunks and gloves. Also, $1,000,000 option on the rematch," he added, "with the stipulation that if the fight loses money I can recoup those losses in the rematch."

As he hung up, Perenchio congratulated himself on his bargaining acumen: "'Boy,' I said to myself, 'You're some negotiator. . . . You've got yourself the Hope Diamond. . . . And all you've got to do is sell it for what it's worth.'"

Within three days he raised a million and a half—Andy Williams pledged half a million; Thomas Evans, retired General Motors attorney, promised to put up a quarter of a million; Sergio Mendes obligated himself for the same; and Perenchio himself kicked in half a million. He was still three-and-a-half million short.

Now he began to experience first-hand the Byzantine intrigue boxing is famous for, where a man raised to believe a handshake was his bond found that "the fight crowd can't vouch for itself through tomorrow." It first manifested itself when, in his quest for backing, he called producer Joseph E. Levine. Levine told him, "I got the inside track on the fight for $3,500,000." Minutes later he received a call from Fried, frantically telling him to get to New York. "The Frazier people are conducting separate negotiations."

Arriving in New York on December 18, just three days after he had supposedly made a deal, he met with Bob Arum and Fred Hofheinz. Arum was Muhammad Ali's legal advisor, but what the hell was Hofheinz doing there? Perenchio asked. "Because Fred and I own Top Rank," Arum answered, naming the closed-circuit operation which had televised the Ali-Bonavena fight. Perenchio retorted he didn't see how Arum could serve two masters. Arum countered by telling him that NBC and Sonny Werblin had matched the offer and that his was only good until six that evening.

It was becoming painfully evident that Perenchio didn't have the rights to the fight after all. In fact, he was beginning to feel as if he were "being used as a pawn," so he called Fried and told him to "arrange for me to sit down with Herbert Muhammad in Chicago" the next day.

Herbert asked Perenchio if he was "prepared to risk your money knowing that a Supreme Court decision against him could knock you out of the box?" (referring to the case on appeal that would rule on Ali's status as a conscientious objector). Was Perenchio still prepared to take the calculated risk? "I told him I was," said the talent agent. "I figured the worst I could lose was a quarter-of-a-million dollars. I was betting in a big game and it was worth the risk." "All right," said Herbert Muhammad, standing up to indicate the interview was over. "We're back in business. Get the money!"

Still three-and-a-half million short, Perenchio continued to make list after list of potential backers, looking for that magic ingredient "OPM." Time was running out. He finally narrowed the hunt down to one name: Jack Kent Cooke.

Cooke was a self-made man. Beginning as Olney Cooke, a radio performer in Canada, he had parlayed that into a string of radio stations. Since coming to the United States in 1960 he had entered the sports world in a big way. A part-owner of the Washington Redskins, he was sole owner of the Los Angeles Lakers and Kings and the building they played in, the Forum. Because his wealth was well known, not a week went by when "some half-assed idea" didn't cross his desk.

To counter such requests for money, he prepared a form letter.

But that letter never went out to Jerry Perenchio, who called trying to interest him in putting up the money for The Fight. A meeting was set for December 22, only one week after Perenchio's first phone call from Fried. Cooke's first question was, "What do you think the fight will gross worldwide?" Perenchio answered with assurance: "$20,000,000 to $30,000,000."

That was enough for Cooke. He answered, "At last I've found a man whose arithmetic agrees with mine." Cooke demanded just two considerations for his money: that he get 70 percent of the profits and that the fight be held in the Forum. But that would come later and be renegotiated to 60 percent. And the fight would be held elsewhere. For the moment, Perenchio had his backer—and The Fight. Almost.

Before he could sign either side to a binding contract, he had to endure last-minute masturbatory maneuvers on the part of both camps. Ali's Chicago attorney, Chauncy Eskridge, told Perenchio: "You may handle the Beatles, but you don't know boxing and I'm not about to put my client's future in your hands. I can't advise my people to go along with you." Meanwhile, Frazier's manager, Yank Durham, fielded bids from other promoters who were trying to get into the act. But Durham finally came around to favoring Perenchio, and the original terms: five million dollars, two and one-half for each fighter and a half-million option for the rematch.

Everything was arranged but the site. Ali wanted the Houston Astrodome, where he had enjoyed some of his biggest successes, while Frazier chose as his home court Madison Square Garden. It was a case of no site, no deal. Perenchio told both sides, "If I don't have one of those by January 15, I'll forfeit the million." That did it for the Ali and Frazier representatives, but not for Perenchio, who had to deliver.

On the day before Christmas, while all through most houses not a creature was stirring, Jerry Perenchio was out hustling to preserve the million dollars he had pledged as good-faith money. He met with Alvin Cooperman, vice president in charge of Madison Square Garden's special events. Within ten minutes they had forged a deal. Perenchio would put up $4,500,000 of the $5,000,000 and the Garden would come up with the other $500,000 as a guarantee against 70 percent of the live gate receipts.

In four short weeks, Perenchio had cornered the "Hope Diamond" and suffered through a crash course on boxing's strange ethics. As he began to plan for The Fight, now just eight weeks away, he could only look back in wonder and say, "If there's a wrinkle here and a straight deal there, the boxing crowd would go for the wrinkle every time."

The scene at 277 Park Avenue was one out of the Marx Brothers' movie—the stateroom scene from *A Night at the Opera*, to be exact. The name on the black marble wall just outside the lobby office read: "Management Tele/Vision Center." But inside it was like Mission Control, with people running everywhere and Jerry Perenchio chairing it from a desk in the middle of the floor.

The scene revolving around Perenchio was pure chaos. Secretaries answered phones "Mr. Pinocchio's Office." Spear carriers pushed pins in an outsized map of the United States indicating closed-circuit locations in three colors—many pins falling to the floor as soon as they were put in, then put back in elsewhere. Publicists who had never pushed anything bigger than a concert or a movie pored over the sports pages trying mightily to familiarize themselves with the names of sportswriters.

This fight was being marketed in a different way from any other closed-circuit fight. Instead of peddling the fight in the traditional manner—taking a percentage of each theater's gross after the fight and depending on big ticket sales for big profits— Perenchio decided early in the game to "franchise" the package to regional buyers who would pay in advance for their guaranteed territories. "We worked out a payment formula based on the number of seats we thought could be sold in each location," he said of his business prescription. The asking price for each so-called "territory" was 50 percent of the estimated total gross, with promoters in each area paying up to 60 percent of their eventual "take." Within days twenty-four "master exhibitors"— including United Artists, Danny Kaye's Concerts West, Loews, RKO, Andy Williams, and other people connected with show business—had paid in a quick $6,000,000 to Perenchio's corporation, The Fight of Champions. Perenchio had almost all his money back at the start and stood to make more, much more, than the Ali-Bonavena fight, which grossed $1,500,000, the Ali-Quarry fight, which grossed just under $3,000,000, or even the greatest closed-circuit money-maker of all time, the first Ali-Liston fight, which grossed $4,200,000. The closed-circuit tail was now wagging the dog.

Closed-circuit revenue was the main feature of Perenchio's master plan. But the show biz entrepreneur possessed other ideas for maximizing his profits. In his own words: "What we have here is the Mona Lisa. You want me to sell it for chopped liver?" So he had programs printed up to sell at $2 each and posters at $1 each at the closed-circuit locations.

Now the purveyor of the modern-day Mona Lisa set his sights on selling between-rounds commercials. With an estimated audience of three hundred million in forty-two countries around the world, he felt he could easily get $4,000,000 more in advertising.

His first stop was McCann-Erickson, the second-largest agency in the world, with such blue-chip clients as General Motors, Coca-Cola, Nabisco, Swift, Del Monte, and Philip Morris. Perenchio suggested that McCann-Erickson buy the entire "package" for its clients. When one agency executive asked him the time-honored question "What happens if it ends early?"—meaning "What happens to all the commercials?" Perenchio fuffumped and finally said, "Ali and Frazier are both businessmen." For the suggestion that money might have an effect on the outcome, Perenchio was shown the door. So much for commercials.

With four weeks to go, Perenchio had failed to sell advertising either in the fight itself or in the program. Now he was faced with yet another problem: theater ticket sales were not moving as had been expected. Burt Lancaster, a client of Perenchio's, had been signed as a color commentator for the telecast and was displaying his dimple on every talk show on which he could be booked in an attempt to hype interest. But more was needed.

Just when he was beginning to question his original judgment in the drawing power of his Mona Lisa-Hope Diamond, the very same world that had spurned his advances to sell them advertising now came to his rescue. For weeks Perenchio had been discussing the possibility of a tie-in with Vitalis Hair Tonic with its agency, Young & Rubicam. Identification with sports and sports events had become one of Vitalis' basic marketing strategies. The hair tonic sponsored NBA basketball, major league baseball, and NHL hockey and had used several famous athletes in its commercials to heighten visibility, including Bob Griese, Don Drysdale, and Jerry Lucas.

With no prospective buyer in sight for between-rounds commercials and the prospect of lagging ticket sales, Perenchio did the next best thing: he gave away his drawing cards for commercials. Vitalis agreed to spend at least a million dollars airing a split-screen commercial of the two combatants during the two weeks before The Fight. As the champion listened on a telephone, Ali taunted him, "Fraz-i-ur, I say this to you and I say it with no malice, when I'm finished wit' you head, you gonna need some Vitalis." The calculated risk paid off. As Vitalis sales responded, so did ticket sales.

But the days were dwindling down to a precious few and Perenchio's dreams still hadn't fully materialized. He needed something—and quick. Although he had several public relations outfits working for him, they didn't understand boxing. One man did—the publicity director of boxing at the Garden, John F.X. Condon—and Perenchio got in touch with him.

John Francis Xavier Condon is a rare bird of a rare breed. In a world in which most wear their clothing as if it were thrown at them in the morning, he is sartorially splendid, looking as if he just walked out of the pages of *Gentlemen's Quarterly*. Most in the broken beak brigade believe that the best idea is a stolen one; but Condon continually comes up with new approaches to old problems. He is part publicity man, part promoter, and partly a throwback to the days when Tex Rickard was generating an idea a minute.

The Garden's basketball public address announcer since 1948, Condon first came to the attention of the boxing department in 1960. He was then serving as a free-lance press agent for a growing group of clients, which included King's Point, Adelphi, and Iona colleges as well as for the New York Athletic Club, when the publicity director for boxing, Murray Goodman, resigned.

Harry Markson, head of the Garden's boxing department, approached Condon about taking the job. Although Condon was harried, he was happy. He turned down the offer. One month later Markson was back. "John, boxing is at its lowest level. It's at the bottom of the barrel and can't go any lower. If you come in here," Markson told the still reluctant Condon, "anything you could do to raise it would be a credit to you." And then in one sentence he wilted all of Condon's resistance: "It's a challenge!" That did it for Condon. Never a man to pass up a dare, John F.X. Condon entered the bright lights of Madison Square Garden.

Johnny Condon started almost immediately to do his thing. He added frills, such as bringing Korean dancers into the ring before a boxer from Korea appeared in the main event, Scottish bagpipers for fighters from Scotland, and marimba bands for South American boxers. By doing so, he added another dimension to the evening's entertainment, a carnival spirit, despite having to endure disparaging remarks from the old "they'll-never go-for-that" school.

206

Condon also improved on Rickard's bringing back the old champs routine and raised it one, putting together entire evenings dedicated to celebrating Jack Dempsey's seventy-fifth birthday and Sugar Ray Robinson's "Farewell to Boxing." It was a feast for the nostalgic fan wrapped ceremoniously around a boxing show.

He attended to everything, from the frivolous to the fundamental. Hearing Oscar Bonavena constantly singing "I Want to Hold your Hand," he dubbed him Ringo, a name that pleased both Bonavena and the press. He pioneered in making the postfight news conference into an organized media event by putting the fighters on a platform to answer questions and structuring the format, in contrast to the grab-ass chaos that prevailed in the small dressing rooms in years past when the less agile were physically excluded from the interview.

But most importantly, Johnny Condon found himself in the enviable position of being able to promote the entire sport and the Garden itself, merely by publicizing a specific fight, in much the same manner as Kodak is able to promote its product—owning 85 percent of the market—merely by publicizing picture taking. Even though he cannot account for his promotions' impact at the gate, his impact on the sport has been substantial and boxing was no longer "at the bottom of the barrel," in part because of John F. X. Condon.

Now, with The Fight fast approaching and the gate still not responding to all his massaging, Perenchio sought out Condon. "Look, John, these guys," meaning his promotion and publicity men, "haven't done a damn thing for me," said Perenchio over the phone. "And I'm paying them all kinds of money. I want you to handle the promotion end of the closed-circuit for me. Will you do it?"

Condon couldn't until he first cleared it with the powers-that-be at the Garden, which meant Alvin Cooperman. Cooperman and Perenchio were, in the words of Walter Winchell, definitely a "don't-invite-'em." Their antipathy towards one another would have been the proper ingredient for a blood fight itself and very nearly came to pass the day of the Ali-Frazier weigh-in when Perenchio, stopped at the door by an overly officious guard, finally got in and physically buttonholed Cooperman, blaming him for his exclusion. Now Cooperman told Condon, "I'm not asking you to work for this guy . . . I'm begging you not to. Because if anything goes wrong with this fight he's going to blame you." Then Cooperman added a few choice pejoratives of his own. Condon got the message and called Perenchio back to turn down the offer.

But Perenchio kept after him. Two days later Condon got another call, this time from Cooperman, who had been called by Perenchio. "John, will your taking a job with Perenchio in any way interfere with anything you're doing now?" asked Cooperman. Condon, who was busy promoting The Fight for the Garden anyway, could only answer the obvious, "It falls right into the same slot, Alvin." Cooperman understood the synergic possibility of promoting both the fight at the Garden and for the closed-circuit locations. He agreed, but before he hung up he could not refrain from shooting one last "zinger": "Just make sure you get your price. Make him pay you for it!"

Condon began to earn his keep immediately. He sat up all one night in a room at the Playboy Hotel in Miami Beach, near Ali's training headquarters, smoking cigarette after cigarette, drinking coffee, and musing: "This guy is a young guy; the country is being run by young people. In a couple of years, the young people are going to have a bigger voice in this country than they ever had before in its history. Ergo, the country needs a young leader . . . and that young leader should be Ali."

Letting out a war-whoop similar to Archimedes' "Eureka" when he first discovered the principle of water displacement, Condon rushed to Ali's Fifth Street Gymnasium at seven in the morning to lay his idea on him. Ali had just returned from the boxer's constitutional, roadwork. Now he lay in bed, hands behind his head, propped up against his pillow, resting. Condon flew into the room and train-of-thoughted his idea: "Look, I'm going to tell you something. Don't talk until I get done talking. When I get done we'll have a chat. But don't say a word 'til then. . . . At twelve o'clock today, you're going to go into the lobby of the Playboy Hotel and you're going to make a formal announcement that in 1976 you're going to run for President of the United States . . ."

Ali leaped straight up off the bed and came down slapping his thighs. "Man oh man, that's just what I need, that's just what I need!" Then, as an afterthought, he added, "But you've got to do one thing though. You've got to check it out with Herbert."

Condon hollered "fine" over his shoulder as he ran into the hall, heading for the phone. First he called Perenchio and, after the same admonition not to interrupt until he was through, went through the idea again. When he was finished, there was no sound at the other end. "Hello, hello. Are you there?" Finally Perenchio came back on the wire and said softly, "Yeah, I'm here. Jesus Christ, John, if you could pull this off, it's the greatest God damn thing that could happen to us!"

Condon's next call was to Herbert Muhammad. He couldn't get through. Instead, he reached John Ali at Muslim headquarters in Chicago. After hearing Condon out, John Ali merely said, "He can't do it, John. No Muslim is allowed to run for public office." And even though Condon argued it was merely a "stunt," the verdict stood.

Still, in exchange for having his plan vetoed, Condon was later able to extract a promise that Ali would predict the outcome of the fight on theater TV just before The Fight itself.

But this gimmick was nothing like the first idea. But then there have been few like it, even from Condon.

The Fight itself was more like a war. A battle to the death. The first time any fight with the pretentious title of The Fight of the Century had lived up to its advance billing.

For fifteen rounds each warrior disdained the other's heavy weaponry and threw himself—and everything he had—into the battle. Until the last round the outcome was in doubt. Then Frazier came up "smokin'" with one of his patented left hooks, leaping off the floor to land it on Ali's jaw. For only the third time in his career, Ali crashed to the mat, his eyes glazed. Almost as soon as his rump touched canvas, his eyes cleared and he was back for more of the same. And then it was over. Fifteen rounds, forty-five minutes, of the best both men could give—and take. The decision was won by Frazier. The people's hearts were won by Ali. In subway after subway, signs could be found etched in the artistic medium of the "little" people, spray paint reading: "Ali Lives."

For the promoters it was a financial as well as an artistic success. While it would be months before the final returns could be tabulated from upstate, initial analyses indicated that gross receipts would set an all-time boxing record. Accountants from Arthur Young & Company were assigned to monitor each of the 369 closed-circuit locations and the Garden as well, to assure "a fair head count." The total gross would be well over $14,500,000—$1,250,000 the "live" Garden gate—more than three times the previous record ($4,747,690 in total receipts for the second Liston–Patterson heavyweight title fight in 1963).

The co-venturers, Perenchio and Cooke, shared some $750,000 in net profits. Postmortems continued to circulate that Cooke and Perenchio had parted company after The Fight, with Cooke allegedly "annoyed at several of Perenchio's business deals," including a few where it was rumored Perenchio had allegedly "turned his back" on a handshake. But Cooke denied the rumors, saying only "I was very happy with Jerry Perenchio. I would be happy to work with him the next time." And, in point of fact, Perenchio made good on those handshakes, paying Condon, among others, "with interest."

But there was to be no "next time"—no Son of Fight of the Century. For now Joe Frazier barnstormed about the country defending his title against a few fighters who didn't bear public mention after sun-up, including Terry Daniels in New Orleans—the night before the 1972 Super Bowl, an old promoter's trick of parasitically attaching its own tail to a larger promotional kite in the hopes of exploiting the "carry-over interest"—and Ron Stander in Omaha. But as he did, the clamor grew for him to defend once again against Ali. Rather than risk going in against Ali, Yank Durham and his advisory group, Cloverlay, opted for a bout in January, 1973, against the Liston-like George Foreman in Jamaica.

Once the arenas had called the tune, pledging the dollars to attract the fighters who would, in turn, bring in the cash customers in sufficient numbers to turn a profit. Now the equation was changing. Closed-circuit television operators were the ones pledging the megabucks. And for the Frazier-Foreman fight a new element had been introduced: a nation became the underwriter of the bout.

A South American impresario by the name of Alex Valdez promoted concerts and tours around the world. One of those tours was by Joe Frazier. Frazier's was not a boxing tour but a musical one, featuring his musical group The Knockouts. Not only did it lose Valdez money, but it was panned dreadfully. One reviewer said of the show, "Frazier should have let the audience in free and charged them to leave."

Valdez was interested in breaking into the *sanctum sanctorum* of boxing. What better way than with the heavyweight champion of the world, Joe Frazier? The heavyweight champion felt beholden to Valdez for having underwritten a losing proposition, his singing group. Valdez was now able to turn his musical due bill into a contract for Frazier to fight anyone except Ali in a place of Valdez' choosing.

The place he chose was Jamaica. It appealed to Valdez for several reasons, not the least of which were its proximity to the United States and its lush closed-circuit market. Equally important was the fact that Valdez didn't want to get involved in stateside taxes.

The island-republic of Jamaica was more than receptive to Valdez' overture. Ten years before the government had formed a company called National Sports, Ltd., with the avowed purpose to "use sports as a vehicle to cure a lot of problems," including the 25 percent unemployment rate, by converting idle energies to constructive uses through sports. This idealistic goal had never been approached. Now it saw a heavyweight championship fight as not only a publicity platform to draw attention to the tiny republic but, in the words of Paul FitzRitson, chairman of National Sports, "to make money so that we can develop sports."

What FitzRitson called "by far the best attraction around" was the Frazier-Foreman fight. It had been fifty years since Shelby, Montana, had pioneered as the first locale to promote a fight, a fight which bankrupted the town after paying Jack Dempsey nearly $300,000. This time it was not a local government that underwrote the fight, it was a national government. Unfortunately, the results were nearly the same.

The Sunshine Showdown—a reference to the island, not the fight, which was fought under the stars—was more a knockdown than a showdown. Six knockdowns to be exact; all by Foreman. The heavyweight title changed hands for the twentieth time; only for the third time in a foreign ring. But there was a profounder implication underlying the bout. Under the aegis of National Sports, Ltd., boxing entered the international economic scene at the governmental level.

Within the year the new champion, George Foreman, was not only elevated to the pantheon of invincibility, but he also became the most important man in international promotional power plays. His first title defense was against a nobody called Joe "King" Roman in Tokyo, his second against a somebody who became a nobody in the second round, named Ken Norton, in Caracas, Venezuela. Boxing's traditional poker politics were now complemented by countries' *realpolitik*.

By the time Foreman had disposed of Norton in Caracas, in March, 1974, contracts and funding had already been arranged for a fight between Foreman and Ali the following September in Kinshasha, Zaire. Whereas intrigue has always been an element of any boxing negotiation, the Ali-Foreman negotiations possessed a touch of foreign intrigue that would have shamed James Bond.

The "promoters" of the Venezuelan to-do were Video Techniques, Inc., a New York-based closed-circuit TV firm which had televised the Ali-Jimmy Ellis and Ali-Buster Mathis fights from Houston, the Ali-Mac Foster fight from Tokyo, and the Foreman-Frazier fight from Jamaica, among many others. With the Foreman-Norton bout already scheduled, Video Techniques was already planning its next move: Ali-Foreman.

But they weren't the only ones. Jerry Perenchio, who had cut his eye teeth on the Ali-Frazier fight, now wanted back into the boxing picture and was hot on the trail of Foreman. He had been "romancing George for months," providing him with "limousines and hotel rooms," even taking him to Las Vegas for one of his promotions at Caesar's Palace. He had, he thought, lined up Foreman for a number of promotions. But every time it was a case of "close, but no cigar."

One of Perenchio's promotional wet dreams had Foreman announcing to a press conference before the second Ali-Frazier fight—with both of them there: "These two men will be fighting for the American championship this coming January [1974]," Foreman announces in Perenchio's fantasy. "I've been criticized for not fighting and been threatened by the World Boxing Association and World Boxing Council. I don't like to train, especially when these fights won't go for more than one or two rounds. Therefore, I'll fight both on the same night. I'll take the winner of the fight on first, and the loser second. And I only want a one-half hour break between fights."

Perenchio had worked out all the details of his "I can beat any heavyweight in the house" variation of the old John L. Sullivan *shtick*. He had gotten the approval of the Texas State Athletic Commission and approached UNICEF to share in the proceeds. Then, to put the evening in its true perspective, he conceived the idea of putting up a circus tent complete with cotton candy, candied apples, and sawdust in the middle surrounded by ten thousand bleacher seats. The crowd was to be blacktie only, $1,000 a seat with 50 percent of the anticipated $10,000,000 to go to UNICEF.

But it was never to be. Again, it was "close but no cigar." Next, he tried to get Foreman's name on a contract to defend his title against Ali. Thinking he had him cornered, he flew to Houston in mid-February, 1974, with a $10,000,000 letter of credit from the Chase Manhattan Bank in his pocket. But he couldn't "get Foreman or his manager, Dick Sadler, to even look at them."

The reason was simple. Although Foreman, Sadler, and his

business manager, Leroy Jackson, had led Perenchio on a merry chase, they had already signed a contract with Video Techniques. More specifically, it had been signed with the man who was fronting the negotiations for Video Techniques, Don King who, according to Video Techniques vice president Hank Schwartz, "Speaks to the Soul."

Perenchio had been "had." As he slowly settled in the West— becoming Norman Lear's partner in TAT Productions— Perenchio the boxing promoter looked back incredulously and said of the boxing fraternity: "The boxing industry as a group can't spell integrity, not even with a small 'i.' On a scale of one-through-ten," he added, "the Ali crowd comes closest to living up to their word; while the Foreman people have a penchant for stealing money and ideas."

Video Techniques now assumed Perenchio's tattered mantle, using Don King effectively as their downfield blocker to speak Soul-to-Soul with Herbert Muhammad and George Foreman. First they had gotten a thirty-day option for $100,000 from Herbert Muhammad to try to put together a Foreman-Ali fight in early February, 1974. Then King had jive-talked Foreman into signing by appealing to his blackness for another $50,000. Out of pocket for $150,000 and with just thirty days to come up with the megabucks to underwrite the fight, Hank Schwartz now embarked on the time-honored boxing odyssey, trying to raise money to stage the fight.

With the meter running, Schwartz began calling everyone on his Roledex. Working from A to Z, he finally got to the name Jack Solomon, three-quarters the way through the alphabet. Solomon, a British boxing impresario, suggested he fly to England immediately to meet with himself and two others who could be helpful in putting together the moneys—textile chieftain Lord Burnam and British closed-circuit promoter Jarvis Astaire.

After inviting Don King out to coffee and never inviting him back to their meeting at London's famed Grosvenor House, the foursome got down to negotiations. They talked . . . and talked . . . and talked. But the glove that stuck in the Briton's craw was the amount of money needed to float the fight. While they talked the realization suddenly hit Schwartz that he was running out of time and that his worthy British brethren were running out of ideas on how to come up with the bread. So he broke off the talks.

Schwartz took to walking the streets of London dejectedly, haunted by the thought that he had taken $150,000 out of a public company for options on a fight that now appeared to be a mental mirage. With nothing to show for it, he feared the consequences, even the possibility of going to jail. Then, as he turned down a side street, he came face-to-face with a sign affixed to an office building that read simply: "Hemdale Leisure Corporation." He remembered having done business with them before. What could he lose by seeing them now?

Hemdale's president John Daly agreed almost on the spot to put up irrevocable letters of credit for $11,500,000, $5,000,000 to each fighter and another $1,500,000 in up-front monies, with a promise to syndicate the fight in Europe. Instead of turning up a loser, Hank Schwartz, Video Techniques, George Foreman, Muhammad Ali, and Don King became winners.

On the basis of the $1,500,000 front money put up on February 28, one day before the option was to run out, Herbert Muhammad gave Schwartz yet another thirty days "to put the deal together." Foreman, who had to defend his title against Norton in Venezuela, reaffirmed his contract.

Hemdale then approached a German businessman who served as the European representative for many countries. In the vernacular he could be called a "bag man," or at the very least a "black attaché man." The German told the Hemdale representatives that "Zaire would back the fight" if they could "sell Premier Joseph Mobuto a 'bill of goods'" concerning the overall effect of black fighters fighting in a black country. It would be a sort of black homecoming. The German and the Hemdale representatives met with a Swiss attorney in Geneva who represented Bernie Cornfeld and IOS. They were joined by a roving minister of Zaire who had been one of Mobuto's commissioners, but had been banished from Zaire because of Communist leanings. It soon became evident to all that the supposed Communist was in reality a capitalist in drag. In fact, according to one of those who sat in on the meetings, he was "the most aggressive capitalist" he had ever seen. With King's help, they sweet-talked Mobuto into holding the fight—soon to become known as The Rumble in the Jungle—in Zaire. Zaire was to underwrite all costs in the name of international public relations.

Together this unlikely group of bedfellows—Hemdale, Schwartz and Video Techniques, the German "finder," and the Zairian commissioner without portfolio as well as the government of Zaire—all formed a Swiss corporation named Rinsella, momentarily sheltering the government of Zaire so that it would not seem to be a party if the project should be aborted.

Meanwhile, back in Venezuela, Foreman finished off Norton in two lackluster rounds and prepared to leave Caracas. The Venezuela government, however, reneged on its promise to the promoters and the fighters to provide them with a tax-free status. Now, while everyone stood around at the airport, the Venezuelan authorities refused to let them leave the country until they paid an 18 percent tax. To insure their getting it, the government put Foreman and Norton under what amounted to "house arrest" and impounded Video Techniques' equipment.

Foreman was furious. Although Video Techniques posted $250,000 to ransom him from the Venezuelan authorities, he held it accountable for his incarceration. Now it was back to square one with the champion. Seeing the fight in Zaire going down for the count, it once more looked to King to rescue its chestnuts from the fire. Again he responded, packing a tooth-brush and flying to San Francisco with Foreman to plead Video Techniques' case. There he "put my well-known talking machin-ery to work" and sermonized Foreman into signing a blank piece of paper. The fight was on again.

King was rewarded for his efforts in salvaging the fight and insuring that nothing went wrong from that point on with a promoter's fee paid right off the top, a position as vice president of Video Techniques, and expense monies. No questions asked.

All was in place. Ali would have his $5,000,000, plus $400,000 training expenses and $100,000 good-faith advance. Foreman would get his $5,000,000, $250,000 training expenses, and $50,000 good-faith advance. Hemdale would have its fight. Video Techniques would have the worldwide television rights. The man who would be King would have his title and expense account. And Zaire would have its place in the sun—or rain, if the fall monsoon season came earlier than expected.

Everyone was happy, that is, except Foreman's erstwhile business manager, Leroy Jackson, who attempted to shake down Hemdale's John Daly for more money just before the fight with a veiled threat that Foreman would "pull out." Daly called his bluff. He not only didn't give in—as so many before him had—but also threatened Jackson with arrest for extortion.

George Foreman was one of those unfortunates who had always gotten caught up in his mental underwear. As street-smart as any ghetto graduate, George was bewildered in the savvy world of freewheelers and spellbinders that the Sweet Science unleashed on him. He once sold one-half of his future earnings to a talent agent named Marty Ehrlichman, who handled Barbra Streisand and promised him great things, including having Barbra sing the National Anthem at all his fights. That arrangement was to cost him dearly in later lawsuits. He had then taken on Leroy Jackson, a former Job Corps classmate, who saw the communal pot of George's money as a windfall and treated it as his own. In fact, the moment Foreman had returned to his hotel in Jamaica after tearing the heavyweight crown off Joe Frazier's head, Jackson had slammed the door shut and screamed at Foreman and his entourage, "I'm in charge now!" He proceeded to read George a financial bill of particulars which Foreman stood still for and bought.

But over and above his financial virginity, Foreman suffered from other misconceptions. He firmly believed that he had a mission and that he had been knighted with invincibility inside the ring and out. He couldn't understand it when the press and some of the public began to tear patches from his hide. He was villified as The Mummy and Ali was hailed as the conquering hero. This mystified him.

On the evening of October 30, 1974—the evening of a day that had dawned some 85 years before in the middle of nowhere in Richburg, Mississippi—two battlers stood in a ring in the middle of nowhere in Kinshasha, Zaire. Boxing and history had merged, coming full circle and halfway around the world. With one deep-dish beauty of a punch, launched those four score and five years before, Muhammad Ali made a mockery of the fight odds and George Foreman's invincibility. His knock-out of Foreman at 2:58 of the eighth round was an upset comparable to the one David had wrought years before by decking the giant Goliath. The Rumble in the Jungle was over. Muhammad Ali—who was alone in his belief that he would, in the words of the old fight announcer Harry Balough, "emerge victorious"—was atop the heavyweight heap again.

With a gross of more than $6,500,000 in the United States and another $3,000,000 worldwide in closed-circuit sales, Video Techniques and Hemdale came out of the Ali-Foreman fight whole. The only loser was Zaire. But then again, it had been worth the $5,000,000 loss to them for the publicity and attention they had gained; a public relations fee, if you will, for worldwide exposure.

Some six months after the fight, a squib tucked away under the shipping news completed the financial arrangements of one of the most bizarre promotions in all sports history. The story told how the country of Zaire, in a true *Mouse that Roared* scenario, had requested—and been granted—a loan of $5,000,000 from the United States for defense assistance, the *exact* amount it had lost on the Rumble in the Jungle.

No longer content to hide his cotton-candy hairdo in someone else's shadow, the man who had upstaged everyone in "The Rumble in the Jungle"—even claiming full credit for the promotion—now advanced to center stage. The character he played was a larger-than-life version of the cartoonesque promoter depicted by Zero Mostel in *The Producers*, a Max Bialystock in black face. But Don King played it to the fullest, combining a street-smart mentality with a penchant for survival. And above all, playing on his blackness, speaking directly to the souls of boxing's spear-carriers, the black boxers.

To the white boxing establishment, this interloper who believes in the spirit of unconventionality—that strain of eccentricity which Susan Sontag calls "Off"—and who not only knew he was a genuine "character," but exploited it, emerged full-blown on the boxing scene. But in truth, the man who immodestly bills himself as "The Modern Day P.T. Barnum" had climbed a circuitous—almost tortuous—path to his Olympian height as the most visible boxing promoter of his day. And his background bore more of a resemblance to Tex Rickard than it did to Barnum.

Born and raised in Cleveland, Ohio, even before the word "ghetto" became fashionable, King was orphaned at the age of 11—the same age as Rickard—his father killed in a smelter explosion at the Jones and Laughlin refinery. With the settlement monies ("in the ghetto we call that tragedy money"), his mother bought a house for the King brood of eight. The rest she put into starting a little cottage industry: the sale of small bags of peanuts with lucky numbers inside. It was there that Don King the promoter was born, pushing little bags that contained hot peanuts and even hotter dreams with an almost liturgical sing-song "Get your hot roasted peanuts and your numbers here. . . . " His evangelical pitch brought Mrs. King customers and little Don a reputation that was to serve as his baptism into the world of hustling. From there it was an easy step for King—like Rickard before him—to eschew the world of formal education for the netherworld of gambling as he set up his own numbers route, peddling "dreams and schemes."

King was fiercely proud of his reputation for honesty. As well as his "turf." And he protected both with his quick payoffs to winners, always commingling the payoff with a patter that took the form of a self-promotion: "Tell 'em where you got it . . . You got it from Don King! . . . " To those whose business he coveted, he gave the old come-on: "Bust me and go to the Hall of Fame. . . . It took Babe Ruth 60 home runs to get there . . . It took Ty Cobb 96 stolen bases to get there . . . But bust me and get to Cooperstown yourself. . . . " It worked. So well, in fact, that he was soon being called by the press "The Numbers King of Cleveland."

That is, it worked until King protected both his reputation and his turf too fiercely.

As King's numbers empire grew, so too did his circle of so-called "friends," acquaintances, and well-wishers. One of them, an old acquaintance who was as much a resident of "Tapioca City" as Cleveland, approached King for a job. King, ever the soft touch, not only set him up in business, but delegated some of his authority as well as some of his "action" to his newfound associate. However, in the classic manner of biting the hand that fed him, King's new ward used the opportunity to go into business for himself, pocketing rather than laying off the money King had collected from his clientele. Sure enough, one of the numbers placed "hit." And come payoff time, neither the associate nor the money was anywhere to be found. King made good on the payoff. But the memory of the money lost and the misplaced trust simmered within him.

That simmer finally came to a head when the miscreant, without bothering to apologize for the previous deceits he had practiced on King, beseeched his former patron and employer once again for help, reinforcing his demands with the menace of proximity. King's anger over the ingratitude, the dishonesty, and the hurt to his reputation boiled over into a physical manifestation of his exasperation. As push came to shove, he knocked down the man who had wronged him and then, by his own admission, "kicked him in the head." The former associate would not bother King again. Or anyone else, for that matter. He was dead. King was tried for unpremeditated homicide. And for being black and "The Numbers King" as well. He was convicted of "Murder Two" and sentenced to the Marion Correctional Institution for up to thirty years. Suddenly, Don King was no longer "The Numbers King." From 1967 to 1971, he was merely No. 125734.

During those three-plus years, in an atmosphere where many men's minds have snapped, souls shriveled, and bodies become bent, King blossomed like a hothouse flower. "I read Voltaire . . . Shakespeare . . . Machiavelli. . . . When I got out of that fucking prison in 1971, I was a dangerous character. I was armed with knowledge."

Upon his release from prison in 1971—after serving his reduced sentence for manslaughter—King determined to make

218

something of himself. And to convert the lemon that fate had handed him into lemonade.

A boxer and a street-fighter in his youth, he turned—like so many blacks before him—to the world of boxing. But King's sights were set on something that had been denied to blacks before him, the promotional side of the street.

After calling on his contacts in Cleveland, and in such nearby cities as Erie and Scranton, King insinuated himself into a position as a sort of roving ambassador with partial portfolio to the Foreman-Frazier fight in Jamaica in January, 1971. As his sponsors watched their closed-circuit screens back in the States with an admixture of shock and amazement, they saw King somehow position himself into the middle of the post-fight festivities in center ring.

For the rest of the decade Don King has stood in that same center ring. First as manager of such worthies as Earnie Shavers and Jeff Merritt. Then, when their careers took a proverbial nosedive, stepping over them to become the foremost boxing promoter in the world, using Other People's Money—as Rickard had before him—to promote fights in faraway places known only to Messrs. Rand and McNally: Kuala Lumpur, Manila, and Kinshasa, to name but a few.

Don King deserves inclusion in the "Who's Who in Ballyhoo"— "How could you keep me out?"—for his addition of a new dimension to boxing: the substitution of entire countries for the boxing clubs of yesteryear; and marketing boxing bouts as national and international promotions.

Today, although known by many things to many people—a man who more often than not goes one-on-one with the English language and loses; who is his own worst enemy; and who has contributed to the undermining of his own brainchild, the United States Boxing Championship, not only by trying to control the fighters but also by failing to monitor the activities of those under him dedicated to boxing's time-honored art of, as he calls them, "trickerations"—Don King stands almost as tall as his Elsa Lanchester hairdo. For he has taken an instrument that has seemed as crude and monotonous as a dime-store flute and produced noisy bass blasts of showmanship and a scale of international overtones.

It was inevitable, in the concentric world that governs man and promoter alike, that two of the brightest lights would ultimately join together in the name of the most common currency known to promoters: expediency. And it was equally inevitable that such a union could take place only in the grab-ass world of boxing, where it is literally every man for himself.

And so, when super-promoter David A. Werblin—the same "Sonny" Werblin who gave you the American Football League and the Jersey Meadowlands—ascended to the presidency of Madison Square Garden, it was only natural that he sought out the one man who could solidify the Garden's claim to being the temple of boxing. That one man was Don King.

In what was the first co-adventure to promote fights that the Garden had struck with any outside promoter since they invited Mike Jacobs to share their bed and board some forty-plus years before, Werblin announced to a packed press conference that "Madison Square Garden has entered into a co-promotional agreement with Don King for the joint presentation of boxing bouts in the Garden on a non-exclusive basis." Each possessed something the other wanted: King was an independent promoter, able to "control" fighters, something the Garden was restrained from doing by court order; the Garden, on the other hand, was what King, like Rickard before him, coveted, "the fulfillment of a dream."

King accepted the scepter and began to trumpet his pleasure at having been brought into the very throne room of boxing, touching on a diverse range of subjects with all the direction of an out-of-control Water Pik. He had just begun to launch into his favorite subject, proclaiming that "Only in America could a Don King happen," when his new boss-associate gingerly pushed a piece of paper in front of him reading: "Cut soon . . . Need pictures . . . They're on deadline."

King read the note, paused, and went on talking about ships, sails, sealing wax, cabbages, and self, assuring all who could hear him that indeed only in America could a promoter like Don King happen.

Muhammad Ali had turned both prophet and profit. The man who had entered boxing with a memory bank, spouting out doggerel, now possessed enough money to start a bank. The $5,000,000 he received for deflating the Foreman balloon was in itself more than the $3,000,000 Marciano grossed in his entire fistic career, more than the $3,500,000 Dempsey earned in the squared ring, and even more than the $4,600,000 Joe Louis earned. He has earned more than $50,000,000 fighting in enough rings around the world to give even the youngest grade-school youngster a crash course in geography. That is more than that grossed by *all* the other heavyweight champions of all time!

But will boxing, as the self-proclaimed Greatest has said time and again, "die when I quit?" Has boxing become a sport hitched to a single trace horse named Muhammad Ali?

While Ali would have you believe so, just as he has made believers of us all for the past two decades, the truth is that he has merely served as a comma—not a period—in boxing's two-and-a-half century evolution.

For today boxing has once again been rediscovered. Whether it was the Hollywood success of *Rocky* or the Montreal success of five U.S. gold medalists is not important. What is important is that boxing has had a rebirth on network TV. It is a ratings winner, which, according to a recent study by McCann-Erickson, "delivers high ratings and showed significant viewing interest among young men."

But this time around, it is not television which is using boxing. Quite the reverse. This time boxing's marrow has changed. Boxing is *using* TV, with promoters and promotions standing in line to sell the three competitive networks live fights, delayed fights and, even entire tournaments to fill the giant maw of some thirteen hundred hours of sports programming each year. And boxing's alphabet soup listing of organizations that control it, including the WBC and the WBA, now must add three more: ABC, CBS, and NBC.

This time around the answer to "the number of asses that are in . . . the seats" may only be told the morning after by Nielsen and not by the gate count.

But regardless of who is counting, boxing has gotten up off the floor yet another time and is ready once again to do battle as a major sport in spite of its own problems—including the lack of small clubs, and the lack of "name" fighters in classes below the heavyweight level.

For, as archie told mehitabel, "There's life in the old girl yet!"

5

From Sweetwater to slam dunks: Basketball for fun and profit

"**T**raining is everything," wrote Mark Twain, in *The Tragedy of Pudd'nhead Wilson*. "The peach was once a bitter almond: cauliflower is nothing but cabbage with a college education." To complete the syllogism, basketball is merely a peach basket with a little professional upbringing.

While Twain was typing these words in the first double-spaced manuscript ever submitted, a few miles from his Hartford, Connecticut, home members of the faculty of The School for Christian Workers, a YMCA training school, were meeting in Springfield, Massachusetts, to discuss a problem.

For forty years the Young Men's Christian Association had dedicated itself to instilling young people with a healthy outlook on life. It sought to attain this high-minded goal through a combination of "physical fitness and mental training" coupled with religious ideals and fellowship. But it had become evident that winter exercises consisting primarily of gymnastics fell far short of instilling anything except boredom.

Now in the fall of 1891, the faculty members of the physical education department of The School for Christian Workers—soon to become known as Springfield College—were meeting to discuss their winter program. The dean expressed his concern: "We're dead wrong to train our students on the horse, the buck, the bars, and the ring, and all this other gymnastic equipment. Frankly, gentleman, it bores them to death after a successful fall of football."

After recounting the growing antagonism of the young men to the routinized program of marching, calisthenics, and apparatus work, he was moved to remark, "We need a new game to exercise our students; a competitive game like football or lacrosse, but one that can be played indoors."

Then, seeking an athletic penicillin to get them through the winter, he pointed his pencil at a thirty-year-old member of the faculty named James Naismith and suggested that he "take the class and see what you can do with it."

The meeting was adjourned. The ball, as the saying goes, was in Naismith's court. Mentally, he began to play every game he had ever seen in the lumbering regions of Canada where he had been raised. Finally, Duck on a Rock occurred to Naismith. The game, as he remembered it, was one where a "hurled ball might send the 'duck' further, but a tossed ball was far more accurate." With this in mind, Naismith designed a mongrelized version. He hung the goal "high enough so that the ball would have to be tossed into it, rather than being thrown." The players' positions were dictated by lacrosse.

Naismith posted his hastily pencilled rules on the bulletin board, summoned the class to the first game, and sent the janitor out to acquire two 15-by-15-inch boxes to serve as goals. When that worthy was unable to find the prescribed boxes, he demonstrated considerable Yankee ingenuity, returning instead with two half-bushel peach baskets, thus insuring that the game, which might have come down to us as "box ball," would be known henceforth as "basket ball."

When the eighteen students in the class assembled the next day, they played the strange new game with an ordinary soccer ball and the two peach baskets hung from the gallery rails. Arrayed in two teams of nine, they raced up and down the floor, stopping only while an attendant on a ladder fished the ball out of the peach basket to put it back in play. The game, it was agreed, was "an enormous success."

Soon after its inception, the game began to grow away from the lofty qualities with which it had been brought into the world. There were the normal changes in its rules. The players dwindled like office hours from nine to five, and metal rims with twine baskets soon took the place of the quaint peach baskets appended to balcony balustrades.

But no amount of tinkering with the rules could change the character of the game, one that was beginning to harden into an indoor version of Johnny-on-a-pony, complete with an un-Christian roughness brought to it by the overenthusiastic company it kept. This, combined with the boisterous behavior of those who befriended it in the gymnasiums of its youth, finally persuaded the Springfield YMCA and other Y's throughout the country to drop its progeny from the program. The YMCA had turned its collective back on its own creation.

Banned from its spawning ground, the game now began a gypsy existence. For the first twenty years of the twentieth century it wandered nomadically from drafty armories to tawdry dance halls.

Touring pick-up teams began to create a following, particularly in New York and Philadelphia areas and the coal mining regions of Pennsylvania. Basketball was becoming a "social'" event. Reduced to renting halls and armories that had once been available to them for free, teams began to charge admission to defray expenses. Extra monies were "divvyed-up" among the players; ergo the teams became, by definition, professionals.

Many games during that era had a surrealistic quality. They were played in a cage. Whether made of chicken wire or steel or netting like the baskets—which bounced back and forth and added to the overall effect—the primary purpose was to keep the ball in play on the small courts of the day, although more than once they served as protection from overzealous fans. Hence, the term "cagers."

Games were scheduled in New York wherever room could be found, at the 369th Regiment Armory and Prospect Hall in Brooklyn; in Philadelphia, at the Musical Fund Hall, the Auditorium, and later at the Braodwood. And just as often at dance halls in the area.

The game itself was part of the dance hall's promotion, part of its floor show, serving either as the preliminary to the evening's entertainment or as the main attraction itself, depending upon the stature of the dance band. With dancing both before and after the game, the management would pour resin on the floor; some clubs, like the Arcadia, put whiskey on the floor and lit it to melt the dance wax before the teams took the floor. They played in an atmosphere where, according to New York Celtics' guard Johnny Beckman's remembrance of the scene, "The smoke was so bad, it was impossible to see."

Perhaps the most fabled dance hall to feature basketball in the 1920s was the Renaissance Ballroom at 138th Street and 7th Avenue, in the heart of Harlem. One fall day in 1922, William Roache, the builder of the Renaissance, was approached by entrepreneur Bobby Douglas. Douglas had a team that had been playing wherever and whenever they could—at the Rockland

Casino at 155th Street or the 369th Regiment Armory—but now he wanted an alternate site, one that would provide his team with a "home" court. Douglas thought Roache might be interested. "They had just built the building and it wasn't going so good. And I told him if you take me there you'll get some good, good business." But Roache wasn't interested. That is, he wasn't interested unless Douglas would name his team of black players Renaissance as a promotion for the dance hall. Douglas could only think, "Now who in the hell wanted to name a team Renaissance." But he did and began playing on a percentage, giving Roache 40 percent of the admissions. New York sportswriters soon took care of Douglas' dilemma by labeling the basketball team the Rens. Still Roache was "tickled to death" by the association, albeit one that was contracted.

Douglas remembers playing the New York Celtics, the Philadelphia Sphas, and the Brooklyn Visitations on Sunday and holiday nights. They played "first and between and around" the breaks of some of "the biggest bands in those days—Jimmy Lunceford, Cab Calloway, Duke Ellington, Count Basie, Benny Goodman, and others."

But the Renaissance's biggest day was Thanksgiving. Douglas would always schedule "my rival," the South Philadelphia Hebrew Association team, familiarly known as the Sphas, led by their coach Eddie Gottlieb. Lines would start forming on Seventh Avenue at five in the afternoon, and "if you didn't get there round 'bout seven, you had a tough time getting in." Then, in front of a packed house of some two thousand screaming fans, Douglas would first offer a preliminary game between two teams of youngsters at 7:30, followed by one of the big bands or some other entertainment, including a boxing exhibition by Harry Wills or Panama Al Brown, capping the evening with a 9:30 game between the Renaissance and the Sphas.

It was a time when basketball teams preferred to "go it alone," aligning themselves with dance halls and armories rather than the loose-fitting combinations of independent teams called "leagues." The Sphas, the Renaissance, and the New York Celtics served as the seeds for the development of professional basketball by taking their act on the road, barnstorming anywhere big enough to have an arena and spreading the basketball gospel.

Barnstorming was a peculiar child of the twenties. It took its shape and its form from those early aeronauts who appeared throughout the country, offering everyone their first look-see at the newfangled machine for just "five dollars for a five-minute ride." And it took its name from a mutual arrangement of convenience where on a slow day the pilot landed in a farmer's pasture and offered him a five-minute joy ride for a place to park his biplane temporarily in the farmer's barn.

Soon the form and the phrase would be adopted.by others, as first baseball and then basketball made the term a part of their own idiom, traveling from town to town "shaking money out of the rubes."

Baseball had pioneered in tours of the great expanses of the United States where major league baseball was only a rumor. Entire teams had even gone abroad as early as 1874. In 1889 "the greatest colored team ever organized," the Colored All-American Tourists, hit the hustings, with eight games in eight states. Their announcement read: "They will travel in their own palace car. The great feature of this club will be their daily parades, which will be in full-dress suits, black pants, white vests, swallow-tailed coats, opera hats and silk umbrellas. By request of different managers, they will play games in full-dress suits." It was the beginning of the Golden Age of Barnstorming. Big-time baseball came to small-town America, with entire teams of traveling major leaguers, black teams, and finally variety teams like the House of David brightening the season of many a fan.

But the team that was to become known as the biggest barnstorming attraction of all time was not a baseball team. It was a basketball team. And it got its start in the incubator of professional basketball, the dance hall. In particular, the Savoy Hotel Ballroom in Chicago.

The Savoy was an extension of the fabled Savoy in Harlem, memorialized in Benny Goodman's "Stompin' at the Savoy." Its owners built a Xeroxed version of the famous club on Chicago's South Side in 1926 and it soon became part of That Toddling Town. But something was missing: the anticipated crowds.

The business agent of the Negro basketball team representing the Giles Post of the American Legion approached the new manager of the Savoy Chicago. "You're right in the middle of a sports-minded area. You oughta cash in on that," he tantalizingly threw out. The manager took the bait. Did he have something in mind?

Of course! "Basketball is a growing sport. You'll do alright at the gate," answered the business agent, letting him have a little line.

"What's the attraction?" asked the Savoy manager. Now he

was really hooked. "We've got a natural," the business agent went on, replaying the plotline pioneered by Douglas four years earlier. "We'll move our team into the Savoy, adopt the Savoy name, and build up a following. It can't miss!" With that, he was able to land his prize catch. The team was renamed the Savoy Five Five and debuted on a blustery night in November, 1926. With them came their coach, Abe Saperstein.

The 22-year-old Saperstein, barely standing one Adler shoe size above five feet tall, had taken over the Giles Post basketball team earlier that year after coaching a 135-pound team at Welles Playground on Chicago's North Side. He shared one ironic characteristic with five others who were the principal shapers of America's most native sport—Naismith, Douglas, Gottlieb, Saperstein, and Maurice Podoloff, the first president of the NBA—he was born in another country, London, England. But the date of his birth—July 4, 1903—made him as American as George M. Cohan, who was actually born on July 3, but believed he was "a Yankee Doodle Dandy/Born on the Fourth of July" anyway.

The young Saperstein looked like a cross between W. C. Fields' version of the "world's tallest midget" with an English accent and a round basketball, complete with cigar—the archetype promoter. He embraced not only America's sport of basketball, but its colors as well, wrapping his teams in the red, white and blue of its flag. Now, as he unfurled his newly named Savoy Big Five quintet on the floor of the Savoy Ballroom, he began to wonder about the wisdom of his adoptive choice of careers. For on that evening that epitomized Chicago's nickname as The Windy City, the players almost outnumbered the patrons.

It got no better soon. No throng of wild-eyed basketball fans beat a path to the Savoy's doors. Finally, after some financial disagreements, the management of the Savoy threw in the towel and made plans to offer roller skating as an added attraction.

Now out of the Savoy and out of bookings, Saperstein had a decision to make. "The boys asked me to go along with them," he was later to remark, "And I said 'yes.'" With that, Abe Saperstein took the first step towards basketball immortality.

If Saperstein temporarily had the "shorts," it wasn't a shortage of wits. Very quickly he came up with two ideas that would form the basis for his troupe and his business. One day he announced to his group, "There isn't much for us in Chicago. We're going to travel and pick up games wherever we can." And then he announced to his black players "And we're calling ourselves The Harlem Globetrotters."

The first part of his announcement sat well with the players. They were hungry. Not just for basketball but hungry, period. But the second part was somewhat mystifying: they were all from Chicago and had never set foot outside the second-largest city in the United States. "Why?" they chorused. "Because," came back Saperstein, who believed a myth is as good as a smile, "Harlem identifies this as a colored team. And Globetrotters makes it sound as if we have been around."

The Harlem Globetrotters hit the road to play in any town large enough to have a town arena. In an old beaten-up flivver Saperstein had purchased from a funeral director—and with Saperstein playing more roles than Alec Guinness in *Kind Hearts and Coronets*, including driver, coach, trainer, business manager, paterfamilias, and even substitute, the only white ever to appear in the Harlem Globetrotters' red, white, and blue uniform—the Globetrotters made their way to Hinckley, Illinois. There, on a snowy January 7, 1927, they played their first game in a little burg of less than a thousand, just fifty miles from Chicago.

That first year Saperstein and his troupe put in more miles than Lewis and Clark as they traveled throughout Illinois and the rest of the Midwest playing the "sticks." By the end of the year, the Globetrotters had played seventy-seven games, winning seventy-one of them for an amazing .922 average. They did it by resorting to the only *shtick* they had—outplaying, outhustling, and outshooting the local opposition. No touring team had been so successful since the New York Celtics had won 720 out of 795 games on the road, and even then they had had *only* a .906 won-lost percentage.

But while Saperstein the coach was pleased, Saperstein the business manager began to feel that the Globetrotters' victories were somewhat Pyrrhic. Not only was the nightly grind wearing his men out, but just as importantly the constant winning, often by large margins, was wearing the Globetrotters' welcome thin. No team wanted to be made to look bad and few if any would invite the Globetrotters back merely to lose by a large score. Something else was needed.

And so Saperstein added one more label to his ever-expanding list, that of marketer. Recognizing the central tenet of the basic marketing concept—that what the customer wants is what you ought to be selling—he added the element of comedy.

Balls began to magically appear from behind backs, off heads, and from between the players' legs. Soon other outrageous vaudeville acts were added as well, including the "baseball act" and the "fluke ball" trick. And the magic was transferred to the box office as well. By merely adding the element of clowning, Saperstein had chanced upon the concept of changing the basic nature of his team and the entertainment they offered. The Harlem Globetrotters had developed a singular place in the market.

The Globetrotters gave the fans both basketball and entertainment. Now the people came from miles around to see the only attraction that would come to their little town all winter. They all came to cheer for their local quintet and gawk at the carnival escapades of the Globetrotters, flocking to their local arena as if it were a circus. It was a circus, a carnival, a traveling variety show. They "oohed" and "aahed" as the Globetrotters came out on the court and went into their signature act, forming a circle and passing the ball around, often looking one way and passing another, or spinning it on their fingers for thirty seconds, or throwing it into the middle with so much backspin that it would come back. As the ball traveled madly up and down the circle for a few wild minutes, the townies laughed and stomped and whistled, trying to puzzle out what was going on. It was entertainment, pure and simple, and the fans loved it.

As the 'Trotters fame grew, so did the bookings and the guarantees. Their itinerary expanded from the Midwest into the Plains states and then the Western states, with an occasional foray into Canada and one into Mexico, thus legitimizing their claim to the title "Globetrotters."

And with increased bookings, Saperstein also increased his troupe. The first years had been marked by Spartan simplicity, five men on the team with Saperstein the only substitute, and one beat-up old Model-T. Now, with bookings and fortunes on the rise, Saperstein added two men and one car, thus giving him both a passenger and a "baggage" car.

Roaring down the highways and byroads of rural and small-town America in their twin flivvers, the Globetrotters finally came into their own as a full-fledged attraction. In 1940 they won the world basketball championship, beating all pro comers, including the champions of the National Basketball League. They were now outdrawing the entire league with their combination of skill and showboating.

By the late 1940s Saperstein had put together the nucleus of the famed Globetrotter team: the incredibly loose-jointed and long-armed Reese "Goose" Tatum; Marques Haynes, the "World's Greatest Dribbler"; Louis "Babe" Pressley; and Ermer Robinson. There still was one man he wanted, Nat "Sweetwater" Clifton.

But getting Sweetwater embroiled Saperstein in one of the few suits he ever was involved in, and this one with his old friend, Bobby Douglas.

Bobby Douglas, now 89 years young and still mentally as agile as he was when he captained and coached the Renaissance, remembers the fracas which took place right after World War II: "Two or three of my players were playing in Europe, and Sonny Wood, one of my good players, wrote back and told me about this boy, Sweetwater. And Sweetwater came in to see me when he got back. Well, Abe sued me. But he lost because he couldn't prove that Sweetwater was his man. And then I got mad and that saved me right after the war, I guess, 'cause I took three of his best men. You see, I paid all expenses for my team—even chewing gum. But all Abe allowed was sleeping. No food!" Douglas added.

"Then, right after the war, 1945 . . . around in there, he played with me from the fall until around February. Then we went into Dayton and Sweetwater jumped the team to play for a colored fella there who had a helluva nice business on Sunday afternoons. He played the best teams there is and he had what he called the Dayton All-Stars. And he enticed Sweetwater and gave him more than I paid him just to play once a week. And Sweetwater stayed there for a while and then he went to the Globetrotters."

After five years with the Globetrotters, Saperstein sold Clifton's contract to the Knicks in 1950 for $25,000, thus making him the first black to play in the NBA—three years after Jackie Robinson integrated baseball, four after Buddy Young integrated pro football, and a full eight years after the first integrated pro basketball team, the Chicago Studebakers, played in the old NBL.

Twenty years old in 1947, the Globetrotters had become the number one attraction in basketball, if not in all of sports. They had traveled hundreds of thousands of miles, entertaining millions of fans. And yet they stood at the crossroads. The 'Trotters were too good to be clowning around and yet clowned around too much to be good. Or at least, so their critics said.

But when the Globetrotters played the professional champion Minneapolis Lakers to a virtual standoff after the 1948–1949 season, many basketball fans and critics alike changed their opinion and came to regard them as the premier touring team in America. The next year they further cemented their claim by playing the outstanding college seniors in a postseason coast-to-coast tour called the World Series of Basketball, with the

Globetrotters winning the series handily. As a promotion, this postseason event was so successful it became an annual affair. The 'Trotters went on to win all eleven tours, taking 146 of the 212 games played.

Within a few years the 'Trotters act took to the road, visiting England, France, Germany, South America, and just about any other free country in the world, becoming in name as well as fact, America's Ambassadors of Goodwill.

As the Globetrotters prepared for the World Championship of Basketball against a group of graduating seniors, class of 1951, New York District Attorney Frank Hogan announced that several of the college stars had "shaved" points or dumped games for pay. Seeing his tour collapsing around him, Saperstein immediately called his old friend, Bill Veeck, a man who seems about as far from a sports promotion as a moth to a flame.

Veeck and Saperstein went back more than a few years. Saperstein also ran the Indianapolis Clowns of the Negro American Baseball League and was instrumental in funneling many black players to Veeck's Indians, including Luke Easter, Harry Simpson, and Minnie Minoso among others. And not only would Saperstein be a stockholder in Veeck's St. Louis Browns team of 1952, but Veeck would almost buy the 'Trotters from Saperstein when Abe was on his deathbed in 1966. "Almost had him conned into selling it, but he couldn't sign the papers. I don't mean figuratively, but literally," adds Veeck, always punctuating a good story.

Now Saperstein was on the phone to Veeck, down at his Arizona ranch. "I'm in terrible trouble," he shouted into the phone at Veeck. "We're just starting this tour and there's a disaster. They just indicted about eight basketball players from Long Island U. The papers are full of it . . . and you know most of these guys are going to play for me. Can you think of something?" he pleaded. Veeck, who was at that time between cups of coffee in the American League, had no immediate answer but promised to meet Saperstein in New York. "We'll think of something by the time I get there."

From Chicago, Veeck called Saperstein at his Empire State Building office, "Abe, look, I'm not coming to New York for another day or two. But I've got it solved." With that Veeck caught the next plane to Washington, D.C.

Arriving in Washington, he went immediately to the State Department and introduced himself as representing the 'Trotters. "I want to play a series in Russia. We'll play winner-take-all, give it all to charity. We'll do anything, anywhere," said Veeck, who can barely keep verbal pace with his motoring mile-a-minute ideas. "The only thing we ask is that we take the same number of referees with us that they have."

The official at the State Department coolly replied, "Oh, yes, that's fine. We'll have to have a meeting on that. You come back."

Veeck, who was not to be denied by red-white-and-blue tape, shot back, "You'd better have a meeting tonight. Because I'm going to the Russian Embassy tomorrow morning. I'd like to have your blessing. But I'm going anyway."

The official lamely answered, "That makes a difference." And Veeck, now walking as briskly as he could towards the door, said, "Yes, Yes, it's a great difference. I'll see you in the morning," and left.

The next morning Veeck stopped back to see the official. "Did you have that meeting?" "Oh, yes, we had a meeting last night and everything is fine. I'll call the Russian Embassy." But Veeck, who had "seen the way you've handled relations with the Russians," just wanted the address. "I'll go over by myself," and away he went.

Arriving at the Russian Embassy on 16th Street within minutes, Veeck asked at the switchboard for the cultural attaché and announced his intention of "playing basketball in Russia." The receptionist looked over the obviously addlepated man without a tie or briefcase and ushered him into a large room containing only a small table and a chair.

Finally, after what seemed like an eternity but was in reality only a half-hour, a personable young blond man came bustling into the room with his hand extended. "Mr Veeck, I'm sorry to have kept you waiting. You want the Globetrotters to play in Russia." Veeck, as surprised by the entry as by the fact that the man seemed to know his name, could only ask, "How did you know my name?" He answered, Veeck was sure only half-jokingly, "You know, we invented baseball."

Veeck half-heartedly laughed and could only venture, more as a question than as a statement, "I hadn't told the receptionist that I wanted to talk about the 'Trotters." The Russian official went on, "And you'd like to play an exhibition series, and you'd like to know right away." Veeck numbly replied in the affirmative by nodding his head.

"Well," went on the Russian, "obviously you know I can't give you an immediate decision. That has to come from Russia. But I will put the request in the diplomatic pouch leaving tonight."

Veeck finally was able to get his voice back to say, "Well, I'd like to be able to say 'We've challenged you.'"

The Russian replied, "That's perfectly alright. You *have* and the question is one we can't answer right away. But I will certainly be in touch and advise you one way or the other."

Then, in a manner befitting Alfred Hitchcock unfolding the denouement of one of his convoluted plots, he confessed, "You know, I'm not trying to be mysterious, Mr. Veeck," knowing full well that he was, "but as Mr. Saperstein knows, we have had observers following the Globetrotters every game they've played in Europe for the last couple of years. We had some of our people at *every* game." And then he added, "I knew the tour was starting in New York in a few days and I knew that you knew Mr. Saperstein, so I just put the thing together and enjoyed baffling you."

Back on firmer footing, Veeck wondered aloud, "While I'm here, could you tell me who to see at the Czechoslovakian and Hungarian and Latvian embassies?" The Russian formerly announced, "That won't be necessary. I'll take care of that for you."

And with that, the interview was over.

Veeck returned to New York where Saperstein made an announcement from the friendly confines of the sporting establishment's favorite trough, Toots Shor's, that they had challenged the Russians. In fact, it was the first time that any cultural group had even suggested going to Russia. The "challenge" got good ink in the New York papers.

But it was all for naught. Some months later, while the Globetrotters were playing in London, a letter was personally delivered to Saperstein. The Russians, so the letter went, "regretfully" couldn't arrange a tour for the 'Trotters of the Soviet Union. However, by this time, Saperstein and Veeck had forgotten about the incident; they had recruited enough players to replace the Long Island U. players and the cross-country tour had been a success, with the Globetrotters grossing between two and three million for the year.

Two years later, Bill Veeck, now the head of the St. Louis Browns baseball team and in Washington to play the Senators for the seventh-place championship of the American League, met the very same Russian attaché one afternoon at the Willard Hotel. Over long steins of beer the Russian finally put the entire picture in perspective: "I'll tell you the reason we couldn't accept your challenge" and then furtively added, "I'll deny ever having said it, as you can understand I must. What didn't occur to me, and did occur to *them*, is that we keep depicting the plight of the

American Negro as being in chains and beaten daily, in our propaganda. It would have messed up the whole thing if you were to bring eight or ten blacks who are obviously having a lot of fun, playing around . . . it doesn't fit the image we're trying to create of what you do to your minority groups."

Although the 'Trotters subsequently carried their globetrotting label to the Soviet Union, the Russian incident underlined one of the basic dilemmas Saperstein faced. For, as the Fifties turned into the Sixties, America began marching to a different drummer and many, including Veeck, began to think the Globetrotters were an anachronism. "What I was worried about was here was an all-black team playing with the same verve and style that is epitomized by an Uncle Tom—'Yassuh, yassuh, boy,'" Veeck punctuated. "And I kept waiting for the black people to picket the Globetrotters on the grounds that it made them look like Uncle Toms. But it has never happened! And that's a phenomenon. They yelled about Stepin Fetchit; they yelled about Old Black Joe, and Little Black Sambo. But no one says anything about the 'Trotters." He paused and said again, incredulously, "And that's a phenomenon!"

But for the Globetrotters, time has been suspended, their activities irrelevant to the beat of the upbeat times. Bill Cosby, who has an honorary contract with the Globetrotters for $1 a year, has always felt that although the 'Trotters have overtones of "Tomism," it provided an opportunity for blacks to make a fairly substantial income. And Larry Kamm, an ABC sports director, felt that same appreciation when he filmed the Globetrotters at Attica State Prison in the summer of 1975. He got the feeling that the black inmates merely felt that "these were black men who made good" and that "these guys epitomized the black man's climb out of the ghetto."

Throughout the years the Globetrotters would remain a symbol, but more a symbol of entertainment than race. It was a symbol Saperstein carefully built, following his own philosophy: "You've got to know what the people want, and then you've got to spend the money and put in the hard work to get it for them." And with that in mind, he added Ping-Pong players, trampoline artists, baton twirlers, and personalities to his traveling circus. He gave a start to Eddie Feigner, now the last of baseball's barnstormers with his famed King and his Court softball act. And he also signed up tennis champ Althea Gibson in 1959 to accompany the tour, a tour in which she "earned over $100,000 in six months" by her own estimation. The Globetrotters, once just five players and coach, had now grown to the point where it was more Barnum and Bailey than basketball.

In 1949, Saperstein put together the last remaining piece in his overall plan. He signed Louis "Red" Klotz, then a 29-year-old 5-foot 9-inch two-handed set-shooting guard who had played with the Philadelphia Sphas and the Baltimore Bullets, to provide his nominal "opposition." Klotz' teams, alternately known as the Washington Generals, the New Jersey Reds, the New Jersey Americans, the Boston Shamrocks, and the New York Nationals, play the 'Trotters an average of 140 games a year—losing almost all of them in as carefully choreographed a piece of balletic artistry as any found in *A Chorus Line*. In fact, the last time the Klotz-led opposition beat the Globetrotters was in 1971 in Martin, Tennessee, when a shot went in at the buzzer for a 98-97 win. When told that the Globetrotters' won-lost record for the past five years was 2,075–0, Dick Young of the *New York Daily News* said, "I thought it was a little better than that."

Today, more than fifty years after Abe Saperstein took those first tentative steps to the little town of Hinckley, Illinois— summoning up "the guts to go on the road," according to Bobby Douglas—the Globetrotters have fully earned their nickname. They have played to more than seventy million fans in eight-nine countries on all six continents, extending those first fifty miles into more than five million miles. And all built on one word: Entertainment.

Ever since the B. T. Babbitt Company offered lithographed picture cards in return for soap wrappers back in 1851, manu- facturers have energetically sought ways to merchandise their products and services, bringing them to the public's attention. They have tied their wares to premiums, events, songs, and just about every vehicle imaginable.

But, with few exceptions, such as the Decatur Staleys and the Green Bay Packers, the naming of entire sports teams for companies remained an overlooked area for tie-ins. That is, until the 1920s and 1930s, when companies tied in to tip-ins, naming basketball teams after themselves was a not-too-subtle manner of merchandising.

It was an age when advertising seemed to be a simpler matter than today: a day of sandwich boards, matchbook covers, and basketball teams. Everyone seemed to be in advertising or an authority on it. One day Stanley Resor, president of J. Walter Thompson, the world's largest advertising agency, took a subway ride down to Wall Street. He found himself seated next to a somewhat disheveled passenger who constantly tried to strike up a conversation. Finally, the man asked Resor, "What do you do?" Resor answered brusquely, "I'm in advertising." "So am I!" the man exclaimed. "And, ain't it hell when the wind blows?" he added. "Really, what do you do?" Resor responded in shock. "Why, I carry a sandwich board, maybe you've seen it, 'Income Tax Forms, Only $1.' " Now everyone was "in advertising." Especially basketball teams, which used their jerseys as sandwich boards.

Only one step removed from industrial teams, the professional basketball teams of the Twenties and Thirties bore so many advertisements on their uniforms that the basketball courts began to take on the look of a running, dribbling, jumping Yellow Pages. The brand and corporate names that bedecked the basketball courts of that era are reflected in some of the names of teams that opened and closed faster than off-Broadway plays:

Indianapolis Kautskys
Cleveland Rosenblums
Pittsburgh Second-Story Morry's
Washington Palace Five
Anderson Duffy Packers
Chicago American Gears
Toledo Jim White Chevrolets
Cleveland Chase Brass
Fort Wayne Zollner Pistons
Akron Firestone Non-Skids
Akron Goodyear Wingfoots
Richmond King Clothiers
Flint Dows
Toledo Jeeps
Warren Penn Oilers
Cleveland Allmen Transfers
Columbus Athletic Supply
Dayton Metros
Ft. Wayne General Electrics
Louisville Aluminates

These marvelously yclept teams advertised goods and services ranging from meat markets (Kautskys) and clothing stores (Rosenblums, Second-Story Morry's Metro, and Richmond King Clothiers) to automotive suppliers. Most were products of a loose confederation called the National Basketball League. The league, formed in the late 1930s by three corporate giants—Goodyear, Firestone and General Electric—from their former entries in the Midwest Industrial Basketball Conference, provided an added dimension to their corporate and product names.

It seemed that everyone was wearing a sandwich board advertising something or other. The Kankakee Gallagher Trojans, who stayed in the inaugural season of the NBL barely long enough for a time-out, came out of the Gallagher Business College in Kankakee, Illinois, and played under the same nickname—the Trojans—they had used in playing other small schools throughout the area. The Evansville Agogans were sponsored by a local Baptist Bible class.

Whatever they were advertising, professional basketball, caught in a frieze during this embryonic period of its development, had established the long-standing relationship between the game and business. Basketball had taken its first step towards becoming a handmaiden to promotion.

Basketball continued to hide its light under a promotional basket throughout the remainder of the 1930s and into the early 1940s, its growth stunted by its umbilicus to company teams, small towns, and unknown talent. It seemed destined to be a permanent second-class citizen in the world of sports.

Then, two things occurred—Irish and ice—which were to change the face of basketball.

The Irish in the mix was Edward "Ned" Irish, a young sports reporter for the *New York World-Telegram* and part-time publicity man for the New York football Giants. He was just 29 years old in the winter of 1934 when he was assigned to cover a game between CCNY and Manhattan College, two of the many schools in the area that had built up a basketball following. Arriving fashionably late at Manhattan's closet-like gymnasium, Irish was greeted by a packed gym, with "no room at the inn" for latecomers. Resourcefully, Irish attacked a small gym window and squeezed through, ripping his pants in the process.

Sensing that "college basketball had to leave the gym," Irish set out on a bold gamble. Quitting his job with the paper, he approached Madison Square Garden to rent the famed amphitheater for a college basketball game. The Garden, which faced many a dark night during those Depression days, was more than receptive to his idea and willing to gamble. Management let Irish have the arena without putting up a cent, risking the $4,000 rent money against a larger percentage of the gross. If it didn't succeed, Irish would forfeit his option to promote more basketball games there.

With his entire promotorial future at stake, Irish decided to try yet another innovative idea. He would couple two college basketball games, giving the fans three hours of entertainment instead of the normal hour and a half. And, not incidentally, with four teams playing, he would have four student bodies and alumni to draw from, thus doubling their pleasure and his house.

At that time, the biggest sporting attraction in the New York area was the Army-Notre Dame football game, played every year to a capacity crowd at Yankee Stadium. If the Fighting Irish were such a draw in football, thought Ned Irish, why not basketball? Especially since they had won 54 and lost 12 during the past three years and featured All-America guard George Ireland and forward John Moir. Their competition? The strongest team in the New York region, New York University. The second game would pit St. John's University, another local favorite, against Westminster College of Pennsylvania.

All answers to the question "Would college basketball draw?" were answered in the affirmative on the night of December 29, 1934, as 16,180 fans crowded into Madison Square Garden to see NYU beat Notre Dame, 25–18, and Westminster administer a beating to St. John's, 37–33. The Irish formula had worked. Basketball had overnight become a major league sport. In eight doubleheaders that first season, the Garden attracted 99,528 fans, an average house of 12,441, more than two-thirds of capacity and almost one-and-a-half times as many as the Garden's supposed "bread-and-butter" sport, boxing.

Irish continued to parlay his gamble into a personal fortune, as he promised sizeable guarantees and previously unthinkable publicity to schools playing in the Garden. In turn, they drew almost half-a-million basketball fanatics each year to his program of doubleheaders and the National Invitation Tourney, added in 1938.

But Irish's contributions might have been restricted to the college arena had it not been for the presence of the other ingredient in the magical mix which was to forge the future of professional basketball: "ice."

The 1920s had witnessed an orgy of athletic plant construction. Not only were Yankee Stadium and most of the college stadia built, but so were many indoor facilities, including Madison Square Garden, Boston Garden, the Cleveland Arena, the Detroit Olympia, the Philadelphia Arena, Maple Leaf Gardens, the St. Louis Arena, Washington's Uline Arena, and several other similar indoor edifices.

But instead of covering their arena floors with sand, as they had in days of yore—the word *arena*, meaning *sand* in Latin, came from the practice of spreading sand on the floor to absorb blood during regularly scheduled bouts between gladiators, making the Roman colosseum the Yankee Stadium of its day— the owners chose ice. Ice was not only a far more civilized substance, but it also was the required base for activities that were becoming quite popular: ice shows and ice hockey.

The game that had been Canada's passion and pastime, ice hockey, had come south of the border, expanding into Boston in 1924, New York and Pittsburgh in 1925, and Chicago and Detroit in 1927 with NHL franchises. Almost immediately thereafter, minor league teams found their way into every cold-weather city of any appreciable size with an arena. Then came the ice shows, skating-and-musical extravaganzas that featured the likes of Sonja Henie, who appeared in the Hollywood Ice Revue and similarly structured shows called the Ice Capades and the Ice Follies. The arena owners were ecstatic. They not only had prime tenants, the ice hockey teams, but also attractions which booked solid a week or more and were every bit as successful financially as they were artistically.

With ice hockey providing the arena owners with both an attraction and a profit during their indoor winter season, this exclusive club, all of whom were members of a fraternity known as the Arena Managers Association of America, began to search for other such attractions. Particularly ones which would fit into the time-honored "Up your profits!"

With the close of World War II, the owners found the answer: professional basketball. Here was a sport that was ready-made for arenas, an indoor game played during the winter months and virtually unknown in major metropolitan areas. Moreover, with the expected postwar boom which would create a bonanza for all sports, could anyone doubt that—properly packaged—basketball could easily become yet another profit center? Especially, if the arena owners who controlled the facilities also controlled the sport?

And so, eleven arena owners, ten of whom had franchises in either the National Hockey League or the American Hockey League, met in New York on June 6, 1946, to form a professional basketball league. Present and accounted for were owners from New York, Boston, Detroit, Toronto, Philadelphia, Providence, Cleveland, Pittsburgh, St. Louis, and Washington as well as the attorney for the Norris family in Chicago. The new league officially adopted the name Basketball Association of America and, as if to perpetuate the lifeline to ice hockey, named the president of the American Hockey League, Maurice Podoloff, as president of the new league. Professional basketball had finally made it to the "big time"—on the coattails of ice hockey.

For the next eight years the league looked more like a dock wallopers' shape-up than a basketball league. The roster of teams took on the madcap comings-and-goings of Grand Central Station, with franchises entering and leaving almost every year. Of the eleven teams in the BAA at the inaugural tip-off, four folded after the first season—Pittsburgh, Toronto, Detroit, and Cleveland—Providence held on for three losing seasons, and Chicago, St. Louis, and Washington managed to make it through four.

Drawing on his ample background as attorney and negotiator, Podoloff, who resembled in shape his product, was always able somehow to round up another team or two to take up the slack. He brought in Baltimore from the American Basketball League in 1947 and Minneapolis, Ft. Worth, Rochester, and Indianapolis in one gulp from the National Basketball League in 1948, thereby adding name players like George Mikan and Chuck Davies. The remainder of the NBL slipped into the BAA's ever-expanding tent in 1949, with Sheboygan, Waterloo, Tri-Cities, Anderson, Syracuse, and Denver taking their place in the league, newly named the National Basketball Association. The results were more of the same: Baltimore lasted seven years, Indianapolis five, Tri-Cities two, and Anderson, Sheboygan, Waterloo, and Denver one each.

If there was such a thing as a watershed year for the NBA, it occurred during the 1954-1955 season. Behind it were twenty-three different franchises in eight years, the end of the Minneapolis Lakers' total domination of the league with the retirement of the first NBA superstar, George Mikan, and the first television contract. Also behind it was the deterioration of the game itself, a game which had become a foul-filled exercise in stalling with little emphasis on action.

The product was one sold to fit the needs of the suppliers, the arena owners, rather than the fans, the potential customers. The men who had assembled on June 6, 1946, had seen few basketball games in their collective lifetimes and were less in a position to judge what should be done for the fans than what they wanted for themselves.

241

As an example of their lack of product orientation, they decided that because they were a professional league, the game should be divided into twelve-minute quarters to distinguish their brand of basketball from high school ball and college basketball. It was that simple; No consideration for what the fan wanted to buy, just what they wanted to sell. They had forgotten the underlying premise of marketing anything: the supplier-producer is not selling a product, he is buying customers.

Caught on their own marketing petard, as stalling and fouling forced games to last as long as three hours, the product provided less and less customer satisfaction. Finding little benefit in watching a game developed without adequate consideration of what they really wanted, the fans reacted in the only way they could: they stayed home in droves, leaving the arena owners to their game and their empty seats.

Maurice Podoloff remembered the situation: "On November 1, 1946, the first game of the NBA was played in Toronto. I don't know how that game went, but I do know this: it wasn't very long before the NBA Governors realized that the game they were playing was definitely not appealing. To put it quite frankly, the NBA game was just sick. Professional sports is actually a business and it's a business of presenting a product which will appeal to the public, and our product was not very good.

"It didn't take the Governors long to discover that the product was not good and they began to think that maybe the rules should be changed. There were a great number of suggestions made, and they were: raise the baskets to diminish the height of the tall players, or lower the baskets, widen the free throw lane, change the values of field goals and free throws and so on and so on, ad nauseum. There was one rule which was brought up quite frequently and that was establishing a rule limiting the time that a team in possession of the ball could retain possession.

"Best as they could, the Governors could not find a remedy or cure to what threatened their game. On April 22, 1954, when the Governors met in New York City for the annual meeting, they were really quite desperate. About half of them made some money, but not too much. And the other half hung precariously on a cliff, threatening to drop them into financial disaster—bankruptcy.

"On that day, Danny Biasone of Syracuse proposed his twenty-four second rule. The rule was adopted unanimously, joyously, and actually in desperation, for the Governors then assembled did not believe there would be a 1954–1955 basketball season."

Biasone's suggestion saved the NBA. Just as importantly, it produced something besides a speeded-up game: it produced goals. And that was what the fans wanted, more scoring. In the previous eight years of NBA play, the total points scored per game was 158. In the first year of the 24-second rule, 1954–1955, more than 186 points per game were scored, 28 more points per game and 10½ more field goals a game. That was the action the fans craved, and they began to come back into the arenas to see the almost totally new product offered them.

Podoloff understood the importance of the rule and the scoring: "This was our main attraction—the goals. In hockey, goals; in football, goals; in soccer, goals; and in basketball, goals. Goals give excitement and interest to the game and raise the reputations of those who make them. The more goals a player scores the greater is his value to his team and to the franchise owner who hires him. It was a magic rule and Danny Biasone will be remembered as the magician who produced the particular miracle. No one else has, as far as I know, ever done anything for any sport as significant as what Danny Biasone did for the NBA."

But perhaps it was Dolph Schayes, a member of Biasone's Syracuse Nationals for fourteen years, who put Biasone's contribution into perspective the afternoon he was inducted into the Naismith Hall of Fame at Springfield, Massachusetts: "The best promotion in the history of the NBA was the twenty-four second clock. It belongs in the Hall of Fame!"

The twenty-four-second clock turned the corner for the NBA. With its adoption, professional basketball quickly took its place alongside baseball and football in drawing power. The boom was on and the NBA was the only game in town. The NBL had struggled for one year after the merger, when the disenchanted teams tried to go it alone, then it quietly passed away. The only competition for the NBA in the years between 1951 and 1967 was a suicidal attempt to establish something called the American Basketball League by Abe Saperstein in 1961.

Saperstein hoped to translate the success of his Globetrotters into the formation of an eight-team league, attempting an extension of his market into major cities without pro basketball franchises—Pittsburgh, Washington, Chicago, Cleveland, Kansas City, San Francisco, Honolulu, and Los Angeles. But the vacuum he had seen was also seen by the NBA and, like the NFL before, the league retaliated in the time-honored manner, establishing competitive franchises in major markets considered vulnerable, moving the Minneapolis franchise to Los Angeles and creating a Chicago franchise to do head-to-head battle with the new league.

Tying the league's success to the 'Trotters coattails, Saperstein attempted to gain a foothold in each of the eight cities by using the two units of the Globetrotters as the first part of a double-header at each of the league's inaugural games and every time attendance needed a "Goose." It was the only time ABL teams were to see a full house, as the sampling of the league's wares failed to generate sufficient fan interest despite the presence of many big-name stars, including Connie Hawkins, Bill Spivey, Larry Siegfried, Bevo Francis, Gene Conley, and Dick Barnett.

Within months the Los Angeles franchise disbanded and the Washington franchise was bought by Tuck Tapes, which re-named the team the Tapers and transferred it to New York. The remainder of the teams staggered through the first year, leaving a surplus of red ink and scant memories: Connie Hawkins leading the league with a 17.5 ppg average; John McLendon, the first black coach in basketball history, sitting on the Cleveland Piper bench between owner George Steinbrenner and former Ohio State star Jerry Lucas, who had been signed to a personal service contract but couldn't play because of litigation; and the three-point basket.

The ABL started its second—and final—season with just six teams: Chicago, Kansas City, and Pittsburgh the only holdovers from the original eight. They were joined by Philadelphia, Oakland, and Long Beach, lineal descendants of New York, San Francisco, and Honolulu.

This time around the league lasted only half a season. On December 30, 1962, league publicist Eddie McGuire released the league's final press release, ending with the valedictory, "Commissioner Abe Saperstein and yours truly join in saying thanks for everything, cooperation of the newspapers, radio and TV, and so on, and wish to wish everybody the happiest of New Years."

The ABL had gone down like the *Titanic*, awash on an iceberg of public ennui.

It's an ineluctable marketing maxim that a successful business always begets competitors. The NBA was no different. Through the years different leagues built on different angles have been conceived to do battle with the NBA. Most have never gotten off the drawing board.

One of those prospective leagues was the World Basketball Association, conceived by Johnny Dee, former head coach at Notre Dame. The World Basketball Association's master plan was to do away with the clock, playing not for 48 minutes, but hundred-point "must" games, the half ending when one team scored 50 points and the game ending at 100. It never got out of the talking stage.

Still another was the United States Basketball Association, a concept fancifully subtitled The Mini League. The proposed league called for a restriction of playing personnel to a "height not to exceed six feet two inches" and a return to the rules of yore, including a center jump after each field goal and successful foul shot. It too died aborning in the fertile and futile mind of its founder.

Only one league was to make a run at the NBA.

Despite the obvious fact that the formation of a professional basketball league was an exercise in monetary masochism, another league came into being in 1967: the American Basketball Association.

The ABA did not emerge full-blown, as Athena did from the brow of Zeus, but instead came from the collective brows of a few young entrepreneurs who lived, worked, and played volleyball together in Newport Beach, California. Anxious to break into the major sports scene in the worst way, Dennis Murphy, Mike O'Hara, Ronald Speth, and Connie Seredin, conceived the idea of capitalizing on pro basketball's burgeoning popularity. Murphy, who had raised millions in the name of political causes, now elicited the aid of an acquaintance, trusts and estates attorney Gary Davidson, who had already acquired the reputation of a supersalesman and super-organizer. "I just happened to be an industrial league basketball player when a couple of people asked me if I'd be interested in helping to form the ABA," Davidson remembers.

Realizing that many people would view the formation of a new league put together by unknown promoters with the same combination of suspicion they reserved toward psychiatry, people with foreign accents, and prohibition spirits, Davidson and company enlisted the services of George Mikan, the man who had been selected by the Associated Press as The Greatest Basketball Player of the first half of the twentieth century. With Mikan confering instant credibility on them and recognition for their league, Davidson and Murphy began a flying cross-country solicitation tour. Arriving in major cities without a basketball franchise, they would seek out the mayor and approach him with "Mr. Mayor, we want to talk to four wealthy businessmen who might be interested in basketball and having lunch with George

Mikan." The mayor and the businessmen would be more inclined to say "Yes" than they would have been for an invitation to have lunch with Gary *Who?*

The luncheon, always accompanied by appetizing facts about the potential of pro sports—and basketball in particular—and a main course on the new league, came with a reasonable bill: only $6,000 for a franchise. The results were rewarding. Pretty soon men of independent means were lining up with their $6,000 in hand, each masochist having his own reason—some for tax write-offs, others for ego edification, and a few, like adman Ned Doyle, "Because the Brooklyn Bridge wasn't for sale."

The ABA held its first league meeting, appropriately enough, at Disneyland, where Mikan was duly dubbed commissioner, Davidson made president, and the last of the franchises were parceled out to Louisville and Denver, giving the ABA eleven teams, the same number the NBA had started with twenty-one years before.

During the course of the meeting, Commissioner Mikan held up an alternately striped red, white, and blue basketball over his head and proudly announced, "This is the ball we're going to use." One of those in attendance, Mike Storen, representing the Indianapolis franchise, could only think to himself, "You've got to be kidding . . . a red, white, and blue basketball?"

The meeting continued with administrative matters the main topic of discussion. First on the agenda was the adoption of the three-point rule, put into cold storage after the collapse of the ABL. Next was the distribution of gate receipts. Should the visiting club receive 15 percent or 20 percent of the gate? Finally arriving at a decision, the owners tried to apply the agreed-upon percentage to teams participating in doubleheaders: should the participants in the first game receive the same percentage, if any at all? How much does the visiting team playing the host team get? At this point, Sean Downey, owner of the New Orleans Buccaneers, slammed his fist down on the desk, and shouted, "My team is not going to play *any* doubleheaders. I'm planning on signing up a lot of veteran stars from the NBA and I don't think its possible for them to play *two* games in one evening."

With that, Mikan just took off his glasses and put his head on the desk, finally excusing himself to go to the bathroom. And so it went. . . .

After a full afternoon of administrative double-dribbling, the meeting finally wound down to a merciful close, giving the members of the closed club an opportunity to meet their fellow lodge members on an informal basis for the first time. Mike Storen remembers talking in the hall with some of his new colleagues when he witnessed a Goldilocks and the Three Bears scenario: "Somebody said, 'Well, Gary [Davidson] owns the Texas franchise.' There were some guys from Texas there who said, 'Hell no, he doesn't own the Texas franchise. We own it. He owns the Anaheim franchise.' And the guy from Anaheim was there and he said, 'Hell no, he doesn't own the Anaheim franchise, we own it!' It was at that point that Gary became the ex-president of the league because all of a sudden it dawned on everybody that he was trying to leverage a position when he really didn't have one."

With that as its keynote, the American Basketball Association—consisting of the Anaheim Amigos, the New Jersey Americans, the Indiana Pacers, the Dallas Chapparals, the Houston Mavericks, the Oakland Oaks, the New Orleans Buccaneers, the Minnesota Muskies, the Pittsburgh Pipers, the Kentucky Colonels, and the Denver Rockets—with a swaggering underemphasis on basketball and a great reliance on promotion, as symbolized by their technicolored ball, went out to do battle with the NBA.

From the very moment Mikan threw out the first red, white, and blue basketball, the ABA was an All-American embarrassment to the point of being a cartoon. When the New Jersey Americans took the floor for their first-ever game, their names were scrawled in crayon on the backs of their jerseys. They ended the season by forfeiting a one-game match for a play-off berth to the Kentucky Colonels because their arena floor was warped, pieces of it missing.

The fundamental ingredient necessary for success, fans, was also conspicuously missing. An average of only 2,804 spectators came out to see basketball played without stars. The league featured, instead, a lot of guys named Jones. The Minnesota Muskies played one play-off game in virtual privacy, before only 661 fans. In a "Suppose-I-threw-a-party-and-nobody-came" scene, the Pittsburgh Pipers threw open their doors and let everyone in free and the fans showed their appreciation for the ABA brand of ball by half-filling the arena.

Unlike normal competition in the marketplace where competitors often deliberately lower the relative value of their goods in order to gain a competitive edge, the obvious inequality of play and talent evinced itself in keeping away the customers. Without a saleable product, the ABA was forced to turn elsewhere to promotions. In fact, starting with its red, white, and blue basketball, the league itself rapidly became merely a promotional shell which featured basketball.

In addition to the multicolored ball—known to some as Mikan's Folly—was the three-points awarded for a field goal shot from twenty-five feet away. In arena after arena, cries rang out. "Steve Jones hit from downtown" or—to mix a metaphor—hit a "home run." The Kentucky franchise signed "jockette" Penny Ann Early to a player's contract so they could claim the distinction of having the first woman player in basketball history. Ms. Early in-bounded a pass and the Colonels called time out to remove her from the lineup forever.

But it was not the on-court promotions that characterized the ABA, but instead the off-court ones. The Dallas Chapparals had a "night" planned for every game until the money ran out; the Denver Rockets front-loaded their promotions into the first three months of the season to overcome the competition with football for the area's attention; and every one of the eleven franchises tried to have something for every halftime, a la football.

Soon the ABA was caught like a Madagascar monkey, an animal captured by hollowing out a coconut, filling it with chunks of raw coconut meat, and tying it to a tree. Although able to put its hand into the hollowed-out trap and remove it without any complications, the monkey, once it has touched the meat, wraps its hands around the chunks, unwilling to let them go. The ABA had its hand wrapped around its promotions, unable to rely on the brand of ball presented on the court and unwilling to let go of its one successful method of selling its product.

ABA franchises had more Nights than ever sat around King Arthur's Round Table: there were Wristband nights (every paying adult got two wristbands, cost 30¢ a pair); Yo-Yo nights (because the team was playing like a Yo-Yo); John Brisker Intimidation Night (with voodoo dolls of the Pittsburgh star given to all attending); Old Ball Night (every fan bringing in an old ball of any type or stripe got an ABA ball, with the old balls going to Goodwill Industries for a tax write-off); Merchants Night; Band Night; Students Night, and every other conceivable night and contest imaginable.

Some worked. At least as many didn't. The New York Nets released a live dove in honor of forward Sonny Dove. The bird flapped its wings twice, did a "Brody," and crashed to the floor, dead. The Carolina Cougars had six members of the local YMCA Karate Club appear at one of their halftime shows demonstrating the ancient art of breaking boards with their hands and feet.

The only thing they broke were their own hands and feet. One member was carried off on a stretcher with a broken foot and another with a dislocated shoulder. The Virginia Squires sponsored a Christmas gift night. Lucky number winners were summoned to center court at halftime to pick up as many of the gifts strewn around as possible before the thirty-second buzzer went off. At the exact second the whistle sounded, hundreds of kids broke from the stands and overran the court like eater ants, taking everything in their wake.

And then there was the Girl Scout Night sponsored by the San Diego Conquistadors, a team created *de novo* in 1972, which featured a halftime game between members of the Girl Scouts and representatives of local businesses. To the accompaniment of "Gorilla My Dreams," one businessman romped around the court dressed in a female gorilla suit, complete with big floppy breasts, posing as The Cookie Cruncher, the Girl Scout mascot. As the game progressed, the businessmen took to holding one another so that the girls could make their shots. Suddenly the gorilla hit the floor and writhed around, tugging at his head. The fans loved it. Just as quickly, the writhing stopped and he lay inert. More laughter. Enter a doctor, court left, who examined the gorilla-businessman and had him carried out on a stretcher. Uncontrolled hilarity. The crowd thought it was one of the greatest comedy routines of all time. But what had really happened was not nearly so funny. The businessman dressed in drag had sweated inside his costume. Because of the lack of ventilation he had collapsed, striking his head on the floor.

The ABA was showing signs of suffocation and collapse as well. The fans soon needed a program not only to distinguish between the Joneses (Jimmy at New Orleans, Larry at Denver, and Steve at Oakland, soon to be joined by Nick at Dallas, Johnny at Kentucky, Collis at Memphis, Rich at Dallas, Wali at Utah, *ad infinitum*), but the franchises as well.

After the first year, the Pittsburgh Pipers became the Minnesota Pipers, replacing the Minnesota Muskies, who moved to Miami for the winter, becoming The Floridians. The New Jersey Americans moved to New York, becoming the New York Nets. The Anaheim Amigos moved to Los Angeles and became the Los Angeles Stars. After the second year, the Minnesota Pipers utilized the other half of their round-trip ticket and returned to Pittsburgh as the Pittsburgh Pipers. The Oakland Oaks moved to Washington to become the Washington Capitols and the Houston Mavericks moved to North Carolina, becoming the first roving regional team in major league sports, the Carolina

Cougars, playing "Tuesday night in Greensboro, Wednesday in Raleigh, and Thursday in Winston-Salem." The third year saw another shakeout, as the New Orleans Buccaneers moved to Memphis as the Memphis Pros, the Los Angeles Stars went to Salt Lake City and became the Utah Stars, and the Washington Caps moved once again, this time across the Potomac, to become the Virginia Squires.

Another auxiliary program could have been sold to keep track of the checkered cast called commissioners who were beginning to come and go with the tide, contributing little to the league's badly needed stability. George Mikan, the figurehead commissioner who had brought the league instant recognition, would not move his offices from Minneapolis to New York, and when the second Minnesota franchise exited after the 1968–1969 season, so did Mikan.

When Maurice Podoloff retired as head of the NBA in 1963, the first question put to Walter Kennedy, an applicant for his job, was the straightforward: "Do you think you can get us on TV?" Using the same logic the ABA selected CBS's Director of Sports Jack Dolph as its next full-fledged commissioner.

Assuming the reins in 1969, Dolph indicated his awareness of his mandate: "The NBA proved to us that televised basketball is exciting—it can be sold. What's true of them is true of us!" Dolph obtained from his alma mater a mini-contract for six games for limited dollars.

The television contract lasted two years. Then, because, as one television executive put it, "With the exception of New York, the rest of the ABA franchises put together aren't even in the top twenty markets in the country," it was cancelled because of anemic ratings.

Dolph lasted one year more, thereby qualifying for the title of Iron Man among ABA commissioners. His three-year reign was characterized by more team moves, more signings of college stars, and more progress than was to take place during the tenure of any of the other five. But his administration wasn't to be remembered for the television contract. Nor even by the infusion of colorful owners into the ABA, like Ned Doyle, Charlie Finley and Earl Foreman—a financial swashbuckler who swashed while his Virginia franchise buckled under his continual dispersal sales of stars like Rick Barry, Julius Erving, George Gervin, and Charlie Scott.

Instead, his reign will be remembered for one magic moment that initiated the inevitable: merger talks. Ever since the day when the ABA had first thrown up its tri-colored ball, hoping for a merger before it hit the ground, all it had gotten for its troubles was an "airball," a total rebuff. Sitting in the proverbial Catbird Seat the NBA wasn't interested in talking to the new kid on the block. They had all the major cities as well as all the top stars. The ABA had failed to pass Square One in approaching the established league.

The NBA's entrenched smugness suffered its first real blow in the spring of 1971 when the four-year-old ABA announced the signing of some of the biggest names in the graduating college crop: Artis Gilmore of Jacksonville, John Roche of South Carolina, and Darnell Hillman of San Jose State. The loss of these three was more than a psychological body blow to the NBA. With only three of the NBA clubs making money during the course of the regular season—and all needing the playoffs to break even—the salary war they had feared had finally come.

Then one day Dolph mysteriously "misplaced" his briefcase. "Discovered" by an NBA functionary, it was found to contain the signed contracts of All-Americans Howard Porter of Villanova and Jim McDaniels of Western Kentucky. That did it! Dolph's briefcase became the catalyst for merger.

Negotiations commenced immediately, with Commissioners Dolph and Kennedy setting up committees to meet with one another and work out details. The first concession by the ABA was the folding of its weakest franchises, The Floridians and the Pittsburgh Condors, making Pittsburgh a three-time professional basketball loser. Still no merger. As meeting after meeting took place with all the forward movement of a treadmill to oblivion, the ABA owners sought someone who could bring the merger to fruition. And with it, stability and success.

Unsuccessful with Dolph, they turned in 1972 to attorney Bob Carlson as their next chief executive. A New York lawyer, club attorney, and part-owner of the New York Nets, Carlson was perceived as the ABA's version of the designated heavy hitter who would see the merger through the Scylla and Charybdis of legal red tape.

It was not to be. At least not yet. For the NBA Players Association stepped in and enjoined the leagues from merging. Carlson's reason for being was gone. And so was he within the year, done away with like the messenger who brought bad news back from the battlefield.

The new commissioner was Mike Storen. With the league since its inception, first as general manager of the Indiana Pacers and then as president and general manager of the Kentucky Colonels, Storen was as much a part of the ABA as the red, white, and blue basketball, because he *was* red, white, and blue basketball.

Storen early on discovered there was a market for the ball. "A big market," he thought. But the league had been unable to exploit the potential of its trademark. So Storen, together with Indiana Trustee Dick Tinkham, set up a company and "went in and made a deal with the league to merchandise them." With the sales rights to the ball secured, Storen immediately located a manufacturer in Taiwan for the all-American red, white, and blue basketball. He also found a sales company which "made a number of sales to a number of petroleum companies to give away the balls as part of a Christmas promotion." But the ball didn't stop there. Everytime an ABA team held a ball promotion, it purchased balls from Storen's company at $2.65 apiece.

Therefore, Storen's tongue must not have been far from his cheek when he uttered his first words as commissioner to the press conference introducing him to members of the New York press establishment: "The first time I ever came here, all I saw at the playgrounds around town were brown basketballs. Today, on the way in from the airport, I counted seven basketballs, and four of them were red, white, and blue."

Frustrated in its attempts to merge with the NBA, the ABA had to resort to type, promoting the hell out of what little product it had. Promotions which had once served as a stimulating form of artificial respiration weren't working their magic any more. And so they installed Storen, one of the league's best merchandisers and promoters, in the commissioner's chair.

What he wrought was less promotional legerdermain than mere administrative tightening. The ABA was going through one of its most difficult years, with rumor begetting rumor that unless a merger was effected—and immediately—it would be their last. The Dallas Chapparals, despite making every night promotional something-or-other night, were in dire trouble. So were the Carolina Cougars. Similar cases of financial malaise also afflicted the Memphis, Utah, and Virginia franchises to a greater degree and the New York and Denver franchises to a lesser one.

Foregoing the promotion of the league and its ball, Storen played the part of the little Dutch boy, keeping his finger in many dikes while devoting the major portion of his attention to the most pressing problems. He oversaw the sale of Julius Erving, at that time the league's only certifiable superstar, to the league's most important franchise, New York; the transfer of the warmed-over Dallas franchise to San Antonio; the sale of the

Memphis, Virginia, and Utah franchises to new owners, who could only improve upon the performance of their new teams; and, finally, the removal of the moribund franchise from Greensboro, Charlotte, Winston-Salem, and all points south, to St. Louis, where it was given the fanciful name of The Spirits of St. Louis.

Then, like the little boy who gives his sled a downhill push and jumps on it while in transit, Storen left his Olympian post as ABA commissioner to go back to the firing lines as president of the newly organized and named Memphis Sounds.

The ABA, as was its annual custom, then named Tedd Munchak as its commissioner of the year for 1974–1975. The former owner of the now-defunct Carolina Cougars, Munchak was brought in as a holding action while the merger continued to stall. Then, with the injunction dropped and the two leagues once again an "item," he was, in turn, replaced by former NBA superstar Dave DeBusschere, the sixth and final ABA commissioner—and the big-name bookend to complement the first one, Mikan.

The ABA had hung on for nine years—longer than anyone had a right to expect—yet, when the moment it had looked forward to almost from its inception finally arrived it resembled, at best, The Incredible Shrinking League. Even Agatha Christie couldn't have scripted this vanishing entity, as the ten teams DeBusschere inherited in the fall of 1975 suddenly became nine with the folding of San Diego. Then there were eight, when the Memphis Sounds shuffled off to Baltimore to become first the Hustlers, then the Claws, and finally the Nonexistents. Then there were seven with the folding of Utah. Then the Virginia Squires staged a soap opera tragedy, floundering in financial confusion. It seemed that every story about the ABA started with the line "The three franchises reported in financial trouble are . . ."

By the time DeBusschere was called to a meeting in the spring of 1976, with the NBA Board of Governors and new NBA Commissioner Larry O'Brien in Hyannis, Massachusetts, he had four somewhat healthy franchises, two with borderline anemia, and one terminal case.

With his clubs already in financial intensive care, DeBusschere now had to face the NBA, which was clinging to the concept of indemnification like a victorious warring nation. The NBA agreed to take in four ABA clubs—for a price. Without bothering to examine the financial records of the ABA clubs, the NBA demanded and got more concessions from the four than the victorious Allies had wrested from the defeated German Empire at Versailles. But not even the Germans had been so thoroughly devastated. The four ABA clubs had to pay $12,500,000 to the existing NBA clubs, another $4,500,000 to the two ABA clubs not included—(St. Louis and Kentucky), and forego their rights to TV monies as well. The NBA had charitably thrown the four already-drowning clubs a financial anchor.

A quick case study in How to Become an Instant Pauper could be constructed just by studying what happened to the New York Nets, once the ABA's showcase team: the Nets paid $3,200,000 as their price of admission to the NBA; another $800,000 to the New York Knicks for invading their NBA Long Island preserve; and a pro-rated portion of the $4,500,000 paid by the four entrants to those two left at the tradesmen's entrance. And all without access to TV income.

For the four clubs the problems—and debts—mounted. Denver tried a public underwriting which failed, forcing them to turn to local banks. Roy Boe of the New York Nets lamented, "I wish I had the same access to banks as Denver," and after finding that even the enforced sale of Julius Erving didn't alleviate the financial pressure, moved the Nets to New Jersey after paying the Knicks *another* $4,000,000 for invading their New Jersey sanctuary. The Indiana Pacers put on a television marathon to raise money and sustain the franchise. Only San Antonio seemed to have been spared the financial burdens brought on by the merger, as the survivors of the red, white, and blue began to sink in a sea of red.

The ABA, which had wanted a merger in the worst way, finally saw its wish come true.

As it nears its centennial, basketball is a hale and hearty survivor of its past. Raised in smoky dance halls, and taken on one-night stands all over the country, it has still blossomed into a respectable member of the sports community, despite its somewhat spotty past.

Where once basketball's cornerstone had been hockey—even the Walter Brown Trophy given the NBA champion was once owned by Lord Stanley—now it has developed roots of its own.

Following the lead of professional football, the NBA's televised Sunday games are now regionalized, an innovation that drew 15 percent more viewers during the 1976–1977 season than in the previous year.

Its promotions, once choreographed to resemble a segment out of "Let's Make a Deal," have now begun to take on some form and dimension, orchestrated by a former baseball executive. Howard Berk, formerly administrative vice president of the New York Yankees, was brought in by the NBA in 1975 to take the dual position of vice president of marketing for the NBA and president of NBA Properties, a promotions arm set by the league in a manner similar to NFL Properties. The league gave Berk a mandate: "Make money, but give us exposure." Berk has turned the phrase and the league's promotions around, providing the NBA what it needed most, exposure, while also making money with promotions deemed worthy of the league's name.

One promotion that wasn't viewed by the NBA as worthy of its name was something called One-on-One.

Deriving its origins from the rich heritage of playground basketball, One-on-One had been conceived in 1968 by George Lois, a New York advertising genius by daytime and Superfan by night. Lois, who had grown up on the playgrounds of New York City playing the individualized game of "one-on-one," foresaw the possibilities of adapting it to television. In effect, reinventing a new sport.

To Lois, the new "game" possessed all of the attributes of man-against-man competition, a macho melding of playground ball with the by-now familiar pro game. To be held at Madison Square Garden, "it was to be an all-day thing, $1.00 and you could go in and out, like the Six-Day bike races." Lois, thinking like an adman, envisioned lots of hoopla, with trucks going around Manhattan blaring out "See West Play Chamberlain." And lots of income from "selling it to the networks."

Lois became more excited the more he talked: "Would a little man play a big man—Calvin Murphy versus Wilt Chamberlain—and what would be the outcome? Would Chamberlain play at all? He might get beat and what would that mean to his ego?"

But that was all that happened, talk. And two years later, after Lois had talked the concept up with both Walter Kennedy and Larry Fleisher, head of the NBA Players Association, the idea still had taken neither form nor flight.

Two years after the idea had come to rest on his desk, Fleisher was approached by Visual Information Systems. They wanted to get into the cassette business and asked Fleisher for his assistance. Instead, Fleisher told them about the One-on-One concept. It was an almost instant "make" as Visual Information saw its potential. Together they went to Pete Spengler of Bristol-Myers—a man who had used sports both as a part of his programming mix and in his commercials, with several athletes extolling the virtues of Vitalis against that no-no, Greasy Kid's Stuff—who bought the overall concept for his brand.

One-on-One became a reality for the 1971–1972 NBA season, with the signing of a package deal between Bristol-Myers, the NBA Players Association, and ABC, the then carriers of the NBA Game of the Week. The half-time filler would feature twenty-six players representing each of the twenty-six NBA teams in an elimination contest, culminating in a play-off between the two finalists with $10,000 to the winner and $7,500 to the second-place finisher; their teammates to share $3,000 and $2,000, respectively.

Produced by a firm with which basketball great Bill Russell was associated, owned by the NBA Players Association, and sponsored by Vitalis, the first year's tournament was won by Bob Lanier of the Detroit Pistons. Known more for his size 22 shoes than for his ever having ever won a major trophy, Lanier had long yearned for a massive trophy to match his size. When he first saw the Vitalis One-on-One trophy—a miniature grandfather clock with each number represented by the numeral "one"—he mumbled, "I always wanted a big fuckin' trophy. This ain't no big trophy." In order to meet Lanier's expectations and specifications, the Vitalis public relations man had to run out and get a bulky marble base to bring the clock-trophy up to the winner's standards. Apparently pleased with his refurbished trophy, Lanier accepted it on national TV.

But not everyone was as pleased as Lanier. ABC was not happy with the production quality of One-on-One. And believing they could do it better, the network produced the tournament the second year, this time around "ringing" in live audiences. Bristol-Myers, while pleased with the brand awareness its association with One-on-One had generated for Vitalis, cut back its sponsorship to half, keeping almost its total identification with the tournament. And more than fifteen different persons wrote to Fleisher's office, all claiming "they had given the idea to so-and-so" and that they were rightfully entitled to a piece of the action.

But none were more displeased than the NBA owners. Some of the purists, like Boston's Red Auerbach, objected to the concept because it wasn't team basketball—as practiced by his Boston Celtics—but just "glorified individual" ball. Other NBA owners objected, less on aesthetic grounds than to the fact that their half-time entertainment was owned by the players, rather than themselves.

By the time Geoff Petrie had put in the last basket to win the second year's One-on-One tournament, the entire NBA-ABC television contract was up for renewal. The owners' television committee not only asked for more money, they also demanded that ABC "stuff" One-on-One. And when CBS outbid ABC—signing a three-year $27,000,000 contract with the NBA to start with the 1973–1974 season—they politically decided not to continue One-on-One, adroitly sidestepping the problem area.

But even though lip-service was given to the fact that One-on-One was discontinued because it was "glorified individual" basketball, CBS was soon putting such so-called team endeavors as 3-on-3, Slam-Dunk, and Horse on at halftime. The main difference was that these exercises in electronic trivia were not owned by the NBA Players Association. And *were* acceptable to the NBA.

The world of promotions was still misunderstood by the NBA. They needed someone like Berk to ally sponsors with basketball. Someone to give them close encounters of any kind, which he did, bringing in Pepsi, Shulton, and Avon among others to underwrite NBA promotions.

But despite his contributions, it is not Berk who epitomizes the arrival of professional basketball so much as those who run the game at the local level. Most notably in Philadelphia.

Philadelphia has long held a special place in the annals of sports. Undoubtedly nurtured by the sorrowful records of the Phillies and Athletics—who finished in last place 22 and 18 times respectively through 1968, nine times mirroring each other's last-place finish in the same year—and aided by the Eagles' pitiful plight of finishing last ten more times, Philadelphia was not only "the most pecksniffian of American cities," according to H.L. Mencken, but the losingest of American cities according to its followers.

The only exception to the Joe E. Lewis line "Show me a Philadelphia team and I'll show you a loser"—excluding the latter-day hockey club—has been the professional basketball team. Over 22 years, first as the Warriors and then the 76ers, it has been almost the entire Philadelphia Story, winning 872 of 1,588 games for a .549 won-lost percentage and finishing in the heady position of first in its division seven times..

In the summer of 1968, Jack Ramsay, then general manager of the 76ers and soon to become head coach, called the general manager of the Spartanburg baseball club in the Class A Western Carolina League and asked if he "would be interested in coming to the 76ers as business manager." The recipient of the call, Pat Williams, although admittedly not having "thought about that end of sports for thirty seconds in my life," confessed to an interest and flew to Philadelphia for an interview. On September 1, 1968, Williams became the business manager of the Philadelphia 76ers, a career that would soon have him taking his place beside all the great promoters as The Barnum of Basketball.

Pat Williams is unique in that small circle of promoters who have been compared to Barnum, no matter how tenuous the comparison. He is the only one of the many who graduated from the field to the front office—albeit Williams was a graduate of baseball, not basketball.

Williams, who hails from nearby Wilmington, Delaware, signed with the Philadelphia Phillies immediately after graduation from college and was assigned to their Miami affiliate in the Florida State League. During the remainder of 1962, Williams hit .292 with 10 hits in 49 at-bats, all but one of them a single. And that a double! The following year, the young catcher was hitting .204 "and sinking" when both the Phillies and he came to a mutual understanding that his future was not behind the plate.

But that understanding was tempered by something that happened to Williams at the end of his first year in Miami. The assistant general manager in Miami was Bill Durney, who had been the traveling secretary for the St. Louis Browns under Bill Veeck. Durney took note of Williams' prowess with an idea, if not with a bat, and suggested he see his old mentor, Veeck, then convalescing on a farm up in Easton, Maryland. On his way home after his first year in organized ball, Williams stopped in on Veeck and spent what he called "the better part of an incredible day" with him. The five hours he spent hearing the old master's voice "electrified my life," and Williams left, yet another disciple of the world's greatest promoter.

Sure of his promotional calling and equally unsure of his future as a player, Williams spoke with Clay E. Dennis, Jr., the Phillies farm director about starting in the administrative end of baseball. Dennis made arrangements with the Miami club for Williams to return in 1964 as the assistant general manager with the understanding that, as Williams recalls, "if the Phillies were happy and I was happy, we'd go from there."

Apparently the Phillies were "happy" with Williams after his one-year apprenticeship—a year which saw Miami lead the league in attendance, despite finishing seventh and fourth dur-

258

ing the halves of the split-season. The Phillies gave him his choice of two openings in their minor league organization: Bakersfield in the California League or Spartanburg in the Western Carolinas League. Williams, who had some background in the South, having gone to school at Wake Forest, opted for Spartanburg. It was a choice that he would never regret; nor the fans of Spartanburg forget.

Williams spent the next four years at Spartanburg, each year leading the league in attendance, one year even accounting for 46.5 percent of the league's total attendance. His efforts also earned him the League Executive of the Year three times, the MacPhail Trophy once, and the *Sporting News* Minor League Executive of the Year once.

It was the year following the recognition of his efforts by the *Sporting News* that Williams received the call from Ramsay. And things have never been the same for Williams—or basketball—since.

Williams stayed in Philadelphia exactly one year. After nine months with the 76ers, a proper gestation period for any embryonic promoter, he received a call from his mentor, Veeck. Bill told his disciple, "A former associate of mine in baseball is an attorney in Chicago and part-owner of the Chicago Bulls." Then he added, in as gross an understatement as Captain Reno telling General Custer, "And there are some problems out there."

Williams followed Veeck's advice, as he was to do throughout his entire career, and called the former associate, Phil Frey, who promptly invited him to Chicago "to talk." Three months later and one year to the day after joining Philadelphia, Williams left one of the most successful NBA franchises to become general manager of one of the most troubled.

Chicago has been represented by eight separate franchises in professional basketball. Each has been struck by the same affliction—a lack of interest.

George Halas—the very same George Halas who was the owner of the Bears and the only man to play baseball, football and basketball on a major league level—was the owner of the first two franchises, Bruins I and Bruins II. Halas' first Bruin team played in the old American Basketball League from 1925 through 1931, disbanding when the league itself cried "uncle" because of the small gates during the Depression. His second entry, Bruins II, played in the new National Basketball League from 1939 through 1942. Deciding that forearms and down-court blocks would never replace goals from the floor, Halas dropped out of the league after three seasons. The Bruins' place was taken during the war years by the Chicago Studebakers, the first fully integrated team in sports. The Studebakers lasted but one year.

With the end of the war in sight, enough manpower was scraped together to field two new teams in the NBL for the 1944–1945 season, one of which was the Chicago American Gears. Sponsored by the American Gear Company, and called the Gears by the writers, they picked up where the previous Chicago teams had left off, compiling a 14–16 record. The next season was more of the same. Then, for the 1946–1947 season they signed DePaul All-American George Mikan to the largest contract in pro basketball history to that point, $60,000 for five years. The 6-foot 10-inch behemoth with the thick eyeglasses and the flailing elbows led the Gears to the league championship. But the following year, leaping before they looked, the Gears jumped to the newly formed Professional Basketball League of America. When the new league folded in just two weeks, Mikan went to Minneapolis in a dispersal draft. Chicago had lost its championship team. And its most vital Gear as well.

The box score for Chicago's experiment with pro basketball read: four different franchises; two winning seasons in thirteen; no survivors.

Oblivious to history, which, according to an old proverb "repeats itself," the fledgling Basketball Association of America, forerunner of today's NBA, naively placed a franchise called the Stags in Chicago in 1946. The Stags proved to be different from their predecessors in one respect: They were a winner. In another respect, attendance, they were not dissimilar to those who had gone down in flames before them. After four winning seasons, the Stags quietly dropped out of the league, fully entitled to sue their fans for nonsupport.

Still possessing its deep-rooted penchant for self-punishment, the NBA created its first new franchise in 1961, placing it in Chicago to compete with Saperstein's Chicago Majors of the ABL. This time the team was named Packers. But the results were the same, horrendous, both on the court and in the stands, as the newly stocked team won but eighteen of eighty games. The fans responded in kind, matching the disappointment with one of their own. By the second year the team was relabeled the Zephyrs and moved to the ancient Coliseum; by the third they had shuffled off to Baltimore as the Bullets.

Then in 1966, ever the gluttons for punishment, the NBA added yet another franchise in Chicago—the Bulls. This time the graft took. A little. The new team in town was actually a passable version of a professional basketball team. Under the guidance of coach Johnny Kerr the Bulls made the play-offs the first year. However, the Chicago jinx held and they lost to the St. Louis Hawks in the opening round, three games to none. But still the fans had ventured out to the International Amphitheater to see their local heroes play.

By the next year the Bulls reverted to form—for Chicago, that is—and won just twenty-nine of the eighty-two games. Still, they made the play-offs, where they bowed in five games. In the third year Dick Motta took over as head coach. But for the first time the Bulls missed the play-offs, which are a financial necessity if any pro basketball team is to come close to making money, since visiting teams do not share in the gate receipts. And yet that was the least of their problems. The first three years of the Bulls' existence had been three years of tumult and controversy. They needed someone in the front office to complement Motta on the court and bring order out of chaos and the fans out of the closets. That man was Pat Williams.

Williams arrived in Chicago at the ripe young age of 29, the youngest general manager in the history of professional basketball. Almost immediately the intolerable situation began to turn around. It would be a gross oversimplification to say that it was Williams' doing alone, for Motta had more than something to do with it. But it seemed that wherever Williams went, like Mary's little lamb, a winning record was sure to follow. In his fourteen years in professional sports the teams Williams was associated with have had a won-lost percentage of .585.

But it was not for his winning record that Williams was known. Nor would that alone gain him inclusion in this volume. For Pat Williams, being a true disciple of Bill Veeck, began to do his thing and would soon become known as the The Barnum of Basketball, thus joining his mentor in the Who's Who of Ballyhoo.

Where Veeck had his easily recognizable talismans—a midget and exploding scoreboards—Williams would soon have his: wrestling bears and trained pigs. Williams fully subscribes to the Veeckian philosophy that the promoter "creates an atmosphere of fun and excitment, a total evening. And when the fan goes out to fight the traffic either it evokes a good memory and he comes back, or it brings on a yawn and he doesn't."

Billed as "Uncle Heavy and the Porkchop Revue," Williams' trained pig act featured "Chick, the Singing Pig." At halftime the fans were supposedly "treated" to the sights and sounds of

Chick as he came down a 10-foot playground slide—less in a graceful glide than in a struggling skid—and joined in with three sibling swine to squeal in unison, emitting sounds that approximated singing almost as much as that offered up by current rock groups. On one occasion, however, the act hardly went as planned, as Chick, the lead little piggie, could only bring himself to huff and puff. And all that came out was one flat, ear-piercing "oink." As the minutes rolled by and Chick continued to do his best charade of "Silent Night," one of his troupe turned critic and delivered of himself at center court. The crowd, taking the other pig's commentary as a cue, turned on poor little Chick and began booing his less than award-winning performance. After the crowd had subsided and the court was cleaned up, Williams himself was moved, and asked: "What did they expect? Grand opera?"

Williams' other introduction was a bear known as Victor the Wrestling Bear, a 6-foot, 700-pound behemoth, complete with muzzle, who bore what Williams called "a resemblance to Dick Butkus." The bear would wrestle just about anybody in the audience. And sometimes he, too, would pee on the floor, ruining the varnish. Victor's real moment in the center-court spotlight happened the first time Williams scheduled him as the halftime entertainment. The local ASPCA threatened to get an injunction against Williams and the Bulls for exploiting the supposedly unprotected mammal. Its concern was that some harm would befall the bear either from his opponent or from, according to Williams, "some overzealous fan who would run down from the stands and mug him." Williams, on the other hand, felt that a parallel society should be set up to protect people because Victor never lost. Finding that his reasoning was getting less than the proper response and respect from the ASPCA, Williams struck a compromise. *He* would wrestle Victor to prove his point. Pat won his point—and the bear his match.

Even though the singing pig act has since been cancelled, every year since he was first introduced, Victor has returned to grace—and sometimes pee on—whatever center court Williams is promoting at that moment.

Williams continued to create a circus atmosphere in Chicago through the 1972–1973 season and then took his traveling circus with him on a side excursion to Atlanta in 1973. But, to his dismay, Williams found that the Atlanta situation "was not stable" with "the ballclub caught up in all sorts of problems—most of them financial." When a call came from Irv Kosloff of the 76ers asking him if he was "interested" in coming back to

Philadelphia to correct the situation which seemed to "be just drifting," Williams jumped at the chance.

And so in July 1974, Pat Williams, rejoined the Philadelphia 76ers as vice-president and general manager. And with him came Victor, by now a fixture with Williams, and his whole menagerie.

Today the two most successful franchises in the NBA both on the court and in the stands are Portland and Philadelphia. Both, not incidentally, are the biggest promoters. Ever since the Trail Blazers entered the league in 1970, they have worked the promotion side of the street. According to Howard Berk, "They've always promoted, from the first day of the franchise. And they do it right now even though they're 100 percent sold out."

The other franchise which can qualify as a promotional "happening" is Philadelphia. In fact, the Philadelphia 76ers are a veritable promotional cornucopia.

First, there is public address announcer Dave Zinkoff, affectionately known as The Zink. Long a fixture on the national scene, associated with the Globetrotters for fifteen years and the Sphas even longer, Zinkoff has been a Philadelphia fixture ever since he broadcast Temple's appearance in the very first Sugar Bowl game back in 1935. The true measure of his contribution to the lore and language of The City of Brotherly Love is the incorporation of his catch phrases, called Zinkisms, into the speech of every sports fan in Philadelphia, down to the playground level.

Zink has been spouting catchy phrases for years to appreciative hometown audiences which, according to the playful Zinkoff, who resembles and sounds like an elf of the Hebraic persuasion, "grab it right away, 'cause they're Philadelphians and have a keen ear." They need a keen ear to absorb the metaphoric mischief Zink works on the English language. Some labels which have survived the passing of time include "Gola Goal," "Dipper Dunk," and "Two-for-Shue." Others that have become part of the local jargon are not-so-easily recognizable, and include "Pair for Share," a reference to Chuck Share, or "Wash on the Line" for Jim Washington, a phrase which, in the words of Zinkoff, "conjures up fantasies of the old days with the clothespins."

Then there is Harvey Pollack, the 76ers' director of publicity. Known as Super Stat, Pollack has taken baseball's greatest enduring promotion, the seemingly inanimate statistic, and applied it to basketball. Long ago baseball discovered that every game could be compared with the never-ending body of data that has chronicled the National Pastime since its founding. More importantly, each game was made more meaningful as part of baseball's unique continuum. Now Pollack has done the same for basketball, breaking down the game into categories that bring it to life in retrospect and allow it to be compared in futuro.

While other public relations directors may haphazardly enter one of Julius Erving's patented flying, backhanded, over-the-head stuffs under the catch-all category of "layups," Pollack enters the feat in his newly created "dunks" column. In fact, Pollack, who has been with Philadelphia basketball teams since the inaugural year of the NBA, has pioneered in breaking out several new categories, all of which were subsequently adopted by the league after they sat at Super Stat's knee and learned "how"—including steals, rebounds, offensive rebounds, individual turnovers, minutes played, and blocked shots. The 76ers' year-book, prepared by Pollack, is rich in statistical detail, containing such esoterica as the most popular months for NBA birthdays, the number of total technical fouls, the most popular uniform numbers, the most common point spread in games played, and everything else which would make any true trivia *maven* weep with joy.

But the real Philadelphia Story is Pat Williams. Seated at his desk underneath a sign which reads "If you don't promote, something terrible happens . . . nothing," Williams analyzed the anatomy of a promotion: "So many people feel that unless a promotion fills the house, it's not successful. The longer I'm around, the more I'm convinced that the promoting end of it comes slowly and that it's a lot of little things meshed together that brings the ultimate results. You know, building in a community a base of support and an interest in a team. And if there is some little thing we do one night, where 100 lives are affected . . . well, that's building something."

The first order of business was to build up the 76ers' woeful identification in Philadelphia, which Williams did, even to the point of obtaining a phone number ending in "7600." Then he went about building up the crowds; crowds which had spent the better part of two years as far away from 76ers games as they could get and now were total strangers.

He did something every night at halftime. He brought in Victor, then a singing group that featured the much-traveled and much-troubled former Philadelphia Phillies' star Richie Allen, bands, midget boxers, preliminary games, Ping-Pong players, jugglers, and just about everything else imaginable—including a one-armed push-up expert. He introduced an act that he originally opened in Chicago, Little Arlene. The diminutive-sounding member of the chauvinistically christened "weaker sex" had manfully taken on five professional athletes in an eating contest and out-eaten all of them, downing 76 hot dogs, 19 Cokes, and 21 pizzas. Then, in an encore, she went back to her hotel room and sent out for room service.

But Williams was sorely aware that "You can only promote to a point. People will come out to see the fleas and the circuses for a couple of years, but you better be building a winner." He knows as all promoters do, that "Winning is the best promotion." Victor the Wrestling Bear cannot win ball games.

And so, concurrent with his crowd-building antics, Williams set out to build a winning team. He drafted (Doug Collins, Lloyd Free, and Darryl Dawkins), signed free agents (Caldwell Jones, George McGinnis), and purchased (Julius Erving, Henry Bibby) enough players to make Philadelphia a contender. And more.

In four short years Pat Williams still stands one step away from the top of the mountain in professional basketball, the championship. But in a promotional sense he straddles the top of the mountain as king of the modern basketball promoters.

If pro basketball were a Broadway show, it would be one that opened on the road, appeared in Off-Off Broadway surroundings, and finally made it to the neon lights of the big time.

Dating back to the founding of the BAA (today's NBA) in 1946–1947, organized pro basketball is only 33 years old as it heads into the 1978–1979 season; the same age organized baseball was in 1908 when Charlie Ebbets enthusiastically announced that the National Pastime was "still in its infancy."

During those thirty-three years, basketball received mixed reviews as it struggled to come of age. Insensitive sportswriters and critics derogatorily called the game "roundball" and intimated that one had only to "arrive in the last five minutes" to see the entire contest. Sociologically snide remarks have been made by many but were perhaps first put into print by Dan Jenkins in *Semi-Tough*. His protagonist, Billy Clyde Puckett, utters the deathless description: "Basketball is nothing but ten niggers in their underwear jumping up and down every five seconds."

Indeed, as the game has changed, so has its complexion. Basketball's roots, once grounded in the YMCAs and the industrial leagues of its youth, have now become an extension of playground basketball played in the inner cities. Some sociologists and sensitive sportswriters view the adoption of The City Game by so many as a desire to escape the ghetto. Others see it as the only recreation available in the crowded slums. But whatever the motivation, no sport—even baseball with its influx of Latin Americans—has experienced a more profound change in its makeup. Today, twenty-eight years after Chuck Cooper and Sweetwater Clifton first integrated the ranks of professional basketball, 201 of the 292 players listed in the *Official NBA Guide* are black.

The dominance of the game by blacks is evident to all observers. Writers like Pete Axthelm and David Wolf have taken a literate look at this phenomenon. Others, such as *Black Sports* magazine, took both a look and a laugh at the situation: "[A] Game in Phoenix saw ten black players on the court at the same time. When Dick Van Arsdale substituted for Ron Lee, a fan behind the Suns' bench screamed out 'Ain't it funny how all these white guys look alike.' "

But social commentary or no, it has also presented a marketing problem. In some cities, the color of a man's skin was sublimated to the color of his uniform, as long as the local team was a winner. In others, it remained a major problem as fans failed to identify with seven-foot blacks playing the game in the name of their city. Robert Lipsyte, in *SportsWorld: An American Dreamland*, tells of how one city surmounted the problem: "[Bill] Bradley was not real—a WASP from Princeton, a Rhodes scholar, a man whose business agent declared before his rookie season that Bradley would some day become President. . . . What could he gain by playing a game that at that time wasn't that popular a professional sport and was dominated by and attended by blacks? It was Bradley's presence that made the game acceptable even to the New York white woman and to the New York executives."

And as the city that looks upon itself as the basketball capital of the universe went—winning the NBA championship in 1969-1970—so too went the rest of the league. The fact that the Knicks beat the Los Angeles Lakers in seven games gave the game exposure in the two largest cities in the country. Moreover, these were the two cities where the local teams were supported by celebrities, which further gave the game a fashionable aura, as people went to see and be seen. Stargazing among arrivistes became a promotion in itself, with stars such as

Robert Redford, Elliott Gould, and Dustin Hoffman found in the stands at Madison Square Garden supporting the Knicks and an equal number of chic Hollywood stars found at the Forum cheering on the Lakers. Pro basketball was suddenly "in."

The atmosphere of the late 1960s and early 1970s demanded a Wham-Bam-Thank-You-Ma'am game to mirror the prevailing attitude of our society. Pro basketball found itself to be the "in" sport, regardless of the color of a player's skin.

In the 1973 survey conducted for the NBA by BBD&O, the fourth-largest advertising firm in the world, NBA basketball was found by 69 percent of the respondents to possess the "fastest action" of any game and 71 percent felt that NBA games had the most "exciting endings" of any sport. Most important to the NBA—today and tomorrow—in the "area of awareness" among 13-to-17-year olds, the NBA stood tallest in the saddle.

But if basketball were to suffer from any overriding problem afflicting it, it would be the emphasis attached to scoring—in contrast to the overall accomplishment of the team. In baseball, when a man hits four home runs, his team wins. In football, when he scores five or six touchdowns, his team wins. And in hockey, when he scores the hat trick, his team (usually) wins. But in basketball, when a man scores 50 or more points in a steady cacophony of sound that goes "swish, swish, swish," his team still may not win. Witness the season-ending exploits of David Thompson and George Gervin, vying for the individual scoring title. Thompson scored 32 points in the first period—a new NBA single-period record—and 73 points in the game; and yet his team, the Nuggets, lost their season finale to Detroit. Later that same afternoon, George Gervin of San Antonio scored 33 points in the second quarter of his game against New Orleans—breaking the hours-old record set by Thompson—and 63 points all together as his team still lost to the Jazz. Somehow, basketball still has too many vestiges of One-on-One. The whole of its many parts are not yet equal to the individual parts. And therein lies one of its weaknesses as a major sport.

Today, although professional basketball continues to have its problems—dissipating its primary resource, the players, by maintaining its time-honored tradition of one-night stands instead of scheduling mini-series as its older brother baseball does and disturbing its financial balance by failing to give visiting clubs a "cut" of the gate receipts—it still has come from far back in the pack to take its place in the forefront of sports in a Silky

Sullivan syndrome of sports. It has become one of the three major sports in the hearts and minds of the fans—and the primary one in those winter months when both baseball and football are "dark." Perhaps it may still become, as its proponents have long held, The Sport of the Seventies. Or, in overtime, the Eighties.

6

Slapshots, service aces, sundry other sports, and the selling thereof

Several other sports hold the same fascination for promoters and fans as baseball, football, boxing, and basketball, but spatial and temporal considerations dictate that, instead of developing these sports with the same loving attention we have devoted to those already covered, we condense them into smaller thumbnail sketches. Sports to be included in our portfolio headed "All Others" include ice hockey, tennis, golf, soccer, auto racing, and horse racing, reflecting their relative importance in the overall sports marketing scene.

The origins of ice hockey are as beclouded as those of baseball. One theory has it that the game as we know it today was first played by members of Her Majesty's Royal Canadian Rifles at the rear of their barracks in Kingston, Ontario, in 1855. If so, it would serve as the proper genesis for a sport that has come down through the succeeding century-plus as an All-Canadian and almost all-warlike exercise.

Starting with the first formal league—a four-team organization started in Kingston, Ontario—leagues and associations blossomed like maple leaves in Ontario, then in Montreal and other Quebec cities, and finally on the Canadian plains and Canada's West Coast. By the end of the first decade of the twentieth century there were two professional leagues operating in competition, the National Hockey Association and the Canadian Hockey Association.

About to run aground because of an early-day bidding war, the two warring leagues merged. The surviving entity, the National Hockey Association, remained the dominant force on the Canadian scene for the next seven years. Then, in 1917, with the country at war and the owners acting much like the Sunshine Boys warring among themselves, the National Hockey Association was dissolved and, in order to freeze out one of the owners, a new entity was brought into existence: the National Hockey League.

The NHL originally faced off with four teams: the Montreal Wanderers, the Montreal Canadiens, the Ottawa Senators, and the Toronto Arenas. Six games into the season the Wanderers' arena burned to the ground and they withdrew from the league, leaving three clubs to skate out the NHL's inaugural season. The same three clubs formed the NHL in its second season, 1918-1919. In 1919, they were joined by the Quebec Bulldogs. Quebec lasted just one year and was replaced by the Hamilton Tigers. This four-team alignment continued for the next four years.

In 1924, two new clubs joined the NHL: the Montreal Maroons, a team appealing to the English-speaking population of Montreal, and the Boston Bruins, the first American entry. The following year, the NHL added the Pittsburgh Pirates and the Hamilton Tigers, who were purchased by a New York group which moved the franchise to New York and renamed it the Americans. And although the Amerks' opening night crowd of seventeen thousand did wonders for the NHL, their very presence in the league did something to the Canadian psyche. Hockey was not only Canada's national sport, but practically its national religion. As a patriotic spokesman for hockey would point out some forty-three years later: "Hockey is Canadian; it's been a vital part of life and concern of an overwhelming number of plain Canadians for several generations."

One of the facts which defined hockey for the first seventy-five years of its existence was that its national and its imperial boundaries were the same. But expansion knew nothing of geographic boundaries and in its tenth year, the NHL further weakened Canada's life-and-death hold on hockey with the wholesale addition of the New York Rangers, the Chicago Black Hawks, and the Detroit Cougars. The NHL then admitted to the partial surrender of its sovereignty by dividing itself into two divisions, the Canadian and the American, for the 1926–1927 season. The American Division housed the New York Rangers, Boston, Chicago, Pittsburgh, and Detroit franchises, while the Canadian Division countenanced the presence of one outsider—

the New York Americans—among the four native teams.

With the exception of some line changes on the fly, the lineup remained essentially the same for the succeeding twelve years as the league fluctuated between ten and seven clubs. Then, in 1939, the Canadian and American designations were dropped. So too was the New York Americans franchise, going first to Brooklyn for one year and then being benched permanently before the 1942–1943 season. That season the NHL put six teams on the ice—Montreal, Toronto, Detroit, Chicago, Boston, and New York—the same six teams that constituted the league for the next quarter century.

But if the overall lineup of clubs was changing, the National Hockey League wasn't. Originally a Canadian fiefdom, it had become an international cartel with feudal overtones. The owners ran the league in much the same way as William H. Vanderbilt ran the New York Central Railroad—with an attitude of "The Public be Damned!"

The small cartel that controlled the NHL consisted of Conn Smythe of the Toronto Maple Leafs, Senator Hartland Molson of the Montreal Canadiens, Walter Brown of the Boston Bruins, and James D. Norris, owner of the Chicago Black Hawks and Detroit Red Wings, and part-owner of the New York Rangers. Expansion was anathema to this quartet of feudal lords.

But soon the old guard passed the torch on to a younger and more progressive group of caretakers. It was more than a mere changing of the guard; it was a new guard. Conn Smythe turned over his interests in the Toronto Maple Leafs to his son Stafford, while Senator Molson did likewise with the Montreal Canadiens and the Forum, passing them on to his son David. The U.S. Justice Department forced the hand of James Norris and ordered him to divest himself of his interests in the Red Wings and the Rangers, along with Madison Square Garden, to the Graham-Paige Corporation, whose lawyer, William Jennings, became president of the Rangers.

Jennings and some of the other Young Turks began agitating for expansion, seeking to cash in on the expansion boom then taking place in other sports. Suddenly the small club known as the NHL was turned into what one Canadian writer dubbed "a really big, American money-making enterprise." In their opaque reasoning, additional franchises would beget additional fans, their growth assured by expansion and a more affluent population.

As the NHL clubs began to play with the possibility of new franchises as though they were building blocks, the reservations of the traditionalists opposed to expansion began to melt in the face of economic persuasion. Montreal and Toronto went along with the growing sentiment on the condition they wouldn't have to split their Canadian TV monies—in excess of one million dollars each per year from their Saturday night package—with any of the other clubs.

Then the building blocks turned literally into buildings and blocks. Stafford Smythe of Toronto let it be known that he would provide both an arena and a franchise to Vancouver if the city would turn over a downtown block to him for the consideration of $1. But the city fathers thought the price too steep for admittance to the closed club and were frozen out in lieu of St. Louis, which hadn't even applied for membership. St. Louis had something no other city had, a white elephant of an arena owned by the Norris interests, who now saw a way of packaging it together with the $2,000,000 expansion fee and making additional money in the bargain.

And so, on June 6, 1967, finessing the Latin admonition *festina lente*, which loosely translated reads "haste makes waste," the NHL Board of Governors embarked upon the most ambitious expansion program in the history of sports, adding an entire division of six teams for the upcoming season. The six teams—the Philadelphia Flyers, Pittsburgh Penguins, Los Angeles Kings, St. Louis Blues, Minnesota North Stars, and San Francisco Seals—were less a clone of the six existing teams than a Xeroxed copy, one generation removed.

Stocked with twenty players from the rosters of the six established clubs, the expansion clubs skated forth to do battle in an expanded 1967–1968 league, playing an expanded 74-game season. Over the course of the season the new clubs won just 40 games and tied 18 of the 144 games they played against the established clubs. They fared no better in the Stanley Cup Playoffs, as the Blues lost in four straight games to the Canadiens, although they extended them to two sudden-death overtimes and lost all four games by just one goal. As Blues' goalie Glenn Hall was awarded the Smythe Trophy, emblematic of the outstanding play-off performer, NHL President Clarence Campbell was reported to have uttered words which must have brought tears of joy to those already looking ahead to their next round of franchise fees: "The expansion was successful beyond our fondest hopes."

The results were the same the next two years, the East Division 4, the West Division—represented by the St. Louis Blues—zip. And getting no closer. Then in 1970, the NHL added two more teams, the Buffalo Sabres and the Vancouver Canucks. This time around the asking price for a new franchise was $6,000,000. In order to realign the now fourteen clubs, the Chicago Black Hawks were placed in the expansion, or West, division, while the two new teams were placed in the established, or East, division.

Hockey was now laying claim to the title The Sport of the Seventies. But instead of being a pennant which flew proudly in the breeze, the rallying cry was taking on the look of an economy telegram.

Attendance, once the NHL's crown jewel, suddenly came tumbling down. Waiting lists for Maple Leaf tickets now became virtually nonexistent. Even in Montreal tickets to the Forum which had been passed on from generation-to-generation like family heirlooms—inherited, unobtainable, and determinants of life's arrangements that only an *habitant* could appreciate—began to lose their luster. According to Clarence Campbell, attendance, which had been "better than 100 percent of capacity for a season" when the league had been a six-team entity, now fell more than 10 percent or twelve hundred paid admissions per game. And, in some cases, more. Much more.

Coupled with this economic setback was yet another, the presence on the scene of a competitor: the World Hockey Association. Almost overnight salaries skyrocketed, going from the lowest average in professional sports—$22,000 a year—to one of the highest, $92,000 plus fringe perks.

The World Hockey Association was another creation of that packager of instant franchises, Gary Davidson, who was turning out leagues almost as fast as Procter & Gamble does soap products. Davidson and his Expansion Mafia—those familiar faces who had already been associated with Davidson in the American Basketball league and would surface again in his next movie, the World Football League—planted the WHA flag in twelve cities. Overnight teams like the New York Raiders, New England Whalers, Miami Screaming Eagles, Ottawa Nationals, Calgary Stampeders, Quebec Nordiques, Alberta Oilers, Chicago Cougars, Houston Aeros, Los Angeles Sharks, Minnesota Fighting Saints, and Winnipeg Jets came into existence. Although the Calgary franchise immediately went bankrupt and the Miami franchise did the same, the Cleveland Crusaders and Philadelphia Blazers joined the fold as Davidson confidently said, "The WHA will open with a twelve-team league in October 1972."

But it was not Davidson's pronouncement or the formation of

the twelve teams that won the begrudging respect of the NHL for the WHA. Instead it was the signing of the Golden Jet, Bobby Hull, to a $2,750,000 contract that did it. His Joe Namath-like signing sent shock tremors down the collective backs of the NHL owners. When that was followed, in quick order, by the signing of Gordie Howe and his two sons by the Houston Aeros as hockey's first family act; local favorites J.C. Tremblay and Maurice Richard by the Quebec Nordiques, the WHA's French-speaking club; Derek Sanderson and Bernie Parent by the Philadelphia Blazers; Gerry Cheevers, Ted Green, and Tommy Williams by the New England Whalers; and more than seventy other NHL near-greats and greats-to-be by all twelve WHA teams, the tremors reached seismographic proportions. The WHA had wounded the NHL in its most vulnerable spot—the pocketbook.

Attempting to find that one distinctive feature that would set the WHA apart from the NHL, Davidson tried tinkering with the tried-and-true coloring of the puck, which was basic black. According to the first *Official WHA Guide*, "the league boldly decided on a colored puck." But, again according to the *Guide*, "early experiments with a blazing red puck were not satisfactory, so the league settled on a deep blue coloring." The Guide little noted or long remembered that blue also proved unsatisfactory and that the league ultimately had to settle for black.

But it was the only time the league would get near black all year, the rest of its ledgers running as blazing red as the puck they had first tried. If the Alberta Oilers had sold out every game in their small Edmonton Gardens (seating capacity 5,800), it still would have guaranteed the owner a $1,500,000 loss. The Philadelphia Blazers played in Convention Hall but experienced problems with the ice, which forced cancellation of some games, starting with the very first WHA game ever played in Philly. For that game the management handed out brightly colored souvenir pucks to everyone attending. But when the public relations director reluctantly walked to the center of the ice to announce that the game was being cancelled on account of melting ice, he was pelted with almost ten thousand pucks from disgruntled fans.

And the Raiders never had a chance in New York. Originally conceived by the WHA to be the second hockey team in New York, one which would do battle with the entrenched Rangers, the WHA's position was woefully undercut when the NHL hurriedly expanded into the Long Island area with a new franchise called the Islanders to preempt the new arena there.

The Raiders were forced to play their games at Madison Square Garden as the tenants of the very team they were to challenge. It was a hopeless proposition from the start. By the second year of the WHA the team had changed its name to the Golden Blades and by the end of that year had gone south to New Jersey, where they were to euthanasically die.

In fact, the entire league began to take on the look of a league playing Follow the Bouncing Franchise. Ottawa went to Toronto then south to Birmingham; New England went from Boston to Hartford and then to Springfield, Massachusetts, after the roof literally fell in on them at the Hartford Civic Center; Minnesota expired and Cleveland moved in to take their place as the St. Paul Fighting Saints, where they too sunk.

The new league's very first program contained an institutional message on the first page which easily qualified for the *New Yorker*'s "Letters We Never Finished Reading" column. It asked "Why the WHA?" and then went on to answer before any smart aleck could interject his own comments: "Competition is the lifeblood of American business and that, more than anything, is why the World Hockey Association deserves to be alive. Forget the booshwah that the WHA has further diluted the quality of big-league hockey. That's National Hockey League propaganda and overlooks the fact that NHL quality had long ago been diluted. What the WHA had done is provide a format for many, many quality players who have been by-passed by many of the Neanderthal NHL thinkers."

Those quality players spent most of the WHA's first year showing the fans how to spend a lot of time sliding on their stomachs, looking like so many George Plimptons on skates. It not only provided an alternative to NHL hockey, it also provided a charade of good hockey. The few superstars who did play quickly showed their superiority, as Mike Walton did in leading the league in scoring and Gordie Howe did in scoring 100 points and being named Most Valuable Player. For the rest, the trip was somewhat of a "bummer." By the eighth game Derek Sanderson had opted to go back to the NHL, while Bernie Parent waited until the play-offs. Many others, like Gerry Cheevers, jumped back after the first year. The play-offs for the Avco Cup—a conglomerate based near Davidson's headquarters in Santa Ana, California, who pioneered in sponsoring the first title trophy in any major sport and the second sports award named after a product (the Chalmers Award, sponsored by a car, given to baseball's MVP between 1911 and 1914, being the first)—pitted Bobby Hull and the Winnipeg Jets against Gordie

Howe and the Houston Aeros. The Aeros won four games to none, the only real winners in the WHA the first year.

By the end of year six, the league had dwindled to seven teams—only two of whom were original member clubs, New England and Winnipeg—and was barely breathing. After having lost $12,000,000 the preceding season, they were taking the next logical step in the progression of new sports leagues: they demanded a merger with the older, more established league. But the hand that had rocked the boat was not about to join the NHL, not if the traditionalists in the NHL had anything to do about it. They had enough problems of their own. The new, compact version of the WHA was reduced, as one wag put it, to copying the now-prevalent Guaranteed Win Night with Guaranteed League Night.

Blindsided by the astonishing surge in salaries and plummeting attendance, the NHL owners now sought ways of extricating themselves from their financial nutcracker. First they raised ticket prices, boosting them from an average of $3.47 upwards to at least double that. But even that wasn't enough. There had to be a better way!

Clarence Campbell watched the twin barometers of attendance and salary pass each other on the financial Richter scales and said, "I can see a time coming when a team like Boston would be forced into an intolerable position unless additional revenue can be developed. As of now, their receipts are fixed because it is impossible to add more seats to Boston Garden or to raise their prices. Under the circumstances, it will be very difficult to go on paying both Orr and Esposito what they deserve."

The magic ingredient—or "ingrediment," as Pogo used to call it—was television. CBS, the original carrier of NHL hockey, had a rough and slow "make" with hockey. Carrying it on Sundays in the first quarter of the year after the pro football season had ended, the network programmed it directly opposite the higher-rated NBA telecasts on ABC. Starting in 1967, NHL hockey generated only a 4.4 share for nineteen telecasts, twenty-seventh out of thirty sports events telecast during the year. It was only during the last two years of the multiyear contract, estimated to be worth about one million dollars a year to the NHL, that CBS made any money.

When the seventh and deciding game of the exciting 1971 Stanley Cup finals between Montreal and Chicago was televised in primetime on Tuesday evening to the largest audience ever to watch an NHL hockey game on television, hockey could take pride in the fact that it was fast growing into its self-annointed title of The Sport of the Seventies. The euphoria was further increased when the 1972 Lou Harris poll showed that of all sports, hockey had made the greatest percentage increase in terms of number of people following it during the previous year. Hockey seemed on its way.

That year, when its contract with CBS came to an end, the NHL practiced what it was then preaching against: it jumped to NBC in a three-year television deal worth more than $6,000,000. The ingredient necessary to the survival of the NHL had been found. For the moment.

Meanwhile something more basic was happening to the game. Whereas once it had been an all-Canadian game, expansion and a new league now found only seven of the thirty franchises in both leagues situated in Canadian cities.

Canadians plunged from chauvinistic heights to icy despair as they witnessed the ruination of their national game. Chris Lang, writing in *Hockey Canada*, issued the rallying cry when he wrote: "This is a ripe issue, a nationalistic issue. The same issue we're going to face with Arctic oil, the Mackenzie pipeline, water, you name it. It's a question of a natural resource getting sold out. Hell, three of the companies that make hockey sticks are now owned by Americans."

But if the game was getting away from the Canadians, it was getting away from the purists as well. Perhaps it all started with expansion. Or maybe it was the upstart WHA. But whatever the reason, the game had changed radically. Whereas once it had been a game of artistry, with well-coordinated lines—like Detroit's Production Line of Howe, Lindsay, and Abel or the Montreal line of Richard, Beliveau, and Moore—flashing down the ice and scoring with precision passing and shooting, now the preponderance of goals were scored on rebounds. And as rebounds gained in importance, so too did measures to counteract them.

No longer were players tolerated who stationed themselves in front of the mouth of a goal to pounce on an errant puck, as Esposito did for so many years at Boston (and whose actions begot the following graffito found on a Boston bank wall: "Jesus Saves/Espo Shovels in the Rebound"). Now there are intimidators patrolling the ice, looking for all the world like German Gestapo agents.

Maybe it was more than a mere coincidence that the chief intimidator for the Stanley Cup champion Philadelphia Flyers was Dave Schulz, whose followers were called Schulz' Army and whose leader wore an old German army helmet to prove his allegiance to this contemporary hero of hockey. The Flyers came to epitomize the new style of on-ice violence during their two-year reign as NHL champions. Their charging, checking, cheeky tactics brought screams of joy to their new breed of followers who dubbed the club The Broad Street Bullies and laughed at the sight of an opponents' blood. From the moment they were turned on by the seemingly spiritual Kate Smith singing "God Bless America" until the collective unconscious bodies of the Flyers' nightly opponents had been less than tenderly carried from the ice, the Flyer fans set up a crescendo and set a pattern for modern-day ice hockey.

In a scene straight out of the movie *Slapshot*, teams now sought out so-called "aggressive" players. The Detroit Red Wings' sales brochure mentioned the newly discovered word no less than eight times as if "aggressive" were the "Open Sesame" to turning around one of the league's weakest clubs. Egged on by organists playing Pavlovian strains and salivating for blood, the new breed now got its "goodies off" by seeking fistfights instead of finesse. It has already witnessed the next tragic step, a stick fight between Wayne Maki and Ted Green, which almost cost the latter his life.

The new breed of fans "turned on" by this pandering to violence was that equally new force in marketing: the white suburbanite. They demanded, and got, blood. Hockey became secondary. They were once again covering the floor with sand rather than ice.

Hockey's current fascination with predators on skates may appeal to some of the more recently converted hockey fans, but it is a far cry from the game hundreds of thousands learned to love, a game once distinguished by balletic motion and fast action. Now that the element of machismo has entered the hockey arena, with men called upon to meet challenges to their manhood constantly, the sport has become little more than boxing on skates. A sport had been completely lobotomized.

But just as the game was deteriorating as an art form—and perhaps even as a sport—it was also deteriorating as a business. It was no longer a "growth" industry. Indeed, far from it. The new fans whom the NHL had first looked to as the fuel for expansion and then as the salvation of the already established franchises failed to materialize. They also failed to materialize in adequate body-count numbers for television. When NBC ran into environmental impedimenta with stations in warmer climes unwilling to clear the Sunday afternoon hockey games—

including Atlanta, which had a team in the league—they cancelled their NHL connection, leaving hockey as the only major sport without the conferred cachet of TV.

Without ancillary income to soften the effect of salaries that had gone up more than 500 percent since the expansion, clubs took to raising their ticket prices up to a league average in excess of $8, over 230 percent in ten years. This in turn brought on the next round of fan defections. By the 1976–1977 season, eleven of the eighteen NHL clubs played not only to less-than-capacity houses, but experienced not a single sellout—a far cry from the proud days of "better than 100 percent of capacity" for the entire league.

The panic of empty seats was further aggravated in many expansion cities by their own special problems, not the least of which was hockey's seeming inability to proselytize additional fans to the fold. St. Louis had to bear the burden of debt financing on the building they got in the expansion to the tune of $1,500,000 a year; Atlanta was woefully undercapitalized; Cleveland's arena in Richfield, Ohio, was convenient to nowhere; and the Minnesota North Stars never regained the fans lost to the WHA's Fighting Saints across the river in St. Paul.

The NHL began to look like survivors from the law of averages; a league which had propagated itself into the endangered specie category. The Sport of the Seventies had barely lasted past 1971.

With hockey now *in extremis* and losses totaling more than $18,000,000 in 1977 in the NHL alone (and another $12,000,000 in the WHA), professional hockey needs to take a hard look at itself and its future. For it is a future in clear and present danger of never happening.

The solution to its deep-seated problems goes far beyond the cosmetic. To realign the eighteen teams into two conferences and four divisions which have little or no meaning for most new or nonhockey fans is masturbatory at best and navel-staring at worst. For all the casual observer knows, the Prince of Wales Conference is named after Captain Ahab. The Norris, Smythe, Adams, and Patrick divisions bear antediluvian names that predate their interest in the game. Even though it might mean something to some Canadian chauvinists, the titling of divisions and conferences after stuffed and mounted busts at the Hockey Hall of Fame is fatuous for a once-haughty sport now in desperate need of appealing to the same general public it has callously taken for granted for so long.

Hockey's complete lack of concern for its customers was

further evidenced during the 1977–1978 season when a league-wide edict calling for all teams to place their players' names on the back of their road jerseys was met with strong opposition, several Cassandrian owners citing the possible "decrease in program sales." One owner, Harold Ballard of the Toronto Maple Leafs, finally capitulated in the face of a fine but gave in on his own terms. With a "public-be-damned" attitude, he put blue lettering on the backs of the blue-jersied Maple Leafs, making them so small that a microscope would be needed to read them. It was but one more instance in the long history of the NHL's studied callousness towards its fans.

Today the NHL urgently needs to establish more intraleague rivalries, to develop a restraint on the violence threatening the very existence of the game, and to negotiate a television contract. Most of all, it needs dynamic leadership.

The league sought that leadership in 1976 when Clarence Campbell stepped down as president after twenty years in office. When the white smoke from the NHL's chimney had cleared, the new president they had selected to lead them out of their troubled times was a throwback to yesteryear, John A. Ziegler, Jr., former legal counsel for the Norris family's large Norris Corporation, a conglomerate of 102 companies, including the Black Hawks, Maple Leaf Milling, Ltd., the Norris Grain Co., Louis Sherry Co., and a huge cattle ranching concern in Homosassa, Florida. In short, hockey has once again handed its reins to a man whose credentials indicate he can best protect the interests of the old feudal lords of hockey.

Sixty-two years old and not wearing well, the NHL is skating on very thin ice and would do well to remember the last words of Cecil Rhodes, who uttered "So little done, so much to do . . . " just before he died. They will cure their own problems, it is hoped, before they too become terminal and follow Sir Cecil with "so little done. . . . "

Tennis has been played in America ever since a Staten Island girl named Mary Ewing Outerbridge returned to this country in 1874 from a Bermuda vacation bearing tennis equipment presented her by English officers. Curious U.S. Customs officials, at a loss to explain the purpose of the strange paraphernalia, seized it and held it for a week before allowing it into the country.

For most of the next century, the American populace has held tennis to be almost as curious and strange as the Customs officials, viewing it less as a sport than as a curiosity out of a

Noel Coward comedy—*Tennis, Anyone?*—or Alfred Hitchcock's memorable scene in *Strangers on a Train*.

However, in the last ten years tennis has been discovered by millions of spectators and participants alike, not to mention businessmen, advertisers, and promoters. The ancient pastime has been translated into a safe, white, surburban game, appealing to the upscale masses and supporting ancillary industries worth millions of dollars. The story hinges on promotion. And on two events that shaped the future of the game.

From the day tennis was first accepted into polite garden society, amateur tennis players have been lionized, reaping adulation and often more from generations of debutante groupies. Over and above all the tennis balls they could eat, these knights in white flannel often accepted under-the-table payments for their efforts. (One latter-day "shamateur," Tony Roche, admitted to earning $25,000 in "expenses" while a member of the 1967 Australian Davis Cup team.) Forced to play as amateurs while being paid as professionals, they not only held a healthy disrespect for the tennis governing bodies that forced them into this uncomfortable and hypocritical position, they also remained eligible for the only competition then available. To them, the word "amateur" was just a word in a dictionary.

Professional tennis, caught up in its own hypocritical underwear, finally came out of the closet in the 1920s, as C. C. Pyle formed a pro tour featuring superstars Suzanne Lenglen and Ellsworth Vines. Through the next three decades, first Bill Tilden and Don Budge, then Jack Kramer, Bobby Riggs, Pancho Gonzales, and finally Frank Sedgeman threw down their erstwhile amateur rackets and took up a new racket for pay. Amateur tennis was no longer the only game in town.

Suddenly in 1968, with tennis nudging its hundredth birthday, professional tennis lost its low-class label. That year Lamar Hunt underwrote promoter Dave Dixon's wild-eyed dream of establishing a male pro tour with contract pros. Together Hunt and Dixon formed World Championship Tennis and signed eight pros they called The Handsome Eight: Dennis Ralston, Butch Buchholz, Cliff Drysdale, Pierre Bathes, Roger Taylor, Tony Roche, and Nikki Pilic. That was the same year four women— including the biggest name in women's tennis, Billie Jean King—signed professional tour contracts.

Hunt's WCT developed the tournament concept along sound business lines. Local sponsors would put up most of the purses as well as front money for stadia, tickets, publicity, and other operating expenses. WCT guaranteed only that the players and WCT staff would appear at the time and place contracted for. This time around, the stars weren't reduced to helping lay down their own court. Pro tennis had become big business, thanks to big businessmen.

But the formation of the WCT did something beyond merely putting professional tennis on a business-like footing. It was the first olive out of the jar, the lever that would ultimately bring tennis kicking and screaming into the twentieth century. For Hunt's tour introduced the world of color to tennis, ending the day when center court looked like a convention of white uniformed Good Humor men. It also provided the necessary stimulant for the abolition of the artificial barriers between pros and amateurs, a difference without a real distinction, but one sought by the staid administrators of the game in the name of status quo. Finally, the WCT also forged a lasting association between tennis and corporate sponsorship.

The game that had been the special province of the monied upper classes now became the new game of the masses, albeit the more affluent masses. Where once the only associative values to be gained from tennis were those that high society could bestow, the commercial world was now beating a path to the door of tennis as its better mousetrap. Advertisers, ranging from wash-and-wear clothing to insurers of wear and tear, lined up, eager for corporate identification with the new "in" sport: Aetna Life & Casualty Company, American Airlines, Avis, Avon, Ban Deodorant, Bonne Bell, Bristol-Myers, Colgate, Commercial Union Assurance Company, Dewar's Scotch, English Leather, Fabergé, Family Circle, INA, Kemper Insurance Company, Kodel Division of Eastman Kodak, L'Eggs, Max-Pax, Pepsi-Cola, S&H Green Stamps, Toyota, and Volvo. It was an all-new game, a game of Corporateball, as the "Tennis, Anyone?" cry of yesteryear became "Tennis Everyone."

But even as tennis was to become the new game of the Wash-and-Wear society, one corporate sponsor was to have the greatest impact, not only on the marketplace but on the entire tennis scene as well: Philip Morris, makers of Virginia Slims cigarettes.

While the history of tobacco is grounded in antiquity, the success of today's tobacco industry is founded on modern-day advertising techniques. Indeed, the whole of the colorful kaleidoscope of advertising history can be seen reflected through the advertising of tobacco products generally and Philip Morris specifically.

Employing a recognizable symbol as early as the 1930s, Philip Morris built up the identity of its flagship brand, Philip Morris, with the use of a rather abbreviated version of a hotel bellboy. For most of the early life of radio, listeners were continually bombarded with "Call for Philip Morris," delivered in the emphatic staccato of an urgent call from "Johnny, Stepping Out of Store Windows Everywhere." Along with the American Tobacco Company's memorable chant from auctioneer L.T. Boone of Lexington, Kentucky, it was one of the two most familiar messages of the 1930s and 1940s.

By 1955 the name of the game had changed to "filtered cigarettes." And Philip Morris was forced to go back to the drawing board to resurrect one of their old brands, Marlboro, to do battle in a new marketplace. Originally sold as a multicolored cigarette aimed at ladies and effete smokers, the brand was repackaged and targeted at the heavy male smoker, complete with the recognizable symbol of a macho tattoo embroidered on a male hand. The result was a huge marketing success, one that took Marlboro straight up the sales ladder to the Numero Uno position.

But a large part of Marlboro's success stemmed from its association with sports. More accurately, its association with pro football. Soon after the reintroduction of the male-oriented cigarette in 1955, Marlboro and Philip Morris became involved with the National Football League as the first national TV sponsor of NFL football.

Even then Philip Morris knew that the acquisition of one-quarter of the TV rights to an event was merely the ticket to the ball game. It had to be properly promoted and merchandised for them to capitalize on their association with sports.

The tobacco industry's stock in trade has long been its intensive trade relations, particularly through its large field sales organizations. Making extensive use of salesmen to do missionary work, tobacco companies have been able to augment consumer advertising by gaining point-of-purchase displays, prominent shelf positioning, and first-hand contact with the retailers. Philip Morris' field efforts were no exception. But now, armed with the pro football connection, they literally ran around their competitors' unprotected ends. And they did the competition one better by becoming the first major national marketer to hire athletes in the off-season to do all-important missionary work.

After the 1957 season Philip Morris hired Sam Huff, Dick Modzelewski, Lindon Crow, Jimmy Patton, Don Chandler, and Art Hunter—all New York Giants, except for Hunter, a Cleveland Brown and Crow, then a Chicago Cardinal. The six were put to work in the advertising trenches, calling on regional Marlboro dealers in areas they knew best and where they were best known.

As a method of merchandising an association with sports, it was an immediate and spectacular success. Jack Landry, executive vice president and director of marketing for Philip Morris, Inc., called it "A faithful extension of our basic concept of 'Let's involve ourselves in the sport.'"

But all this was as a prelude to Philip Morris' most successful association with sports, an association that dated back to tennis' watershed year of 1968.

In that year Philip Morris introduced a brand in the San Francisco area as a test of its potential acceptance by its target audience, women. Marketing has always been less than an exact science. Marion Harper, once head of McCann-Erickson, sought ways of segregating advertising's contributions and hoped that his efforts would be rewarded with the single word "Accountability" engraved on his tombstone. But whether it was the cigarette, its memorable advertising, or a new awareness on the part of women that was responsible for the overall success of the brand is still unknown. What is known is that within two weeks Virginia Slims became an unqualified success, and Philip Morris—eschewing the remainder of its test market activities—took it national.

That very same year, Billie Jean King, The Mother Superior of women's tennis, turned pro. Soon thereafter, true to tennis' tradition of petty politics and pettifoggery, another dispute broke out among the powers that be. Most such disputes were between the alphabet soup-sounding jurisdictional bodies which govern tennis. But this one was different. It was between players: Billie Jean King and Jack Kramer.

The 1970 Pacific Southwest Championships in California offered the backdrop for this dispute, one which would change the face of professional tennis. Outraged at Kramer's distribution of prize money—less than one-eighth of that offered the men was offered the women—Billie Jean threatened a boycott of the tournament unless Kramer came up with a more equitable purse for the women. When he refused, Billie Jean and seven other women pros signed symbolic $1 contracts with Gladys Heldman, the Houston-based publisher of *World Tennis* magazine. It was to be the commencement of a separate, professional women's tennis tour.

Ms. Heldman, as much a businesswoman as a pioneer, not only set up the first all-women's pro tournament in 1971, at the Houston Racquet Club, but also set out to get the necessary financial underpinning for it. And several more like it. She approached Joseph Cullman, Chairman of the Board of Philip Morris, Inc., with the idea of underwriting such a tour. Cullman, who had long been active in the world of tennis, saw it not only as an opportunity to help the game, but also as a chance to help his new brand, Virginia Slims.

Virginia Slims was a natural sponsor for the embryonic pro women's tour. Built around the advertising slogan "You've Come a Long Way, Baby"—a reference to women's new-found role in contemporary society, which, ironically, drew fire from feminists who found the word "baby" pejorative—it now took on a new meaning. Coupled with the John Heldesque cartoon of a symbol called Ginny, the slogan became as much the symbol for the women's tour as for the cigarette itself.

Virginia Slims committed itself to the tour, investing more than $300,000 in what was becoming known as The Slims, the collective name for both the tour and the players. The Slims quickly took flight, moving from high school gymnasiums and dusty old armories into first-class facilities. And the press finally discovered what made Samantha run and elevated The Slims events from agate type under the shipping news to the top of the sports page.

Over the succeeding seven years, Virginia Slims, which started with just two tournaments in 1971, has underwritten the tour to the tune of more than ten million dollars in purses and attendant merchandising. And, according to Billie Jean King—the person most responsible, outside of Joseph Cullman, for The Slims—women who "often outdrew the men and received less than half what they made in prize money now get star billing."

But even though Virginia Slims and the women's professional tennis tour had both "Come a Long Way, Baby" in the succeeding nine years, the Women's Tennis Association decided to turn the sponsorship of The Slims over to a new sponsor in 1979. The new sponsor, Avon, guaranteed an investment of $2 million a year in a championship circuit and another $750,000 a year for a satellite tour—an increase of $600,000 over the total purse monies of the previous years. And one of the most enduring, most successful promotions of all time went up in smoke.

It was only a short step from "Women's Lob" to the next promotion, a Thurber-esque Battle of the Sexes between Billie Jean King and the Happy Hustler, Bobby Riggs.

For years Riggs had been working the hustling side of the street, hustling everything and everybody. By the age of 17, this son of a preacher man had won the national singles and doubles championships and by 21, Forest Hills and Wimbledon, winning $108,000 betting on himself in the process. With little more to conquer, the man who was raised in Los Angeles with Mickey Rooney—and looked more like the winner of the Andy Hardy lookalike contest than Rooney himself—had turned pro and toured with Jack Kramer.

In the intervening thirty years, while little had been heard from him on the sports pages, Bobby Riggs was occupied doing his thing. Which, translated, meant hustling. He devised ways of taking money from willing pigeons who were made "offers they could not refuse" and who regularly lost to Riggs while he was playing with what to others would be overwhelming handicaps. Golf, gin rummy, tennis, anything; it was all the same to this throwback to Bet-a-Million Gates, who would wager on which drop of rain ran down a window pane fastest. Only Riggs was the "Rainmaker."

He played life itself for the buck. He would bet he could hit 20 out of 25 from the foul line, which, of course, he did. He even believed he could beat Bill Bradley in a foul shooting contest. But there Riggs had calculated in an edge—he wanted to use a football!

But it was at tennis that Riggs excelled, on the court and in his hustle. His tennis challenges saw him (A) holding a valise, (B) allowing his opponent two bounces, (C) tethered to a great dane, (D) tethered to two great danes, (E) holding an umbrella, (F) carrying a rock, (G) allowing his opponent to serve to either service box, (H) wearing galoshes and a slicker, (I) sitting on as many as six chairs, (J) all of the above. There were no bounds to Riggs' imaginative ways of winning, only to his opponents' bankrolls. He was the quintessential hustler and the world was his "hustlee."

Seeing the increase in popularity of women's tennis and not incidentally the amount of the purses sponsors like Virginia Slims were making available, Riggs hit upon another scheme. Proclaiming himself to be "the Jane L. Sullivan of women's tennis," the 55-year-old Riggs—still looking like Andy Hardy, even with his Clairol-colored red hair and dentures which gave his boast a sibilant "S"—turned the "I can beat any man in the house" bluster into a "I can beat any *person* in the house" challenge.

First he fired off a volley of insulting come-ons: "Women's tennis? I think it stinks. They hit the ball back and forth, have a lot of nice volleys, and you can see some pretty legs. But it's night and day compared to men's tennis." And "The women only play about 25 percent as good as the men. Their best player couldn't even beat an old man like me!" Then he fired off challenges to the top five players on The Slims circuit. Only one replied, Margaret Court.

At the time she accepted Riggs' challenge for what she thought was a "little hit," Ms. Court was having as good a year as Secretariat. She had won 89 of her last 92 matches and more than $82,000 in prize money during the 1972 Slims tour. She would present a formidable obstacle to Riggs, hustle or no.

The consensus was that the best women's tennis player had little chance against a top-ranking male, basically because of the physical superiority which goes hand-in-racket with the male game of dominant serve and volley. But this time the roles were reversed. Margaret Court played a man's game—serve and volley—rather than the backcourt game associated with women's tennis. Her physical dimensions gave her an edge: she stood 5 feet 8½ inches and weighed 150 pounds, an inch and one-half taller and five pounds heavier than her male opponent. Called Big Maggy and The Arm by her colleagues, Court had an extraordinary reach—three inches longer than the normal woman's—and her grip was equal to that found in most male collegiate athletes. Riggs, on the other hand, was hardly a top-ranking male. Maybe thirty years before, but not now. As a 55-year-old imitation of his former self, he was smaller than his opponent and, more importantly, it was *he* who played a woman's game of lobs, dink shots, soft balls, and off-speed ground strokes.

Almost as soon as the match was announced for Sunday, May 12, 1973, the hype was on. And no one generated more interest or publicity than the self-promoting little man who had started it all. After more than a quarter of a century, Riggs was reemerging from the shadows. Needing his limelight fix, he spent every waking moment—when he wasn't popping his 400 vitamin pills a day—whipping up public enthusiasm for his first public hustle since he had dinked Jack Kramer to death on his second pro tour.

It was a match which polarized male and female into rival camps. It was Right Guard versus Feminique. Supphose versus

Pantyhose. Women's Lib versus Male Id. Suddenly buttons started sprouting up like the first dandelions of spring reading "Bobby Riggs—BLEAH!" on women's blouses everywhere. And males returned the favor by echoing Riggs' sentiments that "there are only two places women belong—in the kitchen and in the bedroom." It had all the makings of a major sports event, or, as *Advertising Age* calls them, a SportsQuake.

The dateline Ramona, California, site of the San Vicente Country Club where the match was to take place, soon took on all the significance of Shelby, Montana, as the public, through the courtesy of CBS, tuned in to watch the biggest sports hustle since Doc Kearns left the former oil boom town with all its resources in an attache case.

After a little scene-setting foreplay in which Barbra Streisand sang "I am woman, you are man" to the accompaniment of shots of both players, the cameras moved to center court. There stood Pat Summerall, ready to introduce the players. But instead of the normal pre-match festivities, the viewers were treated to the spectacle of a little man with glasses bearing a bouquet. The red roses, obstensibly a Mother's Day gift for Margaret, were merely the first psychological shoe, "to soften her up." The psyched-out Court now awaited the dropping of the second one. She didn't have long to wait. Within fifty-seven minutes, Riggs had given her a wide assortment of Mother's Day gifts—lobs, overspins, undershots, drop shots, and a sound drubbing—winning the best two-out-of-three match 6–2, 6–1 in what became known as The Mother's Day Massacre. It was Smokey Joe Wood playing in the uniform of the Bloomer Girls baseball team all over again, as Riggs' shots looked like Hoyt Wilhelm's knuckleball in a wind tunnel. And it was, in boxing parlance, strictly "no contest."

Bobby Riggs had empirically proven the wisdom of Damon Runyon, the laureate of the literate. Enunciated by Sky Masterson in *Guys and Dolls*, his thesis went thusly: "When I was a young man about to go out into the world my father says to me a very valuable thing. . . . One of these days in your travels a guy is going to come to you and show you a nice brand-new deck of cards on which the seal is not yet broken, and this guy is going to offer to bet you that he can make the Jack of Spades jump out of the deck and squirt cider in your ear. But, son, do not bet this man, for as sure as you stand there you are going to wind up with an earful of cider."

Riggs had not only won the match, he had also won the hypothetical "winner-take-all" pot—one of tennis' running in-jokes—and put cider in Margaret Court's ear as well. By treating her "Ms-erably," Riggs had added yet another pelt to his already-overcrowded list of "hustlees." Suddenly male chauvinists had a hero. And, to hear the Ali-like Riggs tell it, "This proves Bobby Riggs is the best women's tennis player in the world."

In the wake of Riggs' victory, everybody seemed to be looking to put cider in someone else's ear. The Battle of the Sexes was heating up into a full-fledged epidemic. Fifty-eight-year-old Lou Nova, former heavyweight contender, issued a challenge to fight "any woman in the world for $100,000"; Jimmy Demaret, winner of three Masters' championships, challenged Kathy Whitworth, the leading money winner on the 1973 Ladies Professional Golf Association tour, to an eighteen-hole winner-take-all match; Brian Oldfield, 270-pound shotputter on the professional ITA track circuit, challenged any woman sprinter to a 30-yard dash; Willie Mosconi, world billiard champion, called for Riggs to engage him in a $10,000 winner-take-all pocket billiards match. Closer to home Billie Jean King defied Riggs to play her in a $10,000 match ("Margaret opened the door, and I intend to close it."). The match that had started as a gimmick was now being taken seriously.

"No way," responded Riggs to Mosconi's challenge. "I know better than to play the other guy's game. But I'd love to get him on a tennis court. Tell Mosconi I might give him two poodles, a pail of water, and an overcoat if he was to play me sometime."

But Billie Jean King? That was cider of another kind. "The women's lib movement in tennis is working quickly to match me with someone," said Riggs. "I want Billie Jean King. I wanted her in the first place!" More to the point, the promoter in him said, "Billie Jean would make the most noise to build up a match."

The idea also occurred to someone else. Jerry Perenchio, who had put together the Fight of the Century between Ali and Frazier, was in nearby Palm Springs with seven other couples on that Mother's Day. "NBC was showing the finals of the WCT with Stan Smith versus Arthur Ashe," remembers Perenchio. "And when the women said, 'Let's go see the tennis match,' I thought they meant the match between Smith and Ashe." But Perenchio found out otherwise to his pleasure. As he admits, "I got caught up in it. Everyone was making bets . . . and I won a coupla hundred."

But that was all Perenchio thought about the match. Until the next morning, that is, when he chanced to "look through the sports section of the Los Angeles *Times*." There he saw a little "boxed item that said 'A Florida promoter would pay Riggs $50,000 to play Chrissie Evert.'" Immediately the man who always thought big, while admitting there "weren't too many things that turned me on," got turned on by the possibilities of another Riggs challenge match. "I had the same reaction as when I saw what they were paying Ali to fight Frazier. It's valuable if it's promotable and self-promoting—like Ali." It was worth "twice as much as anybody else has considered it to be" to Perenchio based on his intuitive feel for public relations: "Many times you have an event that the press envisions as Shruggsville. But if the event is self-promoting, then you have the press in your corner." And Riggs was, if anything, self-promoting.

Perenchio, who had been called "a spendthrift" by Jack Kent Cooke and who admitted to "sometimes getting my zeroes out of focus," nevertheless subscribed to the philosophy that "a promoter can raise something out of mediocrity if he attaches money to it." Ready to move, he thought "I'll just pick up the phone and offer him $100,000." Never having dealt with tennis players—or hustlers—before, he didn't know how to find Riggs. Despite the fact that he was listed in the Newport Beach phone book under "Bobby Riggs," Perenchio called his friend Tony Trabert. "I'll give you $10,000 if you put me in a room with him and I sign him," the by-now excited Perenchio told Trabert. Although he eventually received substantially less money, Trabert was glad to run interference for Perenchio, informing him that Riggs was to be at Caesar's Palace in Las Vegas that weekend, appearing in a tournament.

As in Bingo, where winners have to be present, it was Perenchio's presence at Caesar's Palace that turned the trick. Faced with the insurmountable task of bagging his wary quarry, who let it be known early on in the discussions that he already had a piece of paper in his possession signed by the producer of his match with Court guaranteeing $50,000, Perenchio was forced to abandon all hope for the $100,000 figure. Then $125,000 flew by like another road sign on the Hollywood Freeway. Finally, the figure of $150,000 was arrived at. "That little hustler got me up to that," admitted Perenchio, who now knew how Court must have felt. But despite the cider in his ear, Perenchio had Riggs. Having Riggs, the second round in the Battle of the Sexes was his.

Now Perenchio went looking for what in the world of boxing would be known as the "worthy contender." He didn't have far to look. She had been there all along in the person of Billie Jean King. Long an articulate activist for all things feminine—both on and off the court—Mrs. King had been one of the first four women players to sign professional tour contracts; the leader in the well-publicized demonstration against Jack Kramer that led to the establishment of the Virginia Slims tour; the "up-front" representative who had agitated for equal prize monies at the U.S. Open for women; and the organizer at Wimbledon in 1973, of the Women's Tennis Association, a group that spoke collectively for all women players' interests in tournament and television rights negotiations. In short, she *was* women's tennis; the aptly named Mother Superior.

The Battle of the Sexes Match of the Century was announced in July, to be held "sometime in September." It would pit King, who had just won her fifth Wimbledon singles championship the preceding week, against Riggs, who had won the 1939 Wimbledon singles championship, before Billie Jean Moffett King was born. It was a match that could just as easily come out of Central Casting: the Libber versus the Lobber.

Billie Jean, who had publicly stated "I can't just play for money, I've got to play for a cause," now had both. Her cause was that of feminists everywhere, who were tired of Riggs' outrageous remarks that his job was "to keep our women at home, taking care of the babies—where they belong." Her money was to be the same as Riggs, $150,000, an amount which reflected King's belief that because women's tennis provided "an entertainment value as good as men's," they should be paid accordingly—equal.

If the amounts the participants were getting for the match were identical, the amounts they were generating for endorsements weren't. In an Orwellian sense, all hustlers are created equal, except some more so than others. And Riggs was more so. An incredible range of marketing executives representing Hai Karate, Supphose Stockings, Sunbeam, and Sugar Daddy candy bars flocked to his door. A Swiss firm even paid him a $10,000 advance to mint a sterling silver Male Chauvinist Pig coin.

Riggs got $50,000 from Sunbeam for his part in a dual commercial with King. But when Billie Jean, who had gotten only $25,000, found out, she went back to Sunbeam and told them "You misled me!" She eventually got her $50,000.

The rest of the monies were hacked up like so many cattle in an abattoir: for playing with a certain kind of gut, Bobby got $5,000; for using a certain racket, both got $10,000; for the court surface, Perenchio got $10,000, and so on. "We got the last ounce out of it," said Perenchio, obviously relishing his wheeling and dealing in commercial by-products.

Perenchio selected the Houston Astrodome as the site of the match where, with 46,000-plus seats, he could attain his $400,000 house by scaling the seats down from $100; and he put it up for competitive bidding by the networks as well, hoping to get what John Wayne and Julie Andrews were getting—and "even more." Despite the claim by CBS that it had the right of first refusal by virtue of its having telecast the Riggs-Court match, NBC and ABC entered into the spirited bidding. NBC was the first network to drop out, bowing out at $400,000. CBS bid $500,000 based on their contention they had the right of first refusal. But ABC Vice President of Sports, Jim Spence, saw the match as prime time entertainment and enlisted the participation of the ABC Entertainment Division. ABC ponied up $750,000 and won the rights to what Roone Arledge called "the classic tennis battle of the sexes." It was the most ever paid for a single tennis event, but still "was under the one million dollars we were shooting for," noted Perenchio.

The scene at Houston the week of September 20 was pure carnival. Devotees, dilettantes, and denizens of the world of the unusual all descended upon the city from points east, west, and north, ready for almost anything. Any "action."

And there was plenty of action to be found. All the high rollers were in town. Jimmy The Greek was there along with an assortment of Texas millionaires and hundreds of hangers-on, all who came with money that seemed to be crying out "Bet me! Bet me!" The odds were 7–5 Riggs, and everybody was trying to get into the act—writers, photographers, and onlookers alike. Even Perenchio took some of the action, betting $1,000 on King with Sidney Shlenker, head of the Astrodome.

But despite the satellite activities, the main attraction was Bobby Riggs. The little self-promoter was a publicist's dream. Appearing on the covers of *Time* and a score of other national publications, he had made a whirlwind tour of the United States to "hype" the upcoming match, which rode on the wings of his wind. Now back in Houston, the hype continued unabated. While King remained in seclusion, Riggs appeared every day in the air bubble that had been placed outside the Astrodome for practice. The faithful were charged $5 a head for the privilege of watching him, a takeoff on the old boxing gambit of charging to see fighters work out. Riggs took the opportunity to hustle anyone and everyone. He played writers, giving them two poodles, a raincoat, and a chair. He played a heart surgeon with six chairs and a rock on his side of the court against a free examination for a member of his family. He even played Billie Jean's husband, Larry. It was a hustler's paradise.

The twenty-four hours of September 20 started, appropriately enough, with a Hai Karate pep rally for Bobby Riggs and segued into another promotion, a celebrity tennis tournament held that afternoon at the Astrodome as a showcase for a covey of celebrities flown in by Perenchio, which included Glen Campbell, Rod Steiger, Andy Williams, Karen Valentine, Claudine Longet, Jimmy Brown, Janet Leigh, Merv Griffin and a cast of thousands. The atmosphere was less Perenchio than Cecil B. De Mille.

As the first of the throng of 30,427 began filing into the Astrodome—passing concession stands laden with $2 programs, T-shirts, commemorative racquet covers, tennis sweatbands with male and female biological symbols, and all manner of knick-knacks, paddywacks and *chatzkas*—many of the $100 courtside patrons were upstairs at a party hosted by Virginia Slims. There, in the very city where the women's tour had been served up three years before, Gladys Heldman and the entire Slims entourage toasted Billie Jean, while several of her cultists, admiring colleagues, and members of the camera crew sported "Billie Jean" T-shirts.

Finally, with the countdown to the seven o'clock match minutes away, the University of Houston band took its place on the floor of the amphitheater. They were joined by cheerleaders in red hot-pants and an assorted grouping of Disney-like dancing bears, chipmunks, and other fuzzy-eared costumed characters, all jumping up and down in rhythm to the upbeat music. Also taking their collective place in a very obvious manner were the courtside ticket holders, many wearing tuxedos and carrying glasses of $1 champagne purchased from their neighborhood "bubbly" dispenser, a bar conveniently set up just outside the perimeter of the $100 seats, and catty-cornered from a chuck-wagon selling roast beef. The entire courtside began to take on the look of a crowd associated more with "openings" and ship-sailings than a tennis match. But to many of those in the V.I.P. section, it was just that, their ship finally taking off after many lean years when the crowds at tennis matches could have fit into phone booths rather than the Astrodome.

Many of those in what was called the "cheaper-priced spread"—the $50 and $20 seats up in the stands—wore buttons or carried banners to show their preference, as if it were not obvious from their gender. Several men sported pig-like hats bearing the legend "Male Chauvinist Pigs for Riggs." "Women-Power" T-shirts as well as those reading "WORMS" (for "World Organization for the Retention of Male Supremacy") were everywhere. One of the many banners hanging over the railings proudly proclaimed: "East West North South, Ms. King's Gonna Close Bobby's Mouth." Others, while not as eloquent, screamed out, "Beat him, Billie Jean" or "Win one for the bedroom, Bobby." It seemed that the match had captured the imagination of the country, and those in Houston on September 20 were its standard-bearers.

As 7:00 came up on the oversized electronic Texaco billboard high atop the Astrodome, all of the bit players got into position to act out their parts in what was taking on the semblance of a Fellini movie. The band struck up "Jesus Christ, Superstar." The menagerie of masquerading mammals began vamping it up for the crowd. The six ballboys and ballgirls, an equal number chosen for the "honor" by a local Houston sporting goods store, took their appointed spots. And, on a perch overlooking the court, Howard Cosell and Frank Gifford, together with Gene Scott and Rosie Casals, got ready to render the unbelievable setting to the television audience of some sixty-five million viewers just as soon as the opening commercials were done away with and the sponsors paid tribute to.

All was in readiness for the stars of the show. For this Perenchio had saved his best promotional touch, stealing a page out of the Mike Todd handbook on "How-to" stage a Bacchanalia. To him the match resembled something out of "Ancient Rome," and he intended to reflect that "Feel." First, to appropriate strains issued by the University of Houston band, six barechested men dressed as Nubian slaves, emerged from the runway bearing a feathered litter right out of *Cleopatra*. Their cargo: Billie Jean King. She dismounted onto a long red carpet leading to center court as once again the band struck up and out of the runway came six girls all wearing red T-shirts reading "Bobby's Bosom Buddies," looking as if they more than adequately filled the part, drawing a Chinese rickshaw. There, sucking a huge Sugar Daddy candy bar and wearing a Sugar Daddy warm-up jacket, was the quintessential sugar daddy of them all, Bobby Riggs. He jumped off onto a second carpet and approached Billie Jean at courtside. There hadn't been anything like this since the chariot races of Nero's time.

Riggs handed her the Sugar Daddy, and Billie Jean practiced her own patented version of "one-upwomanship." She produced a little piglet whom she had named Lorimer Hustle, after

Robert Lorimer Riggs. As she handed the pig to Riggs, an appreciative audience howled.

A few more ceremonial offerings, an obligatory interview for each with Frank Gifford serving as the interlocutor, and it was time to get down to the business of the evening. Billie Jean King won the toss, and the first serve. It was itself to serve as a portent of things to come.

With Billie Jean serving, the first game went to deuce, as both players played tentatively, feeling each other out like two wary boxers, thus maintaining the original metaphor Perenchio and others had used to describe the match. Then, at ad-in, Ms. King blazed a backhand shot by Riggs to win. Riggs, still wearing his by-now unnecessary affectation—the Sugar Daddy warm-up jacket—served and unbelievably lost the second game when he double-faulted. The hustler had choked! Removing his jacket Riggs returned to his chair at the sidelines to have his legs massaged. And, amazingly, to make a few more wagers with some of those at courtside. Momentarily rejuvenated, he went back out to break Billie Jean's service in the third game. It was not only Riggs' first big moment it was also to be one of his last, as Billie Jean ate up his soft, inviting lobs with overhand blasts to the far corners, alternating them with bullet-like line shots that had him wrong-footing. Hitting nothing but winners, King won the first set going away, 6–4, and set off screams of sheer delight from her followers. And most tennis fans, regardless of their preference.

The second set proved to be more of the same, King winning 6–3. And when the third went to five games to three, King, Riggs serving, he double-faulted, then hit a weak backhand return which meekly became enmeshed in the net, it was all over. Billie Jean threw her racquet high in the air and an obviously tired old man of fifty-five attempted to jump the net to congratulate her, almost impaling himself as he straddled it. The Texaco board flashed the results heard 'round the tennis world: "King 6–4, 6–3, 6–3." Sex and the Singles Match was over. The man who had executed the neatest hustle of a female since the first time a car just happened to run out of gas on Lover's Lane, when he beat Court, had himself run out of gas. And, in the process, gotten an earful of cider besides.

Later that night as the day's festivities wound down, the distinguished and beautiful people shared the hospitality of Jerry Perenchio at the opulent Astroworld Penthouse, hovering around groaning boards containing mounds of chicken salad, drinking champagne, and staring at a miniaturized version of the electric scoreboard that carried the evening's results. In a nearby room, a disconsolate group of entrepreneurs tried to arrange a picture of Bobby and his Bosom Buddies around bags full of the MCP sterling silver coins that would never see the light of the marketplace. While in the lobby, two youngsters from Oklahoma carried around Lorimer Hustle and would ultimately take it home to raise it.

Jerry Perenchio reflected on the promotion, comparing it to his first, Ali-Frazier: "Well, I'm profit-oriented, and for my favorite promotion it's no contest," referring to the Ali-Frazier fight. "But I'm entitled to be conceited. The Ali-Frazier fight was a major event and it was going to be put on no matter who did it. But I had a lot to do with making the Riggs-King match. . . . Being ambitious enough to go for prime time, holding out for the right money and for making Chicken Salad out of Chicken Shit."

Tennis, in its one hundredth year, had been seen by more people on television than had watched the game in person its previous ninety-nine, many of whom didn't know a baseline from a clothesline. As former great tennis player Pancho Gonzales said, it was "an outstanding show. . . . A lot of people who'd never viewed tennis before watched and enjoyed it. It helped tennis." Tennis had its centerpiece.

As centerpiece, the Riggs-King match provided the table setting for a boom in tennis over the next five years. By 1978 as many as fifty of the top hundred men on the Association of Tennis Professionals ranking list earned at least $100,000 in prize money, joined by no less than ten women. Ten years before, the top five amateurs were making, at best, $50,000 a year under the proverbial table, and the man ranked fiftieth took his expense money and ran. In 1978, according to *World Tennis* magazine, thirty-three million people play tennis at least three times a month, almost triple the number before 1968. And by 1978 players had leased their name to various and sundry firms wanting to tie-in with the new national passion, including various brands of balls, shoes, socks, tennis bags, gut, sunglasses, suitcases, tennis gloves, sports clothes, ball machines, and even watches, cameras, and razor blades for upwards of $125,000 a year.

The game had even been changed in specie as it dripped down into such alloys as platform tennis, paddleball, and something called World Team Tennis.

World Team Tennis was the dream of a Pittsburgh newspaper-broadcasting syndicator named Chuck Reichblum, along with Larry King, Billie Jean's husband, and the ubiquitous Newport Beach promoter Dennis Murphy. It featured an entirely new concept of team play—a radical departure and sporting *non sequitur* from the individualized sport of tennis—and other equally alien ideas: a six-set, two-half format with something called "halftime"; one-two-three-four "no-ad" scoring, and the abolition of time-honored terms like "love"; colorful uniforms; as well as patchwork courts of red, blue, green, and chocolate brown. It was all designed to capture the attention of new fans and of television as an "ideally suited" 2½-hour package of brightly colored entertainment.

From the very first "Off-Broadway" try-out of the new format—when a six-foot racquet spun to determine which mixed doubles team would serve first went out of control striking Philadelphia's Billie Jean King in the face, cutting her under her left eye, to the first official game in Philadelphia on May 6, 1974, where early arrivees witnessed league officials hanging up their own banners in an attempt to simulate the typical setting for team sports—World Team Tennis (or WTT as it has come to call itself) was an exercise in organized chaos. Coupled with its educational problems were those of the more mundane variety: financial, media coverage, and attendance. Embarrassingly low crowds of 176 in Chicago and 454 in New York were the rule rather than the exception. And its TV package was canceled after just one match. Perhaps the only good thing to come of the WTT during its first year was a Ball-Girl contest held by the Florida Flamingos which chose eight girls, according to the contest rules, to go around the court "grabbing loose balls."

One team, the New York Sets, even went so far as to engage an advertising agency, McCann-Erickson, to study its marketing potential. And then promptly ignored them. The agency dutifully reported that "no market existed for the product known as World Team Tennis" and that they "couldn't trade on professional tennis elsewhere," such as the tournament held at Forest Hills. Instead, the agency found that because "the tennis participant was not necessarily the tennis spectator," the league and the team should direct their appeal to those who weren't hidebound to the tradition of individualized play. But the Sets' owner, Jerry Saperstein, Abe's son and someone who should have known better, "thought they were completely wrong," and "rejected the study out of hand." It was but another example of the marketing myopia that plagued the WTT.

But with the addition of several glamour players to the league—including King, Ilie Nastase, Rod Laver, Vitas Gerulaitis, Chris Evert, Virginia Wade, and Bjorn Borg (whose signing by the Cleveland Nets begot the banner: "A Nets Star is Bjorn")—the league found firmer footing in its second and third years, league attendance increasing to 3,053 a game. Its future seemed to be not so much wrapped up in its stars or its attendance so much as in commercial sponsorship. Corporate sponsorship climbed from $14,000 the first year to almost $2,000,000 by the third as commercial enterprises once again sought out a relationship with an upscale audience.

It is questionable, as the WTT now concludes its sixth year, whether the league can reeducate the general tennis fan who cherishes the traditional crescendo of a tournament or the identification with a player rather than a city. It might just be that the customer satisfactions the WTT is offering are, in many respects, similar to the old salesman's joke about trying to sell "iceboxes to Eskimos." Based on its past cold reception, there is no reason to believe it will ever heat up to the point of becoming a major sports entity.

Another outgrowth of the Riggs-King match was the "Heavyweight" challenge rounds pitting Jimmy Connors against the likes of Rod Laver, John Newcombe, and Manuel Orantes in "winner-take-all" competition. But Jerry Perenchio had found that while "the life-or-death struggle of 'winner-take-all' appeals to people, it is not going to be promotable to the participants." And so while these challenge matches, like Riggs-Court and Riggs-King before them, were held out to be the first "winner-take-all" events since John L. Sullivan lost his championship to James J. Corbett back in 1892, they were somewhat less than advertised. Although they were promoted as $300,000 "winner-take-all," in reality the monies were split 70 percent to 30 percent with Connors getting the lion's share of the pot—*even* if he lost.

Perhaps the only thing tennis gained while losing a little of its believability were the trappings promoter Bill Riordan wrapped the "Heavyweight" challenge package in. He borrowed the setting from boxing, the original mano-a-mano sport, even to the point of introducing assembled champions at courtside. Tennis had become the mano-a-mano sport of the civilized world of the 1970s, filling in for boxing in a world where civility is widely regarded as a gauge of progress.

Once having attained its own Everest in the form of the Riggs-King match, tennis now began to suffer its own peculiar form of marketing vertigo. It did everything it could to fall off its lofty perch. Tennis matches began to show up on television during every available time slot. Sometimes taped reruns of players playing in a stale, weeks-old tournament competed against those very same players in a live tournament on another network. McCann-Erickson, in its yearly sports analysis, called tennis "a national pastime" in its 1976 report. By 1977 it could only say "The proliferation of tennis tournaments has fractionalized the potential TV audience to the extent that the big matches in Men's and Women's tennis are no longer a guarantee of a good rating. Additionally, the time of year that these events appear and the nonguaranteed aspect of the biggest names playing in the finals detracted from their overall potential."

Tennis had begun to devour itself. According to spokesperson Billie Jean King, "Four or five years ago everybody got greedy. Shows were packaged poorly and there weren't enough live events. So we got what we deserved."

If tennis intends to maintain its proud position at the top of the marketing mountain, it had better listen to Billie Jean. It did once before. And benefited by it.

The polyester leisure suit of sports is auto racing—although there are many who agree with Red Smith when he asks "This is a sport?" Spawned by big business, it owes its very existence to this continuing relationship. In many ways it is both a sport and an industry.

The answer to "why" can be found in simple economics. With Indy-type mechanical monsters running as high as $100,000-plus and others, from drag racers to stock cars, representing a sizeable investment, the purse put up by the track alone is totally inadequate in financing a professional racing team. The basic economic truth is that the costs of auto racing are so high that no amount of winnings can keep a professional team in business. Sponsorship by advertisers is imperative, from the total underwriting of the car and its crew to the garish decals that adorn the cars and uniforms.

And the advertisers with deep pockets who support auto racing get what they consider to be *quid pro quo* in exchange. They gain exposure for their product. From a patch on a driver's patch-laden uniform to a decal on a decal-clustered toolbox in gasoline alley or the overall identification of their sponsorship of a car—"And now leaving the pits in his 'STP Oil Treatment Special,' Car Number Four, is Richard Petty"—the name of the game is exposure.

If necessity is the mother of invention, then it also was the mother of auto racing. Ever since Charles Duryea used a radical invention, the gasoline-powered internal combustion engine, to win the *Chicago Times-Herald* race in 1895, a man's courage has been contested in magnificent duels between the thoroughbreds of the automobile. That victory fueled the imagination of young Henry Ford, who saw it as a road to his own success and resolved to get backing for his *avant* ideas through the vehicle of auto racing. "Advertising," he was to write in *My Life and Work*, "of the only kind that people care to read."

In the year after Duryea's win, the 33-year-old Ford constructed his first car. Three years later he became superintendent of the Detroit Automobile Company. But Detroit's automotive industry at the turn of the century was in its infancy, with almost every corner carriage and bicycle builder turning out automobiles in an attempt to catch lightning in a bottle. And as is so often the case in fledgling industries, a marketing survival of the fittest resulted in the shakeout of companies ill-prepared to compete in the brave, new world. The Detroit Automobile Company was one which fell to the wayside. And with it, Henry Ford. For the moment.

In a day when winning races was directly translatable into sales, Ford determined upon a course that would underwrite his dream. He entered the Detroit Driving Club's 1901 race. The favorite to win the race, as he had so many races before, was Alexander Winton, a Scottish immigrant who was building cars in Cleveland. He had captured all of the races that season. Smart money said that the Detroit Driving Club would be no exception. But Ford, piloting a car of his own design, lighter and lower than the Winton, won the twenty-five-mile race around the Detroit Driving Club's one-mile oval and with it $1,000 and the start of his company. "It advertised the fact that I could build a fast motor car," Ford was to write. "A week after the race I formed the Ford Motor Company."

Other companies have based their existence, in whole or in part, on their association with auto racing. The Firestone Tire and Rubber Company became involved in the Indianapolis 500 in its inaugural year of 1911, using the racing oval as its testing facility in the absence of its own. The STP Corporation practically created itself and its product through its association with auto racing. And so many other companies have tied-in with auto racing, making the cars flying billboards with their clutter of identification patches and decals, to the point where, as one wag says: "If you were to take off all the decals, there'd probably be no car underneath."

Those who have sought identification with auto racing usually are automotive products for the primary or after markets, including Firestone, Goodyear, Champion, Sunoco, Wynn's Friction Proofing, Diehard Batteries, Valvoline Oil, Steed, Castrol, Pep gas treatment, and a host of other racing-related products. But recently just as many nonracing-related products have gotten into the act as beers (Schaeffer, Carling Black Label, Schmidt's, Miller High Life, Olympia), cigarettes (Winston, Marlboro, Viceroys), hotels and resorts (TraveLodge and Sheraton), and assorted other products including the Atlanta Falcons, Thermo King, Coca-Cola, Johnny Lightning, Samsonite, and Sugaripe Prunes.

Fans are constantly bombarded with product mentions. Asked to what he attributed his speed, one driver told the audience, "Goodyear has made some tremendous tire improvement this year. They're just fantastic. And those Champions didn't miss a drop [of fuel]." Another, when asked by the incredulous announcer if he really meant that he was going to relax after his run with a Coke, responded, "Yes. I mean Coca-Cola. There, I got the plug in again."

Of paramount importance in the marketer's mind is that quality and performance are carried over directly from the race itself. In what advertisers call a Torture Test—"If it works that well on the track, under those conditions, think what it will do in your car under normal conditions"—sponsors seek to translate performance on the track into increased sales, much as Henry Ford did more than seventy-five years ago. For advertisers are aware of the fact that what the people in the grandstand and on television see on the track applies to their cars as well.

One of auto racing's continuing dramas had been between Firestone and Goodyear, as each seeks to associate with the winning Indy driver every year. Their infighting takes the form not only of signing up as many of the starting drivers as possible, it proceeds to the last logical absurdity, placing tires on the pace car. A compromise was once struck that called for Goodyears to be on one side of the pace car and Firestones on the other, so that when pictures were taken, each company got its share of exposure.

But that solution became less than satisfactory to both and another compromise was agreed to: there would be two pace cars, a Goodyear car and a Firestone car, each with four tires of the sponsoring manufacturer. Each was used alternately during practice and time trials to give both companies equal exposure. The "official" pace car was then determined by the brand of tire on the racing car which won the pole position in the qualifying trials. In 1974, Firestone, however, citing increasing costs as well as the diminished relationship between handmade racing tires and auto tires, dropped out, leaving the field—and the pace car—to Goodyear.

Ever since that magic day of January 1, 1971, when the FCC banned cigarette advertising from the airwaves, cigarette manufacturers have decreased their advertising expenditures while pouring the dollar savings back into company profits and into promotions. For roughly the price of twenty prime-time network TV minutes costing $1,000,000, a brand can now dominate a sporting event. For that million dollars several manufacturers have tied into everything from golf to auto racing and even tennis in an attempt to capitalize upon the exposure and association with a tournament named after their brand—The Winston 500, The Marlboro Trail, and others too numerous to name.

Sometimes, in their anxiety to gain exposure and the associative values they feel sports can give them, cigarette manufacturers get carried away. L&M once had plans to fly a hot air balloon, complete with a Lark insignia, over a Super Bowl-packed stadium. Then, so the proposal went, while the balloon hovered at midfield, a professional daredevil known as Sponge-man would dive into a sponge made to look like an oversized Lark pack. The proposal got all the way to the top management before someone asked the obvious: "Suppose he misses?" With that the plan was aborted and all copies of the proposal burned. Another L&M sports tie-in, The L&M Lady Eve Golf Tournament, actually made it to fruition only because a top marketing executive wanted to play golf with Kathy Whitworth.

But most cigarette manufacturers, despite their obvious cash-long positions, have exercised a degree of selectivity in their associations. Marlboro, once a major sponsor in auto racing, began to feel that it couldn't gain the exclusivity it was seeking because of an almost terminal case of sponsor "clutter," and dropped out.

Suddenly, in the face of the 1973 energy crisis, the sport-cum-business faced other defections. The almost-comical irony of competing for higher speed records at the same time the country was cutting speed on the highways to 55 came home to haunt advertisers. One dropout was Liggett & Myers, the cigarette manufacturer, which had been the prime backer for Formula 5000 races for three years. After having spent more than a million dollars, L&M withdrew because "1974 marketing plans for the L&M brand do not complement any racing involvement." Behind their ambiguous statement was the fact that L&M had gained little exposure for its money and, in fact, had only one ad which in any way tied into auto racing—and that featured a mock-up of a Porsche.

Today, although the sport draws an estimated fifty million people a year, according to Triangle Publication's prestigious *Survey on Sports Attendance*, it faces a serious crisis. Auto racing finds itself at a crossroad as it comes to the seventh decade of its existence.

The mystique that fueled its growth over the decades is still working. Men who see themselves as a carbon copy of Bert Jones or John Havlicek or Muhammad Ali have only to look at their out-of-shape frame for the fantasy to click off. But they identify with the Richard Pettys, the A. J. Foyts, and the Mario Andrettis, whose talent is the ability to keep their right foot on the floor longer and harder than anyone else. They are in control of their vehicles. As Vance Packard pointed out, cars are the personification of virility, representing one of the few socially acceptable ways of ventilating aggression and hostility. And while men view the machines as the macho portion of the sport, women are interested more in the drivers. The groupies, the Madonnas of the Grease Pits, see the drivers as sex symbols racing for speed records in a fast and violent world.

But if the mystique is still working for its followers, all of whom look like refugees from a Tupperware party, the other important underpinning of auto racing, the financial, isn't. The sport has lost its attraction for the high rollers of advertising whose one-time affection for it as a vehicle to sell products has been corroded by the high costs of supporting it. Even the sponsor that spawned it, Detroit, has pulled out. Today, auto racing is operating under a yellow flag, the fading emblem of a waning era.

If auto racing is the sport of the Silent Majority, baseball the pastime of the beer drinking segment, and basketball the province of the underprivileged minorities, then golf is the exclusive preserve of Big Business.

Companies which once bought commercials within the framework of a televised golf tournament now buy the entire tournament. Through the years tournaments such as the Monsanto Open, the Firestone Tournament of Champions, the Benson & Hedges Classic, the MONY Tournament of Champions, the Marlboro Open, the Buick Open, the Thunderbird Classic, the

American Airlines Golf Classic, and hundreds of other so-called "classics"—as well as some not-so-classics—have been subsidized by major corporations.

Those "classics" not totally underwritten by major sponsors are often named for celebrities, starting with the late Bing Crosby and including such luminaries as Bob Hope, Danny Thomas, Déan Martin, Andy Williams, Sammy Davis Jr., Glen Campbell, and others. It has become what you give a celebrity who has everything!

It wasn't always thus. Before 1913 golf in America was an exclusive game for rich socialites. But that year a 20-year-old amateur named Francis Ouimet, playing in the United States Open Championship at The Country Club in Brookline, Massachusetts, tied Harry Vardon and Ted Ray, two British golfing immortals, at the end of seventy-two holes and then defeated them by five strokes in the play-off. The victory of the local ex-caddy "from the wrong side of the tracks" revolutionized the game of golf in America. It suddenly became a game "for the people."

Ouimet's victory not only captured the imagination of the American public, it also captured the imagination of an eight-year-old boy from nearby Cambridge, who was then just beginning his career in golf as a 50¢-a-round caddy. That little boy who witnessed Ouimet's startling win was Fred Corcoran. And most of golf's current success as a sport-slash-big business is attributable to his promotional acumen.

Corcoran devoted his entire life to golf. From caddie he rose to tour manager of the Professional Golfers Association in 1952. Corcoran built the PGA, and with it golf, step-by-step, using sponsors' money as mortar. During the twenty years he was associated with the PGA total purse money for one year went from less than $100,000 to well over $1,000,000.

He alone was responsible for converting the game from peanuts to pay dirt, constantly lobbying the heavy hitters of big business on the benefits of tying into the pastime of the upscale. Before Corcoran the big money was in exhibitions. But Corcoran changed that. As a result of his efforts, Elmer Ward of the Palm Beach Company underwrote the Palm Beach Round-Robin Tournament; Teachers' Scotch sponsored the Teachers' Seniors' Championship; and George S. May of the department store Mays financed the richest event up to that time, the Tam O'Shanter World's Championship, with a $50,000 top prize.

Corcoran used his skills as a fund raiser and impresario to start the International Golf Association World Cup Matches—

formerly known as the Canada Cup—with the best two-man teams from up to fifty-four countries competing for the prize monies made available by General Dynamics, American Express, and Time-Life. He conceived the Westchester Classic and its predecessor, the Thunderbird Classic, enlisting the aid of American Express and the Ford Dealers of New York and New Jersey to put up the richest purses in the history of the sport. And he developed the women's tour, bringing not only the greatest woman athlete of all time, Babe Didrikson Zaharias, into the pro ranks under the Ladies' Professional Golf Association banner, but also Alvin Handmacher, proprietor of a line of women's clothing, into the tour to sponsor a major tournament. By the beginning of World War II, "sponsors were standing in line for dates" because of Corcoran's unstinting efforts.

Corcoran wasn't successful in everything he touched, however. He failed to sell golf to television in 1953 when he had a piece of the television rights. Tom Gallery, then head of NBC Sports, told him, "Don't bother me. Golf is not a television spectator sport."

But it soon became so, without Corcoran or Gallery. Today golf, according to a McCann-Erickson study, "continues to represent an excellent vehicle to present corporate messages to an upper income male audience." It is an upper-income audience that soon became followers of a whole new pride of professionals, including Arnold Palmer, Gary Player, and Jack Nicklaus, following their every move, both on and off the course. In fact, one equipment manufacturer, a major sponsor of golf programming, once attributed a softness in his sales to Nicklaus: "Nicklaus is so deliberate in approaching his shots, yet so successful, that soon duffers everywhere were patterning their moves after him. What happened was that they inevitably slowed up the game and backed up players who couldn't get on the course, ergo our sales dropped."

Most advertisers continue to associate with the PGA tour despite the relatively low Nielsen numbers, believing it not only to be a prime place for prestigious product and corporate messages but also that more people are watching than Nielsen gives it credit for. One corporate executive tells why golf telecasts are Nielsen-proof: "Many members of country clubs watch the golf match after coming in off the course and those bodies clustered around the bar are not translatable into Nielsen numbers."

But above merely tying into the event, most are still following the course set out by Corcoran: Sponsoring entire tournaments. One is Colgate-Palmolive, which underwrites the Colgate-Dinah

Shore Winners Circle. Before Colgate came on the scene in 1972, women golfers were similar to their sisters-in-sports, the women tennis players. They played for small purses, to small press coverage, and to still smaller television coverage—one hour a year for the U.S. Women's Open. Colgate "saw few opportunities on the men's circuit" and got involved in women's golf because, in the words of one spokesman, "There was more opportunity there and we could make a name for ourselves."

The Colgate-Dinah Shore Winners Classic was the idea of Colgate Board Chairman David Foster, himself an avid golfer. He not only saw the opportunity to capitalize on the vacuum, but also to package women's golf so that it sold his packaged goods: Colgate toothpaste, Cold Power, Ajax, and other women-oriented household goods. The proof that—in the words of Carol Mann, president of the Ladies' Professional Golf Association—"Colgate has done a super job" is that while showcasing women's golf, they have also showcased their own products.

Thus had Colgate joined the long list of sponsors who have become willing handmaidens to the sport of golf. And benefited by it. Vincent Draddy, president of David Crystal, one of those who "has tied into golf, makes no bones about crediting the success of his company to golf," observes Guido Cribari, longtime writer on the golf scene.

And those 450 traveling entrepreneurs, the players? Have they benefited? "Where would we be without sponsors who promote the game?" Super-Mex Lee Trevino asks rhetorically. "I'll tell you: Julius Boros would be a bookkeeper in Connecticut, Arnold Palmer would still be in the Coast Guard, and I'd be back in Texas picking cotton."

For sponsors and players alike, the system set up by Fred Corcoran has worked. Both ways.

Once the horse moved man's physical presence and articles of commerce from one place to another, pulling chariots and wagons, stagecoaches and surreys, and carrying pony express riders, policemen, and cowboys. Now it moves a part or the whole of the bank accounts of millions of horse fanciers whose hopes and dreams ride with it.

Today more than eighty-two million of those fanciers attend both thoroughbred and harness tracks to see the horses run. And to bet. Therein lies the real *raison d'être* for horse racing. It is the only major sport in America today which is at once a spectator and a participatory sport; the participation being in the betting.

But it wasn't always a sport based on betting. Back around the turn of the century, horse racing formed the backbone of the then-embryonic sports page as well as the focus—along with baseball and boxing—of the sports fan. And it produced the first national sports celebrity, with the possible exception of John L. Sullivan.

That hero was Dan Patch. The same Dan Patch more recently remembered in Meredith Willson's rapid-fire "Ya Got Trouble" number in *The Music Man*. "And the next thing you know your son is . . . listening to some big out-of-town jasper here to tell about horse race gambling—not a wholesome trotting race, No! but a race where they sit down right on a horse. Like to see some stuck-up jockey boy sitting on Dan Patch? Make your blood boil? Well, I should say!"

Dan Patch was a pacer who made the collective blood of America boil for the first decade of the twentieth century. As a celebrity he outshone them all. At state fairs, Teddy Roosevelt, William Jennings Bryan, and even The Burning of Moscow fireworks display ran poor seconds to this four-legged national monument. Foaled in 1896, Dan Patch was a gaunt, scraggly colt with knees too knobby, hocks too curved, and legs too long. In short, he had neither the looks nor the temperament of a racer. His owner, Dan Messner, a village storekeeper in Oxford, Indiana, envisioned his horse as a "pretty fair delivery horse" and thought so little of his chances that Dan Patch was four years old before he ever competed in a race.

Finally, worn down by the importuning of Dan Patch's trainer, Messner entered his horse in a match race against two speedsters of modest reputation around Oxford. The bay colt won in straight heats. Dan Patch never lost a race from that day on.

Messner sought to cash in on his prize horse and sold him for $20,000 in 1901. The following year the new owner multiplied his investment threefold, selling Dan Patch to Marion Willis Savage, a Minneapolis manufacturer. The record amount paid by Savage was mere seed money to create a walking, running, and pacing advertisement for his company, the International Stock Food Company, and his wares.

From that day forward, wherever and whenever Dan Patch raced—traveling the Midwest and the Southwest in his private railway car—he became the prime attraction at local fairs, his appearance preceded by advance men who papered the countryside with huge signs advertising "Dan Patch, the Wonder Horse." His fame spread. And with it the sales of International Stock Food Company.

Soon local farm publications were filled with ads offering "The Racing Life of Dan Patch" for the price of a 1¢-stamp, stock-food literature enclosed free of charge, of course. That was followed by "genuine Dan Patch horseshoes" at $1 apiece, Dan Patch cigars, Dan Patch sleds, Dan Patch coaster wagons, Dan Patch hobbyhorses, Dan Patch farm machines, Dan Patch foods, and Dan Patch buildings. Even a railroad was named in his honor. The horse called by *The Horse Review* "so phenomenal as to defy comparison," was to make more than one million dollars in purse monies and another million from merchandising his name.

Retired to stud in 1910, Dan Patch still inspired millions of his faithful followers to make pilgrimages to his stable outside Minneapolis to take one peek at this living legend. But his passing from the scene marked the last time horse lovers were to show interest in the animals outside of their mutuel prices. From that time on—with the notable exceptions of such worthies as Man O' War, Citation, and Secretariat—affection has been peddled at $2 a heartthrob, less take and breakage.

During the next few years horse racing would change radically. Harness racing, born in the farmlands of the Middle West, soon became the victim of progress. Increasing urbanization accelerated its decline and thoroughbred racing, the so-called Sport of Kings, eclipsed its younger relative in the Roaring Twenties, a decade dedicated to fast action, glamour, and the chance for a quick buck.

Even in those days horse racing was, perhaps more than any sport, an entrepreneurial enterprise: race tracks were privately held, horses were owned by individuals, even the betting was carried on with individual bookies who set up shop near the paddock or in the infield. It was a democratic world. Rich and poor alike had an equal opportunity to lose their shirts.

Then, in the late Thirties and early Forties, the introduction of the automatic Totalizator changed the game completely. The Tote allowed the tracks to form and administer pari-mutuel pools which pitted all the players against one another rather than against the "books." Its immediate effect was to put the tracks in the gambling business and the bookies out. A secondary and perhaps equally important effect was that it attracted new players to the game, those who previously had been wary of the mysteries of betting with a bookie. Finally, the most profound change of all, state governments all across the nation, eyeing the fabulous profits being garnered by the track proprietors (in a pari-mutuel system, the house has an absolute edge, one akin to zero and double-zero on a Las Vegas roulette wheel) stepped into the picture and made themselves partners. Racing has never been the same since. It has been transmogrified from the Sport of Kings into a Sport of One-Eyed Jacks, deuces wild, as the various states have regulated it, deregulated it, raised the take, changed the racing dates, extended the season year-round, and picked it clean all in the name of raising revenues for the sake of the general welfare.

To many, horse racing consists of just three races every year: the Kentucky Derby, the Preakness, and the Belmont Stakes. They are racing's crown jewels. And yet, for many years, these three races for three-year-olds were unconnected, sometimes even conflicting with each other. Man O'War did not run in the Kentucky Derby, his owners preferring to enter him in the Preakness which was held on the same day.

The Kentucky Derby, started in 1875, was something that came out of the very air and the land and the people who lived on it, a celebration of the true horse country of America in a race that pitted aristocratic horses against one another. And the powers that ran the race for the bluebloods of the Bluegrass country thought little about doing more than promoting it within state boundaries.

Even when Omaha won the sixty-first running of the Derby, the fifty-ninth running of the Preakness, and the sixty-ninth running of the Belmont, they were just three races, not necessarily connected. The catch phrase that would make them racing's greatest promotion came not from within racing, but from an outsider, Charlie Hatton, a writer on the *Daily Telegraph*. Tired of writing the names of the races over and over again, Hatton invented a term to link the three together: The Triple Crown. Thus horse racing's greatest promotion was born by Charlie Hatton out of his typewriter and not by the racing establishment itself.

When the racing authorities did anything at all, like establishing the Thoroughbred Racing Associations of the United States in 1942 as a unified body to coordinate the sport's adjustment to war conditions, it was for its own protection, preservation ringing truer than promotion.

Sitting in their collective counting rooms counting out their monies, they were smugly assured that the best promotion was no promotion at all, the wisdom of their nonefforts reflected by soaring attendance figures—thoroughbred attendance going from eight-and-a-half million in 1940 to more than fifty-one million in 1976. But few dared to look behind the computer curtain. For what they would have seen was that attendance, as a function of the proliferation of tracks and additional dates, was in truth declining on a daily basis, as was the betting handle.

And just as disastrously, what figures existed at all on the average trackgoer—horse racing being the only sport that had never undertaken research to discover the demographics of its fan other than checking out-of-state license plates in its parking lots—would show that the average racing fan was 52 years of age. Today, racing is in jeopardy of becoming an extinct species, its fans lost not to competitive entertainment, but to hardening of the arteries, the same affliction that was now consuming the powers-that-be.

When something happened, it was usually from outside the closed ranks of racing. One such serendipitous happening occured in 1969 when Bill Veeck—who had vowed in his autobiography *Veeck—as In Wreck* "Look for me under the arc lights, boys, I'll be back"—came back. Playing in every joint where he could get a bet down, Veeck was back, this time not back to baseball, but to horse racing, as president and part-owner of East Boston's rundown racing emporium known as Suffolk Downs, a track which had been built some thirty-four years before on the site of an East Boston dump and had reverted to its original state.

Veeck was astonished at what he found both at Suffolk Downs itself as well as within the racing establishment. Believing that "anything you do to enhance sales is a promotion" and that "refurbishing is a promotion, of sorts," he immediately initiated a million dollar renovation program designed to make Suffolk Downs presentable—even personally attacking the dingy washrooms and pay toilets with a sledgehammer. He then took off with his personal sledgehammer after some of racing's most cherished, antiquated customs. Discovering that the average age of the racing fan was somewhere near retirement age and that racing, like boxing in some states, bans children from attending the event, Veeck went to the Massachusetts Superior Court and won a decision reversing the Massachusetts Racing Commission's ban on children at the track. "I may not know much about horses," Veeck admitted, "but I do know that we've got to get the young ones to develop new players." Besides, the pixyish Veeck, father of nine, added, "Why shouldn't kids be able to see what their old man is up to?"

Veeck not only brought color to the sport, he brought it to the racetrack itself, opening Suffolk Downs with a $10,000 Lady Godiva Handicap featuring the then-controversial "jockettes"— "Eight fillies on eight fillies." He gave out the by-now recognizable Veeckian gifts to those attending: two thousand coloring books, a lifetime supply of balloons, and one thousand hot dogs. Minstrels strolled through the grandstands and, to lure more women into the track, he designed a program to exchange trading stamps for losing tickets. It was vintage Veeck. And it was promotion, something horse racing had never seen, borrowed not only from Veeck but from another successful sport that promoted itself, baseball.

But the conglomerate that owned Suffolk Downs went broke, and with it the racetrack. And so Veeck retired from racing, leaving it some of his ideas and the sport basically unchanged.

Still odds-on favorite to continue its holding pattern, horse racing was suddenly assaulted by another outsider, one destined to leave its mark.

The outsider was something called Off-Track Betting. Conceived by the state of New York to raise revenues painlessly, it was sold to the legislature as a way to put the neighborhood bookie out of business. What it did was almost put the New York tracks out of business. Starting in 1971, OTB offices began sprouting up on every corner in New York City, offering $2 bettors a chance to lose their money in a more convenient manner. No longer did he or she have to spend a day at the races, paying for transportation, food, and other incidentals. For a 5 percent surcharge on top of the 18 percent take and breakage, they could march into any one of 200 neighborhood OTB shops and put down their money.

The results were predictable. Whereas the average daily attendance at thoroughbred tracks had declined from 8,706 to 8,215 in the previous decade, it immediately took a 19 percent drop, with the first Aqueduct meet showing more than 5,500 fewer fans per day and the average on-track betting handle down 14 percent, or more than $500,000 a day. Harness tracks suffered equally.

Like touts watching the Tote, politicians in Albany, who had for years assumed the sky was the limit, began watching OTB's effects on the New York racing industry. They realized that they would either have to come to their senses quickly or that racing would come to its knees—almost as quickly. They began to generate legislation to combat OTB. First they legalized Sunday racing. Then they lowered the betting age from 21 to 18 and, finally, gave the New York Racing Association flexibility in ticket pricing. No longer would New York tracks be required by law to charge $8 for a ticket to the clubhouse, a law based on the reasoning that anyone who could afford to play the horses could afford an $8 ticket.

But OTB was not the only problem for racing in New York, one of the only five states with year-round racing. Across the river in New Jersey the state legislature had created a sports complex known as The Meadowlands. Run by Sonny Werblin, who had converted an entire state into his personal playground, it had already enticed two of New York's most prestigious sports properties to join it, the football Giants and the basketball Nets. Now it was running head-to-head against the New York tracks, both flats and trotters, and beating them to the wire. Horse racing, unlike most other sports, can stand competition with other forms of entertainment, but because it has not brought additional converts to its fold, it cannot stand competition within its own family. And the Meadowlands was cannibalizing the sport, drawing away the hard-core fan who was New York's $2 staple.

Faced with outside competition as well as intra-industry rivalry for their $2 bread-and-bettor, the New York Racing Association—a state-chartered nonprofit organization which owns three of the four thoroughbred tracks in the state and controls the greatest number of racing days—could no longer afford to hide its head in the backstretch sand. It was faced with a drastic deterioration of its basic product: good horse racing.

The quality of horse racing is predicated upon the maintenance of a self-perpetuating cycle. Large attendance begets large purses which, in turn, attract quality horses, ergo good racing. But if the most basic element in that roundelay—attendance—is declining, the remainder of racing's syllogism must also decline, including the quality of the horses and the races themselves.

The New York Racing Association had to try something. Anything. Even promotions once considered anathema and beneath them.

It authorized exotic betting, with perfectas, superfectas, and quinielas, all designed to bring the OTB parlor player out to the track. But each was copied by OTB. And sometimes even

312

improved upon. It advertised the pleasures of attending beautiful Belmont and less beautiful Aqueduct. But those who regularly attended the OTB parlors were not interested in spending money for track admissions, programs, transportation, and other incidentals that could be plowed back into a $2 bet on a "sure thing." Finally, the NYRA accepted the inevitable and reluctantly invoked the use of promotions in an attempt to attract younger people and families to the tracks.

The product of the efforts was something called Bonus Week, a promotion-a-day carnival in the fall of 1977, marketed under the umbrella theme, "Don't Miss the Most Exciting Week in the History of Belmont." Bonus Week started off with Tip Day on Monday, with everyone getting felt tip pens, a book entitled *The ABC's of Thoroughbred Racing*, and an opportunity to hear Jimmy The Greek demonstrate why he was not in a class with Nick The Greek. Tuesday was something called Big Apple Food Festival Day, with courses of ethnic foods served up to those in attendance. This was quickly followed by Priceless Day III on Wednesday, a day when free admission was granted to the grandstand. Thursday featured the sale of binoculars at wholesale prices and the opportunity of getting one's picture taken with the jockey of his or her choice. Friday was Doubles Day, a euphemistic handle for a promotion that has been known for years as "two-fers," with two tickets to the grandstand available for the price of one. And Saturday was Glen Campbell Day with the Wichita Lineman singing for the benefit of those players who had enough left after Bonus Week to still lay it on the morning line.

It was not possible to turn around years of erosion with a one-week effort. The NYRA's former constituency, weaned away by OTB, were not about to return en masse because of Glen Campbell, Jimmy The Greek or two-fers. Something more was needed. Something that would bridge the ever-widening gap between the on-track and off-track horse player.

One possible solution would be for the legislature, which not only oversees both the NYRA and OTB but which put them into competition against one another in the first place, to make them full and equal partners before the parasite they created sucks the life from the sport it lives off. A second would be reducing the takeout cut at the tracks from 17 to 14 percent. And still another potential solution is the infusion of promotional monies from outside sources into horse racing, much of which has already flowed into and underwritten other sports.

True to its heritage, the NYRA is still operating in the

maching age of the Totalizator as if it were back in the days when betting could be placed through private commissioners or "beards." When Philip Morris, in the person of Jack Landry, the executive vice-president and director of marketing, determined upon a course similar to what was prevalent in Europe, "of firms sponsoring horse racing," he was greeted by Jack Krumpe of the NYRA "as if I had just escaped from the Creedmore Mental Institution."

Landry envisioned a stakes race for the finest horses in the country, one decisive event called The Marlboro Cup. Pledging to conduct a race that would "Maintain the dignity and class of horse racing in a way that would reflect on both the sponsors and the authorities," Landry won over Krumpe—whom he credited with "pushing for a good idea . . . or we'd never have had it"—and finally got the NYRA's approval for a pilot race in 1973, with a $200,000 purse, $150,000 to be put up by Marlboro and $50,000 to be put up by the NYRA.

The seven horses that went to the post at Belmont on September 15, 1973, for the first Marlboro Cup included "the season's finest horses": Secretariat, Riva Ridge, Cougar II, Onion, Annihilate 'Em, Kennedy Road, and Key to the Mint. It was as advertised, "The Thoroughbred Race of the Year." Secretariat started from post position seven and won by a length and a half over his stablemate Riva Ridge.

Afterwards, as Mrs. Penny Tweedy accepted the Cup and $120,000 for her horse Secretariat, Landry was receiving the thanks of the trustees of the NYRA who, in the words of Landry, "showed visible relief when it was over and expressed thanks at the class we had shown."

If there was a drawback it had to do with the press, which adhered to the paleolithic practice of not identifying a commercial sponsor of a sporting event and went through the charade of referring to the event as The Cup. It was just such progressive thinking that once prompted the Louisville Courier-Journal to refer to the Buick Open Golf Tournament, which was then being played in Pontiac, Michigan, as The Pontiac Open.

Once considered a rank outsider to the regal ranks of racing, Marlboro became a fixture, so much so that Classic Magazine selected the fourth running—in which Forego defeated Honest Pleasure by a head—as the Greatest Horse Race in the World for 1976. And other race tracks, impressed by Marlboro's handling of the race and its success, now beseeched them to sponsor races. But Marlboro turned down all such requests from the jockeys-come-lately, determined to retain exclusive association with The

Marlboro Cup, which they now believe to be in a class with such classics as the Kentucky Derby, a view shared by many within the industry.

Now that the commerical camel has successfully gotten its nose into racing's tent and has proved itself to be worthy of inclusion, it is up to racing to pursue that association. Racing needs all the exposure and help it can get. In a day when every bowl game short of the Toilet Bowl is televised, and baseball is a staple second only to soap operas, the networks devote just five telecasts a year to racing. And those average just fifty-six minutes per telecast, the least air time of all sports.

Horse racing must do something to gain exposure, otherwise it is on the track to losing its fans—and not to any other competitive sport, but merely to the grim reaper—as the audience, and the sport as well, grows older and starts dying.

For seventy-five years soccer in the United States was like the subcontinent of Greenland: everyone knew it was there, but nobody gave a damn. It was a great public yawn.

The game of soccer was alien to most Americans. It was a game that differed radically from the traditional American game. It featured long interludes of playing interspersed with brief spurts of action; a game in which the defense was held to be more important than the offense; and a game where the ball was "untouched by human hands." It was a sport played by hyphenated Americans who viewed the playing of *their* national sport as the next best thing to a letter from home.

Suddenly in 1967, during the sports franchising craze, two soccer leagues sprang onto the scene. But the unfamiliar game with unfamiliar names—featuring a babel of immigrant booters sporting three-syllabic last names playing a defensive game in an offensive-oriented society—was seen less as the "real" game of football its sponsors would have the public believe than as spinach, and the public said "The hell with it." The next year the two leagues merged into one, the North American Soccer League. But even that proved one league too many.

By 1969 the league had dwindled to the ridiculous number of five teams, one of which was Lamar Hunt's Dallas Tornado. Hunt, the man who had bankrolled the AFL and the WCT, now bankrolled the NASL. Believing that he had an obligation to those people he had begun with, his very presence gave professional soccer whatever credibility it had left.

With Hunt's oil money providing the lubrication, the league began to grow like crazy. From the faithful five it grew to eight, then to nine and finally to twenty-four, as the world's most popular game literally went on tour to most of the major—and even some of the not-so-major—population centers of North America.

Most of the teams in the NASL were in cities with high ethnic populations, including Miami, New York, Washington, and even Toronto, where the very name of the team—the Toronto Metros-Croatia—played on the loyalties of first and second generation immigrants. But a few franchises even found their way into such maiden territory as Seattle, Atlanta, Minneapolis-St. Paul, and that uniquely American city, Las Vegas.

Together with the invasion of the game into American cities, the game was undergoing a strange metamorphosis. It was becoming Americanized. Players with pronounceable and even recognizable names were beginning to dot the playing pitch. In Dallas the Great American Hope was Kyle Rote, Jr., the NASL's Rookie of the Year and league's leading scorer in 1973, a vestigial remembrance of his famous father who had gained fame playing American football at local Southern Methodist University. In Ft. Lauderdale, it was Mike Seerey, son of former baseball player Pat Seerey. In Hartford, two former local All-Americans, Kevin Welsh and Hugh O'Neill, joined the Bicentennials. No longer did the NASL look like a carbon copy of the United Nations. Nor would fans have to content themselves with locomotive cheers for players whose names they couldn't spell.

And, finally, the NASL, recognizing the peculiar American fascination for scoring—and watching fans' eyelids close as if they bore twenty-pound weights—actually designed their game to appeal to the offensive-minded general public. They installed a "shoot-out" to decide ties and scoreless games and structured the point system to determine standings on the basis of scoring as well as won-loss record. The game became more wide open and attractive than the imported one.

Something was beginning to happen off the field as well that would hasten the arrival of soccer as a major sport. Kids were turning to the game at the grass-roots level. Discovering that soccer's continuous action accommodated all of the players on the field, that size and sex were no longer deterrents to participation in sports, that it was inexpensive to clothe the participants, and that the sport was both safe and inexpensive, youth leagues began to blossom in suburb after suburb. Where there were less than fifty thousand registered players in youth leagues at the advent of the NASL, ten years after the start of professional soccer well over a million kids belonged to some sort of an organized league, including both boys' and girls' teams—a figure half as large as the Little League enrollment. Colleges too were discovering soccer, as the number of schools fielding teams doubled during the decade. Soccer's future was assured.

But the arrival of soccer in America was to await the arrival of the King of Soccer: Edson Arantes do Nascimento, better known as Pelé. An international hero at the age of 16, The Black Pearl had led Brazil's national team to the World Cup championship three times and in doing so had become the most recognizable figure in the world, symbolizing soccer to the billion fans in 147 countries around the globe who called soccer their national sport. At the age of 31, Pelé had retired from the national team to play with his local Santos team and to become a businessman, signing a six-year, million-dollar contract with Pepsi-Cola as a consultant to Pepsi's worldwide youth soccer program.

Pepsi had made good use of Pelé's popularity, showing instructional films which featured his readily identifiable skills to an average of seventy thousand kids each week, around the world. Still, something was missing, both from Pepsi's promotional program and from Pelé's personal prestige, if not his position as soccer's goodwill ambassador. That something was the United States.

The story of the NASL is also the story of the New York franchise. Originally two separate franchises in two separate leagues in 1967—owned by Madison Square Garden and RKO-General Tire—the surviving entity in the 1968 merger was the New York Generals, owned by General Tire. But when, after two years, General Tire's investment went flat, the franchise was returned to the league by the corporate giant with a sigh of almost audible relief.

Two years later, Warner Communications—the same entertainment firm that had brought the general public *The Exorcist*, *Mad Magazine*, and the Rolling Stones, and whose president Steve Ross had once tried to buy the Jets—bought the dormant franchise from the league for the bargain basement price of $10,000 and dubbed them the Cosmos.

For three years the Cosmos struggled, playing first at Yankee Stadium, then at Hofstra University, and next at Downing Stadium. Finally, in 1976 they switched their games to Giants Stadium in the New Jersey Meadowlands and became a success story heard 'round the league. It was a "slow make," but one which epitomized the slow, but sure, growth of the NASL.

In a scene that came right out of an international diplomacy textbook—complete with the intercession of Secretary of State Henry Kissinger, who assuaged the Brazilian government that rather than it being a *norteamericano* buy-out of a national treasure, the signing of Pelé would actually improve relations between the two countries, and a face-to-face meeting of officials of Warner Communications and Pepsico, assuring Pepsi that Pelé's contributions towards increasing the public's awareness of Pelé and soccer in the U.S. would redound to its benefit—Pelé was signed to a six-year, $4,750,000 contract, three years as a player for the Cosmos and three as a public relations consultant for Warner Communications.

That was to be the beginning of soccermania in America, the one promotion that would forcefully bring the game to the public's consciousness.

As a major sport on the American scene, soccer can trace its true date of birth to that June day when Pelé became a New York Cosmo by contract and a roving stump preacher converting millions to the global religion known as soccer by contact. Almost immediately his presence began working its magic: the five games the Cosmos played at Downing Stadium before his arrival attracted an average crowd of 6,500; the first home game featuring The Black Pearl drew 21,000; the second a capacity crowd, with thousands more turned away. It was like that everywhere, as Pelé evangelized as no one else ever had—with his feet.

The next season—Pelé's second—the Cosmos moved into the 76,000-seat Giants Stadium in the New Jersey Meadowlands and the same thing happened, only on a larger scale. Pro football-size crowds began to materialize, 57,191, 62,394, and then an unbelievable 77,691 to see the Cosmos play for the NASL championship. Not only had Giants Stadium become The House that Pelé Built, but when similar crowds turned out around the league, the NASL became The League that Pelé Built.

Everywhere attendance seemed to be on the wing. Total attendance increased 29 percent in his first full year, and some franchises which had never seen the light at the end of their financial tunnel suddenly became profitable. In the space of a single season, Pelé had turned soccer into a major sport, making it not only instantly profitable, but also instantly respectable as other international superstars joined him in the new "in" sport, including England's George Best, Germany's Franz Beckenbauer, and Italy's Giorgio Chinaglia.

But if the promotion known as Pelé was half the story, the new breed of soccer fan was the other half. No longer was the crowd a predominantly male, immigrant, or ethnic one. Now, drawn by the presence of the high priest of soccer and fueled by the spreading conversion at the grass-roots level, the soccer crowd was a white suburbanite social gathering, with demographic measurements that Madison Avenue would drool over, much as Miss America judges would over a 44-28-36: white, middle and upper-middle class, almost ninety percent under 44 years of age, almost three-quarters college-educated, and almost half women and a third children.

In just three short years soccer had changed from ethnic to chic; from fluency to affluency; and from ignored to ennobled.

And as soccer's mushrooming growth takes it past many older sports on the popularity scale—much as supply and demand curves intersect on an economist's chart—it faces only one serious obstacle to its ever becoming King of the Sports Mountain: the lack of a television contract. For, in this modern electronic age, the hallmark of a successful sport is its television exposure. Not only will it bring additional converts into the fold, but also cash into the clubs' coffers.

Twice before—in 1968 and in 1976—it has gone before the network cameras and come away wanting in Nielsen numbers. But even with its newfound popularity, it still faces a major hurdle in adapting to television's needs: its nonstop action is irreconcilably unsuited to television's need for built-in commercial stops every ten minutes or so to underwrite the cost of the telecast. Once CBS employed the use of "official time-outs" as players groveled on the ground with referee-inspired injuries. Another time TVS cut away for a commercial just as one of the three goals in the NASL Soccer Bowl was being scored. It's a problem that doesn't possess a ready solution, other than the one facetiously proferred by TVS President Eddie Einhorn: "We have to hope that when the ball is kicked out of bounds it gets lost under a seat for more than fifteen seconds."

But whatever the final answer is, it will also answer the question of what will be the Sport of the Eighties. For then—and only then—will the sport known around the world as the most popular sport also take its place in the last remaining outpost, as much a part of the American landscape as other imports, such as the hot dog, apple pie, and even motherhood.

If anyone had any doubts about sport's full-time bed partner, business, they would have been permanently dispelled at the 1977 All Star Baseball Game. Every accredited member of the press received his credentials to the forty-eighth "Midsummer

Classic" together with a tote bag filled with giveaways that would have done Monty Hall justice.

Inside a blue vinyl bag stamped with the All Star logo, were the following items, less essential to the enjoyment of the game than to the basic understanding of the true meaning of the games of baseball and promotion: a package of Bazooka gum; a box of Chiclets; nail clippers embossed with the name Getty Gas; a Windsor Supreme Canadian litterbag; a Burger King soft drink holder; a current copy of *Cue Magazine;* a roll of Rolaids attached to a card heralding the Ace Reliever of the Year award; a package of Topps Baseball Cards and bubble gum; a Champion Spark Plug; a small bottle of Pinch scotch; two Paper-Mate pens with "All Star Game" printed on the side; a package of Planters dry roasted nuts; a thread box caddy with "Windsor Supreme Canadian" printed on the cover; a Dellwood Milk pen; a box of Dutch Masters Cameroon Whiffs; a package of Dutch Masters cigars; an album of New York songs, compliments of Manufacturers Hanover Bank; an album entitled "Yankee Stadium/Sounds of a Half Century," compliments of Magnavox; an inflatable Goodyear Blimp; a bottle of Fabergé cologne spray; a Gillette Atra adjustable razor and five cartridges; a Zippo money clip; a knife engraved with the Miller High Life logo; a Chrysler-Plymouth key chain; a Baby Ruth bar; and, just what everyone needed, an autographed photo of the Muriel girl.

The All Star Game, which, according to the bard of all sportswriters, Red Smith, had "started 45 years ago as a circulation-builder for the *Chicago Tribune*, has developed into the Trac II Classic."

The worlds of athletics and commerce had become totally indistinguishable.

7

The greening of America's athletes

Willie Mays, who once verged on the brink of financial ruin after a costly divorce settlement, best put into words the financial plight of the athlete: "The financial careers of most professional athletes can be summed up in these words: short and sweet . . . but mostly short."

From the day in 1869 when Harry Wright became America's first salaried athlete—receiving the then-princely amount of $1,400 a year—America's athletes have provided escapism and entertainment for millions of their non-athletic brethren. All for a fee.

But almost as soon as they had acquired the pulpy fantasies of fame and fortune, their careers were over. And with it their earning power.

By comparison, a doctor—or any one of a thousand other working persons—is just about to embark upon his professional career at the time the professional athlete is enjoying the peak of his earning power. And by the time the doctor's practice—or the worker's skill—is well developed, the all-too-brief career of the athlete has flamed out and he has been retired to the dusty files of nostalgia along with his clippings; his place taken by a new name.

Faced with such a short period to exploit their fame and maximize their fortune, many athletes resort to a time-honored practice: trading on their names.

The first American athlete to successfully trade his momentary renown for monetary reward was baseball's first superstar, Mike "King" Kelly. Sold by the Chicago White Stockings to the Boston Reds in 1887 for the Croesus-like price of $10,000, thereby earning the nickname The $10,000 Baby, Kelly demanded and got the unheard of salary of $5,000 a year from his new employer. But that was only the beginning for the man celebrated in song and verse as "Slide, Kelly, Slide."

Kelly, like so many other athletes, was stagestruck and became the first of an army of athletes to try his luck in a minor character role in a play called *The Tin Soldier*. He was so made up that, in his own words, "My own grandmother wouldn't know me"; but when he was recognized, as he was in New York, the crowd reportedly sent up a "a roar that sounded as if the roof had caved in."

The only player who rivaled Kelly's popularity in the early days of The National Game was Adrian "Cap" Anson of the Chicago White Stockings. Dubbed Cap because he was playing captain of the Chicago nine when captain was not merely a titular position, Anson became playing manager of his world championship team. Bitten by the stage bug the first time he brought his team to New York, he took his entire club to the theater to see a few friends perform in a production called *A Parlor Match*. Invited backstage before the performance by friends who knew Anson's weakness for the stage, they asked him if he'd like to have a bit part in the show that evening. Anson replied he'd like to try and was given a part as foreman of a crew digging for treasure.

When Anson appeared onstage, one of the workmen, instead of greeting him with the line "Good Morning," shouted "Good Morning, Captain Anson." The audience, seeing one of their heroes onstage, whooped it up, and Anson became so flustered he forgot the line and hurriedly exited into the wings. Other members of the cast surrounded the agitated Anson and began walloping him with bladders and bouncing sawdust bricks off his head in the name of fun as the whole episode ended in an affable offstage riot.

That incident not only failed to cure Anson of his mal-de-stage, it actually propelled him on. He later starred in a baseball play called *The Runaway Colt*. The climax called for Anson to hit a home run, dash off into the wings on his way to first base, and reappear soon after from the opposite side of the stage to slide into home. The actor playing the part of the opposing catcher was to receive the ball from a stagehand positioned in the "flies" above the stage and lunge at the sliding Anson, whereupon the actor playing the umpire would cry out dramatically "You're Safe!" Final curtain. If nothing else, the name of the play provided the Chicago team with a new, albeit tentative, nickname—"the Colts."

Other turn-of-the-century athletes also turned to the stage, yesteryear's version of appearing on the Johnny Carson Show. So many, in fact, that the theater began to take on the look of a locker room as every ball player or boxer of consequence went on tour.

Turn-of-the-century vaudeville was comprised of so many gradations that when promised a spot on a bill, one entertainer inquired, "Which one is it? Small-time, medium small-time, big small-time, little big-time or THE BIG TIME?" Suffice it to say that most athletes-turned-actors appeared in the small-time or medium small-time showcasing their so-called "talents." They appeared as hoofers, comics, actors, singers, and, in the case of boxers, as "bag punchers." Some even had full-fledged productions written for them as starring vehicles. Hired on the basis of the drawing power of their names, they strutted, grimaced and, not incidentally, exhibited their athletic prowess with a minimal of professional skill. But no matter how much the critics groaned, the fans loved it!

John L. Sullivan toured in *Honest Hearts and Willing Hands* and *East and West with Parson Davies*. James J. Corbett found a vehicle in *Gentleman Jim* and also appeared as a "Champion Bag Puncher." So did his successor, Bob Fitzsimmons, who generally started with light taps and wound up with a blow that would break the small rope to which the bag was tethered, sending it flying out into the audience as a souvenir. Jess Willard was a rodeo performer, Jack Johnson a performing aborigine.

But they were nothing compared to the ball players who each year took to the road with their acts. Germany Schaeffer and Charlie O'Leary of the pennant-winning 1907 Detroit Tigers put together a postseason "triumphal" tour with snappy patter that went something like this:

O'LEARY: Have you heard the tale of a baseball?
SCHAEFFER: Don't rib me. A baseball hasn't got a tail.
O'LEARY: Well, it sure seams sew.
SCHAEFFER: Get to cover.

And so it went, everybody, as Jimmy Durante said, was "trying to get into the act." Rube Waddell appeared in a period melodrama called *The Stain of Guilt* in which the great eccentric saved the leading lady from a stage "fire," carrying her down a ladder as easily as a mother would carry an infant in her arms. Rube's affection for fires must have, in the words of the manager of the show, "affected his mind. For later he spent most of his time in the fire department houses, and when an alarm came in he not only went to the fire, but he was the first man to climb if there was any climbing to do." Ty Cobb appeared in *The College Widow* as Billy Bolton, All-American halfback who attended a Baptist school. The highlight of the show came when Bolton/Cobb's stage father returns from abroad to find his son enrolled at a rival Methodist college where he is courting the president's daughter and confronts his son with "Well, you're a hell of a Baptist."

Rube Marquard appeared with his wife, Blossom Seeley, and when they were divorced formed his own traveling company. Bill Hallman, a second baseman for fourteen years, mostly with Philadelphia teams in three different leagues, was a regular on the Keith Circuit. "Turkey" Mike Donlin retired from baseball after twelve years in the big leagues to play the Orpheum Circuit, one of the few athletes ever to choose the stage over the diamond as a career.

But unbeknownst to most, vaudeville was soon to go the way of the village smithy, to be replaced by something called the "movies," invented by Thomas Alva Edison in 1889. Fittingly, Edison's first practical use of his invention, the Kinetoscope, was the filming of a boxing match between then-champion James J. Corbett and Peter Courtney at his Orange, New Jersey, studio in 1894. Edison's studio was a jerry-built barn-like structure called The Black Maria. Mounted on a pivot, it rotated slowly to follow the changing position of the sun—the only light for the cameras—and contained a mobile padded stage, fifteen feet wide and six feet high. The two pugilists were to fight six rounds of one-and-a-half minutes duration equalling the cameras' film capacity—with two minutes between rounds to give Edison's crew time to reload. Corbett won by a "knockout" in the sixth and final round and received $4,750 for his efforts against $250 for Courtney, proving again the drawing power of a superstar.

Almost from that moment movies, or "flickers," became the primary source of entertainment for tens of millions of Americans. By the second decade of the twentieth century there were more than twenty thousand movie houses, where some 150 miles of film were shown each week to an estimated hundred million viewers. And despite the dire predictions of several, including Detroit Tiger manager Hughie Jennings who advised his players that "picture shows" were bad for their eyesight and were forbidden, many a ball player threw his baseball cap into the nickelodeon ring.

Ty Cobb was one of the first to take part in the new phenomenon, starring in a potboiler called *Somewhere in Georgia*. Cobb played the archetypical hero who, finding himself in some death-defying danger, somehow manages to overcome this momentary adversity and triumph by the end of the second reel. Bound hand-and-foot by thugs in a remote cabin, Cobb engineers his escape and, after commandeering a mule team, races to home plate just in time to save the game for his ballclub. During the Twenties, screens were filled with the likes of Red Grange, Bill Tilden, Gene Tunney, Jack Dempsey, and many more, all appearing in suitably named vehicles like *One Minute to Play*, *The Fighting Marine*, and *Daredevil Jack*. It was, as one critic noted, "some of the worst acting ever seen on American screens." But it made money for both the producer and the player.

And then there was Babe Ruth. The Bambino had already tried his hand at vaudeville. Smashing his way through a large paper drop in front of the stage, he *almost* sang an old standby called "Little by Little and Bit by Bit," accompanying himself with the nonrhythmic beat of his bat (and adding the impromptu verse, "I'm making a vaudeville hit"). While his audiences, which paid up to $1.50 a seat, sat still for such amateurish shennanigans, the critics didn't. The reviewer for the *New York World* said of his act: "All lip-rouged like a tight-wire lady, with a voice as sweet as a furnace shaker in action, hands that could not find a place on that whole stage to rest comfortably, a grace of carriage somewhere between John Barrymore and an elephant, Babe Ruth came out yesterday at the Palace."

Now the Babe turned to movies. His first film was *Headin' Home*, a "quickie" shot across the Hudson in the cradle of the movie-making industry, New Jersey. Not only had Edison developed the motion picture camera and film in the Garden State, but the first feature film, *The Great Train Robbery*, starring the Lackawanna Railroad, was filmed there in 1903. D. W. Griffith made seventy-five pictures in New Jersey and Theda Bara forty. From Pearl White's *Perils of Pauline* to Mary Pickford's *Rebecca of Sunnybrook Farm*, the dream factories of New Jersey turned out thousands of films against a backdrop of the Palisades and the Passaic River. But while Ruth was shooting *Headin' Home* in the morning and commuting to the Polo Grounds in the afternoon (he would more often than not arrive too late for batting practice still wearing makeup, to the amusement of teammates and the annoyance of his manager, Miller Huggins), most moviemakers were packing their grips and moving west to California, where better weather and cheaper labor beckoned. It was a telling commentary on Ruth the businessman, as the $50,000 he had hoped to receive became only $15,000 before the film company collapsed.

Ruth made his second movie, a creatively titled soap opera *The Babe Comes Home*, in 1926. It was largely ignored by critics and public alike. Aside from instructional films and a cameo part in the 1942 tearjerker *The Pride of the Yankees*, the story of the life and the death of Lou Gehrig, it was to be Ruth's last movie.

But despite the fact that his movie career could hardly be termed distinguished, Ruth's incandescent presence lit the way for many sports stars to follow. He kindled a celluloid subindustry with swimmers (Johnny Weissmuller and Buster Crabbe), skaters (Sonja Henie), boxers (Billy Conn, Max Baer, Arturo Godoy), football players (Johnny Mack Brown, Glenn Davis, Doc Blanchard, Jimmy Brown, Timmy Brown, Joe Namath, Rosey Grier, O.J. Simpson), and baseball players (Johnny Berardino, Ernie Orsetti, Chuck Connors, Mickey Mantle) all turning Hollywood into one big locker room. Most were, as one critic described Conn in *The Pittsburgh Kid*, "Unfortunate," but a rare few—like USC football star Marion Morrison, better known as John Wayne—were able to transcend their backgrounds. And only Max Baer, who cameoed in *The Prizefighter and the Lady*, boxing a few rounds with heavyweight champion Primo Carnera, seemed to pick up more than just money. "I got the feel of him, no problem!" said Baer. A little more than a year later he put his theatrical training to good use, knocking down Carnera eleven times and taking his title.

It was a quantum leap from movies to television, as the tube found athletes in everything from semi-documentaries such as Prudential's "The Violent World of Sam Huff" to guest shots on variety and talk shows. Just hours after he had picked up the ninth perfect game in baseball history, Jim Bunning picked up $1,000 by being introduced from the audience by Ed Sullivan, "And heeeeere in our audience too-night. . . . "

Today athletes have come to view show business as one more ancillary opportunity to play "Up Your Income"; one in which prior training is not needed—just stardom.

King Kelly was not only the first athlete to turn to the stage, he was also the first to turn a buck in the business world. Capitalizing on his fame, he supplemented his already substantial income through endorsements—his handsome Irish countenance beaming down from billboards in every city, recommending everything from streetcar companies to cigars to baby foods.

Kelly's second rule of economic survival was not lost on his baseball brethren. By the turn of the century players were hustling almost as much off the field as on with a variety of schemes that looked like offerings from the Scam-of-the-Month Club: Chick Stahl of the Boston Red Sox obtained a patent on a combination washstand and ironing board and spent his spare hours on the road scouting agents to sell his product; Johnny Evers, of Tinker-to-Chance fame, perfected a method of making it possible "to iron a celluloid collar without setting it on fire" and peddled his invention to a company interested in cashing in on Evers' personal publicity; Cleveland manager Nap Lajoie published baseball literature on the side; teammate Harry Bemis carried an extra valise filled with books on the art of enbalming to sell at any propitious moment; and Leaping Dave Altizer of the White Sox invented a postcard bearing the likeness of perennial presidential candidate William Jennings Bryan, which when held up to the light, showed the White House alongside his head. Prizefighters, true to their heritage, made their money outside the ring as saloonkeepers when not touring with some theatrical troupe. Everyone sought to "make hay while the sun shines," in the vernacular of the day.

But all these methods were small change compared to what would become the traditional way of increasing a player's income: the rental of his name for product endorsement. The first recorded instance of a modern athlete leasing his name occurred on September 1, 1905, when Honus Wagner, shortstop for the Pittsburgh Pirates, gave the J. F. Hillerich & Son Company permission to use his name on its Louisville Slugger bats for a consideration of $75.

Pursued by commercial suitors, Wagner was careful of what he endorsed. He lent his name to a Gillette ad which quoted him as saying "I shave with a Gillette. I know of nothing that could induce me to change the system." But, as a nonsmoker, he sued the American Tobacco Trust which put his countenance and name on a Sweet Caporal baseball card without his permission. He demanded the tobacco company recall the cards which he believed constituted his implicit endorsement not only of the company *per se* but of smoking generally. All but fourteen of the cards were recaptured and today, according to the authoritative *Sports Collectors Bible,* each of the few cards extant are considered to be card collecting's Upside Down Airplane, commanding prices of up to $4,200 apiece.

Wagner's act against the tobacco interests won him not only the praise of Pirate owner Barney Dreyfuss, who tolerated no smoking on his club, but a bonus as well. Dreyfuss felt so strongly about smoking that he had previously sold a promising young outfielder who smoked rather than compromise his standards. That outfielder was Tris Speaker.

In 1907 J.F. Hillerich & Son signed Nap Lajoie to endorse its bats. In 1908 they approached the 21-year-old phenomenon who had led the American League in six categories while repeating as batting champion: Ty Cobb of the Detroit Tigers.

Cobb, already displaying a keen understanding of leverage in business made the company a counteroffer: "I'll give you my name for nothing," Cobb wrote, "if you'll provide me with selected bats. I want you to agree to set aside the best wood that comes into your plant. I want my own bin right at the factory. And I'd like the privilege of specifying the kind of lumber to be used."

The world of merchandising had become an extension of one of the oldest forms of advertising. It was common in patent medicine shows for the elixir salesman to place a couple of minstrels on the tailgate of his wagon to play the banjo and sing and dance. When this attracted a crowd, the old Doc would come out and sell his bottled-in-the-back nostrums. Twentieth century sports extended his tailgate. The minstrels had become professional athletes used—with or without their permission—to provide an audience for the "pitch."

Merchandising tie-ins took many forms. Coca-Cola introduced a series of ads in 1907 heralding "The Great National Drink at the Great National Game." It pictured Honus Wagner and Ty Cobb (years before Cobb "bought" 300 shares of Coca-Cola with $10,800 put up for him by the company's president and reaped a profit of more than a quarter-million dollars) drinking a modification of what had once been called French Wine Cola containing "the tonic properties of the wonderful Coca Plant and famous Cola Nut" and "caffeine," references which have since been deleted. Cobb also had a cigarette named after him by the American Tobacco Company and a candy bar named for him by the Benjamin Company of Detroit.

Bull Durham Smoking Tobacco bought all the outfield signs it could and offered any player who "hits the giant 'Bull' sign with a fairly-batted flyball in a league game" $50. This was the precursor of many signs on ball park walls promising free gifts if hit.

One sadistic and opportunistic manufacturer of female wraps actually marketed the Snodgrass Muff, named for the unfortunate Giant outfielder who dropped a flyball during the 1912 Series, costing his team the championship.

Everyone wanted their products wrapped around sports and sports stars.

In 1920 Babe Ruth proved to be the salvation of organized baseball, beleaguered as it was by rumors of a fix in the previous year's World Series. The Bambino had the greatest year any batter ever enjoyed in the history of the game: he led the league in home runs, runs-batted-in, and bases on balls; finished second in total bases and fourth in batting with a .376 average; and posted the highest slugging average (.847) and home run percentage (11.8 percent) in history. His name became the most heroic in a decade devoted to heroics.

Suddenly manufacturers raced to hitch their products to Ruth's parabolic blasts, with such products as Babe Ruth cigars (which Ruth himself had an interest in), Babe Ruth underwear (which Ruth endorsed but never wore, eschewing *any* underwear, even his own brand) and Baby Ruth candy (which he had nothing to do with financially or, according to the company, in name).

More than other public personae the athlete is dependent upon his reputation for fame and fortune. With the intangible known as a "name" he can both demand a higher salary and attain ancillary deals to add further to his earnings. Without that "good name," he is, as Shakespeare said, "Poor indeed."

Yogi Berra, unhappy with the Hanna-Barbera character Yogi Bear, was told he had no legal recourse inasmuch as his legal name was Lawrence, not Yogi. Elroy "Crazylegs" Hirsch sued the Johnson Wax Company for marketing a women's shaving cream called Crazylegs without his permission, claiming it caused him "embarrassment and humiliation" and won a settlement. Bill Bradley sued the Manhattan eatery, The Steer Palace, for using his picture and implying his endorsement and settled for a donation of the money to charity. Chicago Cub third baseman Stan Hack had his name taken in vain on Smile with Stan Hack mirrors, used to blind opposing batters in the 1935 World Series. And skier Suzy Chaffee recently prostituted her name, signing it away to the Miller-Morton Company, to front for its product as Suzy Chap Stick.

Others felt that if their names hadn't been taken in vain, at least their images had. Two NFL greats, Joe Namath and Johnny Unitas, were both moved to institute legal proceedings after seeing their pictures—or what they took to be their pictures—in connection with publications. Namath sued *Sports Illustrated* magazine for using a picture of him in conjunction with a subscription ad. He lost when the New York State Supreme Court ruled that it was "in the public domain." Unitas was equally litigious, feeling that a rendering of an unidentified football player by artist LeRoy Neiman on the cover of a book was him and also sought redress. His action begot the following reaction from the *New York Post:* "It's the worst thing an aging athlete can imagine: missing out on a commercial endorsement. So Johnny Unitas, ex-quarterback for the Colts, has slapped Hawthorn Books with a $100,000 suit over what he claims is unauthorized use of his picture on the cover of the recent book, *The Thrill of Victory: The Inside Story of ABC Sports.* Not only is Unitas a CBS commentator, but he says this photo has caused a 'dilution of the value of his endorsements and image'—which could be the saddest story we've heard all week." A New York State Supreme Court judge denied Unitas injunctive relief, holding that he was not denied future income on the basis of the drawing appearing on the cover of the book.

But the athlete whose name was first taken in vain was the very first whose name had come to mean something, Babe Ruth. He tolerated and was even flattered by some adoptions of his name, such as Anthony Shettine, who boxed under the name Babe Ruth. Ruth himself would rarely miss one of his namesake's fights. But another use of it bothered him: the appropriation of his name by the Curtis Candy Company for a candy bar.

The wrapper on the Baby Ruth bar lists the ingredients as: "Sugar, corn syrup, hydrogenated vegetable oils, sweetened condensed milk, dextrose, cocoa, soy flour, whey, salt, sorbitol, lecithin (emulsifier), sodium caseinate, artificial flavor and color, potassium phosphate, mono and diglycerides, and carrageene." But nowhere does it include the basic ingredient: pure bull.

The Curtiss Candy Company, a four-year-old firm with just four employees, "introduced the Baby Ruth bar in 1920," according to a press release from its successor company, Standard Brands. It was named not for Babe Ruth—"although millions associate Baby Ruth with the great baseball figure"—but was instead named for President Grover Cleveland's daughter Ruth, who had, it was claimed, "visited the Curtiss Candy Company plant years ago when the company was getting started." Charles Tate, director of Standard Brands' Confectionary Division's publicity further volunteered that the name came out of "an employee contest conducted by the predecessor company." In 1972, when Marshall Smelser was writing *The Life that Ruth Built*, he received a note from an administrative manager in response to a query. The letter claimed that Baby Ruth had made its initial appearance "some years before Babe Ruth, the ball player, became famous. The similarity of the names, therefore is purely coincidental."

While the story took on a life of its own, appearing in books like *The People's Almanac*, it was not true to life. It doesn't require a Sam Spade or even a Maxwell Smart to put the lie to the confectioner's concoction. Although there *was* a Ruth Cleveland, the eldest child of President Grover Cleveland—born during the time he was out of office on October 3, 1891, ironically on New York's Madison Avenue, home of most such myths—she died of diphtheria on January 7, 1904, fully twelve years before the company's own publicity handouts date the opening of its doors. It would, therefore, have been very difficult for "Baby" Ruth ever to have "visited the Curtiss Candy Company plant." And nowhere in the many books of Cleveland, including those by such scholars as Rexford Tugwell and Horace Merrill, or even in Allan Nevins' complete *Dictionary of American Biography* is Cleveland's daughter ever referred to as "Baby Ruth." Furthermore, it would have been farcical to have conducted an "employee contest" among four employees, the number cited in its own publicity releases. Thus, the Curtiss Candy Company's tongue could not have been far removed from its corporate cheek when they put forward such a candy-coated fabrication.

The plain fact was that the nation was captivated in 1920 by the sight of this gargantua hitting gargantuan homers "with the greatest of ease," 54 in all, almost double the record. His feats created millions of followers who had ignored the game before Babe Ruth. Curtiss meant to cash in. In a move of consummate corporate *chutzpah*, one of their first ads was a massive outdoor sign overlooking Chicago's Wrigley Field, another place Ruth Cleveland never visited.

Curtiss suddenly was busy on two fronts. On one they exploited their new product, sponsoring women's basketball teams, a twenty-six-man air circus to rain thousands of candy bars on major urban centers, and a radio program featuring Guy Lombardo, who introduced a new song, "A Rose and a Baby Ruth." Baby Ruth bars were even sent on North and South Pole expeditions. On the other front Curtiss waged a successful holding action, denying the claims of one George Herman Ruth. They even thwarted his attempts to register the George H. Ruth Candy Company and its product, Ruth's Home Run, appealing to the U.S. Patent Office and getting an order enjoining his application.

Now over a half-century later—based upon an offhand remark by Reginald Martinez "Reggie" Jackson that if he played in New York "they'd name a candy bar after me"—the ball has turned. Standard Brands has named a candy bar called Reggie! after the Yankee outfielder, even though some insist Standard Brands wasted its money, reportedly in seven figures, because they already had a bar, Butterfingers, named after him.

But on Opening Day 1978, Standard Brands got a promotion within a promotion. Handing out thousands of Reggie! bars to those 50,000-plus in attendance, it saw them scaled onto the field after Reggie hit a home run in his first time at bat, making it "the first game ever delayed by candy bars."

Athletes began to spend more time chasing the buck than the ball. Moving into commercial ventures with the case of a Joe DiMaggio, they endorsed, invented and became associated with all manner of commerce. Indeed, as DiMaggio—himself a monument to a ballplayers' use of his name as negotiable currency, renting it to everything from cigarettes to banks to coffee makers, and even possessing a contract from Heinz to endorse their 57 varieties the day his hitting streak was stopped—once said: "Now the name of the game is: How much can I make outside?"

But fame in one arena did not guarantee financial success in another. As many times as not the athlete experienced difficulty translating his attainment into instant economic success. Joe Louis endorsed and invested in a soft drink appropriately named Joe Louis Punch in the postwar 1940s. It went the way of all Louis' ventures—Joe Louis Milk Co., Brown Bomber's Chicken Shack, and others too numerous to name, even by the IRS.

Bill Russell, hero of eleven Boston Celtics' championship teams, lost a major portion of his championship checks in an ill-fated rubber plantation endeavor in Liberia. And Lance Alworth, one year after being named chairman of a California conglomerate with interests in motels and dry-cleaning establishments, filed for bankruptcy.

For every successful entrant into the world of business, there was at least one casualty: Billie Jean King's winnings from her match with Bobby Riggs were invested in *WomenSports*, a magazine which lasted just two-plus years; Joe Namath's fast-food chain and employment agency both floundered within months; and even Muhammad Ali's fame could not help his fledgling chain of Champburgers, which went down almost as fast as some of his early opponents. The landscape was littered with athletes posing as accident cases.

And then there is Jerry Lucas, he of the magic memory, whose computer-like mind enabled him to write a book on the art of memorization and demonstrate it on quiz shows. Before he became an updated version of Hitchcock's Mr. Memory, Lucas tried his hand in many other ventures, one of which was a fast-food operation called Beef 'N Burger. He fared no better than Ali or Namath. (In fact, the only former athletes to make a go of it in the capricious world of carryouts have been former Baltimore Colts Gino Marchetti and Alan Ameche, whose association with the chain is somewhat disguised, it being called simply Gino's.)

During one period when Lucas was actively seeking participation in the business community he approached John Galbreath, president of the Pittsburgh Pirates and, according to Vernon Alden, head of the prestigious Boston Company, said, only partly in jest: "John, we're both interested in making money. Why don't we go into a joint venture drilling for oil? If the well comes up dry, you can have it for a tax deduction. And if we strike, it'll be mine!"

Obviously, someone was needed to guide the fortunes of the athletes off the playing field almost as much as a coach or manager was needed on. That "someone" was to be the agent.

The word agent, by its classical definition, means "One that acts for or as the representative of another" and is derived from the present participle of the Latin word *agere*, which means to act, drive, or do. For centuries men have been acting, driving and doing, all in the name of someone else and in anticipation of their client "Growing rich beyond the dreams of avarice."

Many years after agents entered other fields, they found their way into sports. One of the first sports agents was Christy Walsh, an ex-sports cartoonist who had formed a stable of sportswriters to ghost the words of major sports figures, including Ty Cobb, Knute Rockne, Lou Gehrig, Jack Kearns, Honus Wagner, Pop Warner, Amos Alonzo Stagg, Fielding Yost, and hundreds more. While ghostwriting was hardly an American institution, the slender Californian whose ambition had been "a blend of sport-cartooning, peddling publicity, and working for an advertising agency" brought it to new heights. In the bargain he became an agent.

In 1921, Walsh, temporarily out of funds, laid plans to ensnare the new idol of American sports, Babe Ruth, as his first client, finding it "amazing that such a gift from the gods of exploitation should be on the loose." He set up camp at New York's Ansonia Hotel, then the domicile of Ruth, prepared to offer "him everything imaginable for his signature. Correction; everything but money, because of money I had precious little."

Ruth, besieged by promoters and hustlers of every kind, had set up his own escape system to flee their constant harassment. He had one of New York's first unlisted phone numbers, rarely opened his own mail, and made full use of the three exits leading in and out of the Ansonia—particularly the trades-man's—to elude prospectors. One of those he successfully eluded was Walsh. After camping out for two weeks on the Ansonia doorstep with a contract in his pocket, Walsh looked for another way to insinuate himself into Ruth's presence, especially since the morning papers had shown Ruth packing for his trip to the Yankees' training camp.

But as with all great promoters, Lady Luck took a hand. Walsh momentarily adjourned from his perch at the hotel and walked down to the corner delicatessen, which just happened to be the neighborhood bootlegger, including Ruth's. The phone rang. The deli owner answered, uttered a few guttural sounds and hung up, dejectedly. "Baby Root vants a case of beer. Right avay, right avay, and mine boy is gone. Oi! Oi! Oi!" he moaned, sure he was going to lose his best bootleg customer. Walsh volunteered for the chore and in ten minutes was in Ruth's kitchen, counting out bottles of beer with the Babe. Walsh decided to press his luck and asked Ruth if he recognized him. "Sure I know you, kid! Ain't you been bringin' our beer for the last two weeks," said the man who rarely remembered a face. Walsh explained it was his first and only experience as a beverage runner and Ruth, now in on the joke, signed the contract to get rid of the "kid."

It was a marriage made in heaven. Ruth, who only the season before had made just $270 for permission to use his by-line every time he hit a home run (54 homers at $5 each), now saw his earnings multiply to the point where within a few short years Walsh was able to establish an irrevocable $250,000 trust for him. Writers prospered as well. Ford Frick, then a sportswriter for the *New York Journal*, made, according to Walsh, "nearly $10,000 for his twice-a-week collaboration" with Ruth, one of four to serve as Ruth ghosts. Other Boswells cut up approximately $100,000 over sixteen years. Together they turned the press box into a haunted house and included some of the biggest names in sports journalism: Bozeman Bulger, who wrote John McGraw's copy from 1922 to 1932; Warren Brown, who ghosted for Jack Kearns and Joe McCarthy; J. Roy Stockton, who sat in for Dizzy Dean; and Hype Igoe, Gene Fowler, Bill Slocum, Bugs Baer, Westbrook Pegler, and Damon Runyon among others.

But that was only part of Walsh's contribution. He acted as counselor and financial "father confessor" to several of the big-name stars of the era, closing movie deals, tying them into products, and arranging for them to serve as consultants to major corporations. He also set up the All America Board of Football and Baseball to select annual all-star teams for a syndicated sale to magazines and newspapers.

It was Walsh who negotiated a deal for Knute Rockne to be hired as consultant to Studebaker, a struggling auto company in the days when everyone else was prospering. At his very first meeting, Rockne walked into a room where all the top sales executives had gathered for his first lecture. Ignoring them, he walked over to the window and stood there for almost ten minutes, staring down at the parking lot below. Then he turned slowly to the gathered group of salesmen, anticipating one of his patented Win-One-for-the-Gipper speeches. Instead, he turned his Gatling-gun delivery on them: "I see a lot of cars out there! New Cars! Shiny cars! Executives own them. The men who draw their pay from Studebaker. You men! And what do I see? Not one Studebaker in ten parked out there! If you men don't have confidence in the product you're selling, why don't you quit?" And with that Rockne walked out, leaving the flabbergasted executives staring at their hands.

Walsh's success in creating opportunities for his clients to earn a livelihood over and above their on-the-field endeavors paved the way for others. The term "agent" became as synonymous with sports as it was in the entertainment industry. So much so that fifty years later Bill Veeck would only half-jokingly quip: "Attorneys and agents should wear numbers on their backs."

However, like the Holy Roman Empire—which was neither Holy nor Roman nor an Empire—today the term agent is a misnomer. No longer does it mean one who creates outside opportunities for his clients, but something else entirely.

The word began to take on an entirely different coloration in the 1950s. Frank Scott, a former traveling secretary for the New York Yankees, went into the flesh-peddling or agentry business when he asked Yogi Berra the time and was astounded to see Berra pull back his sleeve to reveal three watches. Scott, getting over his momentary shock, inquired and found that Berra had been making Bulova commercials and was being paid off in all the watches he could eat. Right then and there, Scottie decided to go into the business of handling athletes and getting them money instead of "freebies." By the 1960s and 1970s, the classic definition had changed even more as a new breed followed the suddenly burgeoning salaries of stars. Most of the modern agents are, in reality, attorneys acting under the guise of agents, hiding their true purpose of trolling for clients behind the façade of agent to escape the American Bar Association's former prohibition on actively soliciting new business. Instead of seeking outside opportunities for their clients, they function as representatives who negotiate their clients' salary demands and little else.

During the sixties and seventies so-called agents came out of the woodwork, attaching themselves to the quick dollars made by the modern athlete and, in many cases, writing themselves into the contract for payments to be made directly to them. Included in the cast of characters were a businessman who had been so successful handling his own money that he had been bankrupt at least twice; a dry-cleaner who, having spent his life cleaning uniforms for an NBA team, began a new career because of his friendship with some of the players; a sportswriter who ingratiated himself with several athletes and was subsequently convicted of defalcation of their funds; and a schoolteacher who had studied law in the evening and never practiced, but became the legal representative of a number of athletes. The word "agent" was not only becoming a new word; it was becoming a bad word.

One of the more successful and most respected representatives is Larry Fleisher, not only the NBA Players Association attorney, but also attorney for several basketball players on an individual basis. Fleisher himself admits he is *not* an agent: "In most instances, it's just going in and negotiating a salary. I don't think of that as being an agent, but more as either an attorney or an advisor."

Still, there remain a few who can rightfully claim to be agents

336

worthy of the name—seeking outside opportunities for their clients.

There is Bob Woolf, who doubles in brass as a representative and handles the affairs, both at the negotiating table and at the commercial conference, of a stable of athletes. There is Jimmy Walsh, who has built Joe Namath into a one-man conglomerate. And there is Mark McCormack, who pyramided the representation of Arnold Palmer into a multimillion dollar business.

André Maurois, the French writer and satirist, called business "A combination of war and sport." Indeed, by the seventh decade of the twentieth century, the deadly serious game of business had begun to mirror sports. So much so that businesses were lining up to attach themselves in any way possible to the new glamour area.

Commercialism totally pervades the sports arena. Blimps carry the Goodyear name. Zamboni machines that clear the ice between periods of hockey games sport commercial messages for beers and magazines. Ball park walls look like a billposter's dream, cluttered with signs carrying messages for everything from razor blades to movies to local tailors.

And then there are the awards. Everybody, so it seems, gives out an award for something or other: Hickock girds the Professional Athlete of the Year in a belt; Dewar's serves up a cup for outstanding contributions to tennis; Beech-Nut, Inc. tosses out the Life Saver of the Month trophy; Rolaids pitches in with the Fireman of the Year award; Seagram Distillers dispenses the Seven Crowns of Sports awards for "productivity and consistency under pressure," derived from a series of computer ratings requiring a Ph.D. to comprehend; and Datsun, the Japanese automaker, once gave away a car in a tie-in with the most American of games, baseball, at a banquet held on December 7.

The first sports award given for product publicity dates back to 1910. That year the Chalmers Motor Car Company offered its most expensive touring car, the Chalmers 30, to the batting champion of the major leagues. The company immediately became embroiled in a controversy.

With one month left in the 1910 season, only one thing was certain: that the car would go to the American League batting champion, with the leaders hitting more than fifty points higher than those in the National League. Anything beyond that was uncertain, as the two contenders for the Chalmers 30, Cleveland's Nap Lajoie and Detroit's Ty Cobb, continued to exchange the lead. The Chalmers Contest held the fascination of the nation more than any other current happening including the political rift between former President Roosevelt and President Taft and the Supreme Court's trust-busting.

With two weeks to go, Lajoie led Cobb by a mere four points, .375 to .371. Cobb was riding the bench because of an inflammation of the eye when Lajoie went on a hitting spree, collecting 23 hits in 10 games to push his average up to .380. Returning to the lineup, Cobb went 7 for 13 against second-place New York. Before the eye flared up again, forcing him to sit out the last two games of the year, he had built his average to .385. With two games remaining for him to take the Chalmers away from Cobb, Lajoie went into St. Louis for a season-ending doubleheader against the hapless last-place Browns. There the Hate Cobb faction of the American League did its best to deny him the batting championship—and with it the Chalmers. On orders from their manager, Jack O' Connor, the Browns played back, allowing Lajoie to beat out seven infield bunts and convert a short outfield fly into a triple for eight hits. For his connivance Jack O'Connor was barred from baseball for life. It almost cost Cobb the Chalmers. But even though the *Chicago Tribune* statisticians gave the batting title to Lajoie, .385 to .382, and the *Cleveland Leader* gave it to him .382 to .381, when the official tabulations came out they read Cobb .3848, Lajoie .3841, a margin of seven ten-thousandths of a percentage point—a result more than slightly tainted by the discovery some 65 years later by the Society of American Baseball Research that one of Cobb's 2-for-3 days had been double-counted by the American League office, and that his average, without the more-than-compensatory help from the league, was in reality .383, a thousandth of a point less than Lajoie's.

The Chalmers Motor Car Company, glad for the publicity, but equally glad their travail was over, gave both players automobiles in the interest of good publicity, which is what it had been about from the beginning.

The next year, determined not to get caught in the same publicity pincher, the Chalmers Company resculpted its award. This time the car would go to the player deemed by the writers to be "most valuable to a team in his league," the first regularly organized vote by writers for the leagues' most valuable players. The winners were Frank Schulte of the Chicago Cubs and Cobb, who was a unanimous choice, having led the American League in batting with .420, hits with 248, doubles, triples, runs, runs-batted-in, and stolen bases.

The Chalmers Award was discontinued in 1914, but it was to

prove to be the first product award. And the model for many to come in later years.

But awards were not the only answer for businessmen who wanted to tie into sports. They wanted something more direct. They wanted the athletes themselves.

By the 1930s the rush to find gold in California became small in comparison to the headlong rush of advertisers to find gold in athletes' names.

In the cereal industry, Purity Oats advertised alongside eight members of the 1932 Yankees. Quaker Puffed Oats and Quaker Puffed Rice advertised an exhaustive list of Babe Ruth premiums, redeemable for cereal's negotiable currency, the box top, but soon encountered one of advertising's hazards and had to change Ruth's team emblem in every ad and on every premium when Ruth changed clubs, leaving the Yankees for the Boston Braves. And Lou Gehrig endorsed Post Toasties.

Gehrig was selected by Post Toasties, a brand introduced in 1930 to do battle with the market leader Wheaties, to endorse their product on Robert Ripley's NBC show "Believe It or Not." Ripley wound up the program of unusual facts by turning to his guest, the Yankee great, and asking, "What do you have every morning, Lou?" Gehrig answered without missing a beat, "A heaping bowlful of Wheaties!" Aghast at his mental error, Gehrig offered to give back the $100 Post had paid him to plug its brand, but Post gallantly refused to take it and turned even that gaffe into gold by getting the story into a "serialized" form in most of the country's newspapers.

Soon other admen were also listening to the happy sound of sales coming from their sports-related advertising, waves of exhilaration spreading over them the way it spread through the Indians with their ears to the ground upon first hearing stampeding buffalo. Most notable were the cigarette industry's execs.

The cigarette industry, an early adherent of the advertising school that held "Appeal to reason in advertising and you appeal to about four percent of the human race," had long since seen the wisdom of tying its advertising to famous personages. Led by that advertising swashbuckler George Washington Hill, president of the American Tobacco Company (immortalized as a supreme vulgarian by Sydney Greenstreet in the movie *The Hucksters*), who was reputed to have uttered "There's absolutely no difference among products. The difference is advertising," cigarette companies sought that difference. And they found it. In athletes.

In a world of T-zones, toasted tobacco, and taste tests, each brand sought the sports connection that would make the most difference. Naturally or unnaturally. The most farfetched and irrational connection was a 1935 Chesterfield ad which featured an outsized picture of the world's champion Detroit Tigers' catcher-manager Mickey Cochrane. In type the size of boxscores, Chesterfield had the balls to run the following copy: "We don't know what Mr. Cochrane smokes and he is not endorsing our cigarette . . . but he is an outstanding man in the baseball world and has won his place on merit. In the cigarette world Chesterfields are thought of as outstanding—they have won their place strictly on merit."

Camel was far more direct, buttressing its sports association with direct endorsements from players. In a switch on the old "I'd Walk a Mile for a Camel" slogan, the 1939 major league base stealing champion George Case of the Washington Senators was sought by the advertising agency to complement the progression of pitchers who had, up until 1940, formed the brand's mini-campaign. Not only was Case young and attractive but the speed merchant who had just pilfered the second-highest number of bases in twenty years was as all-American as his full moniker—George Washington Case. Most importantly, he was a legitimate Camels smoker.

The spokesman for the advertising agency, William Esty, who had been following Case around the league for an entire year and, in his own words, "was impressed with the fan reaction with you. . . . You're the kind of person we want to advertise our product because the fans come out to see you play," made Case an offer he couldn't refuse. If he would endorse Camels for one year, he would get "a thousand dollars and a carton of cigarettes every week for fifty-two weeks." Not bad for a player making just $15,000 a year.

With the opening of the 1940 season, the campaign broke on the back covers of national magazines, including the *Saturday Evening Post*, *Life*, and *Liberty* among others, all showing Case in a Washington Senators' uniform sliding into an ersatz version of second base. The headline read simply: "I'm George Washington Case. I Smoke Camels."

Almost as soon as the ads saw the light of day Case was innundated with letters from parents all over the country. They had one theme running throughout: Case was a bad influence on American youth. Case could only figure out that although there had been several players before him, "they had mostly been pitchers. I think it was because my name was associated with running speed that so many people became so upset. Kids were probably saying to their parents, 'Hey, George Case smokes cigarettes and he can run like the devil.' "

Whatever the reason—an implicit promise of speed because of smoking or whatever—other letters were simultaneously arriving on the desk of American League president Will Harridge voicing the same complaint. Harridge called Case and "invited" him to stop by his office the next time he was in Chicago. On the Senators' next western trip Case visited the league offices when they arrived in Chicago to play the White Sox. Case was greeted by Harridge and a pile of mail. "I know, Mr. Harridge, I've been getting the same thing," volunteered Case. "Well, we can't have any more of this," replied Harridge, reaching for the telephone. And with that Harridge called the William Esty Agency in New York to tell them that no American League player was ever to be photographed in a baseball uniform endorsing a cigarette.

But the matter didn't end there. Camels, which had too much money invested in the campaign, struck a compromise with Case and Harridge. Case would pose for a new series of photographs in street clothes; same headline, same endorsement.

By the late 1940s and early 1950s cigarettes had become an integral part of the baseball scene. Chesterfield signs were part of several scoreboards, with the "H" or the "E" lighting up to denote a hit or an error on close calls. Cartons of cigarettes were given out for Chesterfield Satisfiers, home runs by members of the home team—a relatively inexpensive promotion in Washington in 1945, when the only home run hit by a Senator at Griffith Stadium was an inside-the-park blast by first baseman Joe Kuhel. At the Polo Grounds, a carton of Old Golds was tossed down the screen for every Old Goldie. It was a toss-up between smoking and baseball on which was the National Pastime; and sometimes the two were indistinguishable.

By 1948, Chesterfield, which had once tried to incorporate Mickey Cochrane into an ad, now went the direct route and got players actually to endorse The Baseball Man's Cigarette. They had six stars: Ted Williams, Joe DiMaggio, and Bucky Harris of the American League and Stan Musial, Bob Elliott, and Ewell Blackwell of the National League, all endorsing the product. Four of them had the cigarette in their mouth, one held it aloft, and only three were in uniform—all National Leaguers.

If sports has good years like wine, 1948 was just such a year, with several of its moments heady enough to be put away for future use. It was the year of the first nationally televised World

Series and of the first regionally televised NFL championship. After that, it would be a whole new ball game. Particularly for advertisers.

With sports a highly visible weekly staple on television, no longer would $100 be the going rate for endorsements. No longer would Post Toasties be able to get a great like Lou Gehrig for a C-Note; or Coca-Cola—which did a series of festoon hangers of greats of the Golden Age of Sports in 1944—be able to get the permission of Samuel Riddle, owner of Man O' War, for just six cases a month of Coke, in short supply during the war years, which he opted for in lieu of the $100; or Hart Schaffner & Marx offer Ty Cobb a mere $100 for his endorsement—an offer Cobb turned down because "I can't see a firm like the 'Cleveland Boys' Hart S. & Marx in such a cheap class as $100. Coca-Cola yes, but that would be the 'only one.' . . . Please deal me out. The boys in the 'Evangeline league' might sign."

In the media age, superstars were no longer defined by deeds alone. Their accomplishments on the field were only passports to the world of commercial opportunity. Their selection for commercial tie-ins was no longer predetermined by the Divine Right of Athletes, but by advertising executives. With so many to choose from—and so few chosen—advertising executives had the power to select the athletes they wanted, and in so doing make them first personalities, then celebrities, and finally superstars. And all through media exposure.

To athletes such commercial tie-ins were their faint approximation of a Johnny Cash one-night stand at the Iowa State Fair for $25,000. They came running. First they came two-by-two, advertising the expected: athletic supporters, gloves, and gear. But the trickle became a dam burst when Madison Avenue—following the precept of Jules Alberti, president of Endorsements International, counseled, "If you don't have anything important to say, have someone important say it."—discovered that the athlete had become the modern version of the movie star.

Advertising has long been the thyroid gland of free enterprise. It has functioned to make the general public think it has longed all its life for something it has never heard of before, selling less a product than abstractions—desires, hopes, promises, identifications, reputations—as it dictates our mores, social habits, and even our scents.

And what better reputations to sell then those of personalities or superstars? In the early 1960s General Foods pioneered with the use of Hollywood heavyweights Edward G. Robinson and Barbara Stanwyck as spokespersons for Maxwell House Coffee. Ever since, advertisers have borrowed interest for their product from the stars endorsing them in a direct translation of Alberti's theorem. But sometimes the advertising has dwelt on the glamour of the presenter to the detriment of the product and the premise. The modern-day commercial has often been a hero sandwich wrapped around a slice-of-life with the product serving as mere garnish.

The search was on for celebrities who were as available as they were believable. Promiscuous pitchmen (such as Arthur Godfrey) who had discredited themselves by endorsing everything down the pike were called "whores." Those who had not yet succumbed to Madison Avenue's siren call were "virgins." And the search was on for the few "virgins" remaining, no matter. what the cost. Sometimes the negotiating became comical, as when Jack Haley, Jr., bargaining on behalf of his wife, superstar Liza Minnelli, told Kenyon & Eckhardt executives "For $100,000 you get 'Liza,' but not 'Minnelli'"! But most times if the money was right, the right celebrity was, like Dickens' Barkis, "willin.'" And none were more willin' than the last remaining "virgin" beachhead: the athletes.

Athletes and their agents began besieging the bastions of Madison Avenue seeking a piece—any piece—of the action. The business manager of Mike Thomas, the NFL Rookie of the Year in 1975, called a talent recruiter to crowbar his client into commercials. "Nobody would even know his name," said the talent agent and hung up. Stan Musial, rated highest in "likeability" and "trust" by a New York research firm in a study completed in 1973, washed out when an auto manufacturer tried him in front of a camera. Although The Man had antagonized the fewest number of the twenty-five hundred respondents, winning the Mr. Congeniality Award, he was found to be "good hit, no spiel" by the advertisers.

Agents tried any way they could to get their clients in on the Madison Avenue gravy train. When Pillsbury's agency BBD&O came up with a new concept for a biscuit called Hungry Jack to be targeted to the black market, they called in a marketing consultant who was supposedly expert in reaching blacks. He took one look at their proposed copy line, "Hungry Jack (Tatum) Likes Hungry Jacks," and told them that the Oakland Raider was all wrong for their product and that he was an Uncle Tom and not respected in the black community. The consultant's alternative was to use Alan Page of the Minnesota Vikings and even, he proposed, change the name of the product to Hungry Alans or Big Man. BBD&O came to find out that the so-called consultant was, in reality, Alan Page's agent.

Even Mrs. Lou Gehrig saw herself in a commercial. In a letter to Frank Scott in 1973, she wrote: "Many times during the year I get requests to endorse products—some good, some weird. It occurred to me to come up with one of my own. One idea I tried out on several friends who came back with enthusiastic reactions. It is this: Pose Mrs. Ruth and Gehrig in full gay nineties regalia—pompadour, bird of paradise, bustle, etc., seated at a small table in a café, or even in the Stadium for that matter, and have one of us coyly turn to camera and say: 'Make mine Schaefer's' or 'This ain't Marlborough [sic] Country' or almost any crack. I think it could be not only surprising, but the two names are valuable. What do you think?" Whatever Scott thought, the advertisers didn't think much of it. The idea died aborning.

But despite those who never made it into the commercial arena, many did. By 1973, according to a study by Gallup & Robinson, fully 15 percent of all prime-time spots featured celebrities. By 1978, the number of commercials featuring celebrities had jumped to one in every three—many of whom were sports stars who had lent their gilt-edged names to commercial endeavors for a buck.

All of a sudden the benches cleared as the global village McLuhan has foreseen became instead a global locker room. In a world of parity, where products claim little more than that they are "unsurpassed," the message was, purely and simply, media macho. And the word "athlete" joined the list of words most often used in commercials, which are, in order of frequency: you, good, wonderful, better, fine, best, effective, and natural.

With athletes used as shorthand for social acceptance, advertisers changed their emphasis from a locker room crusade against body odor into an appeal to virility and sex. Viewers could "score" with the ladies just as the spokesman scores on the field. A steady stream of commercials sought to unload a billion dollars' worth of Closet Queen ointments on the American male by using supervirile superjocks. Dave DeBusschere dyed his hair in the shower for Clairol's Great Day Concentrate; Jerry Lucas gave his hair the Vitalis 60-Second Workout; Muhammad Ali spritzed his underarms with Right Guard; Bobby Hull gave his transplanted dandruff an Enden shampoo; Joe Frazier slapped his own face in a "Thanks, I needed that" commercial for Mennen Skin Bracer; and Hank Bauer and Yogi Berra sprayed their hair with a repackaged women's hair spray. Even the lack of hair didn't stop a helmeted Brooks Robinson from endorsing Vitalis. The advertiser sold an alchemist's dream, changing the base metal of an ordinary consumer into the gold of a superstud by tying his message to a sports star.

But even though most sports stars provided the mental cockleburs that held the advertisers' message in the viewer's head—sometimes to the point where the athlete, but not the product, was remembered, a marketing malady known as Vampire Video—most advertisers were still rewarded with a one-minute dosage of Valium. Athletes lined up with Naugahyde smiles and gripped the English language in a full nelson, delivering endorsements that were crimes, if not indictable felonies. One had Larry Csonka, who did a campaign with Tom Seaver and Hank Aaron for Gillette Platinum-plus blades, giving the unbelievable words, in tandem with a voice-over:

> "I, Larry Csonka . . . "
> "I, Larry Csonka . . . "
> "Do Solemnly Swear . . . "
> "Do Solemnly Swear . . . "
> "To always Faithfully use . . . "
> "To always Faithfully use . . . "
> "The New Gillette Platinum-plus . . . "
> "The New Gillette Plutonium-platter . . . "

One man who dared to be different in the way he used athletes—and profited by it—was George Lois.

George Lois is a feisty Greek posing as an art director who is as ready to pick up the cudgel for a cause or crusade as he is for a campaign. The tall, good-looking Lois—sporting a broken nose as a badge of honor—resembles a Hellenic version of Dave Brubeck. But it wasn't his looks so much as the look of his work that epitomized advertising's creative revolution of the 1960s, giving birth to the school of advertising that sought to "provoke, challenge, interest, entice, snare, grab, infuriate, seduce, [and] motivate" an audience in twenty-eight seconds of air time or one page of print. Lois also gave birth to four agencies bearing his name: Papert Koenig Lois; Lois Holland Calloway; Creamer Lois FSR; and Lois, Pitts, Gershon—more corporate progeny than even Alexander Graham Bell.

While most advertisers search for a "hook" or logical connection on which to hang their use of a sports personality, using athletes like dental floss with hygienic regularity, Lois has developed his own ingenious and indigenous hook. That hook is the use of arresting attention-getting devices. In one of the very first commercials he ever made featuring sports personalities, Lois had Yogi Berra talking to a cat for Puss 'N Boots Cat Food. Berra, facing the camera and the cat, told the exercising cat he was "incredible" and asked him what he attributed his prowess to. The cat, positioned so that only the back of his head was visible, replied—naturally enough—Puss 'N Boots Cat Food. What wasn't natural was that the voice was unmistakably that of former battery mate Whitey Ford.

A gifted raconteur, *saloniere*, and man of infinite *bonhomie*, Lois has almost as wide a collection of friends from the sports establishment as he does winning creative efforts. His outside activities have included designing *Esquire* magazine covers— posing Sonny Liston as a black Santa Claus and Muhammad Ali as a martyred Saint Sebastian among others—package designs, and logos. But as a true sports enthusiast, his favorite activities have to do with sports, no matter how tenuous the association.

One day in 1966, Eddie Rohan, production manager at Papert Koenig Lois, who knew boxer Joey Archer's brother and manager, Jimmy, came in to see Lois. "I just talked to Joey and Jimmy Archer. Poor bastards. They're going crazy trying to get a shot at the middleweight crown," he said. "They've got a couple of hundred bucks put away. Could we get them a P.R. guy?" Lois, never at a loss for words, even if they are expletives, shouted back, "Bullshit! We'll create an ad for them!"

And he did. Falling back on the time-honored practice of publicly challenging the champion to either force a fight or the recognition of the challenger as the uncrowned claimant—a ploy that hadn't been used in almost fifty years—Lois designed a fifty-line ad in the form of an open letter to the then middleweight champion, Dick Tiger. The small-space ad, which ran on the sports pages of both the *New York Daily News* and the *New York Times*, opened with "Dear Dick Tiger . . . " and went on, "Here's why I think I deserve a shot at the middleweight crown: The last time I fought you, I beat you," referring to his ten-round decision over Tiger in 1964, closing "Respectfully, Joey Archer."

Then, in Lois' words, "Everybody went nuts." The results of the $200 Archer spent was a million dollars worth of self-generating free publicity. The *New York Daily News* ran a front-page picture of Archer next to a Bronx Zoo tiger, Johnny Carson had him on the "Tonight Show" and sportswriters, led by the *New York Post*'s venerable and respected Lester Bromberg, began to write that Tiger was "ducking Archer."

But despite the public agitation, Archer still couldn't get a rise out of the champion, who planned to defend his title against welterweight champion Emile Griffith. So Archer invested yet another $200 into placing another Lois fifty-line ad. This one read: "Dear Dick . . . You should meet the best middleweight around, not the best welterweight . . . Respectfully, Joey Archer. P.S. How 'bout a fight, Dick? I'm going broke running these ads."

That did it. Suddenly Archer's phone was ringing off the hook. Tired of the criticism he was getting in the press for "ducking" Archer, Tiger had risen to the bait and would give him a fight. Griffith, sick of the needling, wanted Archer for himself and would fight him instead of Tiger. And finally, Cus D'Amato, the shrewd manager of light-heavyweight champion José Torres, saw the publicity as creating a "natural" between his fighter, the leading Puerto Rican boxer, and Archer, the leading Irish boxer. It would "pack sixty thousand into Yankee Stadium" in D'Amato's estimation.

Archer, who couldn't get a bite before was now offered a virtual banquet. He had his choice. Instead of accepting Tiger's heated offer to fight he backed off. "Let's think about it," he said, fishing for the biggest return on his $400 investment, a shot at the light-heavyweight title. In the "couple of weeks of nonsense" that followed, as Lois called it, the now greedy Archer negotiated with D'Amato; and Tiger, saying "Screw it!" signed to defend against Griffith. But the New York State Boxing Commission ruled that Archer, barely a full-fledged middleweight, could not fight for the light-heavyweight championship. And Archer was out in the cold. Even more so when Griffith dethroned Tiger on April 25 for the championship Archer had coveted and publicly advertised for. As a postscript to the story, Archer got the first shot at Griffith's new crown and lost a fifteen-round decision on July 13, 1966, losing not only his gamble but his $400 as well.

Soon thereafter Lois opened the doors of Lois Holland Calloway without a client to speak of—or to. But his contacts in the world of sports would soon provide him with the agency's first client.

Lois sought a small investment firm he could make famous. Quickly. He found it when he ran into his old friend Dick Lynch at one of their favorite Manhattan refreshment stands. Lois told Lynch of his new association. Lynch told Lois that after eight years with the New York football Giants he had retired and followed the army of ex-athletes to Wall Street, an army so large that it had given rise to a common joke on the Street that you can tell all of the former athletes by hollering "Watch the Tape"—referring to the unbroken line of stock exchange symbols and figures crawling across the wall—and catching them look at their ankles instead. Lynch had invested $10,000 and was a junior partner in a new firm called Edwards & Hanly.

In the third week of the agency's existence the Edwards & Hanly campaign went on the air. The first commercial featured none other than Dick Lynch ("reee-tired"), implying he had made money in the stock market and was working for the two men he introduced at the end. "We got away with it," remembers Lois. The second spokesman was Mickey Mantle admitting he "was just a country boy." That is until he met Messrs. Edwards & Hanly, whom he introduced at the commercial's conclusion. "One take, exactly right," recalls a proud Lois. The third spokesman was Joe Louis who was supposed to say "I just want to say one thing—Edwards & Hanly, where were you when I needed you?" But Louis hadn't said "Where *were* you . . . "; he had said "Where was you at," then "Where was you. . . . " To avoid making him a stereotype, an embarrassed Lois had to cheat and clip the "Z" sound out of the word "was" to make it sound like "were," even after more than 20 takes.

Lois Holland Calloway put $160,000 behind the campaign in news time, running just two flights. But after tripling the firm's business Edwards & Hanly cancelled the rest of the campaign. They simply couldn't handle the business.

Founded on the cornerstone of sports, Lois Holland Calloway continually employed it in its memorable campaigns for such advertisers as Braniff, Maypo, Ovaltine, Olivetti, and OTB, among others.

When his agency acquired the Braniff account from Wells, Rich, Greene, Lois decided to translate the marketing proposition—if you have style and class, you'll fly them—into the airline's advertising campaign. It came out "When You've Got It, Flaunt It." And to "flaunt it" Lois put together the greatest assemblage of stars this side of the MGM lot in the Thirties: Satchel Paige, Dean Martin, Jr., Andy Warhol, Sonny Liston, Whitey Ford, Salvador Dali, Pucci, Mickey Rooney, Gina Lollobrigida, and Joe Namath. But the hook wasn't their mere presence; it was how they were used.

Paired off in some of the most fascinating and incongruous twosomes since Groucho Marx last peered down Margaret Dumont's décolletage, the stars were seated next to each other in airplane seats—fish and foil alike—to give evidence that they had flaunted it. On Braniff, naturally.

The most memorable of the twosomes who "flaunted it" were Sonny Liston and Andy Warhol. While Warhol rambles on— "The anatomy of a soup can can be as interesting as the human body by Michelangelo"—Liston stares into the camera with one of his patented "What's that flaming faggot talking about?" looks. It set the style for others, as the stars paired off against each other for just such hijinks, all punctuated by the campaign's overall message: "When You've Got It, Flaunt It!"

Another Lois client to get the sports treatment was Maypo, a maple-tasting cereal. Before coming to Lois Holland Calloway, the cereal, with its cartoon character, Markey Maypo, who ran around hollering "I want my Maypo," was a cereal for the ages— four through eight. Lois wanted to reposition it to extend its appeal to kids in their early teens. So he redesigned the package to show how to build muscles and got together a group of athletes as spokesmen: Mickey Mantle, Oscar Robertson, Johnny Unitas, Ray Nitschke, Don Meredith, Wilt Chamberlain, and Willie Mays, all in one commercial.

In order to assemble his cast of jock characters, Lois first approached Mantle, whom he had used in the Edwards & Hanley commercial. Mantle had told Lois after the shooting was completed, "If you ever want me again, call me." He did. Then Lois approached Chamberlain. Wilt turned it down, but when he found out Mantle was in it, he accepted. "If Mantle's doing it, I'll do it!" Lois, whose philosophy is "The way to get 'em is through a guy's friend. If you go through an agent, he wants a lot of dough and doesn't want to call them up himself, 'cause they might tell him to GFY," proceeded to line up the others directly, offering $1,000 against double scale.

On the day of the shooting, all seven congregated at the studio for what would be five or six seconds on-camera tearfully pleading "I want my Maypo!" That is, all except Mays.

According to Lois, who has a special way of getting everything an athlete has to give out of him, "When we got to the take, Mays said, "Whadya mean cry? Willie don't cry!" This went on for fifteen minutes. 'Willie don't cry. You don't unnerstan'. Willie don't cry.' I couldn't believe it, he was either dumb or fuckin' pompous." Finally Lois asked Mays if he'd mind a tear in his eye. Mays said no. "So I got some glycerine and put it on his cheek and it was okay."

But of all the athletes he has ever dealt with, Joe Namath is Lois' favorite. Together with Mickey Mantle, Lois' agency and

Namath started an employment service called, appropriately enough, Mantle Men and Namath Girls. In the commercial, Namath says, "I'm not really a full-time typist. But I know if I was, I'd be the best I could be." And Mantle, marveling over Namath's ability to type faster than Elizabeth Ray, says: "Golly, he really can type." Unfortunately the employment agency, started just prior to the 1969 recession, soon encountered financial difficulties, not so much from its failure to place people as from its inability to collect from firms they placed people with. And shortly after the recession started, the business folded.

Jimmy Walsh, Namath's lawyer and representative, remembers clearing up the by-now defunct firm's business and calling one of those associated with the agency to retrieve some of the missing assets, several electric typewriters. The former employee, who had been related to someone at Lois Holland Calloway, provided Walsh with one of the classic lines in business history: "If I give you back the typewriters, can I keep something you don't know I have?"

Out of the ashes of Mantle Men and Namath Girls, which Lois is quick to point out "Neither had put anything into it. I wouldn't do that to friends," came a lasting relationship with Namath. Lois was to use him in a series of Ovaltine commercials directed to a generation of prepubescent kids who hadn't heard of Little Orphan Annie or Captain Midnight ("My old pal Ovaltine") and in a campaign for Olivetti typewriters.

Lois created the Olivetti girl campaign, the forerunner of such feminist targets as National Airlines' "Fly Me" campaign. Petitioned by NOW, which demanded he "use male secretaries" and "female executives," Lois cast Namath as an Olivetti girl in drag. In the commercial an officious woman executive hands Namath a letter to be done "Immediately, pleeease . . ." and Namath proceeds to bang it out on an Olivetti, all the while typing "Fuck you, George. Fuck you, George. Fuck you, George." Then, in the "turn around is fair play" department, the woman puts the make on Namath. Taking off her glasses and letting down her hair, she says, "I'm very pleased with your work, Joseph. By the way, what are you doing tonight?" Namath caps the moment by staring into the camera with a hopeless look. It was theater-of-the-absurd at its best. "Most athletes are embarrassed doing commercials. You see them and you have to feel sorry for them," Lois says of his experiences with most run-of-the-mill performing athletes. "But I've never seen Namath embarrassed in a commercial."

The sixties were super cool, hip, chic. Their high priest, Marshall McLuhan. They were the days of *Easy Rider*, a parable showing the superiority of doing-your-own-thing over the establishment's rules and regulations. In a day when society's members were depersonalized, reduced to social security numbers, zip codes, and area codes, two men gave the world of sports a personal touch. They marched to their own drummer, guaranteeing success on and off the field.

One was Muhammad Ali. But his color, his unfamiliar name, and his un-Christian, unpatriotic stances all combined to make him unbearable to many and unacceptable to most. The other was Joe Namath. In a world of counterculture hippies he was the verbal champion of Motherhood. In a world on dope, he was a drinker. He became the symbol of the rise of the Blue Collar Ethic. The Establishment Greaser, with long hair, white shoes, and a hangdog look reminiscent of a cross between Jean-Paul Belmondo and Elliott Gould, he possessed that certain indefinable something that in the Twenties would be called "it." Now it was called "charisma." He became the hero of the late Sixties. And with it, the commercial hero of businesses trying to reach those unalienated, but uninterested people who followed his every move.

And just as he shaped the future of pro football, Joe Namath shaped the sports celebrity business, more so than any other— Palmer, Player, Nicklaus, Ruth, or even Simpson. He would become, under the guidance of his attorney-agent and former college fraternity buddy Jimmy Walsh, the public persona of many an inanimate product, the Sultan of Shill.

Walsh, a redheaded version of a Pillsbury doughboy with enough leprechaun thrown in to make for a mischievous twinkle in his eye and a mercenary tinkle in his pocket, turned Namath into a money-making machine. In fact, he incorporated him into Namanco Productions, Inc., a corporate anagram for Namath and Company. Namanco, and its wholly owned subsidiary, Planned Licensing, Inc., existed for one purpose and one purpose only—to command Attention, Bucks, and Commercials for Namath, the necessary ABCs of a successful commercial spokesman.

Just before Super Bowl III, Walsh got $10,000 for Namath from Schick for shaving off his Fu Manchu mustache. "And that commercial was only shown three times by contract," said Walsh, proud of his handiwork.

Other lesser lights, like San Diego's shaggy Tim Rossovich,

tried to get into the act. Rossovich offered to let his hair go for $5,000 and his mustache for another $5,000 but there were no takers. Rossovich's agent was willing to have his client undergo any sort of torture to get into commercials "If a shaving cream or razor company isn't interested, maybe we could get a lighter fluid firm. Tim has a reputation for setting himself on fire, you know." But it was Namath, and Namath only, the advertisers wanted.

Walsh has had Namath creamed by Noxzema (in a commercial with the then unknown Farrah Fawcett-Majors), flaunted for Braniff, type-cast by Olivetti, popped for Hamilton Beach, and hosed by Hanes. And he has done it by adhering to three criteria for selecting the product Namath will endorse: the quality of the product itself, the quality of the people who make the product, and the quantity of the money offered. Put them all together and they spell success.

George Lois once said, "Joe doesn't do commercials in which he comes off strictly as an athlete. In fact, I'd be very disappointed if I ever saw Joe in a standard commercial." One commercial that was anything but standard was the Beauty Mist pantyhose commercial for Hanes. The commercial opens with a long caress shot of pantyhose worn by a reclining pair of legs which, as the camera pans up to the face, belong to—lo and behold!—Joe Namath. Walsh was very proud of the results. "It increased their brand awareness factor unbelievably in the trade and there was a 40 percent increase in sales."

Walsh has carefully choreographed the commercialization of Namath, presenting him in what Walsh calls "glamourous circumstances unlike other football players, without his football attire on." Most importantly, Walsh has selected vehicles that heighten Namath's celebrity, avoiding mundane commercials and contracts.

One such contact was with Fabergé, Inc., a fragrance and cosmetics company that was seeking a strong masculine image for its line of men's toiletries. With overall sales declining 12 percent in the first quarter of 1975, Fabergé approached Walsh to sound him out on the possibility of Namath becoming the corporate representative of the company. Walsh, equal to the task, engineered a package deal whereby Namath would become the Overall Sports Advisor for Fabergé, Inc., appear in its television commercials, and develop a line of fragrances potentially bearing Namath's name—all for a minimum of $250,000 a year plus incentives under an eight-to-twenty year agreement. Almost immediately the Namath-quarterbacked promotion worked and Brut 33 and total corporate earnings both took off. The Namath "magic" had worked again.

Namath's association with the Hamilton Beach division of Scovill came less from Walsh's efforts than from the fact that during one of Namath's annual pilgrimages to the hospital for knee surgery a squib appeared in the *New York Times* telling how the Jet quarterback was clamoring for popcorn while convalescing. An opportunistic account executive at Hicks & Geist, the advertising agency for Hamilton Beach, saw the item and rushed over with the Popper Upper. Plugging it in next to a thankful Namath, he made points and a contact. Later Walsh made the contract, a contract which today has Namath pushing Popper Uppers, Little Macs, and Fry Alls, as well as serving as Scovill's spokesman to the financial community.

Together with Hamilton Beach and Fabergé, other staples in the Namath stable include Franklin Sports Industries, which produces Joe Namath equipment; Calvin Clothes, a division of Palm Beach, which manufactures a line of clothing called, appropriately enough, the Joe Namath line; Arrow Shirts, which manufactures the Joe Namath Signature Collection of Shirts; and Dynamic Classics, which makes a limited line of gift luggage bearing the Joe Namath name on the tags. Add to these the Joe Namath Football Camp, his previous endorsements for Dingo Boots, Borg-Warner Chemicals, La-Z-Boy Recliners, Fieldcrest sheets, and you have a minimum of a half-a-million dollars in off-the-field annual income for the mini-conglomerate known as Joe Namath.

Once all that was necessary to insure a product's success was the mere association with an athlete's name. Now the physical presence of the athlete himself is in demand, both to provide a feeling of manhood for men who carry their sports memories around like little jars of ashes and for the transference to the product of the athlete himself.

First it was the regional beer companies employing the off-season athlete as a "public relations" man, going from bar to bar to insure the stocking of their product. One story has it that Roosevelt Brown, the huge Giant tackle, once toured a Ballantine sales territory with some new point-of-sales displays that were given him to hand out to his accounts. Although these were, like most beer displays, to be offered to retailers free, Brown had misinterpreted a Ballantine marketing executive's comment that they cost a certain amount to produce and thought he was to sell them. He sold every last one.

Soon every automotive dealer in every town with a major league franchise had off-season ball players on the showroom floor commingling friendly fanny-rubbing with fancy financial footwork. Then companies like Marlboro, Celenese, J. P. Stevens, and Ford's Lincoln-Mercury Division hired athletes on a corporate level. Finally the shit hit the fans with fan fetishism being served up at such businessmen's Woodstocks as trade shows ("Hi, meet Max McGee, Green Bay Packers"), conventions ("Y. A. Tittle will be in Booth Number . . . "), and plain old sales meetings ("After the slide presentation have a drink and introduce yourself to Bobby Mitchell . . . ").

By the 1970s it was no holds barred as company after company tied into the allure of sports. First, sales promotion agencies designed to put together sports packages for companies that could pay the freight sprang into being. The Gucci of such agencies, Robert Landau Associates, has counseled Ford, Fabergé, Thom McAn, and many other clients on how to tie into the glamour of sports. Landau has conceived such successful promotions as Thom McAn's "Pitch, Hit, & Run"—baseball's answer to "Punt, Pass, & Kick"—as a traffic builder and Ford's MVP, an internal program for Ford's fifty-thousand mechanics and service people throughout the country.

Then, companies made sports an integral part of their customer and public relations programs. American Airlines brought in top-name pro golfers to play with key customers in the American Airlines Astro Jet Classic. The Chrysler Leasing Society, a club sponsored by the Fleet Division of the Chrysler Corporation, gave its thirteen thousand members an opportunity to attend such events as the Olympics, the World Series, the Super Bowl, or the U.S. Open golf tournament in the company of such legendary sports names as Bob Mathias, Stan Musial, George Blanda, and even quasi-sports star George Plimpton. Bob Lilly took winning entrants to the Cotton Bowl for Rath; Terry Bradshaw took them to the Super Bowl for EverReady; and everywhere advertisers sought to have the universal fascination with sports rub off on their products.

Over and above the internal industry benefits that accrue from celebrity charisma, the only thing left was the naming of an entire brand after an athlete.

To those who work on New York's Seventh Avenue, the garment industry is known as the *schmata* or "rag" business. It is a world apart from other endeavors, possessing a fun side— filled with Myron Cohens, "Cut Velvet" jokes, and noon-time *hondeling* and *schmoozing* with ally and competitor alike—and a serious side, epitomized by the agonies suffered by Jack Lemmon in *Save the Tiger*.

But above all else, the clothing business is an ulcerous and treacherous trade, one that rides the winds of fashion dictated by the fickle tastes of the public. With such inbred insecurity, those in the trade are constantly on the alert for "sure things" that will sell and sell continuously.

The surest way to catch the proverbial lightning in a bottle is to tie into sports. This has taken many forms throughout the years. First there was the purchase of the Indianapolis franchise of the National League in 1887 by John T. Brush to "advertise" his clothing store, The When Clothing Company, an association that would subsequently take Brush first to Cincinnati and then to New York as owner of the Reds and the Giants. Basketball teams in the 1920s and 1930s kept the tradition alive, being named after their clothing store sponsors: the Cleveland Rosenblums, the Pittsburgh Second-Story Morry's, and the Richmond King Clothiers.

Then came the "giveaway" promotions, as clothiers and tailors everywhere offered suits of clothes in exchange for free publicity. The most classic "giveaway" was Abe Stark's sign in Ebbets Field which read simply: "Hit Sign Win Suit." Stretching across the bottom of the scoreboard to a height of no more than four feet, the sign was barely readable, let alone hittable. And yet, despite countless thousands of Dodger fans dating back to the early 1930s who thought it only possible to hit if someone shot the rightfielder first, four men did hit it on the fly and collected their 3G's suits: Hack Wilson, Mel Ott, Junior Gilliam, and Carl Furillo—twice. One bounce begot only a free pair of pants, and that was negotiable. In Philadelphia, Sam Gerson gave away a $19.95 suit to a lucky number patron at the Philadelphia Sphas games and threw in the free printed programs for good measure. And in Baltimore, it was the Fineman Tailor sign at old Oriole Park. All over the country clothing signs became so much a part of sports—particularly baseball—that George Price immortalized it in *The New Yorker* as a national pastime in its own right, depicting a middle-aged tailor with gloves on both hands standing in front of *his* free-suit sign ready to protect it if the outfielder missed the ball.

Perhaps the ultimate in tie-ins occurred at a recent Providence College basketball game: A credit line under the Providence lineup read: "Coach Gavitt's wardrobe by Harry Litwack Men's Wear."

Fashionable outfitters early on began to incorporate athletes into their ads as endorsers-models, showing off their threads. First it was trade advertising only, with Walter Johnson pictured on Crack-a-Jack uniform ads and any one of twelve major league clubs, depending upon who the current winners were, shown sporting their Bradley Big League Sweaters. Soon they began to show up in consumer advertising as well, first as endorsers and then, in the 1950s, as models. One of the first consumer ads had Gil McDougald, Lew Burdette, and Del Crandall all posing with their sons in Mayo Spruce underwear ads for Ellington, Inc., fully fifteen years before Yogi Berra and his three sons were found in a Jockey underwear commercial arguing the virtues of white versus colored briefs. Frank Gifford, Paul Hornung, and a cast of bronzed athletes all posed in Jantzen swimming togs during the 1960s. And in the early 1970s, Sears turned around their *déclassé* fashion image by having Bob Griese, Gale Sayers, Tom Seaver, and Johnny Miller model fashions for the Sears Men's Store. Everyone, it seemed, was modeling something or other, except jockeys, who, according to one industry spokesman, "are not favored by clothing makers because of their small physiques."

Clothing and apparel manufacturers lined up trying to sign anyone they could. The Wolverine Shoe Company bought the gilt-edged name of Jack Nicklaus for $50,000 a year to endorse its Hush Puppies brand, then were forced to ask, in one of those guilt complexes that sooner or later strikes every advertiser, "Great! Now what are we going to do with him?"

But more than merely using sports as a backdrop, the clothing industry has mainlined it. They pioneered in incorporating sports into their overall business: naming entire lines after athletes.

It all started with René Lacoste. The French tennis star was one of France's famed Four Musketeers who dominated world tennis between 1922 and 1931, accounting for six straight Davis Cup championships and six Wimbledon singles and four doubles titles. Lacoste won match after match with machine-like steadiness, including the French National championships three times and Wimbledon and Forest Hills twice each. In a day when anyone who exhibited such constant excellence—"outsteadying his opponents," as one French observer called it—was called a "crocodile" by French tennis buffs, Lacoste was known as "le grand crocodile." It soon became his symbol and when a friend of his made a shirt for him it was decorated with a little crocodile insignia. Later, when he became a shirtmaker in his own right, he adopted the symbol as his own.

Lacoste's creation caught on almost immediately in France, but had very few takers elsewhere. In the 1950s Bill Talbert approached his friend Vincent dePaul Draddy, chairman of the board of David Crystal and its subsidiary Izod, and asked him to take a look at the all-knit shirt with the crocodile crest. The distributor, also a friend of Talbert's, couldn't, in the words of David Crystal's publicity department, "give the shirt away in the United States." Draddy bought several thousand shirts to see what he could do with it. But Draddy soon encountered the same sales resistence. Instead of being stymied, Draddy gave the shirt away to several of his influential friends—celebrities like Bob Hope, Bing Crosby, and the Duke of Windsor. The "crocodile"— or, "alligator" as it has become known in the U.S.—almost overnight became a status symbol and today adorns a dazzling variety of apparel, from shirts to sweaters to dresses to socks and shorts to outerwear.

With the success of the "alligator" shirt came other manufacturers seeking to merchandise the sports relationship. Jack Nicklaus' name adorned Hathaway shirts and Hart Schaffner and Marx clothes and his Golden Bear emblem was soon seen on a line of select clothing; Sears made a line of Johnny Miller clothing; Joe Namath had an entire line of Arrow shirts named after him. "Name" clothing has become "in" as manufacturers sought out the sports connection, some even "pressing their bets," like Draddy, who gave golf pros $1,000 for wearing the Lacoste shirt on the final round of televised golf tournaments.

But while companies were falling all over themselves to form associations with sports—naming products like Right Guard spray deodorant, Fast Break isotonic drink, World Series candy bar, Instant Replay breakfast food, and everything short of Pit Stop for an underarm deodorant—there was one athlete still out there whose very name was that of an entire product category: Orenthal James Simpson, better known as O.J. or The Juice.

At the University of Southern California O.J. had broken every Trojan and Pac-8 rushing record on his way to the 1968 Heisman Trophy and the gold that lay ahead in the National Football League. His career as an advertising spokesman began in 1969 when, just out of USC, he signed a three-year $250,000 contract with the Chevrolet Division of General Motors. According to insiders, however, it was a costly agreement, for General

Motors then leaned on Simpson's agent, Chuck Barnes, to sign a multiyear contract with Buffalo at $70,000 a year, implying that they might not use him. Without the GM relationship, he would most certainly have commanded a great deal more.

Barnes quickly signed Simpson up with Royal Crown Cola and then went looking for other "naturals," including an orange juice company. He first approached the Florida Citrus Commission, but was told they were happy with their spokeswoman, Anita Bryant. Minute Maid was equally pleased with Bing Crosby. Barnes tried other companies, but the answer was always the same: "Thank you, but we're not interested." It became what one source called "a joke in the industry" that the man whose name was virtually synonymous with Orange Juice couldn't find a company to associate with.

Finally there was one: TreeSweet Products Co. of Santa Ana, California, a regional distributor. When O.J., now acting as his own agent, approached them in 1976, the company decided to take the plunge—both with O.J. and in the national waters. Euphorically describing the signing of "Orange Juice" Simpson as "the teaming up of two great juices," TreeSweet immediately expanded its distribution. Riding on Simpson's powerful shoulders—together with an occasional downfield swivel of his hips—TreeSweet expanded its distribution into the heretofore unexplored markets of Boston, Texas, and the Pacific Northwest. Its goal: national distribution within five years.

The anatomy of the deal called for Simpson's services for the five-year rollout period on many levels—radio, TV, print, and personal appearances as well as working with the sales force. In return he was to receive $200,000 a year plus a percentage of the company's increased profits over the life of the contract. But perhaps the greatest plus of all was TreeSweet's: "Here we've got a guy with the built-in advantage of having a name the same as our product!"

But Simpson's most visible and memorable association has not been for lending his readily adaptable name to a product, but, instead, in renting his superstar status to "The Superstar in Rent-a-Cars," Hertz.

Stung by Avis' "Number Two" campaign, Hertz wanted to mount a campaign that would convey the already subliminal message that they were number one. They couldn't communicate the message with men falling out of skies into drivers' seats. What they needed was a real flesh-and-blood spokesman; someone who was himself number one.

According to a spokesman for the advertising agency, Ted

Bates, "the search began and ended with O. J. Simpson," who besides his credibility and epitomization of the necessary requisite of speed was also at the top of his profession, Numero Uno. And so, from that first week in September 1975, O. J. Simpson has been leaping, running, twisting, and hurdling through more yards of airports than he ever covered on a football field, all in the name of The Superstar in Rent-a-Car.

O. J.'s airport dashes have increased public awareness of the company by 20 percent, a 56 percent increase in the number of car renters who believe Hertz is the best rent-a-car company around and an increase over rival Avis to 14 percentage points in its market share at major airports. And, not incidentally, they have also provided O. J. with a renegotiated contract worth $350,000 a year.

By the thirtieth anniversary of television's wedding with sports, the wet dream of athletes and advertisers alike had become a continuing fantasy of having O. J. Simpson hurdling over Joe Namath's luggage, upsetting it and strewing the floor with Johnny Miller slacks, Golden Bear golf shirts, and Reggie! bars. To many, this had become the true meaning of sports.

But while advertising has provided many with dreams of gold and glory, to just as many it has been a nightmarish experience.

One such was Roberto Clemente. The proud great—so proud in fact that he would not hit into a mock triple play for the movie *The Odd Couple*—thankfully didn't have to bear witness to what was done in his name, having lost his life aboard a relief plane bound for earthquake-torn Nicaragua on December 31, 1972. But it happened to his memory nevertheless.

For Clemente's death fueled a million-dollar industry in *chatzkas*—Clemente books, Clemente albums, Clemente songs, Clemente coins, Clemente posters, Clemente plaques, Clemente T-shirts, Clemente medallions, Clemente pens, and even a Clemente rock concert. And while many who were inspired to commemorate the fallen great were honest if misguided citizens trying to raise money for Clemente's cherished dream, Sports City, just as many had the moral fiber of the South Vietnamese army.

One group of entrepreneurs from San Juan, calling themselves the Bronze Chilean Arts Co., descended on Pittsburgh like seven-year locusts with plaques bearing the likeness of Clemente created by an illustrator for U.S. Steel. They tried to hawk the plaques at Three Rivers Stadium. When they were refused permission they began taking them around to shops like Fuller

Brush Men. One shop owner bought them on the representation that they were approved by Roberto's widow, Vera, and found some to be defective. He was sued by the man who created them for an infringement of copyright. The Bronze Chilean Arts Co., a separate defendant in the action, was never heard from again. Another entrepreneur diverted $186,000 in funds for his own use while trying to hustle something called the Roberto Clemente Memorial Album. Still another offered his day's take to the Sports City fund, but was refused when they found out his establishment was a dog track.

All in all, the proud man's legacy was one of fraud, fast-buck artists, and something he rarely met with in real life—failure. It's a sorry commentary that the man who always took the first pitch was posthumously taken by pitchmen.

But just as serious as the rip-offs and come-ons practiced in the name of advertising are the misuses and even the non-uses of athletes in commercial situations by advertisers.

The Ghosts of Failures Past include advertising's almost total failure to use black stars for many years for fear sales would be hurt in the South. Bob Gibson, one of baseball's most talented and articulate stars, was always quick to note that the reason he had had only one commercial opportunity—for Pittsburgh Plate & Glass—was because of the color of his skin.

One advertiser, Lever Brothers, the marketers of several brands which at one time or another have tied into sports, was slow to make use of blacks even where it was perfectly natural. Their almost total absence was noted by a group of blacks which during the late Sixties picketed the swank Lever Building on Manhattan's Park Avenue demanding more blacks appear in their commercials. It was during this period of time that Lever was advertising that their newly reconstituted bath soap Lifebuoy provided 38-hour protection. And to illustrate the soap's selling proposition they had several athletes, including Mickey Mantle, Gil McDougald, and Don Drysdale, all sporting "38s," a shorthand way of referring to the copy point.

Even while the screaming was taking place on the sidewalks below, upstairs Lever was screening one of the recently completed commercials in the pool. As they watched Don Drysdale being mobbed by his "teammates" after a supposed "win," the Lever product manager turned to his counterpart from the agency and asked him if those were the real Dodgers. "No," responded the BBD&O advertising executive, those were members of the UCLA baseball team. The product manager replied he could see that, because if there was one place blacks could be used, it was as members of a team that had as many as four blacks on the starting team. And here he was looking at nine white faces. The agency reshot the commercial.

As the sixties turned into the more-enlightened seventies, more and more blacks started invading what up until then had been the province of white athletes only: the commercial world. They shaved (Hank Aaron), put on underarm deodorant (Muhammad Ali), and even doused themselves with cologne (Joe Frazier). But still, the more personal the product, the greater the risk. And blacks were reduced to talking about hair care products rather than rubbing them into their scalps.

The first black athlete to totally transcend the black spearchucker image was Bill Russell. The 6-foot 9-inch former Boston Celtics standout had pioneered before as the first black coach in the NBA and the first black announcer on a regularly scheduled sports series, ABC's telecasts of NBA basketball games. Not only had Russell added color to the telecasts—no pun intended—but he also had added insight and humor as well, almost always punctuated by an infectious laugh that came all the way from the bottom of his king-sized frame. Just as his addition had made the Celtics an immediate winner, his contributions also made ABC's NBA series a ratings winner, with Nielsen figures reflecting the growing enchantment with Russell's wit and wisdom.

The general public as well as the cognoscenti fell in love with this oversized ebony elf. As did one viewer in particular, Dan E. Hutchins, who just happened to be the advertising director for the Long Lines Division of AT&T. It occurred to Hutchins that the personable Russell might well make as effective a spokesman for his company, promoting direct dialing of long-distance calls as he had for ABC.

Together with his advertising agency, N.W. Ayer, Hutchins conceived a campaign that called for Russell to be seated at a desk in shirt and tie—rather than in the basketball player's regulation underwear-cum-uniform—spouting the party line: "As a coach, I tell my players not to pass off if they've got the shot. So don't pass off to the operator. Dial direct."

Russell, by now the coach of the Seattle SuperSonics, agreed to shoot the commercial on Seattle's first trip through New York during the 1972–1973 season. The setting for the commercial was the baronial second-floor library of the Lotus Club, a club dedicated to the arts and literature. But it wasn't the arts and literature that made it adaptable for the commercial so much as the 20-foot ceiling which allowed for a backboard and hoop to be suspended from it without cramping either Russell's style or the camera angles.

Seated behind a desk facing the backboard, the normally left-handed shooter had to take his shots right-handed owing to the camera angle requirements. Coupled with this obvious handicap, the man who had made 6,690 field goals and 3,815 foul shots in his thirteen-year career was called on by the commercial to miss the shot in order to set up the punch line "I *can* miss, but you can't with Long Distance."

With the cameras rolling, the man who had made 44 percent of his field goal attempts nonchalantly threw up the first ball right-handed from his sitting position some twenty feet from the rim, and as the ball disappeared into the netting, dissolved in laughter. It was a take! The tag line was rewritten to accommodate Russell's accuracy, "I *can't* miss and neither can you . . . with Long Distance."

At about the same time the Russell commercials were breaking on television in the fall of 1973, a New York market researcher named Alan R. Nelson was issuing the results of a national study in which 2,500 men across the country attempted to rate 260 athletes in terms of recognizability, admiration, likability, and trustworthiness. About the only spinal tap it didn't take was how wet they thought the athletes' noses were. In fact, the study was far more eloquent in what it did not say than what it did. For although several of the athletes included on the list were black—Willie Mays and Muhammad Ali among them, ranking numbers one and three in the "known" category—not one black was among the top twenty-five in terms of "most trusted." And the only blacks who wound up even in the top quartile of "most trusted" were those who could be viewed as Grand Old Men by the respondents, on the safe side of forty and no longer viewed as threatening.

One of those whose name appeared on Nelson's list was Hank Aaron, who had toiled most of his career in the obscure athletic vineyards of Milwaukee and Atlanta, far from the media capitals of New York and Los Angeles where stars are born. But Aaron, who had entered the 1973 season with 673 home runs, was suddenly in the limelight. Babe Ruth's record of 714 was not only within sight, but the countdown was on. And although Aaron ranked only twelfth on Nelson's list of recognizable sports stars, he still was the leading black in that category most important to advertisers—"trust," coming in twenty-eighth.

On the afternoon of September 26, 1973, with Aaron at 712

and holding, the president of the consumer electronics division of the Magnovox Company, Alfred di Scipio, came to the realization that something—anything—was needed to turn his once-proud company around. Once the personal fiefdom of Frank Fryman, founder and guiding light of the company until his death in the late 1960s, Magnavox had built its base and reputation on its fine cabinetry more than its electronic expertise. And on its exclusive dealer network. But changing tastes and technology had wrought a tremendous alteration in the market, something Magnavox had not seen. By 1973, Magnavox was getting its proverbial chassis handed to them by Japanese imports and in danger of losing its dealers. Its stock, once as high as 62 in late 1968, was now all the way down to 7 and sliding. And its share-of-market was 7.5 and in danger of becoming the invisible shrinking share.

A little light bulb went off over di Scipio's head indicating an idea, much as it had illuminated comic strip panels for decades. His idea was simple. He would extend an offer to Aaron for each retrievable bat and ball from each home run from that day forth and for evermore, as long as he remained a major leaguer. He called in his secretary and dictated a telegram: "On behalf of the Magnavox Company. . . . "

But even as Aaron was closing in on Ruth's record, he was falling behind in the fan-mail department. And di Scipio's telegram was just one of the more than nine hundred thousand personal letters and telegrams he received during his assault on the heretofore unassailable fortress known as "714." Try as she might, Aaron's personal secretary, Karla Koplin, could only answer so many of them, sending each response out with an autographed photo of Hammerin' Hank. The rest of the mountain of mail was sorted into ranges—requests for autographs, well-wishers, hate mail, and offers. Di Scipio's telegram fit into the last category and was filed in Aaron's "tickler" file for future reference.

It would ultimately be referred to by Koplin and Aaron's new agent, Berle Adams, the head of William Morris' sports subsidiary. Aaron announced his new association with Adams at a press conference called in Atlanta on September 29, three days after de Scipio tendered his offer, and the day of his 713th homer.

According to Adams, whose office also handled Mark Spitz, Triple Crown winner Secretariat, Jim Brown, Bobby Murcer, and George Foreman, Aaron would make more money off the field in the next few years than he had made in his entire professional career—between $1,500,000 to $2,000,000, exclusive of his $200,000 annual salary as a ball player.

Before Aaron named Adams as his agent, he had been represented by Mattgo Enterprises, a New York firm consisting of two partners, whose names, Matt Merola and Paul Goetz, formed the anagram "Matt-go." Mattgo also handled such blue-chip stars as Nolan Ryan, Bob Griese, and Tom Seaver. In spite of the fact that one observer described them as "ulcerous" and another, the Braves' publicity director, characterized them with "Every time I ever talked to them they seemed to start shouting," they had been relatively successful in securing contracts for Aaron with companies like the Ward Candy Company—makers of Oh! Henry—Brut, and Lever. Still, Aaron was less than pleased with their total effort in his behalf.

In fact, one of their contracts, the one with Lever Bros., came apart at the seams. It seems that Lever signed Aaron to a contract that promised to pay him more than $100,000 to promote Lifebuoy—$250 for each homer between the 650th and 699th, $1,000 for numbers 700 through 714, and $25,000 for No. 715, the record-breaker—and made a commercial with Aaron endorsing the soap. But the commercial, never shown nationally, was soon aborted. As was the contract. Aaron wound up suing Lever Bros. for the promised $100,000 on the basis that "It became apparent that the defendant was not going to comply with the spirit and the intent of the contract."

Other Mattgo endeavors in Aaron's interest fared almost as well. Equitable Life Assurance had used a picture of Aaron in its 1972 advertising and had paid $750 for the privilege. When they approached Mattgo in 1973, Mattgo raised the ante to $10,000 and Equitable decided to forego the pleasure of Aaron's company.

Aaron, who was suddenly enjoying his fame after it had eluded him for so many years, shared the belief of many that his name was a name that was made for manufacturers with products to merchandise. A marriage, if not made in heaven, at least made at the cash registers. Now, with Mattgo running his affairs, he began to wonder if that marriage would ever be consummated.

That's where Berle Adams came in. And the first thing Adams did upon his appointment was look through the "tickler" file Karla Koplin had been keeping, honeycombed with offers, looking for the ones with the sweetest potential. His eye fell upon the telegram sent by di Scipio. "I figured he had to be interested in something more than bats and balls," reflected Adams, who called him immediately to outline a prospective arrangement whereby Aaron would become the Magnavox spokesman for five years at $300,000 a year.

Di Scipio, knowing that some sort of artificial respiration was needed and hoping that Aaron would provide the same spark for Magnavox that Shirley Temple had for the moribund Ideal Toy Company in the Thirties, still was interested, even at that price. Finally, in January 1974 a deal was struck: Magnavox would pay Henry Aaron $1,000,000 for the next five years, payable at the rate of $200,000 a year, the same as his baseball salary—and $40,000 more than the president of Magnavox was receiving.

There were other residual benefits for Aaron over and above the $200,000 a year. Now that he belonged—body, soul, bats, and balls—to Magnavox he didn't have to concern himself with what he calls "little bitty commercials," explaining "they paid me this money to be associated with Magnavox and that's the way it has to be." In another respect, it also was a Godsend. Aaron had taken a dislike to spending his winters on the rubber chicken circuit eating meals he didn't want so that he could get up and tell a lot of stories he didn't remember or like to people who had already heard them before. Now he only went when Magnavox requested him to in the name of public relations, prefering instead to stay home and watch his Zenith color TV in his den.

But if it was a Godsend for Aaron, it was also a blessing for Magnavox. At least for the moment—that moment being 9:07 P.M. EST, April 8, 1974, when Aaron clocked an Al Downing fastball for Number 715. For that moment, and the delicious moments that followed, the country became almost as Magnavox-conscious as it did Aaron-conscious. With tie-in contests to name the time and the day of the record-breaking home run and giveaway replicas of his bat, ball, posters, and "autographed" photos of Aaron available only at franchised Magnavox dealers, dealer traffic increased beyond even the wildest dreams of di Scipio. And when the ball and bat that felled the Mighty Ruth's record were transported to New York and then to a bank vault in an armored truck to await their ultimate destination—dealers' showrooms and then Cooperstown—it was dutifully covered by the press. Hailed by the advertising trade press as The Promotion of the Year, it was everything di Scipio had hoped it would be.

Then came Number 716, then 717, and all of a sudden Number 715 had all the glamour of the second man to fly the Atlantic by himself. It became as old as yesterday's news as it faded from memory. Magnavox had bought one line in the

Guinness Book of World Records, not a personality. By the end of their first season they were actively seeking ways to "use Hank Aaron." And also seeking a way out, unable to recoup their lost market share. Finally, on October 1, 1974, less than ten months after committing the million dollars to buy Aaron's name, 84 percent of Magnavox's capital stock was sold to North American Philips Corporation. The promotion had not taken. The patient had died.

Marketing problems come in almost as many assorted colors as can be found in a Crayola box. They come in the white of bureaucratic paperwork issued by the National Association of Broadcasters which precluded Sunoco from using live football players in a commercial selling NFL stamps because the NAB thought the implication from the message delivered by spokesman Don Shula was that the kid would get a live player. They come in the green of additional money wanted by Joe DiMaggio who would only allow the Xography Company to use his likeness on 3-D cards for $10,000 when the company was only making two-cents apiece on 30,000 cards to be made for Frito Lay in-pack premiums, and could ill-afford more than the $300 paid to Lefty Grove and nine other players. And they come in golden failures like that of Mark Spitz, hero of the 1972 Olympics.

Even while Spitz was performing perfectly in Munich with seven world records in seven events for seven gold medals, agents and offers were lining up poolside for what one suitor called "the first world-wide hero since Lindbergh." But when Spitz was asked to pose with his seven gold medals by photographers, he struck a diaphanously greedy stance, giving them the back of his stroke, and opted instead for a deal he had struck with a German poster firm for a similar shot. That was to be the beginning of the legend of the man who admitted "I'm a commodity." And the beginning of the tarnishing of the gold.

To some Mark Spitz became merely a footnote to an Olympics remembered only for the tragedy of the massacre. For others, more commercially minded, he *was* the Olympics. One of those who remembered the Olympics for Spitz and Spitz alone was Norman Brokaw, a senior vice president of the same William Morris talent agency which represented Hank Aaron. He saw Spitz as a merchandising phenomenon and set out to package him accordingly—in red, white, and blue wrapping, topped with seven gold discs.

Within the year the man who had garnered seven gold medals had also accumulated seven commercial endorsements estimated

366

to be potentially worth five million dollars. He signed to endorse water games for Kransco; swimming pools for Spartan; goggles, snorkels, and swim fins for Rochester Elton; swim trunks to be manufactured by Arena, a subsidiary of Adidas; milk for the California Milk Producers Advisory Board; the Mark Spitz Shirt for Media Sportswear, a division of Regal Apparel; and razors for Schick. His major contract was the one with Schick which called for Spitz to receive $100,000 annually for five years and $50,000 a year for the rest of his life.

Other offers came flooding in from those wanting to get in on the swim of things: biographies, shoes, television appearances, an animated Mark Spitz television series for children, a commercial to shave off his Jerry Colonna mustache for $25,000, a Mark Spitz swimming doll, a tie-in with a brewery, and three movie proposals, including one where Spitz would appear as, in his own words, "the first Jewish Tarzan."

Spitz had already received his baptismal under kleig lights, receiving $10,000 for his acting debut on a Bob Hope special and $7,500 more for doing a Bill Cosby show. Add to these his appearances with Sonny and Cher and Merv Griffin and you have what looked to be a budding career in television. But his words were laid down like fragile tiles, his movements those of a totem pole. One critic wrote: "To describe him as dull is to describe pneumonia as sniffles."

Spitz continued to have his trouble with the critics. He developed an "us-against-them" bunker mentality and the press returned the fire in kind. When asked how many endorsement offers he had received, he replied flippantly, "How many clouds are in the sky?" It even got to his agent, who said, "For some reason, these smartasses are starting to ask dumb questions. Like asking Mark when he's going to endorse hemorrhoids. Can you imagine this country's greatest living hero having to put up with that?" It had devolved into sniper warfare, Spitz and Brokaw on one side, the press on the other, reminiscent of the Goldwaterite who cried out upon seeing reporters taking notes during one of her hero's speeches: "There are men out there writing down every word he says."

But the critics weren't Spitz' only problem. All of a sudden, in a reverse Midas syndrome, the gold had begun to turn to dross. The supposed Blue Chip Deal with Spartan Pools was in almost as much jeopardy as the company, which was foregoing future advertising plus cutting back on some of its items because of lack of funds. The Federal Trade Commission cracked down on his commercials for the California Milk Producers Advisory

Board, directing the Board to tone down Spitz' claims extolling the virtues of milk drinking.

The biggest debacle in the Spitz endorsement portfolio, however, was the one that was considered to be the cornerstone—Schick. In an attempt to take over the top spot in the electric shaver market, Schick had committed approximately $3,000,000 to Spitz for "advertising and appearances" and backed their bet with another $6,000,000 in promotional monies.

Problems soon started bubbling to the surface. The *Chicago Daily News* quoted an unidentified Schick executive as saying that his company's relationship with the Olympian was a costly mistake. "That guy is so dumb I can't believe it," was the reputed executive's comments in the *Daily News*. "He fouls up public appearances and it's devastating." Equally devastating were the Schick commercials, an all-time low in brand identification, with Mark Spitz pushing the Flexamatic razor while the competition was Remington's Mark III.

Predicated on its campaign, Schick sold tons of merchandise into the retail pipelines, waiting for demand to take it away. But they were soon undermined by the plastic shortage which raised costs and a 10 percent price hike which priced its razor out of the market. Coupled with these setbacks were a $6,000,000 damage suit by Remington charging misleading and deceptive advertising and, not incidentally, flaccid advertising which, if it worked at all, worked against them. The results were predictable; Schick lost $5,200,000 in the first nine months of 1973 and suffered its worst year in history. They were left with a large shaver inventory, a $6,000,000 lawsuit, and Mark Spitz for life. But not for long.

As the financially ailing company continued to lose money from its ill-considered marketing moves—up to $7,800,000 in 1975—they came to the realization that they could hardly afford the luxury of a Mark Spitz. And so, in the fall of 1975 a one-sentence statement was issued from the Lancaster, Pennsylvania, headquarters of Schick Inc., that read: "Schick Inc. and Mark Spitz have mutually agreed to the discontinuance of their relationship as of Dec. 31, 1975."

The only success story of Spitz' balance sheet was the German-made poster. But for all the wrong reasons. Standing almost life-size in his red-white-and-blue swimming briefs sporting the seven gold medals and grinning like a Leon Spinks with teeth, the poster made Spitz the most popular pin-up since Marilyn Monroe's calendar shot. The poster—which sold almost four hundred thousand at $2 or more apiece, with Spitz' cut of each

15¢—appealed to many swimming groupies and also, in large numbers, to homosexuals who viewed Spitz as a cult figure.

Mark Spitz once said, "American people love heroes, and they love to tear them down, and then build them up again." Spitz is still waiting to be built up again. And so are the companies he was once identified with.

But the advertisers' biggest problem is not the active, or "shelf," life of the athlete-endorser. Nor even his being traded. It is his off-the-field conduct. Ideal found this out when their star endorser, quasi-sports personality Evel Knievel, took a baseball bat to the head of his former publicity man, and its sales dropped precipitously. And athlete Tony Dorsett, whose agent "was negotiating some very lucrative contracts—one with NBC television to do some commentary at the 1980 Olympics and the other with Fabergé"—now found them both to be "off because of negative publicity." The negative publicity Dorsett alluded to was to his disorderly conduct charge for assaulting a policeman. Soon, all endorsement contracts may contain what may become known as the Evel Knievel Clause, a contractual provision which allows the advertiser to suspend the contract in the event of the endorser's moral turpitude.

However, despite the problems inherent in using sports as a hook, several companies and industries benefited from the situation. The biggest beneficiary of all: the beer industry.

For generations the beer industry was dominated by German families who survived and thrived by merely producing a good beer and getting it out on the market. If people liked it, they bought it. If they didn't, there was something obviously wrong with the beer and the brewmeister went back to work concocting a new batch. His brew was basically the same golden, translucent beverage that had been made as long ago as 6000 B.C. by the Babylonians—barley malt, rice or corn, grits, hops, yeast, sugar, and water, boiled for a period of time, then filtered and fermented for three or four weeks.

Prior to World War II, the best-selling American beer was made with rice. But that produced a bitter taste that went out of fashion as tastes changed in the 1950s. The new formula to meet those changing tastes included corn, which made a lighter beer, both in taste and in color.

Something else was changing too. During World War II a handful of brewers obtained contracts to supply the military. And a large number of Americans found out for the first time what some of the then small national brands tasted like. They liked what they tasted more than their local brands and when they came home they wanted more of it.

At the time there were more than a thousand regional brands, large and small alike, servicing the local tastes of their equally local customers. Each had built a franchise on its umbilicus to its local market more than taste—an umbilicus sometimes included in its name (Fort Pitt), its hometown waters (Olympia's "It's the water" from nearby Tumwater, Washington), or its sponsorship of local sporting events.

Regional beers had been so profitable up to that time that when the estate of Jacob Ruppert came up for probate in 1945, the family opted to keep the brewery rather than the New York Yankees because it was deemed to be far more "valuable."

But as the patterns of advertising changed along with the country's taste, and radio and television became part of the media mix, national brands were able to advertise to localities at a more efficient rate than even the local brands. It was the beginning of the end for local beers. Faced with the megabucks of national brands and the media weight they could summon to do battle, local brands went the way of the local Mom & Pop shop forced to compete against national supermarket chains. Those who resisted were beaten by aggressive marketing by the national brands, extra dealer allowances, heavied-up media weight, and all those marketing tools they themselves didn't have in their marketing arsenals.

Several tried to retrench, extending their marketing boundaries by shipping truckloads of beer further and further away to make up for the lost clientele at home. Soon they found themselves overextended, shipping a product whose water content was so high that the transportation cost beat them before they started, especially in the face of national breweries building satellite plants close to population centers they wished to annex as sales territories.

But the beat went on. By 1965 there were only 197 breweries. Twelve years later the number had dwindled another 40 percent. The local brewery was on the verge of extinction, an endangered specie.

All of a sudden the conventional barometers that had for so long governed the beer business were no longer applicable—simple marketing methods, sales that rose reliably in good times and bad, and tradition. The new measure of success was cash. And sales as well as cash, continued to concentrate in the hands of the big brewers—Anheuser-Busch, Schlitz, Pabst, Blatz, Falstaff, Miller, Carling, and Coors among others.

Then, in 1970, the Philip Morris Company purchased the down-at-its-heels Miller Brewing Company and the beer industry once again underwent a radical change.

For Philip Morris did not know the beer industry. They only knew the packaged goods industry and how to market products successfully. Unfettered by the traditional do's and don't's of beer marketing, and not beholden to the old advertising saws that saw commercials running with obscure catchwords ("Gusto") and subliminal reminders of their product's place in the market ("The King of Beers"), they immediately set out to make Miller number one.

Some of those transplanted to the Beer Capital had been in New York before going to Milwaukee and had witnessed an interesting phenomenon in the beer business—a light beer called Gablinger marketed by the Rhinegold Brewing Company. They had been fascinated by its high trial rate based upon its message of low calories. However, while Gablinger and similar beers like Meister Brau's Lite in Chicago got what Larry Williams, vice president of marketing, calls "a pretty good trial," they did not sustain themselves, experiencing very little, if any, repeat purchases.

Still a low-calorie brew was of interest to the Philip Morris marketers. And in 1972 it acquired Meister Brau beer and the rights to the trademark "Lite." Almost immediately Philip Morris did what it does best—reformulated the product; analyzed the marketing, packaging, and pricing of the beer; and, in the words of Williams, "really went through our homework."

One of the first things that occurred to Williams and the remainder of the Philip Morris men who were just learning their barley and oats was that low-calorie beers had sold primarily to so-called diet-conscious people. In fact, it had been aimed primarily at women. With less than 15 percent of the beer drinkers making up more than 80 percent of the volume consumed—in effect, the so-called "heavy-user" segment—it was decided to go after this market. Basically, the male beer-drinking market.

. As they reformulated their product they also concentrated on repositioning it as well. Something was needed to attract the "heavy-user," the macho market. With a chicken-and-egg ratiocination, they reasoned that "We wanted beer-drinker types. And one of the areas, of course, was sports figures." However the reasoning went, the conclusion was almost as crystal-clear as the reformulated brew: sports was to bring the macho image to Lite.

Sports had been relied on as an ingredient in the marketing brew of beer companies since time immemorial, and almost always successfully. Some who had turned their backs on sports soon found that their sales—and even their companies—had gone flat. It had happened to Ballantine, once the largest-selling beer on the Eastern Seaboard, and to Goebel, the largest regional beer in the Detroit area. Both had dropped their associations with their local baseball clubs, the Yankees and Tigers, and the fans had dropped them almost as quickly.

But no national beer had tied directly into major sports since Falstaff in the early 1950s. It was a total vacuum. One Miller was soon to exploit.

Miller determined to go into test markets with a pool of commercials made up of believable "virgin" spokesmen. They eschewed actors because they felt "it would come across as just another actor endorsing a product and possibly lose some of its believability." Subscribing to both the governmental and voluntary codes that held that active athletes could not endorse alcoholic beverages because it would imply that it increases their physical prowess, Miller opted for several ex-athletes and a few manly characters who exuded machismo.

With a pool of four test commercials featuring Matt Snell, former New York Jet, Ernie Stautner, former Pittsburgh Steeler, Runyonesque Mickey Spillane, and Buddy Rich, drummer supreme, Miller took its Lite show on the road in 1973 into four test markets—Providence, Knoxville, Springfield-Decatur, Illinois, and San Diego. The results were more than edifying; they were astounding. Beer drinkers were responding in large numbers to the message espoused in the commercials: "Tastes great/Less filling." Repurchase rates almost kept pace with trial. After one year of testing, the decision was made to go national in 1975.

Miller now turned its attention to developing an entire campaign devoted to its dual marketing strategy. "Everything you always wanted in a beer. And less." Its agency, McCann-Erickson, did the legwork, generating the ideas for stars and situations, subject to putting the personalities on tape to see if they had that intangible known as "camera presence." Then, assured they had a presenter, the writers began spawning script after script of different situations for the star-presenter until one was found that "worked." Ultimately they developed no less than thirty-four presenters—some of whom served as "interrupt-ers"—all found in the "sociability of a bar setting to establish the necessary beer-drinking situation."

Together the thirty-four characters—the highest use-of-athlete quotient in the history of sports advertising—provided a veri-table smorgasbord of the most outrageous, outlandish, and out-standing situations since the Pete Smith Specials of the mid-1940s: Wilt Chamberlain bellied up to the bar less than he kneed it; Nick Buoniconti was recognized, or not recognized, as the case may be; Rodney Dangerfield "Got no respect"; Deacon Jones promised in commercial pentameter to "punch" someone in the nose; Bubba Smith easily opened the easy-open can; Boom-Boom Geoffrion and Jacques Plante discussed the finer points of Lite Beer in French, accompanied by English subtitles; Dick Butkus liked the short little pants worn by a rugger; and, in the most delicious one of all, Marv Throneberry simply couldn't "under-stand" what he was even doing in a commercial.

Throneberry, the quintessential Met during their early years of futility—and the most singular of baseball's legends—was in many ways the favorite. According to Williams, "He was as-tounded that any commercial product would want to use him." And, unlike most former athletes, who seem to be just waiting around to cash in on commercial opportunities, Throneberry, true to his heritage, was a supervisor of a glass factory in Tennessee and didn't know whether he could make the commer-cial or not because he had to get time off. In fact, "on the day we were going to film him," remembers Williams, "he had to go down early to open up the plant and then get on a plane to fly up to New York."

The commercials not only "worked" artistically, they "worked" commercially. In a marketplace where a six-pack of beer was suddenly cheaper than Coke, Miller Lite took an almost nonex-istent category up to 2,500,000 barrels in its first year of national distribution. By 1976 it had doubled to 5,000,000. And in 1977, by the best guesstimates available, it had more than doubled again to 12,500,000 barrels, or between eight and ten percent of the total beer market—which was in the ball park of 150,000,000 barrels a year—Lite accounting for two-thirds of the entire low-calorie category.

Called by some a Madison Avenue creation and by others a stroke of genius, Miller Lite has created the low-calorie market much as Xerox created the photocopier market. And the success story behind the success story of Lite has been their effective use of sports and sports stars—so effective that one agency head which represents a rival national brand admitted the campaign was "driving the client up the wall!"

If Golden Jockies were awarded for promotions that advance the cause of promotion and Leaden Jockies for those that almost as prodigiously retard the cause of sports, the awards would be given out to the following. . . . The envelope, please!

Golden Jockies for

Best promotions using sports

1. The Gillette Cavalcade of Sports—for employing sports as a catalyst in building an entire brand name over the longest period of years.
2. The Virginia Slims Circuit—for mating a new product with a new sports phenomenon, women's tennis, making both "Come a Long Way, Baby."
3. The Miller Lite Campaign—for using athletes in a dazzling manner while building an entire product and product category.
4. The Ford Punt, Pass & Kick Contest—for exploiting an exploding sport to provide identity and high traffic to retailers.
5. The Chalmers Automobile MVP Award (1911)—for pioneering in both product awards and most valuable player selections.
6. The Marlboro Cup—for entering a sport unaccustomed to promotion and performing with class and excellence.
7. The Labatt's Purchase of the Toronto Blue Jays—for using a sport to leverage a market while making a profit.
8. The Colgate-Dinah Shore Winners Classic—for sponsoring a sporting event which, not incidentally, gave it a sales platform
9. Bull Durham Smoking Tobacco—for discovering a new advertising medium, baseball scoreboards.
10. The Baby Ruth Bar—for having the *chutzpah* to name a candy after the most popular sports hero in the world and then selling it as if it were named for a president's daughter to escape paying for the privilege.

Best sports promotions

1. The Harlem Globetrotters—for devising a running, dribbling, and clowning takeoff on a major sport that brought millions to its founder and untold pleasure to millions.
2. Bat Day—for pioneering in the merchandising of a sport.
3. The Riggs-King Tennis Match—for providing the platform for the growth of a sport in a once-in-a-lifetime sports spectacle.
4. Night Baseball—for making baseball entertainment as much as a sport.
5. The Importation of Pele by the New York Cosmos—for using the most famous soccer player in the world as an ambassador of good will to build an entire sport.
6. The Ali-Frazier Bout—for packaging the titanic fight between two undefeated heavyweight champions in a total media manner.
7. The American Football League—for the most successful media-sponsored major league.
8. The Exploding Scoreboard—for adding an extra dimension to traditional ball parks, not to mention added advertising revenue.
9. The Rose Bowl—for introducing a chamber of commerce promotion that not only brought glory to its sponsors but also a tradition to football.
10. The Indianapolis 500—for providing a showcase for an entire industry while pioneering an entire sport.

Leaden Jockies for

Worst promotions—both categories

1. The Mark Spitz-Schick Razor Promotion—for proving that sports stars in their quest to "up their income" can sometimes work against a company.
2. The World Football League—for illustrating that sports fans are only so gullible and that expansion can only go so far.
3. The Dempsey-Gibbons Fight in Shelby, Montana—for the greatest sack of a town since the Vandals pillaged Rome.
4. The Snodgrass Hand-Warmer Muff—for sadism above and beyond the call of duty in naming a product after a ball player's misfortune on the field.
5. The Jimmy Connors "Heavyweight Championship" Tennis Bouts—for the most misleading promotion in the history of sports.

6. The Datsun Award on December 7—for commemorating a "Day that Will Live in Infamy," from those wonderful people who gave you Pearl Harbor.
7. The Hank Aaron-Magnavox Promotion—for proving that a sports tie-in will not salvage a sinking ship.
8. The Babe Ruth Underwear—for the most aggregated breach of truth-in-advertising: having someone endorse a product he never uses.
9. The L&M Lady Eve Golf Tournament—for spending $150,000 of the brand's money so one executive could play golf with Kathy Whitworth.
10. The Broadway Joe's Fast-Food Chain—for proving that something more than merely a name is needed for commercial success.

Index

377

Braddock, Jimmy, 180, 183, 185, 187
Bradley, Bill, 266, 286, 329
Bradley, Ed, 6
Bradshaw, Terry, 354
Brazil, 317, 318
Breadon, Sam, 48, 53
Brennan, Bill, 175, 176
Britt, Jimmy, 154–155
Broadcasting, 51, 52–53, 124, 126, 127, 178
Brokaw, Norman, 366, 367
Bromberg, Lester, 346–347
Brooklyn, 169
  baseball, 11, 19, 21, 23, 36, 45, 49, 50, 51, 61, 75, 76, 102: beginnings, 3–4, 10
  basketball, 226
  football, 112, 122, 123, 124
  hockey, 271
Brown Bomber, 183, 184
Brown, Jim, 363
Brown, Paul, 122
Brown, Roosevelt, 353
Brush, John T., 10, 355
Bryan, William Jennings, 327
Bryant, Anita, 358
Budge, Don, 281
Buffalo
  baseball, 45, 58
  football, 104, 121, 123, 125, 358
  hockey, 273
Bunning, Jim, 326
Bunion Derby, 114–115
Burke, Mike, 87–88
Burning Daylight, 150, 151
Burns, Tommy, 158
Butkus, Dick, 373

Cagle, Chris "Red," 92
Cain, Bob, 72
Calgary, 273
California, 161–162, 163, 284, 288, 332, 334, 358
  baseball, 78
  football, 23
  movies, 326
California, University of, 90, 92, 111

Los Angeles, 134, 360
Camp, Walter, 91–92, 98
Campanella, Roy, 19, 21, 56
Campbell, Clarence, 272, 273, 276, 280
Campbell, Glen, 313
Canada, 224, 240. See also Montreal, Toronto
  baseball, 6–9, 31–34
  hockey, 6, 269–270, 271, 272, 277, 279
Canada Cup, 305
Canadian Division, NHL, 270–271
Canadian Hockey Association, 269–270
Canadian National Exhibition Statium, 8–9, 30
Candlestick Park, 11, 12, 13, 14, 15
Candy bar, Babe Ruth and, 330–332
Canham, Don, 136–137
Canton, 98, 99, 100, 101, 104, 107
Caray, Harry, 28
Carbo, Frankie, 193, 194
Carlisle, 92, 99, 100, 116
Carlson, Bob, 251
Carnera, Primo, 180, 181, 183, 187, 326
Carpenter, Robert, 25
Carpentier, George, 52, 176–179, 182, 188
Carr, Joe, 105, 106
Carson, Johnny, 346
Carver, Robin, 3
Case, George Washington, 340–341
Cash, Norm, 76
CBS, 195, 196, 221, 250, 257, 276, 277, 288, 292, 319, 330
Centre College, 92
Cepeda, Orlando, 11
Cereals, 339, 349
Chaffee, Suzy, 329–330
Chamberlain, Wilt, 255, 349, 373
Chance, Frank, 75
Chattanooga, 63–64
Cheevers, Gerry, 274, 275

380

Haley, Alex, 3
Hall, Glenn, 272
Hallman, Bill, 324
Hall of Fame
  baseball, 1, 3, 10, 68
  basketball, 243
  ice hockey, 279
Harlem Globetrotters, 225–226, 227, 228–236, 243–244
Harness racing, 306, 308, 311
Harper, Marion, 284
Harper's Weekly, 168
Harridge, Will, 65, 341
Harris, Bucky, 341
Harris, Lou, poll, 277
Hartford, Connecticut
  basketball, 223, 275
  soccer, 316
Hartsfield, Roy, 25–26
Harvard University, 90, 92
Hatton, Charlie, 309
Hawkins, Connie, 244
Hay, Ralph, 101, 103
Haynes, Marques, 230
Hearst, William Randolph, Mrs., 181–182
Heavyweights, 37, 141, 150, 158, 159, 167, 171, 174, 179, 180, 181, 183, 184, 185, 187, 190, 193, 195, 197, 199, 200, 211, 212, 220, 326
"He can run, but he can't hide," 139
Hecht, Ben, 92
Heeney, Tom, 180, 182, 187
Hefflefinger, William Walter "Pudge," 97–98
Heisman Trophy, 120, 134, 357
Heldman, Gladys, 284–285, 293
Hemstead, Harry, 10
Henie, Sonja, 240, 326
Herseth, Bud, 15
Hershberger, Clarence, 92
Heston, Willie, 92, 99
High, Andy, 21
Hill, George Washington, 339
"Hippodroming," 4
Hirsch, Elroy "Crazylegs," 329
Hockey, 6, 23, 24–25, 240–241, 269–280, 337. *See also* Na-

tional Hockey League
Hockey Canada, 277
Hodges, Gil, 20
Hoffberger, Jerry, 9
Hofheinz, Fred, 200, 202
Hogan, Frank, 232
Holder, Charles Frederick, 134
Hollywood Ice Revue, 240
Holmes, Justice, 42
Homer, poet, 139
Home runs, 28, 36, 40–41, 77
  Aaron, 362, 363, 364, 365
  Campanella, 21
  Chicago, 84–85
  Cleveland, 66
  Huggins, 75
  Milwaukee, 61
  Ruth, 7, 36, 42, 44, 45, 49, 329, 334
Honest Hearts and Willing Hands, 148, 323
Honolulu, 243, 244
Hope, Bob, 357, 367
Hornsby, Rogers, 54
Hornung, Paul, 356
Horse racing, 306–315
Horse Review, The, 308
Hot dogs, 28, 30
Houdini, Harry, 183
Houston, 111, 200, 203, 212
  baseball, 8, 44, 45
  basketball, 247, 249
  boxing, 199, 200, 203, 212
  football, 127
  hockey, 273, 274, 276
  tennis, 285, 292–296
Howard, Elston, 7, 19
Howe, Gordie, 274, 275–276, 277
Hucksters, The, 339
Huggins, Miller, 75, 326
Hull, Bobby, 274, 275, 344
Hunt, Lamar, 125, 127, 281–282, 315
Hurley, Ed, 71–72
Huston, Tillinghast L'Homme-dieu, 40
Hutchins, Dan E., 361–362

Ice hockey. *See* Hockey
Ice shows, 240

San Francisco, 11, 13–14, 15
Toronto, 7–8, 14, 15, 17, 18
Washington, 18, 74
National Police Gazette, 140–141, 143, 145, 146, 147, 148
NBC, 124, 127, 132, 188, 195, 202, 221, 277, 278–279, 289, 292, 305, 339, 369
Neiman, LeRoy, 330
Nelson, Alan R., 362
Nelson, Oscar Battling Matthew, 155–158, 172
Nevada, 153–158, 160, 162–165
Nevers, Ernie, 92, 115, 117
Newcombe, Don, 19, 21
Newman, Harry, 117
New Orleans, 23
  basketball, 246, 247, 249, 250, 267
  boxing, 146, 147, 149, 210
New York City, 362, 371
  baseball, 8, 10–11, 15, 18–20, 26, 33, 35, 36, 37, 38, 39–40, 41–42, 49, 51–52, 53, 61, 64, 75–76, 82, 83, 100, 102, 123, 188: beginnings, 2, 3–4, 10; greening of athletes, 322, 325–326, 331, 332, 334–335, 336, 338, 339, 341, 343, 355, 362, 364, 365, 370
  basketball, 225–226, 229, 232, 234, 236, 238–239, 240, 242, 244, 248, 249, 250, 251–252, 254, 255, 266–267, 361
  boxing, 52, 140, 141, 142, 143, 146, 147, 149, 159, 160, 167–168, 169, 170, 174, 175, 177, 181, 182, 183, 189, 193–194, 195, 196, 197, 198, 202, 212, 346–347
  coast-to-coast marathon, 114–115
  football, 89, 104, 109, 112, 115, 118, 122, 123, 124, 125–128, 131, 132, 239, 284: greening of athletes, 330, 347, 353, 372
  garment industry, 354–355

hockey, 240, 270, 271, 273, 274–275
horse racing, 311
soccer, 316, 317, 318
tennis, 297
New Yorker, The, 355
New York Racing Association, 312, 313, 314
New York State Boxing Commission, 175, 181, 199, 347
Nichols, Kid, 1
Nicklaus, Jack, 305, 351, 356, 357
Night games
  baseball, 44, 45–46, 48–49, 50–51, 56–57
  football, 119
Nitschke, Ray, 349
Norris, James D., 193–195, 271, 272, 280
North American Soccer League, 315–319
North, John Ringling, 174
Norton, Ken, 211–212, 214–215
Notre Dame University
  basketball, 239, 244
  football, 90, 92, 93, 99, 103, 106, 121, 136, 239
Nova, Lou, 191, 289
NOW, 350

Oakland
  baseball, 11, 12, 16
  basketball, 244, 247, 249
  football, 125, 343
O'Brien, Davey, 120
O'Brien, Larry, 253
O'Connell, Dick, 17
O'Connor, Jack, 338
Octopus, Inc., 194
Odd Couple, The, 359
O'Farrell, Bob, 48
Off-Track Betting, 311–313
Oldfield, Brian, 289
Old-Timers' Day, 77–78
O'Leary, Charlie, 323
Olympics, 50, 100, 366, 369
Omaha, 193, 210
  baseball, 45

Stevens, Harry Mosley, 28, 29, 30, 38
Stimson, Henry, 192
Sting Like a Bee, 198
Stock car racing, 299
Stoneham, Charles A., 10, 49, 76
Stoneham, Horace, 10, 11, 13, 14, 76
Storen, Mike, 246, 247, 251–253
Strauss, Eduard, 169
Stuhldreher, Harry, 112
Suffolk Downs, 86, 310, 311
Sullivan, Ed, 326
Sullivan, John L., 36, 141–149, 164, 192, 212, 307, 323
Sunday, Billy, 76
Sunday Blue Laws, 55, 115
Super Bowl, 129, 130, 350
Supreme Court, U.S., 42, 202, 338
Swimming, 326, 356
  Spitz, 363, 366–369

Taft, William Howard, President, 338
Talbert, Bill, 357
Tatum, Jack, 343
Tatum, Reese "Goose," 230
Taylor, Charles, 38
Taylor, Zack, 72
Telephone, 361–362
Television, 326, 358, 359, 367, 370. *See also* Commercials
  baseball, 83, 341–342
  basketball, 241, 250, 254, 255, 256, 257, 361
  boxing, 188–189, 193, 194, 195, 196, 198, 210, 212, 221
  football, 6, 84, 124, 125, 126, 127, 129, 130, 131–132, 133, 283, 305, 306, 342, 357
  golf, 303
  hockey, 272, 276–277, 278–279, 280
  horse racing, 215
  movies and, 43
  Olympics, 369
  soccer, 319

tennis, 291, 292, 294, 296, 297, 299
Temperance movement, 30
Tennis, 235, 280–299, 337, 356
  Pyle, Cparles C., 113–114
Territorial rights, baseball, 11
Terry, Bill, 10, 11
"There Used to Be a Ballpark," 39
Thomas, Mike, 343
Thompson, Alexis, 120
Thompson, David, 267
Thoroughbred racing, 306, 308, 311, 314
Thoroughbred Racing Associations, 309
Thorpe, Jim, 100, 104, 109, 116
Thrill of Victory: The Inside Story of ABC Sports, The, 330
Throneberry, Marvin Eugene, 20, 373
Thydides, 139
Tie-ins, 328–332, 355, 365
Tiger, Dick, 346–347
Tilden, Bill, 281, 325
Time, 292
Time of Your Life, 84
Tin Soldier, The, 322
Tobacco, sports and, 10, 282–285. *See also* Cigarettes
  baseball, 327–328
Toiletries, 352–353
Tokyo, 13, 211, 212
Toledo
  boxing, 171, 172
  football, 107
"Tonight Show," 346
Topping, Dan, 51, 122
Toronto
  baseball, 6–9, 14, 15, 17–18, 22–23, 24, 25–28, 30–32, 32–34
  basketball, 240, 241, 242
  hockey, 270, 271, 272, 275, 280
  soccer, 316
Torres, Jose, 198, 347
Totalizator, 308–309, 314
Tournament of Champions, 193